Opening the Covenant

Opening the Covenant

A Jewish Theology of Christianity

MICHAEL S. KOGAN

UNIVERSITY PRESS

2008

OXFORD
UNIVERSITY PRESS

Oxford University Press, Inc., publishes works that further
Oxford University's objective of excellence
in research, scholarship, and education.

Oxford   New York
Auckland   Cape Town   Dar es Salaam   Hong Kong   Karachi
Kuala Lumpur   Madrid   Melbourne   Mexico City   Nairobi
New Delhi   Shanghai   Taipei   Toronto

With offices in
Argentina   Austria   Brazil   Chile   Czech Republic   France   Greece
Guatemala   Hungary   Italy   Japan   Poland   Portugal   Singapore
South Korea   Switzerland   Thailand   Turkey   Ukraine   Vietnam

Copyright © 2008 by Oxford University Press, Inc.

Published by Oxford University Press, Inc.
198 Madison Avenue, New York, New York 10016

www.oup.com

Oxford is a registered trademark of Oxford University Press

Library of Congress Cataloging-in-Publication Data
Kogan, Michael S.
Opening the covenant : a Jewish theology of Christianity / Michael S. Kogan.
    p. cm.
Includes bibliographical references and index.
ISBN-13: 978-0-19-511259-7 (cloth)
    1. Judaism—Relations—Christianity.   2. Christianity and other religions—Judaism.
3. Judaism—Doctrines.   4. Judaism (Christian theology)   I. Title.
BM535.K614 2007
296.3'96—dc22   2007014739

"Jews and Christians: Taking the Next Step," *Journal of Ecumenical Studies* 26, no. 4
(Fall, 1989): 703–713. © 1990.

"Toward a Jewish Theology of Christianity," *Journal of Ecumenical Studies* 32, no. 1
(Winter, 1995): 89–106, 152. © 1995.

"Into Another Intensity: Christian-Jewish Dialogue Moves Forward," *Journal of
Ecumenical Studies* 41, no. 1 (Winter, 2004): 1–17. © 2006.

"Toward a Pluralist Theology of Judaism," in *The Myth of Religious Superiority*,
ed. by Paul F. Knitter. Maryknoll, NY: Orbis. 2005.

The Little Island by Golden MacDonald and Leonard Weisgard (illustrator) Margaret
Wise Brown, copyright 1946 by Random House Children's Books, a division of Random
House, Inc. Used by permission of Doubleday, a division of Random House, Inc.

For my mother,
>*who brought me to God,*

for my father,
>*who brought me to synagogue,*

for Barton,
>*who shared the journey . . .*

and for 1185, 880, and 1120,
>*with loving memories*

Acknowledgments

I am indebted to many for their help, direct or indirect, in the writing of this book. Professor Gabriel Vahanian has been my teacher, mentor, and friend since we met in my sophomore year at Syracuse University. I studied with him as an undergraduate and returned to take my Ph.D. in the graduate program of religious studies he founded. His creative, luminous thought and brilliant lectures set me on my way in theology. Professor Fernando Molina of the Syracuse University Department of Philosophy introduced me to the field through Kant, Husserl, and Sartre and showed me how great classroom teaching can hone the mind and lift the soul.

So many friends and colleagues encouraged this work. The idea for it came from the Reverend Dr. John Pawlikowski, although he will be surprised to learn this. My dear friends Dr. James Gorney and Dr. Beverly Gibbons gave me years of loving encouragement, as did the Reverend Vincent Rigdon, faithful friend since my days at Columbia University. Professor David Benfield, Professor Stephen Johnson, Professor Eva Fleischner, Professor Lisa Sargese, and the late Professor Thomas Bridges, all friends and colleagues at the Department of Philosophy and Religion at Montclair State University, steadily cheered me on. So did my wonderful students, particularly Dr. Ervin Nieves, Dr. Mario Biera, and Mr. Matthew Dennis, and, of course, the incomparable secretary of the department, Ms. Kim Harrison.

Comrades in the Jewish-Christian dialogue supported and encouraged me: Dr. Leonard Swidler and Ms. Nancy Krody of the *Journal of Ecumenical Studies* and the late, beloved Frank Brennan, founder and editor of the *National Dialogue Newsletter*. I am grateful for the advice of Professor Paul Knitter, leading American pluralist theologian.

I deeply appreciate the helpful suggestions of Rabbi Norman Patz, Rabbi David Lincoln, the Reverend David Williams, the Reverend Lynn Bailey, and the Reverend John Paul Boyer and the prayerful support of the Very Reverend Robert Baker, bishop of South Carolina.

Special thanks are due to those who were kind enough to read this manuscript, my friend Dr. David Bossman, Dr. Elliot Dorff, Dr. Eugene Fisher, Dr. Peter Zaas, Mr. Marshall Steinbaum, and, again, Dr. John Pawlikowski— and, of course, to Oxford's indefatigable religion editor, Cynthia Read, for her great skills and even greater patience.

Finally, my deepest appreciation to Ms. J. Rosemary Moss, a tireless laborer in the vineyard, without whose computer skills, good advice, and editorial assistance this book would not have been possible.

Blessed art Thou, Lord our God, Ruler of the Universe, who has kept me in life, sustained me and enabled me to reach this moment. Amen.

Montclair, New Jersey
January 19, 2007

Contents

Introduction, xi

1. Defining Our Terms, 3

2. The Question of the Messiah, 37

3. Three Jewish Theologians of Christianity, 69

4. Affirming the Other's Theology: How Far Can Jews
   and Christians Go? 85

5. The Forty Years' Peace: Christian Churches Reevaluate
   Judaism, 121

6. Engaging Two Contemporary Theologians
   of the Dialogue, 143

7. Into Another Intensity: Christian-Jewish Dialogue
   Moves Forward, 165

8. Truth and Fact in Religious Narrative, 183

9. Bringing the Dialogue Home, 199

10. Does Politics Trump Theology? The Israeli-Palestinian
Dispute Invades the Jewish-Christian Dialogue, 213

11. Toward a Pluralist Theology of Judaism, 231

Notes, 247

Bibliography, 257

Index, 263

Introduction

According to a well-known account, in the early 1960s, Pope John XXIII was celebrating a Holy Week liturgy at St. Peter's in Rome. Suddenly he gave a signal that abruptly interrupted the worship. The choir had just referred to "the perfidious Jews," a line that had been part of the liturgy for many centuries. The pope announced that never again were those words to be spoken in Roman Catholic worship.

That watershed occurrence is usually seen as a milestone in church recognition of the humanity of Jews, but much more was involved, as later events were to bear out. At the heart of the pope's objection to the phrase was the adjective "perfidious," faithless. The point he was making was not only that Christians should no longer speak contemptuously of Jews but also that Christianity should evaluate Judaism in positive, rather than negative, terms. Jews were to be seen as people of faith, if not Christian faith. This action by a great and farsighted Catholic leader ushered in a new phase of Jewish-Christian reconciliation.

There followed Vatican II and its document, *Nostra Aetate*, issued in 1965, with its groundbreaking statement on Roman Catholic relations with Jews and Judaism. The charge that Jews of the past or present were collectively guilty for the death of Jesus was rejected as historical nonsense and theological poison. The Jewish roots of Christianity were recognized and the kinship of the two faiths was affirmed. The validity of Judaism as a relationship between humankind and God was upheld.

Following *Nostra Aetate*, organized Roman Catholic efforts to convert Jews
ceased. The Sisters of Sion, an order of nuns previously devoted to bringing
Jews into the church, became an order devoted to fostering Christian-Jewish
understanding. Official Catholic representatives began to take part in interfaith-
dialogue groups around the world. The church appointed officials charged with
meeting with and coordinating common action with Jewish organizational
leaders. Church textbooks were reviewed with the advice of Jewish groups to
remove anti-Judaic and antisemitic statements.

A quarter century later, as if to sum up the years of growing Catholic-
Jewish rapprochement, then-cardinal Joseph Ratzinger, prefect of the Vatican's
Congregation for the Doctrine of the Faith (now Pope Benedict XVI), clarified a
public statement that had been issued in his name. He had said that church
dialogue with Judaism "always implies our union with the faith of Abraham,
but also the reality of Jesus Christ, in which the faith of Abraham finds its
fulfillment." When the statement appeared, it was immediately criticized.
Without hesitation, Cardinal Ratzinger issued a clarification consisting of two
crucial words added to the original. In the revised statement, he declared that
dialogue with Judaism "always implies our union with the faith of Abraham,
but also the reality of Jesus Christ in whom, *for us*, the faith of Abraham finds
its fulfillment." The addition of the two words removed the dimension of
spiritual imperialism that had marred the original statement.

This incident points to an ongoing conceptual problem for Christians: how
to be faithful to the New Testament command to witness for Christ to all peoples and to convert all nations, while, at the same time, affirming the ongoing
validity of the covenant between God and Israel via Abraham and Moses. Can
the church have it both ways? On this question, much more later.

Protestant churches have also been struggling with these issues. The
churches of Luther and Calvin were just as eager to convert Jews as Catholics
had been, and just as nasty when those attempts failed. However, these efforts
were coupled with a reverence for Jews as the Hebrew Bible's people of God
and Judaism as the holy faith of the Patriarchs. This mixed view prevailed in
America and elsewhere, but recently the positive side has become dominant.
For more than a half century now, Protestants have engaged in outreach to
Jews and Judaism. This movement has come largely from the liberal mainstream churches that have made their peace with modern pluralism.

True dialogue between individuals or groups must open each participant to
the influence of the other. Interreligious dialogue requires that those engaged in
it give up long-standing convictions of their own exclusive possession of truth.

Historically Christianity has been theologically exclusive and humanisti-
cally universal, while Judaism has been theologically universal and humanis-

tically exclusive. The average Christian believes that Christ is the one way to God, to salvation, to living a life acceptable to heaven. The Jews who founded the church considered themselves to be the new and true Israel, the saving remnant to whom God had revealed the fulfillment of their Jewish faith and the exclusive path to salvation for all people.

At the same time, Christians' view of humanity has been a universalist one: Christ died for all people. The church is made up of the redeemed from all nations. One need not join a particular culture, nation, or ethnic group to accept Christ. The church brings Christ to you where you are, in your race or culture, whatever it may be. Christianity focuses on the individual and seeks out every person, bringing him or her a particular, exclusive notion of God and God's salvific work in Christ. God may be the God of everyone, but God has come to earth once and for all. There is one path to heaven, and everyone had better get on it. Herein lies the theological exclusivism; it is this that Christianity must be willing to reexamine if it desires genuine dialogue with Judaism.

What about those on the Jewish side of the dialogue? As noted previously, as it is lived and conceived by most Jews, Judaism already has the universal theology Christianity is seeking. There is one God—creator, sustainer, and redeemer—who asks of all persons that they live a life of spiritual attunement and moral sensitivity. Where, then, is the exclusivism Jews must learn to overcome? If many Christians suffer from Christomonism—a single-visioned focus on faith in Christ as the one path to God—many Jews suffer from what might be called "Judaeomonism"—the belief that Israel alone is God's chosen people and that only in the origins and history of Israel is God's hand to be found (in terms of God's involvement with a religious community). That is, only in Judaism do we find a truly revealed faith. As to Christianity, what is good in it is already found in Judaism. The rest is of strictly human origin, reflecting many pagan themes.

Jews desire that Christians affirm the ongoing validity of Israel's covenant relationship with God, which is still valid after Jesus as it was before. In other words, Jews want Christians to see the hand of God in the ongoing life and worship of Israel up to the present day and into the future. But are Jews willing to make similar adjustments in their own religious worldview? Are Jews ready and willing to affirm that God, the God of Israel and of all humanity, was involved in the life of Jesus, in the founding of the Christian faith, in its growth and spread across much of the world, and in its central place in the hearts of hundreds of millions of their fellow beings? If Jews are not, if they view the birth and growth of this great faith as some kind of historic mistake or accident, how are they any more enlightened than those Christians who still refuse to affirm the Jews' ongoing spiritual validity as a religious people?

But how can Jews be expected to see the hand of Israel's God in the spread of a faith whose adherents so often denigrated Judaism and frequently persecuted Jews? Will Jews be able to separate the positive aspects of Christianity from the negative, and from the sinful acts of Christians toward Jews?

The essence of religion is both self-affirmation and self-transcendence. As the great Hillel observed, "If I am not for myself, who will be for me? But if I am only for myself, what am I?"[1] Historically, religious communities have focused much more on self-affirmation than on self-transcendence. But true religion requires both. The religious person seeks to understand his or her finitude within an infinite context, to see the individual as the finite bearer of the infinite life of God. There can be no private religion that is true religion in this sense. To transcend our narrow egocentric selves and reach out to others in shared human community *is* applied religion. If this is true for individuals, so must it be true for communities of faith.

The tendency for such creedal communities as the church and the Jewish people to hide behind exclusivist dogmas and separatist notions is an antireligious tendency. It closes us off from other men and women and seduces us into the folly of imagining that God is ultimately restricted to the images our respective communities have created—a form of idolatry. This parochial narrowness—this delusion that our particular tradition says all there is to say about God and God's relations with humanity—is the opposite of the self-transcending openness that is the hallmark of true religion. Each religious tradition must liberate itself from spiritual narcissism through true and thorough pluralism, not only by encouraging its members to respect others and their faiths but also by opening itself to the influence of those other faiths.

Does it seem likely that any tradition, no matter how old and venerable, says all there is to say about God or humanity or their interrelationship? Perhaps the gaps in Judaism's worldview are filled in by Christianity, and vice versa. The human situation is so varied, so complex, that we need other viewpoints to add to our own insights if we hope to gain some understanding of it. Full, true pluralism can be realized only through such sharing. This does not mean amalgamation of faiths but creative interaction between them.

In the decades since Vatican II, Christian churches and theologians have labored to create a new Christian theological understanding of Judaism and the Jewish people. This work is an attempt from the Jewish side of the Jewish-Christian dialogue to construct a new Jewish theology of Christianity that will offer an intellectual and spiritual foundation for our ongoing journey together.

Opening the Covenant

I

Defining Our Terms

It has been observed that the prerequisite for interfaith dialogue is faith. Before interacting with another religion, we must be familiar with our own. When I came to teach at Montclair State University's Department of Philosophy and Religion, I looked forward to teaching Jews about Christianity and Christians about Judaism. Little did I expect to end up teaching Jews about Judaism and Christians about Christianity. This turned out to be necessary due to the prevailing state of ignorance among students regarding the faith traditions in which they had supposedly been raised. Before instructing them in the beliefs of the other faith, I had to introduce them to their own. Often Jewish and Christian students would ask me, "What do we believe about . . . ?" At first I would respond that neither I, nor anyone else, could tell them what to believe. But soon I realized that what they were ignorant of was not their own view of the religious issue under discussion but what their native tradition had to say about it. They recognized that they were hardly in a position to evaluate another faith when they had no idea what they were "supposed" to believe.

The question of what a great religion teaches can and will, of course, be answered in many ways. A single Christian theological statement will hardly cover the very different belief systems of Roman Catholicism, Lutheranism, Pentecostalism, and assorted denominations in between. And how would one statement of Jewish faith encompass the beliefs of Orthodox, Conservative, Reconstructionist, and Reform branches of the community? Nevertheless, recognizing the inevitable inadequacy of the result, I must, at least, attempt to summarize my own understanding of the teachings of Judaism and Christianity so that the reader might have an idea of the meaning of the terms that make up the title of this book. Only if the reader has some notion of what I take to be the tenets of Judaism and Christianity can he or she make any sense of what a Jewish theology of Christianity might be all about.

Theologies of Judaism

"In the beginning, God created the heaven and the earth." Traditionally understood, before this event, God was all in all. "The Lord of all reigned as King while yet the universe was naught," according to the great hymn "Adon Olam," chanted in the synagogue every day and at the end of Sabbath morning services. God, the Eternal One, brought this world into being either from nothing, as tradition has taught us, or from an eternal, chaotic matter, which more recent translations of the Scripture's opening line seem to suggest. ("When God began to create the heaven and the earth, the earth was [already] a formless chaos.") Either way, God is the source of all that is. The narrative continues as the world develops into ever more complex forms until, at last, humanity is brought into being, clearly the crown of the divine creation. "And God created humanity in his own image" (Gen. 1:27). Has there ever been so noble a depiction of men and women? We are the earthly images of the divine, called in the text to create ("be fruitful and multiply") in imitation of God. Not only reproduction is meant here, but every act of human creativity is implied. "The LORD who created must wish us to create."[1]

Being the image of God also involves exercising "dominion" over the earth and all other life-forms. And it seems to me to suggest another meaning. If, in the Hebrew tradition, it is forbidden to produce any image of God, this is perhaps because God has already produced a divine image—and we are it. And yet, God, as such, is imageless. Thus we are presented with a paradox: we are created in the image of an imageless God. Like God, we cannot be reduced to a picture or a statue. But we can also not be reduced to a mental image or idea, a finite concept or a definition of any kind. Like God, then, we are irreducible, unnamable, self-transcending beings, ever beyond ourselves, always more than we are. "I shall be what I shall be" (Exod. 3:14) is our name as well as God's.

Adam and Eve were created to love and serve their divine Master in the ideal realm of the Garden of Eden. They are given free will and one command to test how they will use that freedom. They disobey, attempting to become

God themselves, "knowing [defining] good and evil" (Gen. 3:5). By trying to be more than they are, they become less. The punishment is that they are thrust out of this ideal world into the earth as we know it, with all its pains and contradictions. They, who were apparently originally intended to be immortal, are now subject to death. Yet the story, as understood by Jewish tradition, is more about morality than mortality. Adam and Eve misused their free will and disobeyed God's command. Although they sinned only for themselves, the consequences affect all of us, their offspring. Their misdeed affected us, but it did not *infect* us. Judaism teaches that we—all of us—still retain our free will. We can choose to follow our good inclination or our evil one. We are born with a blank slate and must choose what we will write on it. However, our first parents did offer a bad example, which seems to have established a moral habit of misconduct which it has been hard to resist ever since. Given that sin emerges from the urge to follow our own whims rather than obey God, we might say that sin is not necessary, but it is inevitable. The arrogance that led Adam and Eve astray is familiar to us all. It misleads every one of us at one point or another.

And yet we are still free. God can still appeal to Cain to choose to emulate his brother Abel, rather than resent and attack him. Cain fails his test and is punished precisely because he could have chosen the right path. He sinned in that he misused his still-operative free will. The tale spirals downward through Lamech's "song of the sword" (Gen. 3:23–24) in which he rejoices at having committed murder. Finally we reach the moral nadir of Noah's generation. Pained by the wickedness of human creatures in the form of either sexual sins or violence (Gen. 6:1–4, Gen. 6:5–8), God determines to un-create the world for which the Creator had entertained such high hopes. But "Noah was a righteous man; Noah walked with God" (Gen. 6:9). Again we learn that the human capacity for good was not lost in Eden. Although Noah was only counted as "blameless in his generation" (Gen. 6:9), that is, in the context of that uniquely sinful age, he is still proof that corruption is not necessary. And so God determines to un-create and then re-create the world. The primeval waters above and below the earth come crashing together, obliterating the space originally made for humanity in the first creation. All is swept away save Noah and his family in the ark.

Noah is nothing less than a second Adam, earthly father of a new creation. In this tale all of us descend from Adam by way of Noah. He will start the world anew as humanity is given a second chance by the Creator.

At the end of the flood, God enters into a covenant with Noah, requiring him to respect the sanctity of life even as God pledges to do the same. Never again will a flood come to obliterate humankind. God comes to the depressing conclusion that the human tendency to sin dominates our deeds (Gen. 8:21). Humanity is in a moral rut, refusing to break the habit of self-centered conduct, indifferent to others. Since man seems unwilling (not unable) to change, God must change tactics in guiding these disobedient children. When Adam and Eve sinned, God expelled them from the Garden; when Cain sinned, God exiled him from the divine presence. Now all of humanity, save Noah and his family, have been wiped out. If God keeps reacting in this fashion, the human race is surely doomed. And so God decides to limit the possibilities of future divine action. God sets into the creation an automatic mechanism—the rainbow—which will appear to remind God of the promise to stop what might otherwise be a deadly downpour in the future. God will not allow such a destructive possibility again. God does not explain the new policy adopted to bring humans back to proper conduct; God only reveals what will *not* be done in the case of future human sin.

It is fortunate that God does so, because the second Adam soon shows himself to be deeply flawed, as is at least one of his sons. In an incident so offensive that the biblical writer, who does not shrink from much, refuses to describe it, sin reenters the world. We are told only that Ham "looked upon his father's nakedness" (Gen. 12:22), hinting at some unspeakable sexual misconduct within the family. But God does not act, and Noah and his children are not destroyed.

This brings us into a new era of mytho-history, inaugurated when God at last decides on a new strategy to deal with these wayward children. The first two Adams having failed, a third Adam will be enlisted in the divine project of bringing humanity back to its proper relationship of obedience to its divine Creator. God decides to choose one man, and from him to create a family, and from the family a tribe, and from them a people. The Holy One will train this man, family, tribe, and people in the ways of righteousness. God will do this by arranging a series of events to test them and to teach them so to act that they will become a witness people, a holy nation, living in such a fashion that all peoples will observe and conclude that this is how people act when God is their ruler. By narrowing the focus from all of humanity—with whom God has had little success—God will concentrate on this one group, educating them as God's witnesses, so that they will proclaim God's word and spiritual message to all the world. God is the Redeemer—the one who desires to bring the human race back to intimacy with the divine—but Abraham and his seed are the earthly agents of God's redemptive plan. Adam failed; Noah failed; Abraham must not fail!

God calls Abraham, promising him and his offspring greatness if he will trust in the Lord, leaving behind his home and native land. With his family,

Abraham goes out into the wilderness, not knowing his destination but determined to reach the as-yet-unnamed land that God will show him. This is an exercise in self-transcendence, a courageous thrusting of himself into the future to which he is called. It is a model for all people. Abraham walks by faith, and he begins a new era in the history of the human race. God assures the patriarch that, through him and his descendants, all the peoples of the world will be blessed.

The tests and lessons begin at once. I will mention only a few of them.

Abraham arrives in the land of promise, tours it, and consecrates it to God. Then, at a time of famine, he and his wife, Sarah, go down to Egypt, where he attempts to pass off his wife as his sister to gain favor with the Pharaoh by clearly immoral means (Gen. 12:10–20). The story is confused, a distorted memory of the awkward fact that Sarah and Abraham were half siblings. But the meaning is clear enough. It is Pharaoh who discovers the plot and denounces it as morally improper. He, the pagan, proves ethically superior not just to any Hebrew but to Abraham, father of the faithful. This Hebrew story, written by a Hebrew author to be read by Hebrews, shows our progenitor to be a deeply flawed character, capable of shockingly improper conduct. And that is the point. The Scriptures, surely the most self-critical body of literature any people has ever produced, has ultimately only one hero: God. This becomes an oft-repeated feature of our texts.

Remember the extraordinary fact that Moses is not ever mentioned in the Haggadah. Here, too, God is the only fully righteous one. In the Exodus account itself this point is driven home by the detail of the rod of Moses. Lest the reader think that the miracles are performed by Moses, we are shown that the divinely bestowed rod is the instrument of God's power. In like manner, back in Genesis, Abraham is no hero. It is he who is the sinner; and it is Pharaoh who puts it all right. The message: God did not choose Abraham and his seed because of any outstanding talent or moral superiority to others. God chose us because God loved us. This was a demonstration of God's goodness, not ours. At the very beginning of our people's story we are warned against "ethnolatry;" idolatrous veneration of our people rather than God. Abraham himself will ultimately become a great witness for righteousness, but he did not begin that way.

Later, when God informs the patriarch of the divine plans to destroy the wicked city of Sodom (Gen. 18:17–33), Abraham, now sensitized to his moral role in the world, risks all—his own life and that of the son as yet hidden in his loins—to plead for sinners who are virtual strangers to him. In this stunning scriptural passage, he convinces God through lengthy negotiations to modify the divine wrath and spare the city if only ten righteous can be found there. The tale is full of both danger and delightful humor as the patriarch, who is but "dust and ashes," actually becomes the conscience of God, intervening before the Highest on behalf of his fellow human beings. This is, in my view, the moral high point of the Torah. It reveals the true and unique role of Abraham and his seed as human redemptive agents.

Israel is to stand before sinful humanity and plead: "Stop! You must not act in this way; there is a holy God here!" And then, we are to wheel about 180 degrees and, pointing a finger at God, cry out, "You stop! You must not act in this way. There are innocent people here!" To plead for God before humanity and for humanity before God, to contend with beings divine and human—that is our role and our holy calling. And when we act it out, the Holy One bestows on us fragile creatures the mind-boggling capacity to affect God's decisions and alter God's plans. And remember that the people for whom Abraham risks everything are not of his blood or his religious community. In this tale the patriarch is courageously acting out the divine commission he received at his initial call to bring blessing to all the people of the world. Surely nothing could give our loving Parent more pleasure than when we act in accordance with the redemptive role to which God has called us.

Following the Sodom encounter, Abraham is faced with the greatest crisis of his life; God's horrific, inexplicable demand for the death of the one person whose life is infinitely more precious to Abraham than his own. Isaac must die, and his father must act as his murderer. For three days Abraham lives with this agonizing expectation. And there seems to be no way out. Isaac had been born in what was clearly a miracle birth to a hundred-year-old man and his ninety-year-old wife. All children are miracle children—gifts of God—but this one is most poignantly so. And thus when God, the giver, demands the return of the gift, Abraham is struck dumb. What can he say? He who was so eloquent in the defense of the Sodomites is painfully silent now. Out of horror? Out of resignation? Out of despair? Who can know? But he prepares, as in a slow-motion trance, to obey. Ultimately more is at stake here even than the death of Abraham's beloved son. For if Isaac dies childless, all of God's promises of land and progeny will come to nothing, and the Holy One will be shown to have been lying all this time. The whole divine-human project of world redemption through Abraham and his seed hangs in the balance. And yet Abraham is obedient even unto death.

But Isaac is spared. At the last moment an angel intervenes, and in a flurry of emotion God pours out the ultimate promises to the patriarch. God withholds nothing from the obedient child who was prepared to withhold nothing from his demanding Parent. What has been learned? Perhaps the lesson central to all of God's teaching: the infinite value of a single human life. By demanding the one life that was infinitely valuable to Abraham, God has seared into Abraham's conscience a teaching that neither he nor his offspring will ever forget. More than this, the heavenly Parent has invited the earthly child to share in the agony of the divine inner life, the life that is "all sorrow and all love,"[2] all sorrow *because* it is all love. Hosea and Jeremiah echo this theme. How God must suffer as we live out our brief lives and then die— and by God's own hand. By making this unthinkable demand on Abraham, God reveals the divine inner agony that the plan for the human race seems to require the lives of human individuals. The more spiritually developed and morally sensitized we become, the more completely we share the divine pathos. Our faith calls us to such sharing.

There is much more to Abraham's story, but we can only touch upon a few highlights that have shaped the Jewish theological self-understanding. As has often been pointed out, there are really no Isaac stories. They are all either Abraham-Isaac tales or Isaac-Jacob accounts. It is interesting that of the two most powerful Jacob narratives, one is a dream and the other is at least dream-like, also taking place at night. Like Abraham, Jacob starts out as a far from admirable character. He takes advantage of his simple brother, Esau, then deceives his father and steals the blessing that was to go to the eldest son. Fleeing his brother's wrath, he travels back to Haran, Abraham's hometown. En route, he falls asleep in the desert. It is as if the rock (*Tzur Yisrael*) on which he lays his head speaks to him. Having closed his eyes in sleep, he sees what he missed all his waking life ("Shut your eyes and see," said Stephen Dedalus).[3] He envisions a stairway between earth and heaven with angels traveling up and down, a living link between the human and the divine, partaking of both. Having heard *about* God, he now hears God directly, assuring him of divine protection and of his role as a link in the ongoing chain of his people's life with God.

For Jacob, God is no longer a mere rumor. He discovers that personal encounter with the Holy One can transform all of human experience and remake the world. He concludes, "The Lord is in this place [this world] and I did not know it" (Gen. 28:16). It is the calling of Israel—ultimately to be Jacob's name—to summon all people to realize before whom they stand and to act accordingly. The third of the patriarchs now understands the living link between the divine and the human, the continuum on which we will find ourselves—if we open the inner eye of faith and see. Israel itself is to become that link between heaven and earth, representing the transcendence of humanity toward God and of God toward humanity. Having had this experience of enlightenment amid the darkness, Jacob calls this human sphere "Beth El," the dwelling of God, the place where the divine and human meet.

Jacob's second great encounter takes him even deeper in his life with God, into a further interpenetration of the two spheres that are seen to be connected in the earlier stairway vision. This divine-human wrestling match is discussed at some length in chapter 7 of this work. It reveals yet another aspect of the living relationship of Israel and God that is at the heart of the Jewish faith and its message to the world.

In the next biblical book, Exodus, the stories of Moses and the slavery in Egypt speak to us of redemptive suffering as God's children undergo persecution to teach them, "You shall not oppress a stranger; you know the heart of a stranger, for you were strangers in the land of Egypt" (Exod. 23:9). How else to learn this crucial lesson save by standing—for hundreds of years—in the place of the oppressed? Israel's sacred history is indeed a series of trials by ordeal, lessons taught in raw, often harsh, human experience.

But there are other lessons. Having learned that God's people will be the first to suffer when inhumane rulers come to power, Israel then discovers God as liberator and lawgiver. At the Sea of Reeds and at Mount Sinai, Israel rejoices in its newly bestowed freedom and then is taught the moral code through which we learn how to live out that freedom. "Out of my distress I called on the Lord; the Lord answered me and set me free" (Ps. 118:5). God as liberator; God as lawgiver: two central aspects of the divine life with humanity as revealed to the world through Israel's witness.

God's moral law is revealed to the whole world through the agency of Israel recommissioned at Sinai for this sacerdotal task: "Now, therefore, if you will obey my voice and keep my covenant, you shall be my own possession among all peoples; for all the earth is mine, and you shall be to me a kingdom of priests and a holy nation" (Exod. 19:5–6). Israel is to the world what the priest is to the congregation. We have received from God the knowledge of God's unity, God's rule over all worlds and authority over all humanity. God has chosen us as God's witnesses. The Holy One has revealed to us a body of law with two aspects: one, for us alone, is the ritual law; the other, the moral law, is for all peoples. By giving us a code of commandments, statutes, and ordinances, God has set us apart for our mission to the peoples. Disciplined by Sabbath observance, dietary regulations, schedules for daily, weekly, and holy day prayers, and other structures for regulating our life with God, Israel lives a rich inner existence that keeps her in sound spiritual health, capable of performing her world-redemptive work. She pursues this work by teaching, through instruction and example, the universal ethical standards God has called her to pass on to everyone.

Is Israel a missionary people? Yes and no. No, she does not insist, or even desire, that all people convert to Judaism, the distinctive faith of the Jewish people. But, yes, she does labor for the day when all will recognize the universal moral law and the Kingdom of God will shine forth undimmed. The goal is recognition of the dignity of every human being, the sanctity of all life, justice for all persons and peoples and reverence for the earth, our home. The spiritual requirements of such a world will be satisfied by a universal realization that our finite lives are expressions of the infinite divine life, to which all the higher religions testify.

I have attempted to sketch here the essential elements of Jewish theology. The One God's unity leads us to embrace the idea of the unity of all humanity, of all life and of all being. All have a common source and are upheld by a common power. The rabbis taught that Adam and Eve were the parents of all people to the end that no one could claim that his lineage was superior to another's.[4] From the Jewish perspective, it is to be expected that different peoples will develop various concepts of divinity. Micah is referred to elsewhere in this work. "For all the peoples walk each in the name of its god, but we will walk in the name of the Lord our God forever and ever" (Mic. 4:5). This does not compromise the unity of God but recognizes that different people will understand the divine in differing ways.

From the second century on, Judaism has held that non-Jews can live lives acceptable to God by adhering to seven laws, extrapolated from the story of the sons of Noah after the flood, forbidding them to murder, steal, to commit sexual abominations, blasphemy, idolatry, or cruelty to animals. They were also required to establish a legal system to regulate their society.[5] Thus, their "salvation" depended on what they did or did not do. I suppose this would be called "works righteousness" by some Protestant critics. This is not strictly true despite the Jewish stress on virtuous human conduct as essential to "salvation." But the element of divine forgiveness of sin is also necessary, since no one can be fully righteous. So God's grace is needed in addition to human deeds. One cannot "win" salvation, but still one must do one's part in cooperation with a gracious and forgiving God who will do the rest.

A word must be said at this point about the Jewish concepts of "salvation." While Judaism is not a religion centered on the issue of personal life after death, this is still a teaching of traditional branches of the faith. Orthodox Judaism is firm in its confidence of divine reward and punishment after death. This has been part of classical rabbinic Judaism since its beginnings. However we are taught in the Talmud not to focus on the coming judgment, but to do the good for its own sake and out of devotion to the Holy One.[6] The overall view of the tradition seems to be that the goodness of a good deed may be compromised if we perform it for a future reward. This is why there seems to be so much less discussion of this question in Judaism than there is in

Christianity. This is the result not of a lack of belief in the *olam habah*, the world to come, but of a reluctance to focus on the reward rather than the good deed. However, future reward and punishment are essential elements of rabbinic Judaism; they appear among the thirteen principles of the Jewish faith formulated by Moses Maimonides.

Of course, today, many Jews are followers of nontraditional, liberal branches of the faith. Most of them probably do not believe in personal afterlife or future judgment. They do not think that this break with rabbinic tradition in any way compromises the authenticity of their Judaism. I believe that such a view is possible because Israelite faith was slow in developing a view of afterlife. The Torah says nothing about it, and it may have come to the religion as late as the entry of Greek thought into the Middle East (ca. 400 B.C.E.). Only after the Israelites of the late biblical period adopted the Greek view of the dual nature of the human person as an immaterial soul within a physical body could the question be raised of what happens to the soul following the death of the body. The Israelite version of personal afterlife affirmed the goodness of the body as well as the soul and thus developed the concept of physical resurrection of the body at some time in the future. This was far from the Greek hope for the permanent liberation of the immortal soul from the body that imprisoned it. For Jews, body as well as soul were created by the holy God. Both are good. Evil is not a function of the body but of the *will* that humans misuse to defy God. Today, many traditional Jews continue to believe in physical resurrection at the advent of the Messiah, at which time a final judgment of the whole human being will be given, with heaven or hell as the sentence for earthly conduct.

But since this doctrine, in a variety of forms, was late to come to Jewish theology, contemporary liberal Judaism views it as dispensable. All forms of Judaism believe that there is a holy spark in all human beings. That divine life has no beginning or end. It takes up temporary residence in us at the will of the Creator; it departs from us when God ordains it. It is eternal, but it is not necessarily personal. Individual consciousness may end with death while the infinite life goes on as God wills. Liberal Jews seek lives not of *eternal duration* but of *eternal significance*. This is what they mean by "salvation." And so, while "eternal life" is always a crucial teaching of Judaism in all its forms, it can be understood to mean very different things. All agree, however, that Jews are called to labor for the advancement of God's reign on earth—a world of universal justice and peace. If there is a future reward for such a life of service to the Holy One, well and good; if there is not, the task becomes its own reward and must be performed for its own sake as our loving response to the One who first loved us.

If, according to Judaism, gentiles are "saved" by a combination of human good works and divine grace, so are Jews, but we must keep many more than seven basic commands. One mathematically oriented sage calculated famously that 613 commandments were given to God's elect people to train them to be "a kingdom of priests, a holy nation." Moses and all his successors have, of course, stressed that this election was due to no virtue of Israel but to the unmerited grace of God flowing from the Holy One's love for us, bestowed for reasons beyond human comprehension. No human pride should result from this, only humble, grateful acceptance of God's commission to Israel to bring blessing to the world.

So Jews must keep as many of the commandments as they can, testifying to God's unity and holiness with every act of every day. Little thought should be given to the reward for such conduct. Serve God out of love; God will see to the reward. This seems to be the general attitude. Traditional Jews do not doubt that reward for "prayer, repentance and righteousness" will be bestowed in the world to come; more liberal Jews, while holding that the infinite divine life lives in all finite persons, say little or nothing about the immortality of the individual personality. The good deed is to be done for its own sake, for love of God and neighbor, with no further reward hoped for or guaranteed.

The key to living a life acceptable to God is therefore the righteous deed done in accordance with God's commandments (*mitzvot*), ethical commands for all, additional ritual commands for Jews. I admire this double-track approach to "salvation" that established a salvific pluralism from the early years of rabbinic thought, hinted at as early as the prophets. However, it does seem to me that the seven commandments given to the sons of Noah (the Noahide covenant) are utterly inadequate as an approach to present-day Christians. Today what is called for is a Jewish theology of Christianity which recognizes that the God of Israel has acted through the Christian founder to open the covenant via a new revelation to the world. Now gentiles can come to Israel's God without becoming Jewish. Through Jesus and his interpreters, Israel's God has revealed the divine desire to welcome all people into an expanded covenant.

Gentiles can join Jews as worshipers and servants of the One God through Christianity. This has been true for 2,000 years. But due to a tragic history, Jews were prevented from seeing Christianity as a new Jewish outreach into the world, and Christians were misled into thinking they had replaced the Jews rather than having joined them in the eternal covenant with God. Through the interfaith dialogue of the last forty years, all Israel—Jewish root and Christian branch—are coming to understand their proper relationship and embrace each other as sisters in faith, not identical twins but fraternal ones. Each has its own distinct appearance and way of life. And surely the high moral and spiritual standards of Christianity cannot be adequately conceived through the seven commands of the Noahide covenant. Jews must try to see Christians as closely as possible to the way Christians see themselves, freed from the error of supersessionism and embracing the expanded covenant in which Jews were once the only human participants.

Essential to the Jewish overview of human life and how it is to be led is the conviction that the error of humanity's first parents did not so compromise human capacity for righteous conduct that "original sin," as conceived by Christianity, can be spoken of. Since, for Jews, people retain freedom of the will, with the power to choose between good and evil inclinations, the Torah's moral laws are an adequate guide on how to exercise our freedom. God has created us, given us freedom to choose, and revealed a body of elevating stories and laws of conduct to guide us in our lives with God and with each other. By Torah we mean the Ten Commandments, the five books, the whole Hebrew Bible, and the vast tradition of commentary and responsa stretching up to the present day. Guided by this body of sacred literature, Jews can live life as God intends. The ultimate purpose of all this striving is what is popularly known today as *tikkun olam*, the healing of a broken world. We are called to put our shoulders to the wheel of history and push forward until this human world becomes the Kingdom of God—or, at least, until it is made worthy to receive the Messiah who will bring the age of peace and justice to flower for all.

Jewish theology can be sketched in many ways. This is my attempt at a brief outline. Some would point to "covenant" as the central concept, some to *mitzvot*, some to "justice," or "Kingdom of God," some to "ethical monotheism" or some other term. All these are involved, and more. But I hope that Jews, reading these pages, will recognize in this brief outline many of the fundamentals of our faith.

Theologies of Christianity

As is the case with Judaism, Christian theology emerges from the story found in the Bible. For Christians, of course, this means both Hebrew Scriptures and the New Testament. One might view the New Testament as part of an ongoing literary tradition. First came the Torah's five books, then the prophets and writings as expansions on Torah themes, then the later commentaries on the Hebrew Scriptures. The New Testament would be seen as the Christian commentary, the Talmud and ongoing rabbinic tradition as the Jewish commentary. But this model would not fully express the Christian conception of the New Testament. It is true that the New Testament would be incomprehensible without the earlier Jewish Scriptures, that the life, death, and resurrection accounts in the Gospels were written to reflect Israelite themes, and that the story of Jesus of Nazareth was composed so as to repeat and recapitulate the story of the people Israel recorded in the First Testament. If Jesus is the single exemplary Israelite whose story gave rise to Christian theology, the people Israel is the collective individual whose story inspired Jewish theology. Both Jesus and Israel are referred to as "Son of God," in the respective texts, both are the results of miracle births, both are sent by God for a world redemptive purpose, and both undergo death and resurrection, once in the case of Jesus, many times in the case of Israel.

But even with all these parallels, and more, the New Testament story is, for Christians, much more than recapitulation or repetition of earlier themes. Jesus represents a new revelation of God to the world, an inbreaking of the infinite into the finite, of the eternal into time. But while Jews and Christians have usually located their differences as focused on the question of who this Jesus was ("What think you of the Christ?" Matt. 22:42), it has always seemed to me that the different responses to this question are the consequence of an earlier disagreement over the conduct of humanity's first parents. In discussing Jewish theology, I stressed that whatever happened in the Eden story, Adam and Eve's sin of disobedience did not constitute "original sin" in the Christian sense. For Judaism, humans remained free after the sin in Eden, still capable of choosing the good and living successfully with God. For guidance in their efforts, Israel was given the Torah to live by and to teach by precept and example to all peoples. The whole story of ancient Israel assumes that while sin may be a bad habit, it is one that can be dealt with by a combination of human obedience to Torah and divine grace through which God forgives us when we inevitably fall short.

It is here, in this initial moral evaluation of the post-Eden human person, that Christianity differs from Judaism. Both faiths include both human effort and divine grace, but the emphases are different. While there is no one Christian theology, we can locate and outline several major strands of thought within the Christian worldview.

The earliest Christian theology was conceived by Paul of Tarsus, the first and greatest of Christian theologians. For Paul, Adam's sin consigned all of humanity and, indeed, all the world to sin and death. Adam and Eve were to have been immortal, their will conformed to the divine will, their actions characterized by perfect obedience to their Creator. They were created to love and serve God, but they were also created with free will. This was a logical necessity even for God. Love is not love unless it is freely chosen, neither is service worthy of the name if it is programmed or coerced. Given freedom by necessity, Adam and Eve chose to misuse their free will and to rebel against God's single command. According to Augustine, Paul's most brilliant interpreter, the root cause of this defiance of God was the sin of pride, which led them to attempt to redefine good and evil according to their whim rather than God's will.[7] Their disobedience constituted "the fall" in which all creation was fatally compromised and ontologically altered. Humanity's plunge into sin changed our nature in a fundamental way. Not only did we commit sin, we *became* sin—and "the wages of sin is death." Humans, created to be immortal, were doomed to death as well as to a life of "thorns and thistles" until their inevitable end.

Through this "original sin" Adam's seed became infected. Self-gratification became our dominant motive for seemingly "good deeds" as well as bad. Since God looks upon the heart—the motive—and the motive of all actions by a corrupted humanity was now self-interest, no act could be truly good. Even if it seemed so to human observers, God knew better. We were truly lost. For Paul, the story of early humanity was one of deepening moral failure. Expelled from Eden, Adam and his progeny fell ever deeper into sin. Cain killed Abel out of jealousy and resentment. His rejection of the fraternal bond reflects the earlier throwing off of the divine paternal authority. All homicide is fratricide, the fruit of rebellion against the Divine Parent.

With Noah's flood God's original plan unravels further. The creation is un-created, re-created, and begun again. But it is no use. Sin continues to be irresistible. In truth humans do not seem even to want to resist. God then inaugurates a plan of redemption that begins with Abraham and comes to fruition in Christ. For Paul the Mosaic covenant, all-important for Judaism, was no more than a moral custodian, a babysitter for a humanity still in spiritual and ethical infancy—a temporary and imperfect attempt to bring some order to the chaos of human affairs (Gal. 3:23–26). Such an ethical custodian may influence external human conduct, but it cannot cure the moral sickness in the heart of a rebellious humanity.

Because that illness is a fatal one, the problem afflicting us all is radical. In Adam all creation fell. True human free will was obliterated by sin. "For I do not do the good I want, but the evil I do not want is what I do . . . Wretched man that I am!" (Rom. 7:19, 24). Sin overwhelms all good intentions. We are in bondage. This radical dilemma requires a radical solution—much more radical than the Jewish solution to what Judaism sees as a far less radical problem. The overall conceptual scheme upon which Pauline Christianity— and, perhaps, all Christianity—rests is that of "fall and redemption." Jews would agree that we are all sinners. That is why God gave us the Torah as a guide to right conduct, containing various mechanisms for repentance and renewal. But "penitence, prayer and good deeds can annul the severity of the decree."[8] Daily prayers of repentance, the great assizes of Yom Kippur, physical and spiritual disciplines are designed to control the wayward human inclination. But for Paul and his successors in the tradition of thought that he founded, none of this can ever be enough. Sin infects every aspect of our being, even our desire to reform. We cannot solve this problem, since the problem is not just a matter of our conduct, but our nature. "Who will deliver me from this body of death?" cries Paul—and answers, "Thanks be to God through Jesus Christ our Lord!" (Rom. 7:24–25).

What does Paul think of the Law of Moses, viewed by Jews as the divinely given guide to righteousness? For him it is quite the opposite. The Law reveals our sins. Its high standards—which we cannot possibly live up to—condemn us and reveal our case to be utterly hopeless from a human point of view. But, fortunately, that is not the final or ultimate evaluation of our dilemma. How, then, does Paul view the great saga of Israel's life in the Hebrew Scriptures? An original in all things, he developed the typological method of reading the Bible stories. They are valuable as symbolic foretellings pointing to the solution God had prepared to the problem of human sin. The Law as temporary custodian points beyond itself to Christ, who will come to offer an effective solution to our dilemma. Hagar is seen to represent the Jewish Law, while Sarah foreshadows the new covenant in Christ. When the latter begets her legitimate child, the servant and her slave-son are cast out (Gal. 4:21–31). So it is when Christ comes and liberates us from the Law of the Old Covenant. The Jews had identified themselves as Isaac, the son of promise; Paul relegates them to the Ishmael role as slaves of an antiquated, ineffective Law.

Later Christian theologians follow Paul's lead, reading in the "Old Testament" typologies of the "New." Noah (Jesus) rescues humanity from the flood (of sin) by building an ark (the church). Get on board if you would be saved! Moses (Jesus) leads Israel (all people) out of bondage to Pharaoh (Satan) to the promised land (heaven). Come along if you want eternal life! Abraham's near sacrifice of his son, is, of course, a foreshadowing of the divine sacrifice of Christ the son in the New Testament. With such reinterpretation, Paul and later Christian thinkers absorbed the Hebrew Scriptures into the "Christian Bible" of Old and New Testaments.

For Paul a fundamental break with Judaism was made in his reading of the Abraham story. He seeks to prove from the Hebrew account that the Jews of his day are wrong in their view that human righteousness is possible and that it leads (together with divine grace) to salvation. In his Epistle to the

Romans he points out that Abraham was chosen by God to found a holy people before he had produced any good works. God chose him out of inexplicable love—pure grace—to be the progenitor of the line that would eventually produce Jesus. Paul seeks to "prove" from Scripture that the Jews are both right and wrong about salvation. They are right in their belief that righteousness leads to salvation; but they are fatally wrong in assuming that the righteousness referred to is *human* righteousness. This cannot be so, since all people since Adam have been consigned to sin and death. "None is righteous, no, not one" (Rom. 3:10; Ps. 14:3).

For Paul the righteousness that saves is God's righteousness, shown forth by Christ's selfless sacrifice on the cross. What is asked of us is faith in God's righteousness—acceptance of the sacrifice for all humanity in the one selfless (thus redemptive) act ever performed. Christ is the second Adam. The first was disobedient, succumbing to sin and condemning all of us, his seed. The second Adam was obedient even unto death, resisting all temptation to sin (Matt. 4:1–11) and redeeming all people who accept what he has done for them. Christ reverses the spiritual rotation of the sinful world, reopening the door slammed shut by Adam's sin. More than that, Christ *is* the door—the gate into the sheepfold of salvation (John 10:7–8). Once we truly accept Christ as guide and motivating force in our lives, we may, with Paul, cry out, "it is no longer I who live, but Christ who lives in me" (Gal. 2:20). Paul, the ultimate pessimist from the human perspective, becomes a supreme optimist when viewing our story from God's point of view. Christ does for us what we could not do for ourselves. We who were lost sinners become sinners saved by grace, a free gift of a loving and merciful God. The ultimate promise is that we will be made new beings in Christ—that he will enter us and live his blameless life in us. Thus, while Judaism holds that righteousness leads to salvation (at least, in part), Pauline Christianity reverses this logic and declares that salvation leads to righteousness. If we accept by faith what Christ has done for us on the cross and believe in our hearts that he has been raised from the dead, he will enter us, remake our sinful nature, and lead us to eternal life with him.

Human fall and divine redemption, radical dilemma and radical solution—this is the essence of Paul's original Christian theology—a brilliant intellectual tour de force that in a fascinating way turns Judaism on its head by reversing the logic of its soteriology. In addition to his theology of the two Adams, Paul outlines a salvific theory of Christ's blood shed as atonement for human sin. This Pauline conception is expanded and given much elaboration by Saint Augustine, Saint Anselm, and others, but the rudiments can be found in the apostle's letter to the Romans.

As has been pointed out, Paul consigns all creation to sin and death following the "fall" and expulsion from Eden. Human corruption is complete. Our will is in bondage to sin, having been deprived of its original freedom by Adam's fatal misuse of it (Rom. 5:12–14). We all became slaves of sin (Rom. 6:17), utterly incapable of the righteousness for which we had been intended. The Law of Moses only increased the trespass by showing forth the high standards required by a righteous God—standards a corrupted humanity could in no way even approach (Rom. 5:20). And so a loving God provided a divine solution to a problem that, from the human perspective, was utterly hopeless and insoluble. "All have sinned and fall short of the glory of God, they are justified by his grace as a gift through the redemption which is in Christ Jesus, whom God put forward as an expiation by his blood, to be received by faith" (Rom. 3:23–25). Christ's blood, shed on the cross, "justifies" us all (Rom. 5:9), that is, this selfless act of divine grace makes us sinners acceptable to God by paying the price for our sins. Prior to this, death awaited us all as a just punishment for sin. But God chose to visit that sentence on God's son instead of on us who deserved it. If we now accept with all our hearts what Christ has done for us, we are set free from bondage to sin.

This does not mean for Paul that our Adamic free will is restored. No, once we have "put on Christ" (Gal. 3:27), we become slaves of righteousness (Rom. 6:18), unable to sin. "We were buried therefore with him by baptism into death so that as Christ was raised from the dead by the glory of the Father, we too might walk in newness of life" (Rom. 6:3). When Paul speaks of "eternal life" (Rom. 6:22), he means the future life we will live in what Jews would call the *olam habah*, the world to come. But when he speaks of "newness of life," he has in mind the life we live here and now following our acceptance by faith of what Christ has done for us. The old sinful person dies with Christ in baptism, his former nature drowned in the waters of death. But those same waters then become waters of life, signifying our rebirth into "new life" with Christ.

The blood is the key. Although Paul does not elaborate on this doctrine, as does the later Augustine, he is its founder. He is also the originator of the account of Jesus' words and actions at the last supper (1 Cor. 10:23–26). The cup signifies the new covenant "in my blood." Here he does not elaborate a soteriology of the blood as payment for human sin; that will be done by Augustine and others. But the foundations of the theory are Paul's, and they are accepted by the great majority of Christians, Catholic, Protestant, and Orthodox. Paul states clearly that Christ "was put to death for our trespasses and raised for our justification" (Rom. 4:25). This once-for-all act of the righteous

God who offers God's own Son on the altar of the cross is the grace that justifies (makes acceptable to God) all sinners who respond with faith by accepting what God has done for them through Christ's atoning blood (Rom. 3:21–26). Now they can walk in "newness of life," freed from bondage to sin, now in bondage to Christ who lives again in each of them.

But surely there is a problem with this Pauline theology. It is a problem that arises from our lived experience in the world. That experience is, in most respects, time bound. We live in time, or perhaps time lives in us. Augustine himself identifies time as an internal condition, the extendedness of the mind itself.[9] "There is no external past, but the present of things past," the *memory*. There is no external future, only "the present of things future," *expectation*. And the present has no duration or extension; it is momentary. He calls it "sight" or "awareness." But even if this is true, awareness occurs from moment to moment, both ever new and ever conscious of its connectedness to itself in remembered past moments and projected future moments that make up a lifetime. But if moments of awareness are connected to each other in sequential consciousness, this does not mean that the attitudes or points of view of the conscious self are necessarily the same or even similar from one moment to the next. Emily Dickinson, with her usual eloquence, reminds us, "One does not know what party one may be tomorrow."[10]

And this is the problem with Paul's designation of the sinless "newness of life," which we put on in accepting Christ. Paul so often stresses the "once for all" aspect of salvation. Christ died "once for all," paying the penalty for our sins. We accept that "once for all" with our whole heart and soul, and we who were slaves to sin are now forever slaves to righteousness. Of course, he says that we are "set free," but this seems to be "freedom to do the right" because our hearts have been conformed to Christ. Having put on a new nature, Christ now lives his sinless life over in us. For Paul, freedom to fall back into sin is not freedom at all but a loss of the freedom-for-righteousness we have in Christ. That would be a relapse into bondage to sin.

But what about Emily Dickinson's dilemma? We are beings extended temporally (whether the time in question is in us or we in it). If this is so, how can any act or decision ever be "once for all"? Jean-Paul Sartre writes of the gambling addict and the alcoholic who pledge in the morning not to gamble or drink that day. But five o'clock comes, and they make another decision. This does not mean that the earlier resolution was not sincere, but that the self of 8:00 A.M. is not able to control the self of 5:00 P.M. In terms of will and desire it is not even the same self. In Sartre's words, it is as if "I made an appointment with myself on the other side of that hour, of that day or of that month." But the self that projects that future rendezvous with itself cannot suppress "the possibility of not finding myself at that appointment, or of no longer even wishing to bring myself there."[11] Paradoxically, the self of 8:00 A.M. both is and is not the self of 5:00 P.M. that same day. This is "the nihilating structure of temporality," which fragments human will and requires that resolutions be made over and over again.

How, then, can even the most sincere commitment to give one's life over to God (in this case, God in Christ) offer any kind of guarantee of future fidelity to this promise? The problem is often referred to as that of "backsliding." Paul must have recognized it. He is not building a theory in midair with no resemblance to the realities of human life. In fact, he does recognize the problem elsewhere. In his Letter to the Corinthians he is addressing Christians who have been baptized and, they believe, made new in Christ. But Paul has discovered that they misunderstood the process in a number of ways. First they grumble about who baptized them, as if that were a significant question; then they misinterpret Christianity as a new kind of philosophy one can grasp with the intellect; finally, at least some of them engage in sexual abominations in the false belief that their souls, having been "saved," are now liberated from their bodies; thus what their bodies do with the local prostitutes is irrelevant to their new spiritual condition.

Paul, of course, is horrified by all this and cries out, "You are not your own; you were bought with a price [Christ's blood]. So glorify God in your body" (1 Cor. 6:20). He urges them to "secure your undivided devotion to the Lord" (1 Cor. 7:36). And he reminds them, "God is faithful, and he will not let you be tempted beyond your strength" (1 Cor. 10:13). Even back in Galatians he urged, "If we live by the Spirit, let us also walk by the spirit" (Gal. 5:25).

So . . . temptation is still possible for the "saved," and even they must be admonished to act out their faith in deeds. Again in Corinthians he includes the famous and beautiful thirteenth chapter, in which he declares, "if I have all faith, so as to remove mountains, but have not love, I am nothing" (1 Cor. 13:2). The faith that marks conversion must be extended temporally by an ongoing loving motivation renewed from moment to moment.

Through conversion we may, according to Paul, become slaves of Christ and righteousness; but all slaves are not good slaves, nor are they always obedient. They may even try to run away from their master. If this were not the case, Paul would never have had to write to the Corinthians. Sartre's "nihilating structure of temporality" dictates that the most profound commitment can be undone by time and by the fractured nature of the human self. Not for nothing did Kierkegaard see religious life as a "perpetual striving." There is and can be no "once-for-all" that does not also recognize the need for an ongoing struggle in which we wrestle like Jacob or take up our cross *daily* as Luke's Jesus requires (Luke 9:23).

There is, of course, a crucial and central eternal element in religion that seeks to tame the devouring power of time and remove the sting from time's ultimate end, which is death. The recognition of the infinite context of finite experience is necessary to the religious vision, but paradoxically it is only in time that the human consciousness can participate in the eternal. Time and space are not done away with but are made eternally significant through the eye that beholds the radiance of all things past and present and to come and embraces them as finite expressions of the infinite totality. At times Paul stresses the "once-for-all" theory of conversion; at times he speaks of the ongoing struggle. But the crucial elements of Adamic fall and redemption through the cross are constant.

It is often claimed that Roman Catholicism does not share the Reformation interpretation of Paul's theory that original sin destroyed humanity's freedom of will and placed us all under absolute and complete bondage to sin. The Catholic Catechism states that through original sin "human nature has not been totally corrupted: it is wounded in the natural powers proper to it ... and inclined to sin."[12] But it continues: "By our first parents' sin, the devil has acquired a certain domination over man, even though man remains free. Original sin entails captivity under the power of him who henceforth had the power of death, that is the devil."[13] As a consequence the world as a whole is in a sinful condition. It is only the "New Adam" (Christ) who can make amends superabundantly for the disobedience of the original Adam.[14] Thus, while a distinction must be made between the Catholic and Reformation Protestant interpretations of Paul's view of the degree of sin's influence over the human will, all traditional Christians agree that *sin dominates individuals and the whole human race*, creating a problem requiring the radical solution of the cross.

Although the great majority of Christians subscribe to some version of this Pauline theory, there are those liberal Christians who today object to one or another aspect of Paul's view—or at least to the elaborations of Paul's themes by Augustine and Anselm. In their dissent from Paul, these liberals are supported by alternative traditions in the New Testament and in the history of Christian theology.

The earliest Gospel, that of Mark, seems to follow Paul in his understanding that the blood of Christ wins expiation for human sin. Mark's account of Jesus' words at the Last Supper seem to point to Paul's meaning: "This is my blood of the covenant which is poured out for many" (Mark 14:24). Matthew appears to share Mark's view, even adding "for the forgiveness of sins" (Matt. 26:28), making the message more explicit. However, Luke seems to have a different concept of what the shedding of Jesus' blood is all about. Here Jesus refers to "this cup which is poured out for you" (Luke 22:20) but goes on to interpret his words as referring to true servanthood. The genuine leader is one who serves. His blood will be poured out as the ultimate act of service to his followers to show them how to serve God. He has demonstrated this in the whole life he has led with them; now, having shown them how to live as servants of God, he will show them how to serve even unto death. No mention is made here of paying the penalty for human sin.

Likewise in John's Gospel, another note is struck. Here Jesus says nothing at the Last Supper about body and blood, but focuses on his life and death as demonstrations of his love for his followers and for God, as well as God's love for him and for all. From these non-Pauline readings of the meaning of Jesus' life and death, an alternative tradition of Christian theology, christology, and soteriology emerged. While Augustine and Anselm followed and expanded on Paul, a Greek father of the church, Irenaeus (ca. 130–202 C.E.), stressed not only the cross but the incarnation and lifelong works of Christ as affirmation and sanctification of all human life. Jesus shows us how to live a truly human life in obedience to the Father of us all. As in John's Gospel, Jesus is the enfleshment of the eternal Word of God who comes down into the human realm to live an exemplary human life, unlike the disobedient Adam, and draws us all back into the eternal life to which he ascends following his sojourn through the world.

Also in contrast to Paul's later elaborators, Peter Abelard (1079–1142) rejects their concepts of Christ's work as paying off an otherwise unpayable human debt to God, owed due to sin. As in the Johannine tradition, Christ's life and death are all about love. The Son of God is incarnated out of divine love for us, he lives a life of loving deeds, teaches us about loving each other, shares our human life in love, and, in love finally pours himself out for us, prompting us to return the selfless love by which he lived and died. So moved by how he has lived and what he has done for us, we are now able to live lovingly, conquering the sin of selfishness that dominated us since the Fall. In contrast to Abelard, the great theologians of the Reformation—Luther, Calvin, and others—followed Augustine and Anselm, who had picked up on, intensified, and spelled out Paul's theory of Christ's expiatory sacrifice.

I have presented these brief sketches of some Christian theories of salvation to introduce the reader to basic concepts of Christian theology—or, better, of Christian theologies, since there are many. Paul, as the first theorist of soteriology, has pride of place, but there are many variations on his themes and, as we have seen, even some rejections of them.

I touched on salvation theories before dealing with christologies because I believe that more important than who Jesus was is the question of what he is believed to have accomplished. That issue leads us directly to our evaluations of what has occurred in the Garden of Eden—in other words, the nature of the human. How deeply were we affected by Adam's sin? Given the Jewish answer to this question, Torah is a sufficient method of healing humanity; starting with the Christian reading of the problem, Christ's work is necessary. But now we must move from Jesus' work to Jesus' person. "What think you of the Christ?" (Matt. 22:42).

Is Jesus the "Son of God" or is he "God, the Son"? Is he divine or human or both? Is he the "human face of God" or the "God conscious man"? Over the centuries Christians have answered these questions in many ways. My own view is that one is a Christian if the person and life of Jesus of Nazareth is at the center of one's life with God. Whether holding a low christology of Jesus, the man with divine qualities, or a high one of Jesus as God become man, Christians always focus on the one who for them is the central figure of human and divine history.

Paul presents Jesus as taking many roles, some of which we have mentioned. It is, in fact, impossible to point to one definitive concept of Jesus' identity developed by Paul. And if we try to point to two such theories, we find that they occupy opposite ends of the continuum of New Testament christologies. Here as elsewhere, Paul is anything but consistent. In Romans 1:3–4 we find: "the gospel concerning his [God's] Son, who was descended from David according to the flesh and designated Son of God in power according to the Spirit of holiness by his resurrection from the dead, Jesus Christ our Lord." Here it would seem that Jesus was a man, a royal descendent of King David, who was "designated Son of God" only after his resurrection from the dead. The title "Son of God" indicates a new "power" bestowed upon him by the Spirit. In taking up this power, he was named "Lord," a title of heavenly authority used for God. But Paul's meaning is hardly clear, especially since, lacking a virgin-birth story, his writings do not include a claim that Jesus had no human father. He is not the "Son of God" in that literal sense. And since "son of God" was also a title used for Israel (Exod. 9:22) and for the kings of David's line (Ps. 2), we would have to classify the christology of this passage as relatively low. Even if "Son of God" was used here as a heavenly name far beyond the titles given to Israel and the Davidic king, it was a designation bestowed on Jesus only after his resurrection. In this passage Paul hints at no divine existence for Jesus prior to his earthly appearance.

But if we examine Paul's christology in his Epistle to the Philippians, he seems to answer the question "Who is the Christ?" very differently: "Christ

Jesus, who, though he was in the form of God, did not count equality with God a thing to be grasped, but emptied himself, taking the form of a servant, being born in the likeness of men. And being found in human form he humbled himself and became obedient unto death, even death on the cross" (Phil. 3:5–8). Here Jesus is seen as a preexistent divine person, one with God, who, in service to humanity, became man and embraced death in obedience to a divine redemptive plan. This is Pauline christology at its highest. I know of no way to reconcile these two passages by Paul regarding Jesus' identity. When Paul, in another context, was accused of self-contradiction, he responded, "I have become all things to all men, that I might by all means save some" (1 Cor. 9:22).

In Mark the picture is quite different. Here Jesus is Son of God, Son of Man, and Messiah. But, taking the last title first, he is not the Messiah his followers think he is. When Peter uses the title on the road to Caesarea Philippi (Mark 8:27–38), Jesus corrects him. What could Peter have meant by the title? Probably he had in mind the idealized future king, foretold by Jeremiah and some of the later Isaiah writers, who ascends the throne of David to rule Israel and the world in righteousness. Jesus responds harshly to Peter and corrects him. No, "Son of Man" is the title he chooses, the apocalyptic judge and redeemer who will come at the end of days with clouds from heaven (Dan. 7:13–14) and be given authority by God. The Son of Man (also spoken of in Enoch) is human, but more than human. Jesus speaks of him in the third person, but Mark is satisfied that he is speaking of himself. What is most important is that Mark's Jesus goes on to identify the exalted Son of Man with the lowly servant of God spoken of in Isaiah 53. When these two images are united in one person, one might say that the Gospels' first christology is born. Jews had identified Israel or some persecuted prophet of the past (perhaps Jeremiah) as the servant. But Mark's Jesus sees him as the other aspect of the Son of Man who will suffer and die and then return in glory.

For Mark, Son of God is a far less exalted title than Son of Man. Son of God meant primarily king of Israel. Mark considers Jesus to be, like David and his line, an adopted son of God, anointed as king by John the Baptist (Mark 1:9–11) with the heavenly voice echoing the Second Psalm, the coronation anthem of ancient Israel's kings, "You are my [adopted] son." But it should be noted that, for Mark, Son of God, in its gentile meaning, signified a divinized man who had the power to perform miracles, drive out demons, and heal the sick. No Israelite king had ever done such things.

For Matthew, Jesus was literally the Son of God, having no human father. Luke agreed but stressed that Jesus was "full of the Holy Spirit . . . and was led by the Spirit" (Luke 4:1). The Holy Spirit is the principle actor in the Luke-Acts narrative, not the man Jesus. In Hebrew Scriptures the spirit moved over the face of the water in the beginning (Gen. 1:2), entered Joshua and the Judges, giving them their military prowess, came into David and his seed, bestowing divine authority to rule, and then into the prophets, empowering them to speak the word of the Lord. In Luke the Spirit enters Mary, impregnating her with the Son of God (no such idea is known to Mark, who sees Jesus as God's adopted son), then comes into Jesus at his baptism, empowering him to resist Satan (as Adam did not) and perform his mighty works. Finally, on the cross, he yields up the Spirit (Luke 23:46), but it descends anew on the disciples at Pentecost (Acts 2:4) to empower the church and lead it on. Luke-Acts is a three-part drama (era of Israel, era of Jesus, era of the church) with the Spirit as its central character. Who is Jesus? He is the vessel of the Holy Spirit in the second act, begotten of the Father, thus both human and divine.

For John, who presents the highest New Testament christologies, no birth or conception story is needed: "In the beginning was the Word, and the Word was with God, and the Word was God. He was in the beginning with God; all things were made through him, and without him was not anything made that was made ... And the Word became flesh and dwelt among us" (John 1:1–3, 14). Here Christ is the incarnation of the eternal Logos (Word) of God. Reflecting both Greek thought and Hellenized Hebrew Wisdom literature, the creative divine word is eternally with God, sometimes conceived as the divine intellect itself. From Mark's relatively low christology to John's eternal Logos, the New Testament and the later Christian tradition contain many christologies. I have attempted in this thumbnail sketch of a few of them and of some of the soteriological conceptions that go with them to present the reader with a short summary of aspects of Christian theology.

Foundations of a Jewish Theology of Christianity

Before we attempt to outline a Jewish theology of Christianity we must be clear about the differences between the two faiths. As noted earlier, it seems to me that we are dealing with two understandings of a single narrative, the mythos of the Garden of Eden. For Jews there was serious error in the disobedient actions of Adam and Eve, an error that affected all of us. For Christians there was a Fall, an ontological event, that *infected* us all. If sin is a habit— what we do—what is needed is an authoritative code of laws that can teach us how to break that habit and reform our conduct. If sin is our nature—what we are—a more radical solution is needed. Another, not infected by sin, must do for us what we cannot do for ourselves. Christ is needed.

While recognizing the disobedience of our first parents, Judaism never gives up on human nature. Of course, God's grace is needed to help us help ourselves. That grace is offered in the calling of the patriarchs, the election of Israel, and the gift of Torah, given as a guide toward righteousness. We must, through our own effort, and with God's help, strive to live as our Creator means us to live. We must cooperate in our own salvation. Of course we cannot achieve full righteousness. And so, once again God's grace is needed to forgive our shortcomings when we fail. Thus, Judaism begins with grace (Israel's election and the gift of Torah) and ends with grace (divine forgiveness). But in between—in the lifelong strenuous human effort to do the good—is where we live our daily lives. *That we live* is God's gift to us; *how we live* is our gift to God.

For Pauline Christianity grace occupies center stage. It is not bestowed to help man in his striving toward the good. Rather, it is given precisely because humans are moving in the other direction. Fatally compromised by sin, they are fleeing away from God. Christ appears, offers himself as an obedient servant, faithful even unto death, and gives us the power to stop in midflight and then to turn and move in the opposite direction. This new power is not our own. It is bestowed by a gracious God on us sinful children. For the sake of Christ's righteousness God offers to put away our sins if we will "put on Christ" by accepting the gift of his righteousness offered on the cross on our behalf.

Paul is not clear whether we ourselves possess the power to accept Christ in our lives. God's Spirit may have to enter us to enable our nature, so weakened by sin, to do even this much (Augustine is certain that "preparatory grace" is needed to make this possible). But now we have been given the power to walk before our God in "newness of life" (Rom. 6:4) as reborn beings in Christ. Is the struggle for righteousness now over (for Judaism it never is), or does it go on? Are we given a new nature incapable of sin as Paul at times seems to claim? Or are we capable of backsliding into sin? Are we who were sinners, now justified sinners, having been made acceptable to God, even in our sin? Or have we lost the capacity to sin—having been once slaves to sin but now slaves to Christ and his righteousness (Rom. 6:18)? The problem is as complex as human nature itself, and Paul is inconsistent in his arguments and conclusions.

The main purpose of all this struggle and the bestowal of grace is, for Paul, individual salvation. It is probably safe to say that this is a crucial consideration in all Christian theology. That is because it was central to Jesus' preaching, reflecting as it did an important element of the first-century Pharisee thought which, in this case, he shared. As I have explained, personal salvation, while still an essential doctrine of Orthodox Judaism, has been widely dispensed with by liberal branches of the faith. Since personal salvation in a future life was a late development in Israelite religion, one can be an authentic Jew today without including it among one's beliefs. The same cannot be so easily said about Christians whose faith tradition has incorporated this central belief since its inception. Christianity—in all its forms, though perhaps in differing degrees—remains a religion of personal salvation. Judaism is much more concerned with personal and communal sanctification. "You shall be Holy!" (Lev. 19:1).

We need only recall the courageous words of the three Hebrew youths, Shadrach, Meshach, and Abednego in the book of Daniel. King Nebuchadnezzar demanded that they prostrate themselves before his image of gold or be thrown into a "burning fiery furnace. "And who," the king asked, "is the god who will deliver you out of my hand?"

> Shadrach, Meshach, and Abednego answered the king, "O Nebuchadnezzar, we have no need to answer you in this matter. If it be so, that our God whom we serve is able to deliver us from the burning fiery furnace; then he will deliver us out of your hand, O king. *But even if he will not*, be it known to you, O king, that we will not serve your gods or worship the golden image which you have set up." (Dan. 3:16–18)

Even if He will not... we will not serve your gods! May every Israelite have the courage to proclaim these words in the hour of testing. If there is a reward for the faithful of God, well and good. But even if not, let us be faithful still and then be willing to "slip into the night, demanding nothing, God, of man or of you."[15] Such fidelity even unto death—with no rewards promised or guarantees given—seems to me to be the purest and highest expression of martyrdom. How many of our people have walked this path since the immortal tale of the three heroic Hebrew youths was written nearly twenty-two centuries ago! Of course, Christianity too has produced its army of martyrs. It is just a distinction to be noted that for Judaism it is sanctification of God's name and of the individual's and community's life that is central, while for Christianity the issue of personal salvation is indispensable.

Although Paul was the creative genius who produced the first and most powerful Christian theology, there were many alternative post-Pauline theories of the faith developed in later years. Paul may have proclaimed the Jewish Law to have been abolished with the coming of Christ, but all Christians did not agree. The authors of the Letter of James and of Matthew's Gospel were "judaizers." In James's view, human good works were necessary for salvation.

"Faith apart from works is dead" (James 2:26). Paul had claimed in Galatians that good works flowed from a prior salvation that was the result of divine grace. But for James, good works came first with salvation as God's gracious response (James 2:18–26). I sometimes picture the author of the Letter of James, sitting at his writing desk with Paul's Letter to the Galatians spread out before him, refuting Paul's argument point by point as he composes his own work with its very Jewish version of Christianity.

Later shapers of nascent Catholicism also departed from Paul or, at least, added much to his thought. Paul's overthrow of the halakha (the Jewish legal system) left a vacuum which they filled with the sacramental system. As in Judaism, so in Catholicism; people must cooperate in their own salvation. There are commandments (*mitzvot* in Judaism, sacraments in Catholicism) to be fulfilled. Without grace—prior grace bestowed on the cross—there can be no salvation. But the sacramental system—like Torah, a gift of grace—must be observed by those seeking acceptance by God. Catholicism is a re-Judaizing of Christianity after Paul. To this extent, the soteriological patterns of Judaism and Catholicism closely parallel each other.

So, too, do the roles of the people Israel and of the individual Jesus parallel each other in Judaism and Christianity. I will develop this thought throughout this book. The key to understanding the relationship between the two sister faiths which emerged from ancient Israelite religion is to be found here. It is often missed because Israel is a collective individual while Jesus is a single individual, but it is crucial. Isaac, progenitor of Israel, is begotten by God through a miracle birth. Surely the hundred-year-old Abraham and the ninety-year-old Sarah were unable to conceive this child of divine promise without a miraculous intervention by God. In a sense unparalleled elsewhere in Hebrew Scriptures, this child is the son not of Abraham but of God. This astonishing insight is stated explicitly by Philo of Alexandria in his first-century commentary on Genesis. Abraham is the father of many nations. But Isaac is the father of the people Israel whose divinely ordained task is to witness to God and upbuild God's kingdom. Israel is called to teach the peoples a universal ethic, preach the unity of God, and heal a broken world. But the world frequently resists, and thus Israel, "the people of Christ, has become the Christ of peoples," suffering, dying, and rising again in sanctification of God's name and its own life. Israel is God's "first born son" (Exod. 4:22) and God's salvific agent on earth, "a light to the nations" (Isa. 42:6–49:6).

Is this not the pattern of the life of Jesus in the New Testament? The authors of the Gospels consciously presented the life, death, and resurrection of the Nazarene as a repetition and recapitulation of the life of the people Israel. This individual, exemplary Israelite, born of a miracle conception, preaches, teaches, and witnesses as did the earlier collective Israel of Hebrew Scripture. He, too, suffers, dies, and is raised up to proclaim the triumph of life and to show us all that world redemption is worth the suffering and dying of the righteous. Israel bears the Torah—the Word of God—within it. Jesus is the enfleshed Word. Both show forth Emanu-El, God in our midst.

The first observation of a Jewish theology of Christianity must be that these stories are so closely related that they represent two ways of expressing parallel redemptive concerns. We come to know a religion by learning its story and then witnessing how its followers act out their narrative in their liturgies and in their spiritual-ethical lives. While this is not a study of liturgical forms and practices, we must mention the obvious similarities between the liturgies of synagogue and church. Many of the words are identical or closely related articulations of the same thought. The ark containing the Word of God on the scrolls is paralleled by the tabernacle housing the Word made flesh. The ingestion of the Word in the elements of Communion is paralleled by the gesture of Jewish worshipers as the Torah scroll is carried in procession through the congregation. As it passes, the faithful reach out, touch it, and carry their hands to touch their mouths, thus expressing their desire to take the Word of God into their mouths that they may speak it and, in a deeper sense, become incarnations of it. This, too, is holy communion.

The many other parallels in liturgy and decoration of church and synagogue, the physical layout of the space, the bodily gestures of the worshipers, are too numerous for discussion here. When I have brought students to witness Jewish and Christian services over the past thirty years, they never fail to comment on the striking similarities. And, of course, where the Mass departs from synagogue practice in the holy sacrifice on the altar, it is only to reproduce the earlier blood sacrifice on the altar of Solomon's Temple (Heb. 9:25–26).

And we need only a paragraph of one sentence to state the obvious about the daily lives of pious Christians and observant Jews: spiritually they are parallel; ethically they are identical.

Returning to Paul, a Jewish theology of Christianity must examine his formulations of the relationship of the two faiths to see what can be used and what must be discarded. Why give Paul all this special attention? Because Paul was a Jew and a Christian theologian familiar with the patterns of thought of both faiths. He was raised in the first, and he created the earliest and most influential version of the second. He also offered two analyses that, I believe, can be partially adopted in our Jewish theology of Christianity—partially adopted but also partially rejected.

First of all, he outlines the earliest theory of who Jesus was and what he was sent to accomplish. I have already discussed Paul's inconsistent christologies: the low version of Romans 1:1–6 and the high in Philippians 2:5–11. In the first, Jesus is a human descendant of David who is then exalted as Son and Lord through his death and resurrection. In the second, Christ Jesus was "in the form of God," possessing "equality with God" prior to his "being born in the likeness of men," emptying and humbling himself as a servant, "obedient unto death, even death on a cross." As a consequence of his self-emptying, he was exalted, his name set above all others as Lord. As Roger Haight has pointed out, the first is a two-stage christology in which the earthly Jesus is raised to divine status, the second a three-stage account in which a divine Christ descends to earth and, having accomplished his kenotic work, is elevated by God to a heavenly status even higher than his original one.[16]

Clearly Judaism cannot endorse either of these Christian theories or incorporate them into its Jewish theology. There is no reason why it should. As Judaism sees the human dilemma, the election of Israel and gift of Torah are fully sufficient to deal with the problem of human misuse of free will (sin). As we have seen, the Christian solution is needed only if one begins with the Christian understanding of sin. That is where the two sister faiths truly differ. But that is not to say that this difference of interpretation of the shared text of Genesis causes them to part company. It is because they share that text—and so many others—but differ as to interpretation, that they have so much to say to each other. And the conversation has proved to be mutually enriching and enlightening.

Torah and Christ are both seen, respectively, as Word of God. So for both faiths the revealed Word is the solution to their two readings of the Eden problem. With its lighter view of sin, Judaism might become overly optimistic about human nature, causing it to fail to grasp the darkness so often found in the human heart. Conversations with Christians on this subject may help to correct such tendencies. On the other hand, Christianity has a tendency to become deeply pessimistic about what it sees as "fallen human nature." Exposure to Jewish analyses of the topic may help to alleviate some of this gloom. Through Jewish-Christian discussion of these issues, a more balanced view may emerge for both participants. The human reality is complex and varied, resistant to a single overall interpretation. We Jews and Christians need each other—and others still—to approach a fuller understanding of the vexing problems of human motivation and conduct. If we allow ourselves to move beyond mutual respect to mutual influence, we may find that both traditions of thought are richer for the exchange. The human reality is greater than either of our interpretations of it.

Such honest and complete exchanges between faiths on this and indeed on all aspects of our doctrinal differences must be genuine and thus open to learning from the other. We cannot assume that we possess all truth. Where our understanding is weak, the other's may be strong, and vice versa. We really do have much to teach each other. Such mutual learning is one of the blessings of the Jewish-Christian dialogue. It forces us to delve into our own tradition while simultaneously investigating the other's wisdom. The ultimate purpose is for Jews to become better Jews and for Christians to become better Christians and for both to become better and wiser human beings.

At its highest level interfaith exchange will include each participant's development of a theological understanding of the other. Once they allow themselves to accept the possibility that the other's evaluation of the problem of sin may contain wisdom, then they will be led to examine the possibility that the other's solution to that problem may contain truth. For example, Christians will come to appreciate how Judaism defines sin and thus how Torah deals with the problem. Jews, for their part, will strive to understand the Christian manner of conceiving Fall and Redemption and begin to appreciate the role of Jesus in the Christian worldview. We do not give up our conviction of the truth of our understanding, but we do leave open the possibility of the truth of the other's account of things. Thus it is not necessary to defend my truth by denying the possible truth of the other faith's insights. God may have acted as the other says God did. How does one open such a possibility while still holding to the truth of one's own traditional understanding?

The answer to this question for Judaism is the development of a Jewish theology of Christianity. In this book a number of historic attempts to do this will be reviewed. They are all *Jewish* ways of understanding our sister faith. That means that we need not adopt the worldview of the other as our own. We may be sisters, but we are fraternal, not identical twins. The Jewish thinker who attempts to understand Christianity must strive to develop a Jewish approach that comes as close as possible to the way in which Christianity sees itself, while still remaining wholly Jewish. What might such an evaluation look like in broad outline?

Starting from within our own Jewish tradition, we recall that the Holy One called Abraham to be a blessing to all the peoples of the world (Gen. 12:1–3). This has happened through the witness of Judaism itself, but also through Christianity and Islam. Today many billions worship Israel's God, only some 15 million of them being Jews. This is either some gigantic accident or the partial fulfillment of God's commission to Abraham. A Jewish theology of Christianity (Islam will have to wait for a future study) must see in this spread of Jewish insights via a closely related faith an opening of our covenant with God to include major parts of the larger human family. Again Paul gives us a model for understanding what has taken place, parts of which we Jews can accept while rejecting others.

In his definitive discussion of Christians and Jews in Romans 9 through 11, the apostle tackles what to him is at once a glorious development and a painful problem. What was happening in his day that so excited him? He saw the Jesus movement, originally one of the Judaisms of first-century Palestine, reaching beyond its original home out into the great world. Significant numbers of gentiles—pagans until that time—were coming to faith in Jesus as the God of Israel's agent of redemption. Together with the earlier Jews who had followed the Nazarene, these newcomers were creating what Paul saw as a new reality—a new people in Christ. Jews and gentiles were uniting; the ancient walls that had separated them for hundreds of years were crashing down. It was not that Jews were converting to Christianity but that gentiles were joining Israel through Christ. God who had covenanted with Abraham, with Isaac, and with Jacob and then with all Israel at Sinai, was now embracing the whole world. It seemed to Paul that all of humanity was becoming a newly expanded Israel, a universal people of God. He addressed gentile followers of Jesus as part of that new reality.

In his attempt to explain to the Roman followers of Jesus what was happening, as well as how they should view the Jews, he used the felicitous metaphor of the olive tree, an ancient symbol of Israel. In coming to Israel's God through their acceptance of Christ, gentiles were being grafted into the olive tree (Rom. 11:17–25). The covenant had been decisively opened to all through Christ. Since Paul affirmed the earlier covenant while adding a development that has manifestly taken place, I can see no reason why Jews cannot accept this part of his picture of what Jesus had accomplished—an opening of the covenant to include gentiles.

Of course, since it was Paul who developed the theory—not Jesus, who preached exclusively or predominantly to Jews (according to Matthew and Mark, respectively)—this opening to gentiles was really the work of Jesus via Paul. Traditional Jews at the time were in no position to understand events in this way. But today it seems to me that we have no reason not to agree that the God of Israel may well have spoken anew through Christianity at a decisive moment to bring the gentiles into an expanded covenant. The alternative to this theory, or one like it, appears to me to be an insistence on the part of Jews that God is involved in and concerned only with the spiritual well-being of some 15 million chosen ones while remaining indifferent to the billions who are left to stumble on without guidance from above. Such an exclusivist view seems to me to be not a religious theory but an antireligious one.

But why was it impossible for Jews at the time to see in Christianity a Jewish outreach into the larger human community? One reason was what most Jews saw as the extravagant claims made for Jesus by his followers. That objection still remains. But if Christians view Jesus as more than human, we need not view him as less than Jewish. We can see Jesus—a crucial figure in Jewish and human history—not as the Messiah conceived of by our rabbinic Judaism but as one sent by Israel's God to open the covenant to gentiles. That was not clear 2,000 years ago. But, today, who could deny that this is what Jesus has accomplished?

Jews of the first century also took exception to the negative attitude held by Jesus' followers, including Paul, toward the Mosaic covenant and the Jewish Law. Paul was rarely anti-Jewish, but he did hold views that could be considered anti-Judaism. He stated that Jews were the original people of the covenant, eternally belóved of God: "I bear them witness that they have a zeal for God, but it is not enlightened. For, being ignorant of the righteousness that comes from God, and seeking to establish their own, they did not submit to God's righteousness. For Christ is the end of the law, that every one who has faith may be justified" (Rom. 10:2–4). Jews did not believe this then. We do not believe this now. I do not believe this. That is, I, a Jew, do believe much of what Paul says I believe, but I do not believe my faith is "not enlightened" or that Christ is, for Jews, "the end of the law." As I have said earlier, Judaism retains its belief (which I share) in the human capacity for righteousness, as well as the revelation of the Torah as our guide in our moral and spiritual striving. This belief, which Paul considers "not enlightened," is, indeed, central to our faith. On this issue, as on many others that divide us, discussion and debate are called for. But Paul is entitled to disagree with traditional Judaism and propose a new reading of certain verses in Scripture that argue against the possibility of human righteousness. He is correct in stating that we Jews do not see why the sacrificial work of Christ was called for. As explained earlier, this flows logically from our definition of sin, as does our Jewish confidence in Torah as teacher and guide.

Jews can entertain the possibility of the truth of Christianity only if we view it as a faith revealed by Israel's God to and for gentiles. Later in this work I will discuss a number of Jewish thinkers of earlier ages who held that worship of Jesus, while forbidden to Jews, was permitted for gentiles. Our ancestors properly resisted Christianity when it attacked our faith and pressed us to convert. We would and should resist such blandishments today. But what is there to reject in an enlightened form of Christianity that has accepted the eternal validity of God's covenant with Israel and the value of the Jewish faith? As long as they recognize the truth of our faith *for us*, we may feel free to recognize the truth of their faith *for them*. How can one believe in the existence of two religious truths? By holding that they were revealed at different times to different groups of people. We come to God via Torah and membership in the Jewish people (Israel, Jewish root); gentiles (who choose not to become Jews) come to God via Jesus and the church (Israel, Christian branch). One God, two revelations, two true religions. Ultimately this same logic will lead both Jews and Christians to be open to the possible truths revealed in the other great religions of the world.

From the Jewish point of view, Paul's olive tree metaphor is also partially flawed. Can we accept the image of gentiles grafted into the tree of Israel through Christ? Certainly. However, Paul goes on to speak of some of the original branches of the tree having been broken off (Rom. 11:17) when Jews declined to include Jesus in their religion. For Paul this was all part of a divine plan. Had the Jews responded positively to the gospel, he claimed that it would never have occurred to him to carry the message to the more receptive gentiles (Rom. 11:11). But for Paul, Christ is for everyone. His redemptive plan has two stages. First the gentiles are won to the gospel, the Jews having declined it. Then the Jews will, at some future time, recognize Christ as Messiah. And so the branches that were cut off will be grafted in again (Rom. 11:25). "A hardening has come upon part of Israel, until the full number of the gentiles come in, and so all Israel will be saved . . . for the gifts and call of God are irrevocable" (Rom. 11:25–26, 29).

Paul is no pluralist, however much some would like to make him one. Judaism's current faith in Torah and Christianity's faith in Christ is not, for him, a simple difference of opinion, even less two closely related truths. Paul holds that our conception of Torah is based on a misunderstanding. Clearly we Jews, who continue in our ancient faith, must disagree. And we must reject the negative aspects of Paul's olive tree metaphor (as do many Christians in today's dialogue). Faithful Jews have in no sense been "broken off" from the flourishing tree of Israel. Today, of course, for those committed to the dialogue, the differences in our religious views are no longer a matter of right versus wrong, but of two valid conclusions arising out of two valid premises. Torah as *etz hayim*, tree of life, or Cross as tree of life: two responses to the dilemma posed by another tree that flourished in a lost Garden once upon a mythic time when the world was young.

Why must we insist on only one reading of a story, on only one understanding of a problem, on only one solution? If God has opened the covenant to include gentiles in a larger Israel, let us accept that, adding this new chapter to the old, old story of redemption. There are two distinct creation stories in the book of Genesis. Both of them convey life-giving truths about the divine and the human and how they interact. Both deserve our attention. Can we not, then, have two—or even more—accounts of sin and redemption? Jacob is said to have wrestled with himself, with another man, with God. All are true. One reading of a rich story does not cancel another; they complement and enhance each other. So it is with Judaism and Christianity. Paul's olive tree allegory— in all its positive aspects—tells us, the stock, to make room for new branches grafted in. And so we should. It is only the negative aspects of the metaphor that we must reject.

The good news is that since Vatican II in 1965, the mainstream churches, one after the other, have also rejected Paul's clam that we Jews are branches cut off. Today Christians have come of age. They do not wish to be saved at the expense of others. Israel is a mighty tree, old and firmly rooted in fertile soil. It has room for many branches. Now that so many Christians have come to understand that they have not replaced us, but joined us, we can feel free to welcome them as ingrafted branches of the tree of Israel reaching out into the world to nourish all people with goodly fruit. Let this be the starting point for a Jewish theology of Christianity that will emerge from these pages.

2

The Question of the Messiah

As usually conceived, the central disagreement between Judaism and Christianity is over whether Jesus of Nazareth was or was not (is or is not) the Messiah. When my New Testament students ask me this question, I usually reply: "Yes and no, depending on how you define the term 'Messiah.'" In Mark 8:29, Peter answers Jesus' question, "Who do you say that I am?" with "You are the Christ (Messiah)." But Jesus rejects this title or at least the title as understood by Peter. The disciple apparently conceived of Jesus as the glorious royal Messiah of David's line who was about to expel the Romans from Jerusalem and mount the Davidic throne of an Israel newly restored to independent life. In contrast to this implied expectation, Mark's Jesus responds by speaking of a suffering Son of Man who will be killed and rise again (Mark 8:31–38). Mark clearly understands this figure to be Jesus himself.

But if the Nazarene rejects the title of Messiah in Mark's account of the exchange at Caesarea Philippi, he reacts to Peter very differently in Matthew's rewriting of the event. In Mark the whole point of the confrontation is to reveal Jesus for the first time as the suffering Son of Man, thus bringing together at the very heart of christology the imagery of Isaiah 53 (the suffering servant of the Lord) and that of Daniel 7 (the glorious "one like a Son of Man"). But in Matthew's version of this exchange Mark's answer is given away in the question. Here Jesus asks the disciples, "Who do men say that the Son of Man is?" (Matt. 16:13). Jesus' self-identification as Son of Man is no longer the central point of the story. It is assumed in his question. Here Peter responds, "You are the Christ (Messiah), the Son of the living God" (Matt. 16:16). And here Jesus accepts the title of Messiah. The truth of his identity has been divinely revealed to Peter by Jesus' "Father who is in heaven" (Matt. 16:17). Nowhere in the following references to his suffering does Matthew's Jesus use the term "Son of Man." He only brings it into his monologue at the end when he is referring to the glorious coming of the one who is to judge the world (Matt. 16:27). Here, as elsewhere, Matthew reveals what can only be seen as a failure to understand the subtleties of Mark's careful and delicate reworking of traditional messianic terminology. For Matthew the Christian community's definition of "Messiah" as the one who suffers and dies for the world's redemption is assumed. Luke goes further by deleting entirely Peter's objection to the new definition (Lk. 9:18–27). He alters the original meaning of the exchange and ignores the complexities of first-century C.E. Jewish messianic speculation.

In reading Luke Timothy Johnson's very interesting work, *The Real Jesus,*[1] I was struck by the author's habit of repeating similar oversimplifications of a complex issue. In several places he writes of the "messianic pattern" of Jesus' life. By this he means the pattern of the suffering Messiah who lives and dies in service to others. According to Johnson, all the Gospels agree on this pattern. He is probably correct in this observation, but in his uncritical assertion that this is the "messianic pattern," he seems to be implying that it is the only one possible. He never examines how this suffering servant Messiah relates to the exalted Son of Man who is to come, and he certainly never even hints of any of the many other canonical and extracanonical concepts of the Messiah abroad in Palestine at the time of Jesus. For him, Jesus is the Messiah, and the Messiah is the one who suffers for others. This is "the messianic pattern."

One can only respond to such a single-visioned definition by pointing out that this is *a* messianic pattern or, rather, one element of a larger and more complicated Christian messianic pattern. And this pattern cannot be properly evaluated or understood except as part of an even larger pattern of Jewish messianism—or, rather, *messianisms* before, during, and after the time of Jesus. Today Jesus' Jewishness and that of nearly all his original interpreters is acknowledged by all, yet many still fail to locate early christology within its Jewish context or to inquire as to its relationship to other Jewish messianic formulations. Christianity, as one of the Judaisms of the first century, must be considered within its proper intellectual and spiritual environment. Examined in this manner, its messianism, far from being alien to Jewish thought patterns, may be revealed as one expression of the rich and varied world of historic hopes and mythic visions that is Israelite messianic speculation. This chapter will attempt a very brief outline of such an examination.[2]

The Royal Messiah in the Canon

Of the several messianic conceptions circulating among Jews in the first century, the one that has proved to be the most long-lived in Jewish circles is that of the idealized Davidic king. This perfect ruler of a future perfected Israelite kingdom is the key figure in many, though not all, prophetic eschatological projections of the end of days. But it must be noted that this image represents a radically futurized and idealized version of a title originally used in a far more mundane and restricted manner. The title "Messiah" occurs thirty-nine times in the Hebrew Scriptures. Not one of these usages refers to a king of the distant future. Rather, the terms "Messiah," "anointed one," and "the Lord's anointed" refer to the Israelite king ruling at the time. From Saul onward, Israel's king was believed to hold office by virtue of a divine anointing. Samuel anoints Saul with oil (1 Sam. 10:1), and God confirms the choice with a spiritual anointing (1 Sam. 10:10). The prophet later repeats this ritual with David (1 Sam. 16:13), and Nathan, David's court prophet, eventually announces that God's choice of David to be his anointed ruler will continue down through David's line forever (2 Sam. 7:11–17). This expansion from the original anointing of an individual to the permanent divine anointing of a dynasty proclaimed in Nathan's Davidic court theology represents the first instance of a futurizing tendency in the messianic idea: "The Lord declares to you that the Lord will make you a house . . . And your house and your kingdom shall be made sure forever before me; your throne shall be established forever" (2 Sam. 7: 11, 16).

As each new king of David's line was anointed by the high priest (who took over this role from the prophet), the great coronation anthem was chanted by the levitical choir. This has come down to us in Psalm 2:1–2:

> Why do the nations conspire,
>   and the peoples plot in vain?
> The kings of the earth set themselves,
>   and the rulers take counsel together,
>   against the Lord and his anointed . . .

But while Davidic kings were to rule Israel forever, there is as yet no idea here of a single ideal king whose reign would be eternal. History is gradually becoming myth in the Davidic theology, but the myth is dynastic, not yet focused on a future individual.

There are, of course, passages in which a great future king is spoken of, but it is interesting to note that the term "Messiah" is not used in them. Many of these passages are presented as prophecies from the distant past and refer to David himself. Actually composed during David's reign, they legitimate the ascent to the throne of the Lord's chosen ruler. The patriarch Jacob foretells his rise from the royal tribe of Judah. In Genesis 49:10, we find: "The scepter shall not depart from Judah, nor the ruler's staff from between his feet." In Numbers 24:17, Balaam offers a similar prophecy. Although Judah is not mentioned, the Davidic reference is clear:

> I see him, but not now;
> I behold him, but not nigh:
> a star shall come forth out of Jacob,
> and a scepter shall rise out of Israel;
> it shall crush the forehead of Moab,
> and break down all the sons of Seth

This prophecy was later reinterpreted as an eschatological vision, but the reference to Moab (and Edom in v. 18) reveals that David, the conqueror of these peoples, is the "star" Balaam "foresaw." In future ages the star image was to be appropriated by one messianic figure (Bar Kochbar) and the vision of the one who rises by another (Jesus of Nazareth). Samuel 23:1, 5 also uses this latter terminology:

> The oracle of David, the son of Jesse,
>   the oracle of the man who was raised on high,
> the anointed (Messiah) of the God of Jacob,
>   the sweet psalmist of Israel ...
>
> Yea, does not my house stand so with God?
>   For he has made with me an
>   Everlasting covenant.

The metaphor of rising or being raised to royal power, used in reference to David, the king who ruled when these lines were composed, will be mythologized and literalized in the Gospel accounts of the resurrection of "great David's greater son."[3] We see a similar pattern in the eventual literalizing of another mythic element of the Davidic theology. The Second Psalm, which celebrates the coronation of the anointed of the Lord, speaks in more personal terms of the relationships between God and Israel's king:

THE QUESTION OF THE MESSIAH   41

> I will tell of the decree of the Lord:
> He said to me [David] "You are my son,
> today have I begotten you." (v. 7)

Originally conceived in an adoptive sense, this image was to be re-visioned by three of the evangelists in a literal and more highly mythical way. Mark alone remains a classic adoptionist in his view of Jesus' sonship. Luke and Matthew literalize the concept, and John goes even beyond this to identify Jesus as the earthly incarnation of the divine Word itself, the son who is, in some mystic sense, one with his father.

The theme of divine sonship is further expressed in Psalm 110. The probable meaning of verse 3 is:

> ...upon the holy mountain
> From the womb of the morning
> like dew, I have given you birth.

However symbolic these words may have originally been intended to be, later Christian interpretation was to give them a more powerful mythic meaning. In all these passages, and in many more, the fact that the word "Messiah" rarely appears should not obscure the "messianic" meaning. It is David and his dynasty that are being described; the "anointed" (as in Ps. 132:17) is the star, the son, the one who is raised up.

All Davidic kings are the Lord's anointed, but not all ruled in admirable fashion. While the failures of individual rulers in no way compromised Nathan's Davidic theology, the human failures of unfaithful monarchs will be punished: "I will establish the throne of his [Solomon's] kingdom forever. I will be his father and he shall be my son. When he commits iniquity, I will chasten him with the rod of men, with the stripes of the sons of men, but I will not take my steadfast love from him" (2 Sam. 7:13–15). Again the reference to an eternal kingdom is dynastic, not individual, nor, as we see, is any particular king idealized. Both David and Solomon sinned and were punished, but the dynasty went on. These inevitable human failings even of God's chosen ones would gradually give rise to the beginning of the idealization of the Messiah-King who would sit on Israel's throne. These early ideal visions were presented by prophets, in contrast to the flawed king who actually ruled at the time.

In Isaiah 7 and 9 the prophet foresees (or is said by a later writer of the Isaiah school to have seen) a soon-to-be-born king who, in stark contrast to Ahaz, the current weak and vacillating ruler, will be perhaps Israel's greatest monarch. In Isaiah 7:14 we read: "Behold a young woman shall conceive and bear a son, and shall call his name Immanuel [God in our midst]."

This next Judean king, Hezekiah (the Lord is my strength), son of Ahaz and his queen (the "young woman" referred to), will "refuse the evil and choose the good." And

> ...his name will be called
> Wonderful Counselor, Mighty God,
> Everlasting Father, Prince of Peace. (Isa. 9:6)

The meaning of the name would be more clearly conveyed by the following translation:

> ...his name will be called
> "A wonderful counselor is the Mighty God,
> The Everlasting Father." [He will be a] peaceful prince.

This name does not imply divinity, but rather indicates that the appearance of this child-king is a sign that God has not and will not abandon the Davidic line no matter the failings of this child's father (and the abominations of his son, Manassah). The ideal picture of Hezekiah's reign is striking; this is the first time that any biblical king has been pictured in such terms of perfection.

> Of the increase of his government and of peace
>   there will be no end,
> upon the throne of David, and over his kingdom,
>   to establish it, and to uphold it
> with justice and with righteousness
>   from this time forth and forevermore.
> The zeal of the Lord of hosts will do this. (Isa. 9:7)

Again, the eternity spoken of is dynastic, but it is expressed in a manner that could easily be taken to point to a future king's eternal rule. And so it would be reinterpreted in later ages in reference to another descendant of David.

Two chapters later, Isaiah, or a later writer of the Isaiah school, offers a vision of an ideal future king that has become a core text of messianic prophecy. Whether the prophet is referring to Hezekiah, as in chapters 7 and 9, or is speaking of a more distant future fulfillment is unclear. I tend toward the latter reading largely because the vision is not only of an idealized reign, as in chapter 9, but of an idealized world in which all conflict within the created order is overcome. This text may be a bridge passage in Isaiah on which the prophet or his heirs pass over from the earlier focus on a current or soon-to-be anointed king to a future ideal ruler of a mythically perfected earth. This ultimate vision of the "Peaceable Kingdom" could hardly refer to conditions expected to be realized soon even under the benign rule of a Hezekiah.

There shall come forth a shoot
   from the stump of Jesse.
And a branch shall grow out of his roots.
And the spirit of the Lord shall be upon him,
   the spirit of wisdom and understanding...

...with righteousness he shall judge the poor,
   and decide with equity for the meek of the
   earth:
And he shall smite the earth with
   the rod of his mouth,
   and with the breath of his lungs he
   shall slay the wicked.
Righteousness shall be the girdle of his waist,
and faithfulness the girdle of his loins.

The wolf shall dwell with the lamb,
   and the leopard shall lie down
   with the kid...

They shall not hurt or destroy
   in all my holy mountain;
for the earth shall be full of the
   knowledge of the Lord
as the waters cover the sea. (Isa. 11:1–9)

The passage goes on to predict the gathering of scattered Israel and Judah "from the four corners of the earth" (v. 12).

A unique expression of the messianic hope is found in Deutero-Isaiah's hymns regarding Cyrus, king of Persia, the only gentile ever referred to as "Messiah":

Thus says the Lord to his anointed, to Cyrus,
whose right hand I have grasped,
to subdue nations before him
and ungird the loins of kings...
for the sake of my servant Jacob,
and, Israel, my chosen,
I call you by your name,
I surname you, though you do not know me. (Isa. 45:1, 4)

In this prophecy we find many of the elements of classic messianism: the righteous and wise king who fears the Lord, who will establish social justice by military might. But these victories are achieved by the Lord's power given to Cyrus. The ultimate beneficiary is, of course, Israel, and Cyrus is ignorant of the divine plan being realized through his conquests. The messianic themes of kingship, conquest, gathering of Israel, smiting of her enemies, and a righteous order reestablished are all present. What makes this messianic proclamation unlike all others is that the Messiah here is a non-Israelite who brings salvation to Israel. We will see an interesting inversion of this conception in Christian messianism, which proclaims an Israelite Messiah who brings salvation to the nations.

Although the prophet Isaiah is identified in the minds of many with the hope for a Davidic Messiah in the classic sense of an idealized ruler of the future, it is probable that Jeremiah was the originator of the idea. As we have seen, the original Isaiah material may have contained references to a great king of the immediate future (Hezekiah), but more long-range and mythologized prophecies were added by later writers of the Isaiah school, probably in the exilic and postexilic period. Thus Jeremiah becomes the most likely prophet to have originated the classic messianic vision of an idealized king ruling a perfected Israel in a future age.

The historical context makes more likely the probability that Jeremiah was responsible for the projection of a mythologized messianic ruler of the future. The need for this transformation of a present ruler into a future one and a flawed king into an idealized image of perfection probably emerged only with the fall of the Davidic kingdom in the Babylonian conquest of 587–586 B.C.E. Left in the ruins of Jerusalem and having witnessed the overthrow of the dynasty, Jeremiah felt called to give new life to the Davidic court theology, which many must have viewed as discredited by the recent tragic history. His previous oracles of doom gave way to new proclamations of hope for Israel's future. In Jeremiah 23:5–6 we find:

> "Behold, the days are coming," says the Lord, "when I will raise up for David a righteous Branch, and he shall reign as king and deal wisely, and shall execute justice and righteousness in the land. In his days, Judah will be saved, and Israel will dwell securely. And this is the name by which he will be called: 'The Lord is our righteousness.' "

His name, "The Lord is our righteousness," is a contemptuous reference to the name of Israel's discredited last king, Zedekiah ("The Lord is *my* righteousness"), who brought the nation and himself to ruin. The prophesied king will rule for the people, not for himself. This anointed one of David's line

("Branch" being a classic messianic term) will gather Judah and Israel from afar in a new exodus from captivity and return to the land of promise (vv. 7–8). In chapter 30 the prophet adds that the returned people will "serve the Lord their God and David their king whom I will raise up for them" (v. 9).

In contrast to this messianic prophecy, Jeremiah's final vision is of a "new covenant" written upon the hearts of Israelites, all of whom will "know" the Lord (Jer. 31:31–34). All this will be accomplished directly by God, with no mention of (or, seemingly, need for) a Messiah figure. In this vision, God has been given the role of redeemer and perfector of history. God' relationship with the people of the "new covenant" is too intimate to leave room for an intermediary or earthly representative. This passage is an example of the many prophetic projections of an eschaton without a Messiah. One cannot say whether this vision is original to Jeremiah or is a later addition to the actual oracles of the seventh-century prophet who had hoped for the coming of David's righteous branch.

Ezekiel followed Jeremiah in many things, including messianic imagery. In chapter 17:22–24 the exilic prophet speaks of a sprig or twig of the cedar that will become a noble tree giving shelter to many. This messianic allegory lacks the usual royal symbols, but it is clear enough in its reference to earlier tree of Jesse language. In 34:23–31 the prophet foretells a future age of a shepherd king of David's line. Following a judgment presided over by God, the shepherd king will be placed on a throne to feed his people, but always under God's authority. A covenant of peace will be established with deliverance both from human oppressors and natural threats (drought, famine, and wild beasts). "And they shall know that I, the Lord their God, am with them" (v. 30).

Here we have a vision of restoration in which a Davidic king (Messiah) is present but hardly necessary. All the major work is done by God, yet the title of shepherd is given to the human prince. One might make the same observation of Ezekiel's famous chapter 37. The dry bones are raised up, clothed with flesh, and given new life. Israel, thus restored, will include both northern and southern kingdoms (the two sticks), but under a single king of David's line (v. 24). The restoration will be permanent under an eternal covenant. Its external sign will be the restored sanctuary (Temple) in the midst of the returned community. Although the king functions primarily as a symbol of the reunification of Judah and Israel, he is a definite element in the vision, and thus this prophecy must be counted among the royal Davidic messianic oracles.

Among these traditional royal Davidic prophecies must be counted those found in Hosea and Amos. Although not regarded as part of the original eighth-century B.C.E. material, the references to the restoration of "David, their king" (Hos. 3:5) and to the raising up of "the fallen booth of David" (Amos 9:11) expressed postexilic hopes for a full and flourishing renewal of national life under a renascent Davidic dynasty. While not full-blown classic messianism, these images were ultimately to be read as such. Significantly, the author of Acts has James refer to the Amos passage at the great Jerusalem council of 50 c.e. Here he seems to interpret the fallen booth of David that is raised up as Jesus' body. As the restored Davidic dynasty was to "possess . . . all the nations" (v. 12), so now the resurrected Davidic heir will come to hold spiritual sway over the gentiles (Acts 15:16–17). Thus the conversion of Cornelius is justified by a radical reinterpretation of ancient prophecy. The mission of the church to the gentiles begins here.

Postexilic additions to Micah also contain messianic material that was to prove central to later Christianity. In 5:2, we read:

> But you, O Bethlehem Ephrathah,
>   who are little to be of the clans of Judah,
> from you shall come forth for me
>   one who is to be ruler in Israel,
>   whose origin is from of old,
>   from ancient days . . .

During a time when no Davidic heir sat upon the throne, the prophet sought to keep alive the hope for a new shepherd king who, like David, would be born in Bethlehem but, unlike David's descendants who once ruled in Jerusalem, would "feed his flock in the strength of the Lord" (v. 4). The prophecy, written in the wake of the overthrow of the Jerusalem monarchy, is both a repudiation and a reaffirmation of the Davidic tradition, a "back to the source" oracle calling for a return to David's roots rather than a continuation of his compromised and dethroned line. I rejected such an interpretation of Isaiah 11 because it seems unlikely that the prophet would announce a divine repudiation of the Davidic line while it was still occupying the throne. There the prophet pins all his hopes on a Davidic heir rather than calling for a new beginning with another line stemming from Jesse. But in a postexilic Judah without any king, the heirs of the Micah tradition might well view the Davidic line as having been abandoned by God and thus call for a return to Bethlehem, where God would raise another king who would fulfill the hopes once placed on the young shepherd-king, David. Needless to say, such subtleties would hardly be noticed centuries later by readers of this prophecy. They expected a Messiah who was both a native of Bethlehem and a descendant of David. This prophecy became a central element of the classic messianic tradition.

In the prophecies of Haggai and Zechariah we find messianic terms once again used to describe living persons currently leading the people. Haggai's central preoccupation was the building of a replacement for the destroyed Temple. For him the stability and reconstitution of the restored postexilic community depended on the successful completion of this divinely ordained project. And it was Zerubbabel, the Judean governor of David's line, who was commanded to accomplish it. Haggai's—and Zechariah's—urgings were effective, and the work was completed. Encouraged by this, the prophet went on to turn his attention to the successful governor and to hail him in messianic terms:

> Speak to Zerubbabel, governor of Judah, saying, I am about to shake the heavens and the earth and to overthrow the throne of kingdoms.... On that day, says the Lord of Hosts, I will take you, O Zerubbabel my servant...and make you like a signet ring; for I have chosen you, says the Lord of Hosts. (Haggai 2:21-23)

This rash prophecy of the destruction of the world political order (the "overthrow" could only be of Persian power) may have proved fatal to the unfortunate Zerubbabel. Rather than being elevated to messianic ("signet-ring") status, he soon disappeared from history altogether, a victim, perhaps, of Persian preventive measures. Jewish liturgical activity at a restored Temple was one thing; Jewish political ambition was quite another.

Zechariah was no less vocal regarding Zerubbabel as soon-to-be revealed Messiah. Despite the poverty and seeming lack of promise of the restored community in the late sixth century B.C.E., the prophet proclaimed that Jewish history was still in God's hands, that God's angels even now patrolled all the earth (1:10), and that God was a wall of fire for the unwalled holy city (2:5). Zerubbabel is "my servant," the Branch (3:8) who "shall bear royal honor, and shall sit upon his throne" (6:13). In 4:14 Zerubbabel is clearly seen as one anointed with holy oil, the royal Messiah. The Branch metaphor is taken from earlier references to the branch of David (Jer. 23:5), an unmistakable messianic formula. As we have seen, the prophets' hopes for Zerubbabel were unrealized. Is this historic failure what prompted the later oracles in the Zechariah corpus? In 9:9 we find:

> Rejoice greatly, O daughter of Zion!
>   Shout aloud, O daughter of Jerusalem!
> Lo, your king comes to you:
>   triumphant and victorious is he,
> humble and riding an ass,
>   on a colt, the foal of an ass.

The prophecy goes on to explain that the Messiah's lowly means of transportation represents God's rejection of chariots, warhorses, and battle bows (v. 10). This king will "command peace to the nations." This peaceful theme is a continuation of chapter 4: "Not by might and not by power, but by my spirit, says the Lord" (4:6). In chapter 4 the Lord is speaking to Zerubbabel. This may indicate that the prophecy in chapter 9 is about the same man. If so, the vision is grandiose indeed, for King Zerubbabel's rule is foretold to be "from sea to sea and from the River to the ends of the earth" (9:10). But is this a prophecy of Zerubbabel's soon to be realized glory, or is it a classic messianic projection of a distant age to come?

In chapters 13 and 14 the prophet speaks of "a fountain opened for the house of David and the inhabitants of Jerusalem to cleanse them from sin and uncleanness" (13:1). This "fountain" would seem to represent a future Davidic king who will somehow cleanse the nation of sin. But in the next lines it is God, not the king, who "cuts off" both idols and false prophets in the land. And in 13:7 the Lord appears to strike the shepherd king and two-thirds of the people—a fearful tribulation indeed followed by a further refinement of the remaining third of the population. Only then will the remnant "call upon my name," leading God to take them back as his people (13:7–9). As if all this were not strange enough, the oracle in chapter 14 foretells "a day of the Lord" in which God will gather the nations against Jerusalem, allow the city's destruction, then fight against the destroyers, and finally reestablish the city as a source of "living waters." At that point "the Lord will become king over all the earth," and all the world will come to Jerusalem to offer sacrifice.

What is most peculiar in all this is that chapter 14, the last oracle, contains no mention of a Messiah at all. On the contrary, it is the Lord who is declared king several times as if in pointed renunciation of any human royal claimant. This oracle belongs with the many in Scripture that are clearly eschatological but manifestly nonmessianic. But, as we have seen in 9:9, the human king of peace does arrive in Jerusalem humbly on an ass. Is this the shepherd struck down by the sword (God's own) in 13:7? If he dies at this point, having cleared the nation of sin (13:1), he would consequently be absent in the final vision of chapter 14. If this is the meaning of this material, we may have here the inspiration of the vision of the Messiah who appears, presumably reigns, and then is killed in 4 Ezra.

But this reading of Zechariah is far from certain. It is certainly not the way the text is usually interpreted. Many read 13:7 as a continuation of the denunciation of the "worthless shepherd" of 11:15–17. According to this reading, the shepherd, whoever he may be, is not a future Messiah in the classic mold but a current community leader of some kind (surely not Zerubbabel) who will soon be struck down by the Lord in punishment for his indifference to "the perishing...the wandering...and the maimed" (11:16). This self-seeking officeholder will pay for his corruption and lack of compassion. But why would the "sheep...be scattered" (13:7) as a consequence of this person's fall? Why would the death of a manifestly evil leader (shepherd) not liberate and encourage the people? This text is full of puzzles.

But whatever its original meaning may have been, this verse must have evolved in the thinking of some Israelites into a messianic prophecy. The evidence for this is found in the Gospels. En route from the Last Supper to Gethsemane, in Mark 14:23, Jesus, thinking of his coming arrest, confides to his disciples his fear that they will all fall away; "for it is written, 'I will strike the shepherd, and the sheep will be scattered.'" Was Mark the first to read the Zechariah text as a prophecy of a future Messiah who will be struck down (as part of God's plan, for it is the divine sword that strikes him in Zechariah 13:7), or was this verse already understood in these terms? Another unanswerable question to add to that of the text's original meaning. All these uncertainties should lead us to leave open the question of whether we have in Zechariah the first prophecy of a future Messiah who dies as part of a divine scenario.

With the prophecies of Haggai and Zechariah we come to the end of royal Davidic messianism in the canonical Hebrew Scriptures. At times referring to a sitting king, at times to a soon to be revealed ruler, at times to a classic Messiah of a mythic future, Scripture's royal messianism takes several forms. But this is not the only messianic tradition in the Bible. We now turn to texts that refer to a priestly anointed.

The Priestly Messiah in the Canon

As we have seen in the canon, the specific term "Messiah" is used in its royal sense to designate the Israelite king ruling at the time. But there is another anointed one often mentioned in the books of Hebrew Scripture. This is the priestly Messiah of Aaron's line whose office was also confirmed with an anointing of sacred oil. In Exodus, Leviticus, and Numbers the anointed priest or priests are mentioned (Exod. 28:41, 30:30, 40:15; Lev. 4:3, 6:19; Num. 35:25, etc.). At times, of course, the king was permitted to perform sacrifices, a duty usually restricted to the priesthood. Saul incurred Samuel's wrath for taking on the priestly role at Gilgal (Sam. 13:8–15), but no objections were recorded when David performed priestly sacrifices (2 Sam. 6:17–18) or when Solomon apparently did the same (1 Kings 8:62–65). At these times the distinction between priestly and kingly roles seemed to blur, but the tradition remains clear as to there being two distinct offices requiring anointing. While prophets and patriarchs are occasionally called "anointed ones," this usage is probably metaphorical (Ps. 105:15; 1 Chron. 16:22; Isa. 61:1; Joel 3:1). In the postexilic period the theme of the anointed priest is found in Haggai (1:1–14, 2:21–23) and Zechariah (4:6, 6:9–14) indirectly and in Zechariah 4:14. Here the prophet visualizes a great menorah with two olive trees or two olive branches to its right and left. In answer to the prophet's request for clarification, the angel explains, "these are the two sons of oil (or, "anointed ones") who stand by the Lord of the whole earth." These two anointed leaders, the governor Zerubbabel and the high priest Joshua, hold distinct, divinely anointed offices. Like Moses and Aaron of antiquity, they both represent divine authority on earth. It is Zechariah's image of the Davidic and Aaronic anointed ones that may have inspired the Qumran community in its expectation of two Messiahs, one royal, one priestly, and even the vision of Jesus as high priest, albeit of the line of Melchizedek rather than Aaron (Heb. 5:10), may owe something to Zechariah's conception of a priestly Messiah. Of course the original picture is of a priest living at the time of the prophet's writing. But like so many of the biblical images referring to contemporary figures, this idea awaited only an age of renewed mythic imagination to transform it into a hope for an idealized future realization.

The Suffering Servant in the Canon

In a very real sense the whole saga of Israel's history contained in Scripture is the tale of God's suffering servant. Abraham, Isaac, and Jacob all suffer for a higher purpose. All are refined by suffering so as to become what God wishes them to be. Abraham is assured that this pattern will continue into future generations. In Genesis 15:12–13 the Lord tells the patriarch: "Know of a surety that your descendants will be sojourners in a land that is not theirs, and will be slaves there, and they will be oppressed for four hundred years."

God's newly created people, guiltless of any crime, will suffer for centuries. One might call this the dark side of the covenant, and Israel has come to know it well. But God's servant nation will emerge from slavery "with great possessions" (Gen. 15–14). What are these "possessions"? Surely not merely the silver and gold thrust upon them at their departure by the desperate Egyptians. No, the Bible itself reveals the treasure Israel mined from oppression: we find it described in Exodus 22:21 and 23:9: "You shall not oppress a stranger; you know the heart of the stranger, for you were strangers in the land of Egypt." The suffering of centuries is not for nothing. Through it

Israel is tested and taught the lesson of empathy. Henceforth the Israelite mission in the world will focus on compassion for the stranger, the helpless, the marginalized. And all this will stem from Israel's life in the world from the very beginning. Israel has a good heart because she has a good memory. This collective individual, the people Israel, will emerge time and again from severe tribulation as a more dedicated servant of God. And all peoples will benefit from the lessons learned by Israel from its trials.

This messianic reading of Israelite history sees the people itself as a collective individual placed on earth to keep God's law, proclaim God's sovereignty, and build God's kingdom on earth. Israel itself takes on the messianic function as it labors for the day when God will crown Israel's historic work with an eschatological epiphany. Until that day it is to be expected that Israel will suffer in the world. This may be an innocent suffering, as in Egypt, through which Israel is to come to "know the heart" of the oppressed. Or it may be a *refining* suffering as both punishment for straying from God's path and purification for future faithful service. Virtually all the prophets interpreted foreign conquests in this way, especially at the time of the Babylonian exile. It is in this light that we turn to the suffering servant passages in Deutero-Isaiah. We have two questions before us. The first is, of course, the identity of the servant. The second is how that identity was understood in the first century.

The first of Isaiah's servant songs (42:1–4) refers either to Israel or to Cyrus, it is not clear which. Either way, there is a messianic theme here, since Cyrus is elsewhere referred to as "my anointed" (45:1) and Israel has often been conceived in Scripture in messianic terms, as noted earlier. But there is no classic messianic theme of an individual future redeemer king to be found here. The servant is the chosen of God who bears the divine spirit. His task is to establish "justice in the earth" (v. 4) for the benefit of all people. It seems to me that this proclamation could refer just as well to the contemporary Cyrus or the future Israel. If the reference is to Cyrus, then the "bruised reed" and "dimly burning wick" (v. 3) that he will not injure is Israel. But the title of "servant," used frequently in surrounding chapters to designate Israel, would seem to indicate that the nation itself is being addressed here. In neither case, of course, is the servant suffering in this first of the songs.

In the second song the servant speaks (Isa. 49:1–13), and the voice seems to be that of the nation itself. This is stated explicitly in verse 3. But in verses 5 and 6 a distinction seems to appear between the servant and the people:

> And now the Lord says,
> who formed me from the womb
> to be his servant,

> to bring Jacob back to him;
> and that Israel might be gathered
> to him . . . " (v. 5)

Is the servant here a particular exemplary Israelite or the personification of the nation as a whole? If he is synonymous with the nation, the statement is puzzling, since the one addressed seems to have a redemptive function to perform *for* and *with* the nation. It is easy to see how the individual interpretation of this ambiguous text could gain ascendancy in the first century when the single individual Messiah so often represented the collective individual, Israel. Here as elsewhere the gathering of the nation from afar and the servant, formed from the womb, will ultimately be a light to all nations (v. 6). The suffering spoken of here is national. Israel is

> . . . one deeply despised, abhorred by the
> nations,
> the servant of rulers . . . (v. 7)

But the Lord "will have compassion on his afflicted," and heaven and earth will exult to see it (v. 13).

The third servant song (Isa. 50:4–11) speaks in the first-person singular. We may be dealing with an extended metaphor for Israel, but the plain sense of the text indicates that an individual is speaking. Is he the prophet himself who, like Ezekiel, confronts "a rebellious house" of Israel? (Ezek. 2:5). Or is he another divine spokesman who is rejected by his contemporaries? If he is Israel, then it is the gentile nations who reject his witness and who will pay the penalty for causing his suffering. And suffer he does, as we see in verse 6:

> I gave my back to be smitten,
> and my cheeks to those who
> pulled out the beard;
> I hid not my face
> from shame and spitting.

The last servant song (Isa. 53:1–12) is the most poignant of all and the most famous due to its later Christian appropriation. Here, too, the servant is presented as an individual, but who can say whether this is, once again, a metaphor for the nation of Israel?

> He was despised and rejected by men,
> a man of sorrows and acquainted
> with grief . . .

> But he was wounded for our transgressions,
>   he was bruised for our iniquities: . . .
> and the Lord has laid on him the iniquity
>   of us all. (Isa. 53:3, 5, 6)

The servant suffers for the sins of others, and with that suffering he becomes an offering for their sin. He dies (v. 12) to make intercession for transgressors. Is the prophet speaking of a historical personage known to his hearers, about himself or Jeremiah, or about a future suffering redeemer? If he means Israel, the collective individual who suffers for the world's redemption, he might have done us all the favor of saying so. As it is, if this is a metaphor, extended in the extreme, it seems to take on a life of its own due to the superb eloquence of the language and the richness of its imagery. It might be said that the metaphorical devices are so poignant that they obscure rather than clarify the underlying meaning. When a metaphor becomes opaque, when it loses its transparency, it becomes self-sufficient; in short, it ceases to be a metaphor. This is precisely what happened to Isaiah 53. Whatever its original meaning, by the first century more than a few saw it as a messianic text. In following centuries both Christians and Jews were to speak of a suffering Messiah, even one who dies, and Isaiah 53 may be the source of this powerful image.

The "Son of Man" in the Canon

No conception in Scripture has undergone a more radical transformation than that of the "Son of Man." Originally the term meant exactly what it says. A human being with all his limitations is designated in contrast to the power and wisdom of God. In Ezekiel the term becomes a virtual name for the prophet, imposed upon him by an almighty deity who wishes to keep the lowly human in his place. "Son of Man," says the Lord to the prostrate prophet, "stand upon your feet, and I will speak with you" (Ezek. 2:1). This form of address continues throughout the book.

But in Daniel 7 we find a vastly different usage. Here we find "one like a son of man" but infinitely more:

> I saw in the night visions,
>   and behold, with the clouds of heaven
> there came one like a son of man,
> and he came to the Ancient of Days
> and was presented before him.
> And to him was given dominion

and glory and kingdom,
that all peoples, nations, and languages
should serve him;
his dominion is an everlasting dominion,
which shall not pass away,
and his kingdom one that shall not be destroyed. (Dan. 7:13–14)

This one "*like* a son of man" is precisely the opposite of Ezekiel's son of man. This is one who appears to be human but is clearly a semidivine being. He comes with clouds from heaven and is given eternal dominion. He is the apocalyptic judge and redeemer who serves God and shares in his divinity. Here is the ultimate supernaturalization of the Messiah-King who has been given divine power and authority in this glorious mythic vision. That this figure was construed in the first century as the Messiah will be demonstrated later in our examination of Enoch.

Postcanonical Messianic Conceptions

As we turn to the postcanonical literature of the Jews, we must recall that we have culled from Scripture four distinct conceptions that can broadly be considered to be messianic. We have reviewed references to a royal Messiah (contemporary or future)—a priestly Messiah, a suffering servant seen as either a single or collective individual (Israel) and a divine Son of Man. We will now see how each of these conceptions, whether or not they were originally intended as classic messianic images (and most of them were not), became in later centuries part of Israel's eschatological messianic expectation.

At this point it should be noted that we have no evidence that all or most Israelites of the intertestamental period expected the coming of any kind of Messiah. Much prophetic eschatology attributed future salvific work directly to God, obviating any need for a messianic redemptive agent. Most of Deutero-Isaiah expresses such thinking, as do several other prophets. We do not know whether most Jews of the first century lived in messianic expectation. Sadducees rejected all such notions as invalid post-Mosaic additions to the true faith of the Torah. And Pharisees focused more on sanctification of daily life than on eschatology. Zealots and Qumran covenanters apparently held messianic beliefs of very different varieties. But of the average person's thoughts on the matter we know nothing.

What we do have are a number of texts produced by communities of Jews who did hold messianic beliefs, and they indicate a wide variety of expectations. Because there was no single Judaism at the time, there was no single conception of the Messiah. All the assorted messianic ideas referred back in one way or another to biblical sources, but the interpretations of ancient texts were nothing if not varied, as we shall see.

The Messiahs of the Pseudepigrapha

The Similitudes of Enoch

Most striking—and most complete—of the noncanonical treatments of the messianic theme is the series of eschatological visions found in chapters 37 through 71 of 1 Enoch. Known as the Book of Similitudes, this material of the first century B.C.E. presents a series of prophetic visions of heaven and earth and of the last judgment. Enoch, the mysterious character from Genesis 5:18–24, said not to have died but to have been translated alive into heaven, is given a tour of his new home by an angel who reveals to him secrets of the latter days.

In chapter 38 we are introduced to a humanity split between the righteous and the sinners who oppress them. These righteous are the elect of God while the wicked are identified as kings and rulers. Soon "the Righteous One" appears, condemns the sinners, and justifies the faith of the righteous ones. In chapter 40 the prophet describes a vast multitude of those "who stand before the Lord of the Spirits" (v. 1). He goes on to speak of four angels, one of whom blesses "the Elect One" and the elect of humanity. Notice that where "the Righteous One" is mentioned the human righteous are also referred to. In similar fashion "the Elect One" appears with the human elect. In each case the former (a transcendent, heavenly figure) will justify and defend his human counterparts. In discussing Isaiah's servant songs I commented on the difficulty of determining whether the servant (called the righteous one in Isaiah 53:11 and the elect or chosen one in Isaiah 42:1) is an individual or a designation of the people Israel, elsewhere called servant, elect, and righteous. In Enoch the issue is clarified. There are elect and righteous people *and* a distinct Elect/Righteous One who, in many ways, can be said to represent them. Why does the author of Enoch portray this figure in such superhuman terms? He explains himself in chapter 42:

> Wisdom could not find a place in which she could dwell; but a place was found (for her) in the heavens.
> Then Wisdom went out to dwell with the children of the people, but she found no dwelling place.

> (So) Wisdom returned to her place and she settled permanently among
> the angels . . . (42:1–2)

In this magnificent poem we may find an explanation for what may be
termed the "supernaturalization" of religious thought in the intertestamental
period. In this literature we find increased emphasis on transcendent phenomena; angels and demons abound and a mythologizing of earlier, more
earthly themes is the rule. Messianic images are no exception.

As the author states, Wisdom (now hypostatized and personified in the
typical fashion of the age) dwells not with humanity but with the angels, not
on earth but in the heavens. Thus traditional conceptions, the Messiah among
them, must be supernaturalized if they are to reveal to seekers the Wisdom
that rules the universe. A human king of David's line becomes a divine personification of Israel's righteousness and election; the Davidic throne in Jerusalem becomes a transcendent throne in heaven; and the Davidic dynastic
requirements, as mere human considerations, can be dispensed with entirely.
Having given us a clue to his thinking, the author of Enoch goes on to introduce us more fully to the heavenly Righteous and Elect One.

In chapter 45 "my Elect One" sits on the seat of glory and judges the
sinners and the holy ones. Following that judgment the Elect One will dwell
on a perfected earth among the righteous. Chapter 46 extends the vision:

> At that place, I saw the one to whom belongs the time before time.
> And his head was white like wool, and there was with him another
> individual, whose face was like that of a human being. His counte-
> nance was full of grace like that of one among the holy angels. . . .
>   This is the Son of Man to whom belongs righteousness, and with
> whom righteousness dwells. And he will open all the hidden store-
> rooms; for the Lord of the Spirits has chosen him. (46:1, 3)

The inspiration of this vision is clearly Daniel 7, the only true apocalypse in
the Hebrew canon. But now the "one like a son of man" (Dan. 7:13) has
become simply "the Son of Man," and a term used in Ezekiel to designate a
merely human being has been transformed into its opposite, the heavenly,
divine judge of the world. We learn more about him in chapter 48:

> At that hour that Son of Man was given a name in the presence of the
> Lord of the Spirits before time, even before the sun and the moon,
> before the creation of the stars, he was given a name in the presence
> of the Lord of the Spirits. He will become a staff for the righteous
> ones in order that they may lean on him and not fall. He is the light
> of the gentiles and he will become the hope of those who are sick in

their hearts. All those who dwell on earth shall fall and worship before him. . . . For this purpose he became the Chosen One; he was concealed in the presence of (the Lord of the Spirits) prior to the creation of the world, and for eternity. (48:2–7)

The Messiah of Hebrew Scripture was said to have origins "from of old" and to have been known by God while yet in the womb. Here he is designated ("named") by the Lord, not since the birth of the Davidic dynasty but from before the world's beginning. His mother's womb has become the womb of creation itself. This universal redeemer will support the righteous of Israel and be a "light to the gentiles" as he receives the worship of all humanity.

In 48:10 he is called "Messiah" for the first time and, once again, the "Elect One" in chapter 49. In chapter 51 the "Elect One" presides over the resurrection of the dead and final choice of the righteous—and all this from his seat on God's own throne (v. 3). The titles "Messiah" and "Elect One" appear together in chapter 52, the "Righteous and Elect One" in chapter 53, and once again in chapter 55 we see the "Elect One" on "the throne of his glory, judging Azaz'el, the wicked angel and his legions" (55:4).

Clearly we are dealing here with one divine figure, the apocalyptic judge and redeemer known variously as the Righteous One, the Elect One, the Son of Man, and the Messiah. If the author did indeed take the titles Elect One and Righteous One from Deutero-Isaiah's servant songs (Isa. 42:1 and 53:11), then we have here the first indication of a pre-Christian reading of those songs as messianic prophecies. Enoch's designation of the Son of Man as "a light to the nations," taken from Isaiah 49:6 (in the second servant song), is a further indication that at least one pre-Christian Israelite community or author interpreted the songs as referring to a redemptive individual, rather than to the nation as a whole. For the first time, titles from Isaiah have been brought together with Daniel's title, "one like a son of man," now transformed into "the Son of Man." The connection has been made between two key texts, both now reading as referring to the same expected one. What is missing, of course, is any suggestion in Enoch of a *suffering* Son of Man. For that missing element we must look elsewhere.

The Davidic Messiah in Psalms of Solomon 17 and 18

At the end of the first century B.C.E. a Jewish sectarian group opposed both to the Hasmoneans and to their Roman successors produced a collection of beautiful psalms that were attributed to Solomon, probably because of their stress on the theme of wisdom with which that ancient king had long been associated. We know nothing about this group outside of what they wrote. But that is enough to tell us what they opposed, how they felt about recent Israelite history, and what they hoped for in the future.

Psalms 17 and 18 of the collection focus on the figure of the "Lord Messiah" who would bring to bear on the nation's desperate situation a new order founded in divine wisdom. Beginning with the praise of God, "Israel's king forevermore" (v. 1), Psalm 17 goes on to remind the Holy One of the eternal promises to David and his house (v. 4). The fall of David's dynasty and rise to royal estate of the usurper Hasmoneans is blamed not on God but on Israel's sin (vv. 5–6). But God overthrew the false claimants by means of the equally loathsome Romans who brought the Hasmoneans to well-deserved ruin but who caused great suffering among the people (vv. 7–18), who were scattered abroad. Following this review of recent history the psalmist appeals to God: "See, Lord, and raise up for them their king, the son of David, to rule over your servant Israel in the time known to you, O God" (vv. 26). The Lord is asked to give the new Davidic ruler strength to destroy unlawful gentile rulers and their sinful Israelite supporters (vv. 23–25):

> He will gather a holy people whom he will lead in righteousness;
> And he will judge the tribes of the people that have been made holy
>   by the Lord their God. (v. 26)

He will restore the tribes of Israel to their territorial allotments, drive out foreigners, and purify Jerusalem (vv. 28–31):

> And he will be a righteous king over them, taught by God.
> There will be no unrighteousness among them in his days, for all
>   shall be holy, and their king shall be the Lord Messiah. (v. 32)

He will rule with compassion, needing no military might. His word will compel obedience (vss. 33–35), and all this will be possible because "God made him powerful in the holy spirit and wise in the counsel of understanding" (v. 37).

Psalm 18 develops similar themes. In these two compositions we have examples of classic messianism within Wisdom literature, a rare phenomenon. And that is what is new in this otherwise typical vision of a royal Messiah, idealized and futurized in the usual manner. Mention of the Holy Spirit's empowering the anointed one is no novelty, but its identification with divine wisdom indicates an updating of the ancient hope in terms of the new stress of a Hellenized age. This text makes clear that some circles in Israel expected a royal Messiah who would rule by virtue of the divine gift of cosmic wisdom bestowed by Israel's ultimate ruler, God himself. And so a new strand was added to the increasingly complex messianic tapestry.

Messiahs Who Suffer or Die

We have been considering the widely varied images of the Messiah found in canonical and extracanonical texts. Few of these texts are free of ambiguity, except those that refer to currently reigning kings or functioning priests. The texts we have called classic messianic prophecies all give rise to major uncertainties. The central question is often: "To whom do they refer?" Is the one spoken of a figure of past or future, is he an individual at all or, rather, a personification of the nation as a whole? Usually these questions cannot be answered with finality. And then we are faced with the further question of how subsequent generations came to read these ambiguous texts as referring to a highly individualized and mythologized future ruler, often possessing divine qualities.

Among the writings most difficult to interpret are those that *may* speak of a redemptive figure who will suffer or die. In Isaiah's servant songs we wrestled briefly with the problem of the servant's identity, whether collective or individual. In Zechariah we found evidence (13:7) of a shepherd king who is struck down (killed) and his people (the sheep) scattered. Gospel writers later read this reference as messianic (Matt. 26:31; Mark 14:27), and so it seems to be. The theme of the death of the Messiah (although this specific term is not used) may have been introduced at that point into Israelite thought.

Daniel's reference to the coming of a Messiah (anointed one; Dan. 9:25), "a prince," and his subsequent statement that "an anointed one shall be cut off" (9:26), is probably not relevant here except in the sense that the death of a Messiah is spoken of. But this is not part of a classic messianic vision. The anointed spoken of here had already come and gone by the time of Daniel's composition (ca. 165 B.C.E.). The two references may well have been to Zerubbabel (the prince and messianic contender), killed in the Persian period.

More relevant may be the figure of the Righteous One in the apocryphal Wisdom of Solomon. This composition of the first century B.C.E. praises wisdom and righteousness and, in several early chapters (2–5), personifies the latter in a figure referred to as the "Righteous One." As with earlier texts, we cannot be certain whether a specific individual is meant or merely any righteous person, but the possibility exists that the former meaning is what the writer had in mind, and so this text bears examination here.

In chapter 2 we are introduced to the Righteous One. For him the wicked lie in wait because he reproaches them for "sins against the law" (2:12). They are infuriated by his claim to know God and even to be God's son. His ways, so unlike theirs, reprove them. They determine to deal harshly with him:

> Let us test him with insult and torture, that we may find out how
> gentle he is and make trial of his forbearance.
> Let us condemn him to a shameful death, for, according to what he
> says he will be protected. (2:19–20)

Did later Christian writers pick up on these themes in describing the mocking of Jesus as he hung on the cross? (Matt. 27:39–44; Mark 15:29–32; Luke 23:35–37). Perhaps, but the earlier explanation (v. 12) of the anger of the Righteous One's enemies being due to his having reproached them for sins against the law would hardly fit the Gospel stories. For in them it is Jesus' opponents who deride *him* for laxity in legal matters, a reversal of the situation in Wisdom of Solomon.

Nevertheless, the Righteous One is delivered to death, but God gives him the ultimate victory:

> Then the righteous man will stand with great confidence in the
> presence of those who have afflicted him...

> When they see him they will be shaken with dreadful fear, and they
> will be amazed at his unexpected salvation...

> ...in anguish of spirit they will groan, and say...Why has he been
> numbered among the sons of God and why is his lot among the
> saints? (5:1–3, 5)

The Righteous One is the persecuted one who dies a redemptive death so that the wicked may come to understand the wisdom of the path he trod. And, of course, his death is really an entrance into the life that is eternal (5:15). The similarities to Isaiah's suffering servant are clear enough. This Righteous One is not a king or priest or ruler of any kind; he is a humble and uncomplaining servant of God who, by his quiet forbearance, rebukes his persecutors. Nowhere is the Righteous One called "Messiah," nor is he seen as a future ruler. But, like the suffering servant, he deserves a place in our discussion of themes that later come together to enrich Israel's messianic imagination.

The Fourth Book of Ezra, from the late first century C.E., is a treasure trove of messianic imagery that gives us further evidence of the wide-ranging character of eschatological speculation within Judaism around the turn of the millennium. Containing seven distinct visions of the end of the age, this creative and colorful book was produced during the dark days (for Jews) following the failure of the revolt of 66 C.E. and the destruction of the Temple. Rather than yield to despair, the author finds hope in God's promises as revealed in his visions, three of which focus on apparently different images of the future redeemer. That the same writer could entertain such varied conceptions may indicate an absence of literalism in his thought, a realization that all such mythical speculation about the future is necessarily metaphorical. And if this is true of 4 Ezra's author, it must be true of other ancient writers who present accounts of the coming apocalypse. In 4 Ezra's third vision we are introduced to the author's conception of the Messiah. Following severe tribulations and cosmic cataclysms:

> The city which now is not seen shall appear, and the land which now is hidden shall be disclosed. And everyone who has been delivered from the evils that I have foretold shall see my wonders. For my son the Messiah shall be revealed with those who are with him, and those who remain shall rejoice four hundred years. And after these years my son the Messiah shall die, and all who draw human breath.
> (4 Ezra 7:26–30)

What was suggested in Zechariah 13:7 is here made explicit. The Messiah is revealed, lives for 400 years (during which he presumably rules the nation, although this is not stated), and then dies together with the whole human race. For seven days the world will be "turned back to primeval silence" (v. 31), following which a new world will arise, a general resurrection will take place, and "the Most High shall be revealed on the seat of judgment" (v. 33). Thus the messianic age will be temporary, and the Messiah will have no part in judging the world. It will be God who will preside at the final assizes.

Did the author of 4 Ezra speak only for himself or for a first-century sect or community of Jews left as part of the remnant residing in what must have been desperate conditions in postwar Palestine? We cannot answer this question any more than we can in the case of earlier Israelite writers. But this striking vision of a dying Messiah does make inescapably clear that such notions were abroad during this volatile period. 4 Ezra was composed at the end of the thirty-year period in which the four Gospels were written. Like those works, 4 Ezra was written in the wake of the Temple's destruction and, like them, speaks of a dying Messiah. Beyond this there is little similarity between Christian messianism and that of 4 Ezra. Although the visions of the latter bear obvious resemblance to Jesus' apocalyptic discourse (Matt. 24; Mark 13; Luke 21) in which the Son of Man foreseen by Jesus comes to judge the world and to reign forever. *His* rule is not to be temporary. And, of course, despite his death, 4 Ezra's Messiah is no suffering servant. But even with these crucial differences, 4 Ezra makes clear that the Christians were not the only Jewish group to incorporate a dying Messiah into its theology.

In 4 Ezra's fifth vision (chaps. 11 and 12), the so-called Eagle Vision, we find an extended messianic metaphor, which we mention here as yet another conception of the redeemer. The eagle is Rome. It rises from the sea to terrify the earth. But then a lion emerges from the forest and rebukes the eagle in a human voice, predicting that it will disappear, leading to an age of refreshment for the world, followed by the last judgment (vv. 36–46).

In later verses the vision is interpreted. The lion (of Judah) is the Messiah of David's house. He has been "kept until the end of days" (v. 32) and will now appear to denounce Rome, judge and destroy her, and deliver the remnant of Israel. Here the Messiah is judge, not king; but he is of David's line, and so elements of classic messianism are present.

In 4 Ezra's sixth vision (chap. 13) we meet another apocalyptic figure, "the Man from the Sea." In this dream vision Ezra sees the man emerge from the deep and fly with clouds of heaven. His voice melts like wax all who hear it. A great multitude gathers to fight him. Without weapons of war, he smites them with his word. A stream of fire issuing from his mouth reduces them to ashes. He then gathers his people of the ten lost tribes, uniting them in peace with the remnant of the holy land.

With three disparate apocalyptic visions, 4 Ezra underscores the fact that Jewish messianic speculation was a rich and various complex of ideas, images, and visionary projections. Any first-century (B.C.E. or C.E.) author or group could pick up earlier strands of thought and weave them as they wished into new and colorful patterns.

The Two Messiahs of the Qumran Community

We noted earlier that of thirty-nine mentions of the Messiah in the Hebrew canon, not a few of them refer to anointed priests. Zechariah picks up on this theme with his reference to the "two anointeds who stand by the Lord of the whole earth" (Zech. 4:14). Perhaps inspired by this text, the sectarians who withdrew from Jerusalem in the Hasmonean age and established the Dead Sea community developed a dual messianic vision of a Messiah, son of David, and a Messiah, son of Aaron. In keeping with their focus on ritual purity, the priestly Messiah seems to take precedence over the Davidic anointed in their eschatological texts. This may also reflect the possible priestly origin of their founder, the "teacher of righteousness." Disgusted with the corruption of the Jerusalem Temple and monarchy, these monastic covenanters projected a classically messianic vision of an idealized and futurized priest and king who would purify the polluted institutions of Israelite leadership.

In the Qumran scrolls an apocalyptic battle takes place, victory is won, the new Jerusalem is established, and the anointed ones appear. As Zechariah had spoken of the two "sons of oil," Zerubbabel and Joshua, so the Qumran texts speak of the dual Messiahs in at least seven passages. The Anointed of Aaron and Israel are repeatedly spoken of as the leaders who will bring on the consummation of all things: "This is the exact [or detailed] account of the statutes in which [they shall walk in the appointed period of evil until there shall arise the Anoin]ted of Aaron and Israel who will atone for their iniquity" (CD 14:18–19). Jeremiah had included in God's promises the assurance that both the Davidic dynasty and the Levitical priesthood were eternal (Jer. 33:17–18). In the first century B.C.E., an age in which such dynastic assurances were often individualized in messianic speculation, the development of the dual Messiah hope was to be expected. The conceptual way station between Jeremiah and Qumran was, as we have seen, the imagery of Zechariah, who spoke of two contemporary anointed ones. All the Qumran covenanters had to do was project this vision into an apocalyptic future. Were they and their eschatological texts themselves another way station en route to the Christian Scriptures in which Jesus is spoken of as both anointed king and high priest? (Heb. 2:17; 4:14; 5:10). And while, once again, the Christian conception can hardly be conflated with that of the Qumran community, a comparison of the two will help us to understand the many-faceted world of thought out of which they and multiple other forms of Jewish messianism arose.

Suffering and Dying Messiahs in Later Jewish Texts

We have seen that the several texts in the Hebrew canon that can be read as prophecies of a suffering or dying Messiah all admit of alternative interpretations. In the servant songs of Deutero-Isaiah the issue is always that of the identity of the servant. Is he a single redemptive individual or a personification of the nation as a whole? This uncertainty is echoed in postbiblical texts in which the Messiah often seems to represent the people Israel both in its contemporary desperate condition and in its projected future glory. It could be said that the concept of the first and second comings of the Messiah developed by the first-century Jewish sect that became the Christian church follows this pattern. Jesus' initial advent as a common Israelite, a man of the people, his struggles, his suffering, and his death reflect the situation of his nation. But this nation, despite earthly appearances, has an origin and a destiny of unequaled splendor. Accounts of Jesus reflect these also. Jesus was chosen by God from of old, as was Israel, and will be exalted in the future, as Israel will be. As Christianity adopted and adapted these elements of classic Jewish messianism (preexistence and ultimate glorification), it was taking unto itself conceptions of the origin and destiny of God's people that were much in the air of first-century Judea. This was because it was always difficult to distinguish talk of the Messiah from that pertaining to the nation.

The original "son of God" was Israel itself. "Thus says the Lord, Israel is my first-born son" (Exod. 4:22). So said Moses to Pharaoh. Only later did the Messiah-King of Israel take on this title. "I will be his father, and he shall be my son," says the Lord of the Davidic heir (2 Sam. 8:14). And later the future Messiah became known as God's son. Thus we see the gradual process by which first the sitting king and then the idealized future king take on titles originally belonging to Israel and, in so doing, become personifications of the nation as a whole. This is, if anything, even truer of messianic visions and prophecies in later ages. As Israel suffers, so does the Messiah; as Israel will be exalted, so will the Messiah. In the Babylonian Talmud, compiled in the fifth century C.E., we find the following parable:

> R. Y'hoshua ben Levi once found Elijah standing at the entrance of the cave of R. Shim'on ben Yohai.... He asked him: "When will the Messiah come?" He said to him: "Go, ask him himself." "And where does he sit?" "At the entrance of the city [of Rome]." "And what are his marks?" "His marks are that he sits among the poor who suffer of diseases and while all of them unwind and rewind [the bandages of their wounds] at once, he unwinds and rewinds them one by one, for, he says, 'Should I be summoned, there must be no delay.'" (Babylonian Talmud, Sanh. 98a)

Some four centuries after this Talmudic picture of the suffering, wounded Messiah, a ninth-century visionary recounts:

> I saw a man, despised and wounded ... and I asked him: "What is the name of this place?" And he said to me: "This is Great Rome, in which I am kept captive in prison until my end comes."... And I said: "I have heard your tidings, that you are the Messiah of my God." And forthwith he appeared to me like a youth in the perfection of his beauty.... And he [the Angel Metraton] said to me: "This is the Messiah of the Lord who is hidden here until the time of the End ... " (*Sefer Zerubbabel*, ninth century)

The Messiah, despised and wounded, sits at the gate of an unheeding world. But at the moment he is recognized, he appears in the perfection of his youthful beauty. So Israel, despised and wounded, will in God's good time be restored to the perfection of youth and beauty that it possessed when the world itself was young.

The ninth-century *Pesiqta Rabbati* presents the Messiah as accepting terrible sufferings "so that not a single one of Israel should perish"(*Pes. Rab.* 161a–b). This text goes on to tell us:

> In that hour the Holy One, Blessed be He, says to him: "Ephraim, My True Messiah, you have already accepted [this suffering] from the six days of Creation. Now your suffering shall be like my suffering. . . . In that hour he [the Messiah] says before Him: "Master of the World! Now my mind is at rest, for it is sufficient for the servant to be like his Master!" (*Pes. Rab.* 162a)

Not only does the Messiah's suffering mirror that of Israel, but it reflects the inner agonies of God. As in Jeremiah, here the Holy One is presented as a suffering God whose condition is brought on by the tragedies of God's beloved people on earth. The divine suffering is, of course, one of the great themes of religious literature. It is an important conception of Jewish theology and the central one of Christianity. If any doubt remains as to the reason for the messianic suffering in this text, it goes on to declare of the Messiah, "you suffered because of the sins of our [the patriarchs'] children." Thus, the suffering of the Messiah is redemptive; it both reflects the current condition of Israel and procures its future glorification (*Pes. Rab.* chap. 36).

A related text of the eleventh century, *Midrash Konen*, explicitly connects this view of the suffering Messiah to the servant of Deutero-Isaiah. Elijah speaks to the Messiah: "'Endure the sufferings and the sentence of your Master who makes you suffer because of the sin of Israel.' And thus it is written: *He was wounded because of our transgressions, he was crushed because of our iniquities* (Isa. 53:5) until the time when the end comes." The *Zohar* pictures the Messiah as functioning in the same way. After quoting the Isaiah verse (53:5), it envisions the Messiah as taking all the diseases and sufferings of Israel upon himself. These sufferings are due to Israel's neglect of Torah; the Messiah must assume them in the absence of the expiatory rites of the ancient Temple (*Zohar* 2:212a). One need hardly comment on the similarity of all this to Christian conceptions, thought by many to be foreign to Judaism. These Jewish texts tell a very different story.

Both Judaism and Christianity have attempted to deal with the seemingly contradictory messianic texts in the Bible: those that speak of a suffering, possibly dying redeemer, and those that present an exalted, glorified king. Christianity solves the problem by splitting the messianic advent into two comings, the first in humility, the second in glory. The same one who entered

Jerusalem on a lowly donkey will return with clouds of heaven in the future. Thus did one first-century Jewish sect deal with these messianic paradoxes. Later Jewish writings express another solution.

Perhaps Zechariah and certainly 4 Ezra had spoken of a fallen Messiah. In Ezra this is clearly the classic Messiah of the future. But how do the inheritors of these texts reconcile them with the more numerous predictions of a glorious, victorious, and totally successful Messiah-King of the future? They might have done so by ignoring the former tradition. But that is not the Jewish way. All Scripture must be dealt with. And so the Talmud picks up the theme of the death of the Messiah: "... *and the land shall mourn* (Zech. 12:12). What is the reason for this mourning?...R. Dosa says: '[they will mourn] over the Messiah who will be slain...'" (Babylonian Talmud. SB. Suk. 52a). Again, Zechariah! Was he indeed the originator of the concept of the Messiah who dies at God's hand? The same Talmudic text reveals that the Messiah who has died is not the Davidic Messiah but the Messiah "son of Joseph." He will be slain as God has foreordained (B. Suk. 52a). This in no way compromises the saving mission of the glorious Messiah, "son of David" who is to come. In fact, in a responsum of Hai Gaon (tenth to eleventh centuries), we find that, following the death of Messiah, ben Joseph, Messiah, ben David arrives and revives him:

> Armilus [the archetypal evil king of the apocalypse]...will slay
> Messiah ben Joseph and it will be a great calamity for Israel...[then]
> Messiah ben David will reveal himself....When Messiah ben Joseph
> is killed, his body will remain cast out [in the streets] for forty
> days,...until Messiah ben David comes and brings him back to life,
> as commanded by the Lord.

What Christianity accomplished with two advents of a single Messiah, later Jewish writers achieved with two Messiahs! For the former group the same Messiah dies and is raised. So, too, with Messiah ben Joseph. But here it is Messiah ben David who raises him, all by the power of Israel's Lord, of course. Thus ultimately, in both Christian and later Jewish texts, it is only the divine source of life that can give new life. The story lines and the number of Messiahs differ, but the final word is resurrection, new and eternal life for God's people, for God's anointed—and by extension for the whole human race.

It will be astonishing to both Jewish and Christian readers unfamiliar with postbiblical messianic speculation how Jewish writers and whole communities elaborated on earlier images of the suffering, dying Messiah. Far from being a barrier between Jewish and Christian worlds of thought, this tradition should, in truth, be seen as a common possession, a shared treasure.

Conclusions

Having reviewed so many messianic passages in the Scriptures, the Apocrypha, the Pseudepigrapha, the Talmud, and the responsa, can we still maintain a view that there was an orthodox messianism—or, for that matter, an orthodox Israelite faith—at any period in the people's long history? The absence of any mainstream messianic idea or expectation is especially obvious in the intertestamental period. Each author or sectarian group that had any concern with eschatology produced its own texts, combining, as seemed best to them, elements of earlier traditions. Not all were messianic. Many, like the author of the earliest strata of Deutero-Isaiah, attributed to God directly all functions of redemption and judgment. No Messiah was considered necessary. But those who wrote of a divine agent of deliverance could choose among Davidic and Aaronic images, animal metaphors, human and divine figures or those who combined both elements, redemptive sufferers or dying monarchs, earthly warriors or heavenly beings who fly through the air and, with no need of weapons, smite the earth with their irresistible word. Glorious or humble, eloquent or mute, the redeemer figures kept coming on well into the Middle Ages, during which rabbinic speculation continued to generate new images of the long-awaited Messiah, even one who suffers and dies.

If we view the Nazarene sect—later, Christianity—as one of the Judaisms of the first century (and how else can we view it?), we must conclude that this group of Jews had as much right as any other to develop its own unique conception of the Messiah. And unique it was—as were they all—but only in the sense that it combined in a distinct fashion elements of Jewish messianic speculation that had been circulating for centuries. The earliest messianic references in Hebrew Scriptures had referred to kings and priests who were contemporary historic personages. Jesus was such a personage. Later messianic language became idealized and futurized. Jesus would come again in glory. All the well-known terms, Messiah, Son of God, Son of Man, shepherd, king, high priest, suffering servant, son of David, et al., were eventually reinterpreted and applied by the Christian sectarians to their redeemer figure. They were certainly not unique in their application of these terms to a living man or to a figure of the future; they *were* unique in holding that one man could be both of these. By conceiving of a first and second coming of Jesus, Christian thinkers found a way to apply virtually every previous messianic name and function to one person. Theirs was certainly the most comprehensive messianism of any of the many Jewish sects that reworked the ancient images into their own speculative patterns.

We have seen that the Christians could hardly be called nonorthodox in their messianism, since there was no reigning orthodoxy (and no orthodox Judaism for that matter). Were they radicals? Perhaps, but no more than the Qumran covenanters or the author or community that produced 4 Ezra. What ultimately led to their break with other Jewish sects was probably more their openness to gentile participation than their messianic views. The question so often asked as to whether Jesus was the Jewish Messiah is therefore the wrong question. He was *a* Jewish Messiah. As were the Davidic king, the Aaronic priest, and their futurized and idealized images; as was the suffering servant and the exalted Son of Man; as was the Lion of the forest and the Man from the sea. The humble man of Galilee who will return in glory takes his place among these and all the other messianic figures of Israelite tradition.

But there is a difference. *This* Messiah who suffers and dies for the re-demption of the world has broken out of his original Israelite context. He has, via his interpreters, brought the salvific word of Israel's God to the gentiles. If for Jews his story was a new expression and combination of familiar themes, for gentiles his message was wholly new—and for many it was convincing.

Has Jesus brought redemption to Israel? No, but he has brought the means of redemption to the gentiles—and that in the name of Israel's God—thus helping Israel to fulfill its calling to be a blessing to all peoples. A Jewish Messiah for the gentiles! Perhaps, as I have suggested, an inversion of Cyrus's role as a gentile Messiah for the Jews. Israel is redeemed by engaging in redemptive work. Perhaps redemption is not a final state but a process, a life devoted to bringing oneself and others before God. To live a life in relationship to the Holy One and to help the world to understand itself as the Kingdom of God—which it, all unknowingly, already is—is to participate in redemption, to live a redemptive life. This has been Israel's calling from the beginning.

Christianity, conceived as one form of Jewish outreach into the world, and Jesus (through Paul) as agent of salvation to the gentiles, constitutes one aspect of Israel's redemptive work. Jesus may not be the redeemer *of* Israel, but we may well see him as a redeemer *from* Israel. Through Jesus the messianic project has been turned outward into a world awaiting the fellow-ship with God already experienced by Israel. The validity of this project rests on the prior and ongoing validity of God's eternal covenant with Israel. Through this outreach, the gentiles come to share in that covenant and in the messianic, redemptive life of the people of God.

3

Three Jewish Theologians of Christianity

Menachem Ha Me'iri (1249–1315)

The history of Jewish-Christian relations includes no more remarkable figure than Rabbi Menachem Ben Shlomo Ha Me'iri of Provence. He lived in an age characterized by narrowness and bigotry, ultimately witnessing the expulsion of the Jews from France in 1306. Yet he defended Christians and Christianity, going so far as to include them under the category "Israel," rejecting all past Jewish claims that Christianity constituted a form of paganism. Many of his statements on the subject bear a distinctly modern character, and some, such as the view just indicated, go beyond what many Jews are willing to concede to Christianity even today. Certain halakhic authorities had earlier developed theories aimed at making possible business dealings between Jews and Christians. If Christians had been categorized as "pagan," such would have been impossible. But Ha Me'iri went far beyond these practical approaches to present a Jewish theology of Christianity that was positive and affirming of the religious "other" in ways unheard of in earlier times or among contemporary Jewish authorities.[1]

Ha Me'iri's theology of the religious "other" went far beyond what might be called "tolerance" and included Islam as well as Christianity. Of course, in France it was Christianity with which Jews would have had closest and most frequent interaction. Ha Me'iri held that the ancient pagans (idolaters), denounced in the Talmud as people dangerous to Jews and unfit for social intercourse, had by his time largely passed from the scene. Therefore, the Talmudic strictures were irrelevant to the situation in which Jewish communities now found themselves.[2] The Abrahamic faiths of his day were to be considered under a new category he created: "Nations restricted by the ways of religion."[3] They were in no way comparable to the idol worshipers referred to in Talmudic tractates such as *Avodah Zarah* (Idol Worship). For him, Christians and Muslims deserved a positive evaluation as peoples devoted to the one true God and to God's universal ethical law.

For Ha Me'iri humanity's most exalted characteristic was its capacity to form a philosophical conception of metaphysical and ethical truth—and this ability was clearly exhibited by Christians and Muslims. Both communities were rich in philosophers, theologians, and ethicists. The work of these advanced minds was responsible for the high level of speculation among them. In this manner, these two non-Jewish communities had reasoned their way to truths similar to those divinely revealed to the Jews. Those additional truths known only by Jews (specific doctrines and practices) could only be the fruit of a particular revelation that gentiles could not, of course, have experienced.

Ha Me'iri often spoke as a philosophical admirer of Maimonides, but on the issue before us he broke with the great philosopher. For Maimonides, Christianity and Islam were extensions of Judaism designed to spread Jewish truths, albeit in strange and altered form, to "the far isles."[4] This universal dissemination of their understanding of Torah would help bring to fruition the messianic day when the pure doctrines of Judaism would shine forth undimmed while the gentile dross would fall away. However, Maimonides added to this largely positive overview the observation that both of the other Abrahamic faiths, especially Christianity, contained pagan elements that led him to categorize them as idolatrous.[5] It was on this point that Ha Me'iri emphatically disagreed.

He never claimed that Christianity or Islam had received direct divine revelations, but he did view the human thinking that produced them as legitimate and admirable. Both faiths were much closer to Judaism than to any other religious community (meaning the vanished, idolatrous systems). Christians and Muslims, in recognizing God and the moral law, reflected the Jewish devotion to orderly human society "restricted to the paths of religion" (thus, to universal ethical principles).

Like Jews in all times, Ha Me'iri was faced with this question: Were Jews better off under an Abrahamic regime (Christian or Muslim) that made a place for them in the divine plan of redemption, or would they have done better and been safer in a pagan society that had developed with no reference to them at all? The question is complicated by the fact that in Christendom, at least, Jews were conceived as playing a crucial role in the divine scheme, but a role that ended, in a positive sense, with the coming of Christ. Following that event, what part could Jews play in the Christian drama of salvation? Augustine offered a lugubrious answer to this question with his twisting of the Jewish self-conception of Israel as God's witness people.

Yes, he said, Israel is a witness—in a wholly negative sense—a witness to the disaster that befalls a once-favored nation following their sinister decision to become at worst a deicide people or, at best, one that willfully chose to oppose God's offer of salvation in Christ. In order to bear such ghastly witness, the Jews must be kept alive but in a degraded condition appropriate to a pariah nation.[6] It may well be that this Augustinian theology of the negative Jewish role in society was responsible for preserving the Jews alive, protected by the church from the fury of the mob so often whipped up by the deicide charges and blood libels of the Middle Ages. But it is also true that it was this poisonous theory that led the church and the secular authorities to maintain the Jews in the most miserable conditions the Christian imagination could conjure up.

Is there any Jewish tourist who has visited Chartres and not marveled at the incomparable cathedral, Europe's most glorious "Bible in stone"? Who has not "read" the luminous windows and splendid stone carvings to learn the eternal story of God's preexistent majesty, God's creation of the world and humanity, the fall into sin and the wondrous saga of divine, redemptive love in the birth, death, and resurrection of God's beloved son? And is there a single Jewish visitor who has not then wandered the medieval streets of that city until coming upon the Rue aux Juifs (Street of the Jews) located along the river in what was the lowest, most noxious and unhealthy depths of the town? Have they not, like me, been suddenly called to a deeper consciousness than that of aesthetics, deeper even than the spiritual exaltation experienced in the cathedral's interior? A lump in the throat and heaviness in the chest call the Jewish traveler to the realization of what accompanied all this beauty. What we confront is how Jews were forced to live in the dark shadow of this magnificence by a church that had incorporated them into its story as accursed and exiled wanderers, rejected by God and living at the pleasure of victorious Christendom. And what Jewish visitor has not thought in that moment of bitter reflection that it might well have been better for our tormented forebears if Europe had been dominated by pagans who had no place for us in their worldview and were therefore willing to leave us alone?

But, as understandable as such thoughts may be, it is not at all clear that Jews would have fared better under pagan rule. It is true that Jews were permitted by the ancient Romans to dispense with prayers *to* the emperor as long as they agreed to pray *for* him in their synagogues. It is also true that the Roman admiration for antiquity in all things frequently led them to a toleration of

Judaism as long as Jews made no attempts at achieving political independence. Yet, at the same time the Jews were expelled from Rome under Claudius and, like Christians, dealt with savagely when scapegoats were needed to placate the restive mob. The first pogrom on record occurred in Roman-ruled Alexandria in pre-Christian days (68 c.e.). Caligula had earlier refused to intervene, to protect Egyptian Jews in 40 c.e., treating the Jewish delegation, led by Philo of Alexandria, with disgust and contempt.[7]

I would say that the question before us must remain an open one as regards the Jewish lot under pagans or Christians. However, it is my belief that God sent Jesus and his interpreters (primarily Paul) for the express purpose of opening the covenant to include gentiles so as to spread the worship of Israel's God to much of the world. Therefore, Christian (and Muslim) domination of most of the lands in which Jews dwelled may have been part of the divine redemptive plan. Needless to say, it would have been infinitely preferable for Jews and Christians alike if the latter had found a way "to tell the old, old story of Jesus and his love," without compromising the message with attitudes of hatred and contempt for Jesus' people and kindred. It has taken Christians nearly 2,000 years to be able to disentangle the positive and negative elements of their inheritance.

It is remarkable that seven centuries before this epoch-making change of Christian heart regarding Jews and Judaism, Ha-Me'iri found it in his heart to develop his affirmative evaluation of Christianity. He certainly would have said that the emergence and spread of Christianity was a positive development, despite the shameful treatment of Jews by so many Christians. Thus, with his forgiving attitude, he was surely a better "christian" than those who laid claim to the appellation.

One reason for Ha Me'iri's willingness to distinguish Christians from the pagans of the ancient world was what can only be called his dynamic conception of history, very much in the biblical tradition, but hard to locate in Talmudic thought or the subsequent period of halakhic writing. Against the often static thinking of his time, he insisted that conditions prevalent in earlier ages had altered drastically. The context in which the Talmud had been produced had changed—in fact, no longer existed—and the gentiles Jews had to deal with in his day bore little resemblance to those of the earlier age. The notion that truth is contextual is a great departure in the philosophy of history and one that religious fundamentalists resist even today. Carried as far as it can go, it would cast into doubt all notions of eternal truth, as it has in postmodern thought. Ha Me'iri, of course, applies the principle sparingly. He never uses it to question what he views as the eternal, revealed truths of Judaism. He does point out, however, that the exterior conditions of the non-

Jewish world have altered and that Jewish thought regarding it must change accordingly.

Sometimes he seems to go so far as willingly to misinterpret Talmudic passages to allow Jews to interact with Christians. The Talmud forbids Jews to trade with "Notzrim" on their holy days.[8] Clearly "Notzrim" translates as Nazarenes, that is, followers of "the Nazarene," Jesus. Yet Ha Me'iri claims that the title comes from the name Nebuchadnezzar, king of Babylonia, and thus refers to Babylonian sun worshipers! He points out that Sunday was their holy day. It was these long-vanished idolaters that the Talmud meant all along. Jews were to have no contact with such lawless people on Sunday so as to give no recognition to their holy day. Thus, he concludes, the Talmud never forbids interaction with Christians.[9] Jews and Christians (and Muslims) are, he said, entitled to equal standing, equal treatment, and equal rights in society. They share a common humanity, a common recognition of God, and a common commitment to a society governed by laws ultimately grounded in divine fiat. In Jewish courts all such people governed by religion and law must be dealt with equally.

Since the second century Judaism had propounded the theory of the Noahide laws, seven requirements for a just and orderly society given by God to Noah and his sons following the great flood. Although not found in Genesis, they were extrapolated from the biblical text by later rabbis in the *Tosefta* (second century C.E.). Christians are not mentioned specifically as Noahides, but it may well be that it was the development of Christianity out of Israelite faith that led the rabbis to develop these universal requirements by which all persons must live. Ha Me'iri's category of "those restricted by the ways of religion" seems to be a synonym for Noahides. Both terms certainly refer to righteous gentiles. But Noahides were required to refrain from idolatry and from blasphemy against God. They were not called on specifically to recognize the one true God worshiped by Israel.

On the other hand, "those restricted by the ways of religion" refers to people who do worship the one God as well as recognizing a universal moral code. Thus, Ha Me'iri may be giving us a more specific and particular definition that would apply only to Christians and Muslims, who are people of positive theistic belief. This would go beyond the category of Noahides, who are not specifically required to hold such a belief. All those "possessed of religion" are Noahides, but it would seem that not all Noahides are "possessed of religion" in the positive, theistic sense of the term.[10]

But Ha Me'iri goes even further in his affirmative Jewish theology of Christianity. Leviticus 25:17 commands Israelites, "You shall not wrong one another." Clearly this refers to the treatment of one Israelite by another. The

Talmud comments on the verse as follows: "another" here means "one who is with you in Torah and commandments" (Bava Metzia, 59a), that is, fellow Jews. Stunningly, Ha Me'iri holds that all those restricted by the ways of religion "are with you [Israelites] in Torah and commandments." Thus he declares that all moral laws governing conduct between Jew and Jew also apply to conduct between Jew and Christian, since Christians "are with you in Torah and commandments." Christians are not only "restricted by the ways of religion"; that religion is the one found in the Torah, not all of it, but at least as far as its ethical laws apply to all people. It is doubtless true that Christianity, rejecting the Marcionite heresy, incorporated the entire Hebrew Bible in its holy texts. Based on this Christian-Jewish sharing of Torah, Ha Me'iri calls for a unified view of Jews and Christians as constituting a single whole as regards their moral and legal standing.[11]

He calls upon Jews to violate the Sabbath for the purpose of saving a Christian life as well as that of a Jew, to refrain from negative thoughts or words on seeing a church or Christian cemetery, to greet Christians courteously, and to be willing to visit their homes on their holy days. He seems to be seeking a broadening of friendly social relations between Jews and Christians and to counsel Jews even against negative, private thoughts about the Christian "other."[12] There are, even for Ha Me'iri, obvious limits to all this. He holds to the traditional ban on interreligious marriage, as well as that on the consumption of wine prepared by Christians, since it was frequently used in their religious rituals. But he holds it to be permissible for a Jew to share his festive holiday foods with a Christian. This would seem to open the way to entertaining Christian holiday guests. Of course, the restrictions of kashrut would prevent the Jew from accepting similar hospitality in a Christian home unless extraordinary preparations would have been made. One is reminded of the kosher facilities, dishes, flatware, et cetera kept available by a few noble German houses centuries later so that Moses Mendelssohn might be able to dine there. It is doubtful that Ha Me'iri had given thought to such a situation. It is also possible that his positive attitude toward sharing Jewish foods with Christians may have had more to do with the treatment of one's servants than with socializing with Christian friends. We cannot be sure which of these situations he had in mind. One would have much more significant implications than the other. If he meant for Jews and Christians to socialize at Jewish holiday tables, he is suggesting a new concept of social relations that would substantially expand the interaction between the groups, so often all but strangers to each other.

But Ha Me'iri ventured even further into territory still controversial today. He interpreted the Talmud, specifically Shabbat 156a, "Israel is not subject to the stars," in a totally revolutionary manner. Since Christians and Muslims do

not worship or consult the stars for blessing or spiritual direction in life matters, "Israel" here is meant to include "all who are restricted by the ways of
religion," that is, Christians and Muslims as well as Jews.[13] This stunning
declaration that Christians and Muslims are included in "Israel" erases completely any racial or ethnic meaning of the term, at least in regard to the
construction of human identity before God. The three Abrahamic religions are
part of one community of faith in the one true God and God's moral commands. Israel has, to be sure, received a direct revelation, which, according to
Ha Me'iri, is not the case with the other two. But since they receive their
legitimacy as continuations of the religious traditions of Israel, at least as regards moral law, they too are "Israel," people of God.

Such a view would be considered progressive even today and rejected as
heretical by many Jews. I should know, having been on the receiving end of
many a shocked look or unbelieving shake of the head when I have suggested
the same move to Jewish audiences. The opening of the covenant to include
gentiles and the expansion of the category "Israel" to encompass them is considered scandalous by many even after forty years of Jewish-Christian dialogue.
Yet it is, I believe, the obvious Jewish response to the new Christian recognition
of the ongoing validity and effectiveness of our covenant with the Holy One. If
Christians now understand that through Jesus they joined themselves to Israel's
still functioning covenant rather than replacing one that had run its course,
why should Jews not agree with this insight and accept Christianity as a branch
of the good stock of Israel? Resistance to this opening of mind and heart—a
self-transcendence that is of the very essence of applied religion—is based, I
believe, on the profoundly antireligious impulse to divide God's world between
"us" and "them," the favored child and the rejected one. The scandal is not that
Ha Me'iri was willing to reject all such self-serving thinking seven centuries
ago—that is the miracle! The scandal is that all these long centuries later, there
are many among us who refuse to make the same move. His astounding expansion of the meaning of Israel surely ranks Ha Me'iri among the great progressive thinkers in the history of Jewish thought.

As I note elsewhere in this book, every religious community generates its
own version of idolatry. Judaism's form of idolatry is "ethnolatry," in which the
people Israel replaces God as the focus of veneration or the absolute principle.
At one point in its early history, the modern Jewish Reconstructionist Movement seemed to be heading in that direction with its emphasis on "peoplehood"
and its denigration of theism. With this movement's rediscovery of spirituality,
a proper balance is being sought. Jewish peoplehood may be an essential component of our faith, but we must never forget that Israel exists for the glory of
the Holy One who is the parent of all and the founder of a number of religious

communities. Ha Me'iri renders Jewish "ethnolatry" impossible by defining "Israel" to reflect his self-transcendent attitudes. Thus he expands the category "Israel" to include non-Jewish worshipers of God—a remarkable and admirable insight. I only wish he had taken one more step and examined the possibility that God may have given birth to Christianity and Islam by new revelations directly to the founders of these communities. That acknowledgment would have placed all three peoples on an entirely equal footing. But, for his day, his formulation was astonishing enough. Perhaps he left it to us to take the next step.

It is no coincidence that Ha Me'iri bases his redefinition of "Israel" on a Talmudic verse rejecting the notion that human life is controlled by the constellations. For, in order to make ethical decisions, Israelites must be, and believe themselves to be, free moral agents. It is this community of conscious moral decision makers that constitutes his new understanding of Israel. It must also be true, he says, that all Israelites believe in *creation ex nihilo*—creation out of nothing—if they are to be, and to act as, free people. Without such an absolute starting point, people would be controlled in their conduct by prior causation or the nature of the preexisting stuff out of which they were made. This would be some kind of eternally existing matter that God may have shaped, but lacked the power to create. Such a Platonic understanding (as expressed in *The Timaeus*) would restrict both divine and human freedom. For Ha Me'iri, God must have created the world from naught and given us freedom to choose, as recorded in the story of Adam and Eve. We are not subject to heavenly influences or irresistible causation. We are accountable for our deeds and will answer to the divine Judge. "Know what is above you: an eye that sees, an ear that hears, and all your deeds written in a book."[14] Without this conviction of the reality of Divine Providence, all moral law and conduct would be impossible. Ha Me'iri is consistent in his insistence that creation from nothing, universal moral law, human freedom, and reward and punishment are the necessary beliefs of all who are "restricted by the ways of religion."

He seemed untroubled by any consideration that this set of beliefs, while theoretically necessary for moral conduct, so often, in fact, failed to produce it. How did Christians—all believers in the theological and ethical principles just enumerated—nevertheless visit cruel persecution on the Jews, their fellow "Israelites"? In the face of this reality, why did Ha Me'iri hold so tenaciously to his theory and, indeed, why did he feel the goodwill toward Christians that led him to produce it? His benevolence regarding people who seldom returned his positive thoughts must remain a mystery. But whatever his reasons, he is among the very few Jewish thinkers to have accepted Christian claims to be part of Israel. Today, in an age when Christians are striving mightily to overcome centuries of anti-Jewish attitudes and conduct, we Jews would do well to follow

Ha Me'iri's positive example and affirm his claim that Christianity has indeed been grafted onto the good stock of Israel as a legitimate branch of an ancient tree. We have much more reason to say this in our time than Ha Me'iri ever had in his.

Moses Mendelssohn (1729–1786)

Moses Mendelssohn was a true son of the Enlightenment and the inspiration for all modern Jews who seek acculturation to Western ways of living in the world without the assimilation that would lead to the disappearance of the faith and people of Israel. This great soul and radiant mind taught us how to share in the wonders of the general civilization, indeed, how to help shape and direct it, while maintaining essential elements of the ancient faith bequeathed to us by our forebears.

Among the new ideas developed by the Enlightenment was the revolutionary concept of the human person as essentially a rational individual only secondarily connected to his religious, ethnic, or national group. Therefore, what people had in common—their basic humanity, that is, their ability to reason—was infinitely more important than the communal distinctions that divided them. Mendelssohn shared this view of human nature but clung to the belief that God had revealed special commandments to Israel that Jews were obliged to obey. It was this act of revelation, rather than a racial distinction, that made Israel unique. In his earlier writings Mendelssohn seemed to hold that while Israel's faith was made up of divinely revealed truths, those same truths could have been discovered by man's unaided reason.[15] The oneness of God, the universal moral law, the eternity of the human soul, and punishment or felicity after death based on one's conduct on earth made up a supremely rational religion and lay at the heart of Jewish faith. But there was more to Judaism: the laws and statutes, ordinances and commandments—in short, the system of ritual and ceremonial *mitzvot*—contained many nonrational elements that could never be discovered by human reason. It was in these areas of conduct that Judaism was unique, for Jews only, and often mysterious in its meaning.[16]

While committed to these laws, Mendelssohn recognized that they were for Jews alone and thus saw no need to convert others to the faith. In fact, Mendelssohn may have been the first since Paul to point out the folly of a gentile who would choose to convert to Judaism. As he was, all he had to do was to obey the seven commands given to the sons of Noah. Once converted, he would be required to keep hundreds of commandments or face divine displeasure. Viewed in this way, becoming Jewish made little sense.[17]

Mendelssohn spoke with pride of Jewish tolerance for other faiths. All the righteous were destined for reward. The laws of nature guide all to worthy living, and human reason is a reliable guide. Maimonides had also valued man's rational capacity, but he did not view it as sufficient to guide people to salvation. In fact, gentiles who kept the Noahide statues were not, according to him, living lives acceptable to God unless they kept them because they believed that God has given them. Since it was possible to follow the Noahide rules without believing in the one true God—and unbelievers were destined for punishment—religious motive was crucial for otherwise righteous gentiles. Those who obeyed the seven laws because they appealed to their reason were doomed to the fate of the godless, according to Maimonides.[18]

Mendelssohn disagreed strongly. All Noahides, regardless of why they kept the seven laws, were destined for salvation. A theistic motive was not neces-sary.[19] Although the law of nature would eventually lead all rational beings to recognize the divine Creator, it was righteous conduct that ultimately counted. Mendelssohn ridiculed the narrow view of some Jews that only members of their tiny nation could be saved. Surely such a view denied human freedom, as well as divine justice. His was a true religious pluralism coupled, as it must be, to an ethical universalism.

Mendelssohn was hesitant to express views on Christianity. As a member of a persecuted minority possessing only the rights granted by the Christian authorities, he was acutely conscious of the danger of putting his people in jeopardy by anything he might say. When pressed, he did express admiration for the moral character of Jesus, an admirable religious teacher who, according to Mendelssohn, never claimed to be divine or a unique conduit to God.[20] The philosopher approved of Jesus but sharply distinguished the rabbi of Galilee from the claims that the church later made for him. As a pious, practicing Jew, Mendelssohn rejected the christology of Christianity. He seemed to believe, as most religious people do, that the affirmation of the truth of one's own religion necessarily entails viewing other creeds as false. But why should that be the case?

A believer might hold that while God had revealed certain truths to his group, the same God had revealed others to other groups. Such a pluralist view is attributed to Rabban Gamaliel, who appears as a character in the New Tes-tament (Acts 5:34–39) and expresses a liberal attitude that would have been unique in his time. He suggests that the new Jesus movement *may* be of God, while, of course, he affirms the ongoing truth of Judaism. Whether or not the historic Gamaliel ever expressed such sentiments, this approach to religious claims could be expanded to recognize the equality of all higher religions and allow for each revelation to be seen as a partial unveiling of the ungraspable divine totality. Each revelation is true as far as it goes and may be confidently followed by the group to which it is given. But each revelation is also finite, giving each finite person or community only a hint of the infinite truth that must remain hidden in God. While Mendelssohn was prepared to speak of a general revelation of divine truth to all via the laws of nature or the seven commandments of God to Noah and his sons, it seems never to have occurred to him that God might have revealed truths to Christians that were only for them, as God had done earlier to Jews. Perhaps this was just a failure of imagination on his part, or perhaps merely the consequence of his belief that since the seven Noahide laws sufficed for gentiles, no additional revelation was needed.

This would include even the revelation of the oneness of God. The command "I am the Lord your God who brought you out of the land of Egypt, out of the house of bondage. You shall have no other gods beside me" (Ex. 20:1–3) was spoken to Israel alone. Because God had redeemed Israel from bondage, because God was the divine Ruler of Israel, Jews owed absolute and exclusive allegiance to the Holy One. Not so with gentiles. Unlike Ha Me'iri, Mendelssohn, with all his tolerance, never included righteous gentiles under the category "Israel." It was to be expected that gentiles would recognize gods foreign to Israel. He held that Christians did worship the same God as the Jews, but they also worshiped Jesus, Mary, and perhaps others. He did not condemn them for this. Only Jews were forbidden to associate God with other entities.[21] Radical monotheism was not required or expected of others. Often, he said, gentiles used various names but really meant God. Since they were never commanded not to do this, such conduct is no sin for them as it would be for a Jew.

Of course the belief in one God that was revealed to Israel is also a supremely rational idea. In fact, all the beliefs of Judaism are rational. Mendelssohn pointed out that the faith of Israel contains no irrational dogmas as does Christianity. Thus Judaism is more reasonable, more tolerant, and more suited to an age of enlightenment than is its younger counterpart. Of course, God also gave us laws and practices that reason could not have discovered. However, these were not dogmas or doctrines, but forms of conduct. One wonders if these regulations, while given without rational explanation, could have been seen by Mendelssohn as *contrary* to reason. While he does not directly address this issue, if pressed to do so, given his rationalist commitments, one suspects that he would not hesitate to come up with sensible reasons to observe dietary laws, Sabbath regulations, and the like.

In his late work *Jerusalem* (1782), Mendelssohn shifts ground a bit and claims that the Torah's doctrines regarding God and ethical conduct are all available to reason and thus not literally revealed. It is the *mitzvot* of a ceremonial nature that came directly from God rather than indirectly via divinely created human reason. One gets the impression that Mendelssohn is appealing to Enlightenment values to prove that Judaism, while tolerant of Christianity, is superior to it, in that Judaism contains no dogmas whatever, only rational propositions (except, of course, for the ritual *mitzvot*).[22] But was it really necessary for him to take such an extreme position? Surely there are ideas in the Jewish religion that are superrational. The election of Israel is certainly such a conception. Moses himself comments on God's curious choice of the smallest and weakest of peoples (Deut. 7:7). If, as Michael Wyschogrod has so movingly put it, the Holy One simply fell in love with Abraham and sees his likeness impressed on every Jewish face,[23] it is not reason that is at work here. Divine love is no more rational than its human counterpart. Kierkegaard, too, saw human love as the closest earthly equivalent to the love between God and humanity.[24] More to the point for Mendelssohn, Hosea pictured God as a loving husband torn by grief over his faithless wife, Israel (Hos., chaps. 1 and 2). Jeremiah pictured a pain-wracked God mourning over the sins of his beloved child and tormented over Israel's coming suffering (Jer. 8:18–9:3). What does any of this have to do with reason or the cold formulations of the Enlightenment?

But Mendelssohn's proclamation of an ethical way of salvation for Christians had everything to do with his view that all people are united by reason and capable of choosing to do the good. If all of God's children are brothers and sisters, it is due to this common rational nature. He might have paraphrased Paul: in rationality there is neither Jew nor Greek, slave nor free, male nor female. It was on such common rational ground that Jews and Christians could meet, join hands, and walk together toward the Kingdom of God.

Elijah Benamozegh (1823–1900)

Elijah Benamozegh, rabbi of the Italian city of Leghorn, was fluent in many languages and was learned in philosophy and in Christian as well as Jewish theology. Although deeply grounded in Torah, Talmud, and Kabbalistic texts, he was very much a man of the world whose broadly based intellect reflected the best of the cosmopolitan character of his native city.

In the last years of his long and productive life he set about writing an 800-page tome defending his faith against charges of narrow tribalism and declaring it to be universal in scope and prepared to lead the world into a new age of human fellowship.[25] In the process of developing his arguments, he produced what might be seen as an outline of a Jewish theology of Christianity. He sees Judaism's daughter faith in terms which are more Jewish than Christian and which ignore or dismiss central claims of the latter religion. Nevertheless, he affirms the validity of some of the basic principles of Christianity and leads Jews to a positive evaluation of its way of life.

As with any Jewish theology of Christianity, Benamozegh begins with basic principles of Judaism. For him the essential verse in the Torah is surely found in God's commission to Abraham: "Get you out of your native land and from your father's house and go to a land that I will show you. And I will make of you a great nation . . . and in you shall all the peoples of the world be blessed" (Gen. 12:1–4).

In these words are found the dual aspects of Israelite faith that are the keys to grasping Benamozegh's understanding of Judaism. He echoes what has been pointed out many times: that the faith called into existence here by God possesses both particular and universal characteristics. But what Benamozegh does with this insight is unique. Abraham is called to go to a particular land and to establish a singular people destined for greatness. However that greatness rests on a universal mission: Abraham's people are to bring a blessing to all the nations of the world. Thus Israel's uniqueness, its peoplehood, and its particular practices exist to prepare and preserve it for its ultimate role as world redeemer.

According to this thinker, the distinction in Jewish understanding between the particular religious practices of Israel and the universal religion preserved by Jewry for the entire world was essential to the faith from its earliest beginnings. He holds that the seven commandments given to the sons of Noah that make up this universal religion at the heart of Judaism are first articulated in the Talmud: "Our sages have said that seven commandments have been prescribed for the sons of Noah: the first requires them to have judges; the other six forbid sacrilege, idolatry, incest, homicide, theft and the consumption of a limb taken from a living animal" (Talmud: Sanhedrin 56b). Although he can point to no earlier specific listing of the seven commands, he, along with other orthodox authorities, believes the Noahide laws to go back to the earliest days of Israelite faith, to Abraham, even if not to Noah himself. Those mysterious righteous gentiles—Melchizedek, Jethro, and Job—spoken of in Scripture must have been Noahides. The "God-fearers" spoken of in Psalms 22, 118, and elsewhere were gentiles who worshiped Israel's God and kept ethical commandments, but who declined circumcision, water immersion, and full membership in the people Israel.

Such people may well have been numerous in ancient times. Why else would they have been mentioned so often? And Israelites recognized their validity as a religious group. Their sacrifices, said Maimonides, were accepted on the Temple's altar, and they were welcome to observe as much of Mosaic legislation as they wished.[26] According to Rashi, their practice reflected an early pre-Sinatic version of Israelite religion. Also according to Rashi, the seven commands alone were kept by the Israelites at the time of the Exodus until the moment of revelation at Sinai. These laws are essential for all civilized society and constitute the universal religion preserved by Israel as a blessing for all humanity.[27]

The Mosaic religion revealed at Sinai, while for Jews alone, in no way implies divine abandonment of all other peoples. Benamozegh denounced the hypothesis that God would so abandon them as "monstrous." The God who had created all humanity would never act in such a manner.[28] God's ultimate plan is for the unity of all peoples under Jewish religion. But for this author, Jewish religion has the dual nature referred to earlier in this chapter: Mosaism for Jews, Noahism for all others. The latter is no secondary, off-to-the-side afterthought. God gave these seven commandments long before God covenanted with Israel. The later revelation does not cancel out the former in any way. At Sinai God gave laws by which Israel was to live, thus preserving Israel for its universal mission to bring the Noahide faith to all peoples. For Benamozegh the seven commands are the headings of a much more comprehensive ethical system divided into seven categories of conduct by which all peoples are required to live. For example, the anti-incest command implies a broader category of rules governing sexual morality. Likewise, the prohibition against eating the severed limb of a living animal implies a ban on all cruelty to animals. All the commands must be expanded in similar fashion. Obviously, the first of them would lead any society to establish a complex court system of various levels and institutions which can hardly be described in a command of a few words.

What is pointed to by these Noahide commands is a decent, moral, humane society reflecting the way God desires that all people live together.[29] Viewed in this way, the Noahide system becomes much more important to humanity as a whole than the particular legal requirements of the Mosaic revelation to Israel. The Noahide laws are surely more rational than the Mosaic. And they alone justify themselves. By contrast, the laws of Moses were given not for their own sake but to keep the Jews a distinct people so they could ultimately bring the Noahide revelation to all humanity. Jews exist for the sake of the world; their particular law exists for the sake of the universal law of which they are the guardians.

Benamozegh is quite specific in his conception of Israel's role in service to humanity. God is the parent of all. God desires the happiness of all humanity. God calls them all to the virtuous life. Israel is God's firstborn son. In ancient times the firstborn was the priest of the family, the teacher of all the younger siblings. This is Israel's role vis-à-vis the world. As priest and teacher, the eldest must cultivate a special holiness via practices of self-mortification and rigorous religious discipline. For this purpose, the Parent has given the eldest son a system of rules to keep his spiritual senses acute and his strength up to his high calling. The younger brothers are rather more like laymen than priests. They receive the teaching of their older sibling. That teaching is a less rigorous, yet still demanding, system of ethical requirements shorn of the ritual practices followed by the priest-instructor.[30]

Benamozegh points out that this understanding of Israel and humanity is already subscribed to by Judaism's daughter faiths. Christian and Muslim ways of life are modeled on the Hebrew original. Their religious texts either contain the Jewish Scriptures, as in the Christian Bible, or paraphrase them, as in the Qur'an. Christianity calls itself the new Israel, and its Gospels are written to reflect passages in their "Old Testament." These two faiths are indeed simplified versions of Judaism, in some ways imitations of the original. Of course Christianity adds its great emphasis on Jesus. For our author this is ironic, since Jesus, the faithful Jew, had no intention of founding a new religion.[31] Benamozegh holds that open-minded Jews understand Jesus much more accurately than do traditional Christians. However, he sees new developments in his day pointing to the emergence of a liberal Christian conception of the person and role of Jesus much closer to the Jewish evaluation of the simple but profound rabbi and teacher of righteousness.[32]

Benamozegh sees the rise of Christianity as riddled with errors in judgment by its early leaders. They misread the dual nature of Judaism. If they had understood the two versions of faith—one for Jews, one for gentiles—preserved by the Jews, they would have seen that their new religion, which had begun attracting large numbers of gentiles, was, in fact, the Noahide faith of ethics and spirituality devoid of the Jewish law code. This insight could have led them to adopt the proper attitude of appreciation for the mother that had given them birth. Instead they turned on her and declared it their intention to abolish the Law of Moses for everyone, Jew as well as gentile. Other early Christians (Judaizers) insisted that gentile converts to Christianity adopt the whole Mosaic law, that is, become Jews and then Christians.

Paul's position on this issue is not clear. He opposes observance of the law for gentile converts; that is plain enough (Gal., chaps. 2 and 3). But, although he himself claims to observe the law (Acts 21:24), he is accused of advising Diaspora Jews who follow Jesus to cease observing it (Acts 21:21). Whether this charge was true is unclear. James is the early church figure who seeks at first to require all converts to observe the Law of Moses, but then, according to Acts, relents and produces a compromise at the Jerusalem conference that sounds in all particulars, save one, very much like the Noahide laws: "Therefore my judgment is that we should not trouble those of the gentiles who turn to God [trouble them by requiring circumcision] but should write to them to abstain from pollutions of idols and from unchastity and from what is strangled and from blood" (Acts 15:19–20).

Other than the order not to eat strangled (not ritually slaughtered) animals, these requirements to avoid idolatry, sexual sin, and killing are all among the Noahide categories. What Jew could object to a religion for gentiles founded on such principles? According to Benamozegh, had the early church not demanded the end of the Mosaic law along with the passing from history of the old Israel, the rise of Christianity could have been seen by Jewry as the fulfillment of Abraham's call to bring blessings out of Israel for all the world's peoples.

But the misunderstanding did take place. Israel had preserved the universal Noahide code at its heart for centuries. In Christianity, this religion for all people came into its own. But few were able to appreciate this. The church attempted to convert Israel to the simplified Noahide religion designed for gentiles, and, of course, Israel resisted. Mother and daughter became enemies, opening nearly two millennia of conflict. But in the late nineteenth century Benamozegh detected liberalization among Christian intellectuals, a lessening of the emphasis on the divinity of Jesus, and the expansion of good relations between Jews and Christians. He may well have been sixty years too early, but his predictions of a new era of Christian-Jewish good feeling have come true in our time. Now many churches have finally come to the realization that, while Christianity may have replaced paganism, it did nothing of the sort to Judaism. Rather, Christianity joined Judaism in the work of advancing the Reign of God. As Benamozegh hoped a century ago, Christians now recognize the universal aspects of Judaism they long ignored. Progressive Christians and progressive Jews are now prepared to share the work of healing the world. Benamozegh expressed this hope eloquently:

> The two religions themselves are and will remain sisters.... If they are fundamentally united and interdependent no power on earth will be able to separate them permanently. Indeed, to the contrary, they will know at the proper moment how to join their energies of spirit and intelligence... they will recognize their original kinship, and through an appropriate alliance resume their common work for the accomplishment of their great destinies.... Why should Judaism and Christianity not unite their efforts with a view to the religious future of mankind?[33]

Why not indeed?

4

Affirming the Other's Theology

How Far Can Jews and Christians Go?

Religious Self and Other

Although this chapter deals with theological issues, it also poses one overriding ethical question: that of self and other. How am I to treat the other? Not the other who is just like me; treating him well is easy enough. In affirming him I affirm myself. But the question—the challenge—is how to treat the other who is truly other, who is unlike me, who disagrees with me, whose very existence calls into question my smug assumptions about the obvious truth of my own position, who forces me to doubt the universality of my own most cherished beliefs. That other challenges my humanity and presents me with the ultimate ethical dilemma. Can I affirm who I am while making room for the other's self-affirmation? This combination of self-affirmation and self-transcendence *is* the ground of ethics. It is also religious humanism in practice.

"Thou shalt love thy neighbor as thyself," says the author of Leviticus (Lev. 19:18), and from the context of the command it is clear that he means "thou shalt love thy fellow Israelite." The author of Jonah expands this command. He sees God as requiring that Israelites love their enemies afar off, even the hated Assyrians in Nineveh. The Israelite prophet is directed to pray for them and preach to them and help them to change their ways. Why? Because they too are God's children—therefore Israel's "neighbors"—and they "do not know their right hand from their left" (Jon. 4:11).

Then comes Jesus, rabbi and prophet of Galilee, who further expands the Levitical charge. You shall love those most-difficult-to-deal-with adversaries. Not the enemies in a distant land but those close by to whom you have denied the status of neighbor. The Samaritan and the Israelite must love and respect and honor each other's humanity. They must become neighbors ethically as well as geographically (Luke 10:29–37).

And so the term "neighbor" first meant fellow Israelite, then distant enemy, and finally the hated other close by. And *now* it must of course mean everyone. If it doesn't mean everyone, then it cannot mean anyone. For we are all children of the Most High who are commanded to seek out and encourage the highest in ourselves and in each other. All are neighbors; a human race of neighbors. The Levite who penned the original command wrote better than he knew, and his words have taken on a power far beyond their original meaning.

Now we know all this. Certainly Jews and Christians in America know this, and we seek to respect each other and to work together on common projects for social betterment, for cultural excellence, for justice for all. We are truly neighbors. Today only a crackpot fringe would deny this.

But it seems to me that the ethical demand confronting us is greater now than we have recognized. It is time to move beyond mutual respect between Jews and Christians and to ask the theological question. Not just what Jews and Christians have to say about each other, but what *Judaism* and *Christianity* have to say about and to each other. A human individual is called to affirm her own worth without denying the equal worth of her neighbor. But what about religious communities? Are they not called upon to do the same? And what about theological systems? Are they not called to self-transcendence as well as self-affirmation?

Thus ethics challenges theology to make room for the other and, more than that, to affirm the value, the worth, even the possible truth of the other and the other's claims. Can this be done? And what happens to the universality of the claims of religion when this is attempted? Can a religion affirm its own truth without denying the truth of its neighbor faith? Can it make room for the other without denying its own origin in divine revelation? Can religion, traditionally so unprepared to deal with the other on the other's own terms, answer this great ethical challenge? Can it survive if it does answer? Can it survive if it does not?

In this chapter I will review some attempts by Jewish and Christian theologians to deal with these very difficult ethical and theological questions. The chapter concludes with my own attempt to confront these problems.

Three Modern Jewish Theologians Reassess Christianity

Franz Rosenzweig

On October 31, 1913, Franz Rosenzweig wrote to Rudolph Ehrenberg, "You witnessed how I began ... to construct my world anew. In this world ... there appeared to be no place for Judaism."[1] This conclusion seemed at first to lead Rosenzweig toward conversion to Christianity, but then he suddenly saw the same reality from a different angle or, better, in an entirely new light. One is reminded of T. S. Eliot's line: "everything is true in a different sense."[2] For now Rosenzweig saw that if the world had no room for Judaism this was because Judaism and the Jewish people had already transcended the world. Dwelling already in the divine realm of eternity, the eternal people Israel could gladly relinquish the dimensions of time and space to Christians and Christendom. From this unexpected vantage point, Rosenzweig's Israel could, in a wholly unprecedented way, affirm all the claims of Christianity.

Did Christians deny the salvific power of Judaism by quoting Jesus' words from John 14:16: "No one comes to the Father save through me"? Rosenzweig could agree, but with a novel and profoundly insightful twist. "No one *comes* to the Father—but it is different when one no longer needs to come to the Father, because he *is* already with Him. And this is the case with the people Israel."[3] This people needs only to stand firmly in its allotted place, the first fruits of redemption for the whole world, already at the end of the historic process through which all others must move to be redeemed. For non-Jews, the guide in that movement is the church, ever active in the world of time and space, calling all nations (save Israel) to the God with whom Israel already dwells eternally. "The synagogue can only see itself; it has no consciousness of the world. Thus, to the church it can only say: we have already arrived at the destination, you are still en route."[4]

For Rosenzweig, the collective individual that is Israel lives in the presence of God, enjoying the divine glory, obeying the divine voice, anticipating redemption for all peoples. The price she must pay for this is removal from the world-historical scene. The world has no place for Israel, and Israel need trouble the world no longer. It is Christianity that now fights for the souls of men and women. It carries the Torah, in its Christian interpretation, to the nations, and in so doing represents a Judaizing of the pagan peoples. While Judaism abides within itself, Christianity "has its soul in its externals."[5] Judaism, in its completeness, reminds Christianity of its incompleteness and of the as yet unredeemed state of the world. It acts as a corrective to the world's complacency and of Christianity's triumphalism. As such Judaism is absolutely necessary for Christianity as Christianity is for it.

Rosenzweig's most familiar images are of the Star of Redemption, with Judaism as the eternal flame in the heart of the star and Christianity as the eternal rays shining out into the world. "The rays shoot forth from the fiery nucleus of the Star. They seek out a way through the long night of the times. It must be an eternal way . . . it must master time."[6] Thus Christianity gives its name to the present epoch, relegating all time before Christ to a perpetual past and the coming time of redemption to an eternal future. Vital and alive as people and nations are vital and alive, Christianity fights for humanity's soul, seeking to lead all to where Judaism already is, alive eternally but not in the world of externals. Jewry reproduces itself, guarding in its blood its eternity while Christianity peoples itself by converting the world.

Flame and rays need each other, but the need is a conscious one only for Christianity, which cannot forget its origins in Israel, while Israel, the flame, is unconscious of its rays, its Christian outreach into the world. In Rosenzweig's theory there is one divine plan of redemption, one plan but with two crucial elements. The world needs both Judaism and Christianity for its salvation. Without Judaism, Christianity would be overcome by the world and its pagan ways, the very world it seeks to win for God. With Judaism at its back, as its source, it is constantly reminded of its origin and its goal beyond time and space and so it is enabled to overcome the world. Without Christianity, Judaism's only life would be a lifeless life of eternally guarding its inwardness, its purity, its spiritual riches. The world beyond Israel would remain unredeemed. With Christianity, Judaism, all unawares, acquires an outward expression bringing salvation "to the far isles." What is accomplished in Judaism by works of ritual is accomplished for the world outside of Israel by works of love.[7]

If Israel is already at the omega point of redemption, the first fruits of the divine reign, awaiting the arrival of the other peoples who come via Christianity, then any talk of Israel's conversion by Christianity is disallowed. Rosenzweig points out that while the gentile individual is born a pagan and must be reborn into the church at some decisive moment in his life, Israel as a collective individual was reborn at Sinai, and thus Jews are born as Jews, having had their spiritual birth prior to their physical birth. "The rebirth of the Jew . . . is not his personal one, but the transformation of his people for freedom in the divine covenant of revelation."[8] The church must understand and accept this, must see that the conversion of Israel to Christianity would be a redundancy. "However, what the church concedes to Israel as a whole, it refuses to the individual Jew; it is on the individual Jew that it will and ought to test its power and see if it can win him over."[9]

Rosenzweig's system is ingenious and profound. He understands that world redemption needs both Jewish and Christian elements of the divine plan and that those elements are related essentially and organically as are flame and rays. But here the analogy begins to break down. This is through no fault of its author. When the *Star of Redemption* was written, vast numbers of ghettoized Orthodox Jews lived lives of piety in eastern Europe, lives rich with internal meaning but devoid of effect on the external world. It was indeed as if they had withdrawn from the pageant of history to cultivate an eternal inner life in the presence of God. But Rosenzweig lived in the waning years of that reality. The ahistorical life of the pious Jews of eastern Europe was soon swept away by history's most barbarous forces. In the wake of that overthrow, Israel reentered history as a nation for the first time in nearly 2,000 years. In this age of Israel reborn, what Jew can recognize himself in Rosenzweig's picture of a people beyond history? And what Jew, even the most Orthodox, would concede to Christianity all "works of love" while focusing Israel's life exclusively on an abstract form of God consciousness and on ritual? That objection would hold true in Rosenzweig's day as in our own.

Rosenzweig may have held universalist Reform Judaism in contempt, but Reform Jews did not invent the idea that Abraham was called to be a blessing to all peoples (Gen. 12:1–3). Reform theologians did not conjure up Israel's mission to the world; God commanded it. Witness to all peoples and active upbuilding of God's moral, ethical, and spiritual reign are as essential to Israel's life as is the keeping of the ritual commandments. "You are my witnesses, says the Lord" (Isa. 43:10). Witnesses to whom? To the world. And not only indirectly via Christianity, but directly as Jews who seek to elevate the level of humanity's life in the world. One cannot avoid the conclusion that Rosenzweig goes too far in accepting Christianity's exclusive claim to be God's witness in the world. He would have done better to say that there are today at least two divinely established witness communities, each in its own way calling the nations to join in laboring for the divine consummation.

In his relegation of Israel to a kind of extraterrestrial eternal life of dreamy self-contemplation, Rosenzweig might be said to be doing for (or to) Judaism what Leo Baeck did to Christianity. In his writings Baeck held that Pauline thought and Judaism (romanticism and classicism in religion) were forever at war within Christianity.[10] Without its Jewish element of ethical action in history, Christianity falls into an ethereal romanticism, shorn of any moral imperative and intent only on cultivating its inner life of faith. This charge is at the heart of Baeck's anti-Christian polemic. But Rosenzweig describes Judaism in much the same way. What for Baeck is a wholly negative picture of Christianity becomes for Rosenzweig a positive, if paradoxical, description of Judaism. Both Christianity and Judaism deserve better.

Christianity need only concede Judaism's continued validity as a living relationship between a people and its God. Judaism should recognize Christianity's divine origin and co-redemptive role. Neither is called upon to abandon the field to the other. And what must be insisted upon by the Jewish side of the dialogue is that Christianity's recognition of the permanent validity of God's covenant with Israel preclude all attempts by Christians to convert individual Jews. Rosenzweig's bizarre formulation that the church's recognition of the covenant status of Israel leaves individual Jews as proper targets for proselytizing must be rejected.

Martin Buber

Martin Buber's analysis of the relationship between Judaism and Christianity is much less complex than Rosenzweig's, and it yields much less to the Christian side in the discussion. The key concept is redemption.

> The Jew, as part of the world, expresses, perhaps more intensely than any other part, the world's lack of redemption. He feels this lack of redemption against his skin, he tastes it on his tongue, the burden of the unredeemed world lies on him. Because of his almost physical knowledge of this, he *cannot* concede that the redemption has taken place; he knows that it has not.[11]

Nor, according to Buber, have individuals been redeemed. To recognize Christianity's claim that believers are redeemed in an as yet unredeemed world would open up a division of soul and world the Jew could not accept. God's world cannot be divided between the saved and the damned, nor can that world be relegated to a condition of lostness. All must remain open to redemption. For Judaism the division between holy and profane is really one between holy and not yet holy. All the earth will be hallowed. This is the message of prophetic eschatology that triumphed in rabbinic Judaism. Meanwhile, apocalyptic eschatology, with its despair of the earth and of worldly ways, won over the Christian mind and heart. Judaism insists on the human role in bringing redemption. No "Fall" incapacitates humanity for that task or necessitates a reliance on grace alone. Thus, as regards redemption—already or not yet—and the question of the human role in the salvific drama, Judaism and Christianity are for Buber forever divided.

The same is true regarding the role of the people Israel: "The Church perceives Israel as a reality *rejected* by God. This condition of rejection necessarily follows from the claim of the Church to be the true Israel. Those of Israel have, according to this view, forfeited their claim because they did not recognize Jesus as the Messiah."[12] But Jews know better. They know it with their very lives. This is no abstract belief, but the central experience and conviction of Jewish life. Our intimacy with God is such that our certitude is unshakable. Israel confronts the church's rejection of its knowledge of itself and its covenant status. This difference cannot be resolved. "We have to deal with each other in the diversity of the human."[13] Jews cannot directly appraise Christian claims. What Jews know they know from within their own being. They know the world is unredeemed, and they know also that in the midst of that world they are held in God's hand as they have been since Abraham.

What can Jews say about Christianity, according to Buber? He is not always consistent on this issue, but his statements are always powerful: "We understand the Christology of Christianity quite definitely as a substantive occurrence between the Above and the Below."[14] What does this mean? Is Buber recognizing in the Christ event an entrance of the heavenly into the earthly realm? Or is he merely acknowledging that christology makes this claim? If he had said that he recognizes christology as attempting to express the meaning of a "substantive occurrence between the Above and the Below," then this would be a stunning statement indeed. But he had already said that Jews cannot evaluate Christian claims from outside. This leads us to conclude, regretfully, that he is probably commenting on the power of Christian doctrine rather than on the Christ event to which that doctrine refers. "We view Christianity as something whose spread over the world of nations we are in no position to penetrate."[15] Here he reflects his usual position that the claims of any religious community can only be evaluated from within that believing group. Jews cannot appraise the significance of Christianity's growth. But, Buber adds, Jews do know that this growth has not resulted in the world's redemption. For Jews redemption cannot come short of the full flowering of God's reign. Keeping in mind God's words from the burning bush, "I will be what I will be" (Exod. 3:14), we must hold open all divine possibilities until the end. God may appear in many manifestations, but God is always superior to any or all of them. Jews do not say that God cannot be revealed in such and such a manner, but no revelation is unsurpassable. According to Buber, an incarnation would be unsurpassable because it would claim to express the totality of the divine. But the divine totality cannot be expressed or exhausted. Here Buber seems to be rejecting the possibility of incarnation because he sees it as a limit placed on future divine possibilities.[16]

It is interesting to note that Buber also points out that Israel's election is not exhaustive of the divine activity in the world, not unsurpassable. The prophets remind the people "that it is nothing more than, so to speak, an experiment of God." First God tried to work with humankind in general. Only when that experiment failed did God call Israel into being as the "beginning of his harvest" (Jer. 2:3).

Despite his focusing on what he considers the irreconcilable differences between the two faiths, Buber does speak of what we hold in common, "a book and an expectation." We can study the book and await together the advent of the One, even as we find each other incomprehensible due to our radical differences over the "already" or the "not yet" of redemption. Yet "every authentic sanctuary can acknowledge the mystery of every other authentic sanctuary."[17] He points out that "the gates of God are open to all. The Christian need not go via Judaism, nor the Jew via Christianity in order to enter in to God."[18] The traditional Jewish formulation, "the righteous of all nations have a share in the world to come,"[19] says nothing whatever about Christianity. It is, rather, a statement about God's moral requirements for all humanity. Here, as is often the case, a Jewish thinker has found it easier to deal with gentiles as human beings in general than as Christians.

Buber seems to accept the church's failure to recognize the present-day validity of Judaism and the mission of Israel as logically necessitated by its view of itself as "the new Israel." At one point he suggests that fruitful dialogue cannot take place unless the church rethinks this position. He indicates that he hopes for a change of heart by the church. But there is no further mention of this. He does not really believe that the church will ever make room for Israel in the world. But Israel is here nonetheless, knowing that the church's view of her is untrue. Unlike Rosenzweig, Buber will not cede the world to Christianity and have Israel retire to an eternal realm outside of historic time. He yearns for the church to give his people recognition as a salvific force in the world. "We are entitled . . . to hope that the possibility for an authentic acceptance of Israel exists in a common struggle hard but blessed."[20] Meanwhile, the best that can be accomplished is a dialogue based upon "the belief in a human community as the royal realm of God." Is this "interfaith dialogue" at all, or a resort to a universal religious humanism that skirts all theological issues save messianic expectation? And even that question cannot be fully explored, since the two parties await a different expected one.

One is led to the conclusion that Buber settled for too little. Of course, the church of his day was prepared to give so little. She, not he, is to be criticized for that. The paradox is that Buber, who was prepared to go so far in the dialogue, accepted the church's unwillingness to move at all. But it must be made clear that Buber really concedes little or nothing to Christianity. It is on the subject of Jesus that he breaks with previous Jewish patterns of thought. And even here he does not do this to affirm any of the several Christian views of Jesus, but to attempt a new Jewish conception of him: "From my youth onwards I have found in Jesus my great brother.... and today I see him more strongly and clearly than ever before. I am more than ever certain that a great place belongs to him in Israel's history of faith and that this place cannot be described by any of the usual categories."[21]

He sees Jesus not as messianic pretender, not as rabbi or prophet but as something new. However, he does not explain what this vision of Jesus might be. His implied question seems not to be "Was this man God?" but, rather, "What must this man have been to lead people to believe him to be God?" After all, no one ever suggested such a thing in the case of rabbis, prophets, or even the Messiah.

But whatever Buber has in mind, he does want to see Jesus in the Jewish context. He makes this clear in the same text when he contrasts Jesus with Paul. In sending his disciples out to "the lost sheep of the house of Israel" (Matt. 15:24), Jesus expresses concern for individuals who have strayed from the flock. It is not the flock that is lost, but the individuals who have strayed from their proper place in the Jewish fold. When they hear the word spoken to them, they will return home to the holy community within which alone they can find the meaning of their individual lives. In contrast, Paul calls individuals out of their native communities (Jewish and gentile), as Buber believes Christianity has been doing ever since. In this distinction between Judaism and Christianity Buber clearly places Jesus on the Jewish side. Finally, Buber leaves unanswered the question of who or what Jesus was in a profoundly suggestive way, which opened a door in Jewish-Christian dialogue that had never been opened before.

Why did Buber assume that the church could maintain its own claim to be the new Israel only by denying Israel's claim to ongoing validity? What about Romans 9 through 11 about which we hear so much today? It is understandable that the church of the 1930s might overlook it, preferring the chauvinism of Galatians, but why would a Jew familiar with Paul's epistles not notice the possibilities here? At least Rosenzweig conceived a divine plan requiring both Israel and the church in the work of salvation. Buber stops far short of that. He makes no suggestions for reconciling opposed views or even softening them. Could he not see in God's election of Israel an element of the "already" in the "not yet" of the Jewish view of redemption? And could he not find in the Parousia hope something of the "not yet" in the "already" of Christianity's salvific conception? In not going far enough, Buber went too far in making his peace with differences that are not absolute or necessary. Perhaps the lure of a universal religious humanism led him to take refuge from Jewish-Christian differences in a realm he felt transcended both. This "solution" cannot provide a model for authentic theological dialogue.

And yet Buber has one more word to speak on the subject of possible Jewish-Christian dialogue. In *Two Types of Faith* he offers a comparison of Judaism and Christianity. Typically he points out what he sees as fundamental differences, this time in terms of their respective understandings of faith itself. For him Judaism's faith, *emunah*, must be understood as "trust," leading to perseverance through the lived experience of history. This existential trust arises in the context of a people's ongoing journey of life. All individual Israelites gain their *emunah* within the context of the communal experience of the people of faith. It is this faith, shared by the whole house of Israel, that unites in solidarity all its members into one pilgrim people en route to redemption.

Christian faith, *pistis*, by contrast, is born outside history in the soul of the individual who accepts a belief that lifts him in his new faith-centered self-definition out of his community or nation. As a Frenchman or a German the Christian believer has a twofold being, the Christian dimension being radically ahistorical or transhistorical and individual. As such Christian *pistis* is exactly the opposite of Jewish *emunah*, which unites the individual with his people (Israel) and its historical life.[22]

In his insistence that for the Jew faith and nation are one, Buber agrees with Rosenzweig, but he turns the latter's thought upside down in insisting that *emunah* arises in and remains in the flow of history, while *pistis* removes the Christian from historical self-understanding insofar as he is a Christian. But is the Christian's faith as radically individual as Buber states? It is surely more so than that of the Jew, but the ethnic churches of eastern Europe and the complex interweaving of faith and nation in, say, Irish or Spanish Catholicism escape his notice. He also shows little understanding of the church as the living body of Christ of which all believers are members. He is pointing to a real contrast, but as usual, he overstates it. This does not lessen the poignancy of the hope with which he concludes his thoughts.

> The faith of Judaism and the faith of Christendom are by nature different in kind. . . . But an Israel striving after the renewal of its faith through the rebirth of the person and a Christianity striving for the renewal of its faith through the rebirth of nations would have something as yet unsaid to say to each other and a help to give to one another—hardly to be conceived at the present time.[23]

Here indeed are the seeds of dialogue. As James Parkes had noted, Judaism's style is more communal and Christianity's more individual.[24] This is not the absolute difference Buber imagines, but one of emphasis. In any case, on this issue the two faith communities have much to say to each other. Christianity can help Judaism develop its own often latent individual spirituality, while Judaism can teach the church how to become a closer-knit community of faith. This is a bright hope indeed that makes all the sadder Buber's last words, "hardly to be conceived at the present time." The fact that we can so easily conceive such an exchange today—the fact that it is actually occurring— reveals just how far we have come in a few fateful decades.

Abraham Joshua Heschel

Abraham Joshua Heschel was both a friend and a critic of Christianity—a critic because he was a friend. Seeing Christianity as a potentially great force for spiritual and moral renewal in the world, he urged the church to reform itself in quest of its highest potential. He believed that the problems between the church and the Jews started when Christianity began to define itself in contrast to Judaism. This was an inevitable result of the increasing gentile presence in the church and the eclipse of the earlier Jewish branch of the movement. "The Christian affirmation and culmination of Judaism became very early diverted into a repudiation and negation of Judaism."[25] This was expressed in various triumphalist doctrines in which a degraded parody of Judaism was contrasted with an idealized Christianity. Thus the daughter faith dishonored her mother and even sought her destruction.

Church renewal can only take place today if Christians are willing to reverse this sad process: "The vital issue for the church is to decide whether to look for roots in Judaism and consider itself an extension of Judaism or to look for roots in pagan Hellenism and consider itself as an antithesis of Judaism."[26] Heschel decried the Marcionite heresy still alive in the church and cited the views of Rudolf Bultmann to prove it. He warned against the Hellenized individualism exhibited by the church in its stress on personal salvation at the expense of world redemption. "Only a conscious commitment to the roots of Christianity in Judaism could have saved it from such distortions."[27] He found fault with the un-Jewish tendency in the church to concern itself with "mystery" as opposed to "history," a tendency that allowed the church to withdraw from the struggle for social justice. A healthy dose of Jewish prophetism could have prevented this.

But the eclipse of the prophetic dimension is a Jewish as well as a Christian problem. "In biblical days prophets were astir while the world was asleep; today the world is astir while church and synagogue are busy with trivialities."[28] And so Jews and Christians both need renewal in their religious lives. That renewal must take the form of individual and institutional self-transcendence. The problem for Heschel was not the preservation of the church (or synagogue) but, rather, the preservation of humanity. The issue was not the incarnation (or any other doctrine) but the elimination of God from human consciousness. All dogmas are tentative; none is final. But humanity's need for a sense of the living God and of a divine moral imperative is the central problem of this age. And here church and synagogue can join hands and point the way.

In his essay "No Religion Is an Island," Heschel insisted that the time of parochialism had ended. Religions are no more self-sufficient than individuals and nations. Judaism and Christianity together face the abyss of nihilism and must fight it side by side. How can any religion feel triumphant when all have been defeated by the horrors of the twentieth century? Jews and Christians may differ in their conceptions of God, but they share something much deeper: the image of God. In this human-divine dimension we meet and act together. We are divided on issues of law and creed. We say "No" to each other here. But we may together say "Yes" to God as he calls us to help heal the world. The call is the same, and so are our consciences, our sin, and our shame at our failures. Dogmas differ; God is One.

As regards Christian doctrines, "Jews and Christians are strangers and stand in disagreement with one another." But we are both children of a commanding God. How do we affirm our differing faiths while, at the same time, reaching out to one another in a common cause? Heschel insists that "the first and most important prerequisite of interfaith is faith."[29] For him interfaith dialogue "must remain a prerogative of the few. It is not for the half-learned or spiritually immature." Syncretism is a constant danger to authentic Judaism and Christianity. Each must be and remain what it is. Yet each, loyal to its own tradition, must learn reverence for the other. How is this to be done? "A Christian ought to realize that a world without Israel will be a world without the God of Israel. A Jew, on the other hand, ought to acknowledge the eminent role and past of Christianity in God's design for the redemption of all men."[30]

Jewish critics of Christianity should ask themselves what other non-Jewish religion would we prefer for the world? We can only flourish in a world that reveres our Scriptures. Of all non-Jewish religions, only Christianity does that. We gave birth to Christianity; she is our child. We have a stake in that child's future. The church brought the Scriptures and the God of Israel to the nations. Clearly Christianity possesses great truths. So does Israel. The task of building God's kingdom requires many hands. God has willed it so. "In this aeon diversity of religions is the will of God." But the ultimate truth remains in God and is not expressible in words or possessed by any one individual or tradition. This forces on all persons and on all traditions the humility necessary for healthy religious life.

The church must see Israel as Israel is now ready to see the church. Thus the "mission to the Jews" must be abandoned. No Jews should be asked "to betray the fellowship, the dignity, the sacred history of [their] people."[31] Christians must come to see the ongoing history of Israel as a demonstration of God's faithfulness. Is it possible that Christians really believe that the world would be the better if the spiritual treasures of Judaism, its practice, and its faith were swept away? What the church has considered Jewish stubbornness must now be seen as Jewish faithfulness to God. And Jews must open themselves to "the glory and holiness in the lives of countless Christians."[32] Heschel cited Reinhold Niebuhr and Paul Tillich as voices raised against a continuation of "the mission to the Jews." He goes on to remind Jews of the words of Yehuda Halevi and Maimonides, who held Christianity to be a *praeparatio messianica*. Maimonides pointed out that through Christianity the Torah and commandments have been brought to the nations. Christianity (and Islam) are not "accidents of history or purely human phenomena." They are "part of God's design for the redemption of all men."[33]

In his positive evaluation of Christianity, Heschel considers that the church plays a crucial role in God's plan of salvation. In this he is closer to Rosenzweig than to Buber, who discerns in the spread of Christianity no redemptive results. Heschel too acknowledges the failure of Christianity but sees this as the shared failure of Jews and Christians to accomplish their salvific tasks. This failure does not deny the divine origins and missions of both faiths but rather points to the pressing need for both to live up to their high callings. Apparently it did not occur to Heschel to comment on the grace/works controversy in the church. The liberal Christians with whom he dealt believed that human beings must cooperate in their own salvation. For his part Buber talks as if no Christians believe this. Of course Roman Catholics and many non-Lutheran Protestants do not hold that "grace is sufficient." Heschel's objection was to the overly individualized form of Christianity that neglected the goal of world redemption. Here Judaism could help the church gain a new focus. Interaction with Jews would also force Christians to take Israel seriously as a present-day laborer in God's vineyard. Heschel would not make his peace with the church's illusion of being the only redemptive force operating in today's world. For him Christians and Jews must recognize that they are both striving toward the Kingdom, both doing God's work.

Heschel affirms the divine calling of Judaism's Christian partner in redemption and will not tolerate a Christian refusal to recognize Judaism in a similar way. He feels close enough to Christianity to make demands that neither Rosenzweig nor Buber managed to articulate. For Heschel these possibilities were opened by the American climate of religious tolerance and interaction. His close friendships with Christian theologians and the growing cooperation between his Jewish Theological Seminary and Union Theological Seminary across the street opened up vistas unknown to Rosenzweig or even Buber. And yet Heschel, who had no hesitation in criticizing what he took to be Christian errors of thought, never allowed himself to comment on positive Christian doctrines. He adopts a policy of silence regarding Christian claims while demanding that Christians affirm basic Jewish doctrines. For example, he insists that Christians endorse the Jewish claim to be a covenant people acting today in fidelity to a divine calling. He asks Jews to say the same of Christians. But these moves are not parallel. In the Jewish covenant, Israel, the collective individual, is created and called by God and is placed in the world as God's redemptive agent to bring the divine reign to fruition. In the breaking open of the covenant accomplished by Christianity, that salvific role is given to a single individual, Jesus, who is the new agent of world redemption.

But Heschel says nothing positive about Jesus or about Christian claims regarding him. He assumes that to be a Jew is to deny all of these claims without realizing that a corresponding denial on the part of Christians would lead them to refuse to recognize the present-day redemptive role of Israel. Heschel is quick enough to recognize the holiness and integrity of the lives of individual Christians, as well as the church's role in the divine plan. But for Christians the church is the body of Christ with its raison d'être in the one about whom Heschel remains silent. Buber had said that Jews cannot evaluate the phenomenon of the church and its spread in the world. Heschel disagrees and evaluates it as an agent of God. But he seems to be saying that Jews cannot evaluate the role of Jesus or say anything positive about this gigantic figure in the history of Israel and the world. Where Buber had so much to say, speaking so eloquently of "my great brother," Heschel is silent. And, curiously, where Heschel speaks freely of the church and its divinely appointed task, Buber refuses to comment. Until Jewish theology is willing to speak more freely of *both* the church and the one to whom she points—and in language in which Christians can recognize themselves and their faith—full interfaith dialogue on the theological level will not develop.

Three Modern Christian Theologians Reassess Judaism

While the churches have been laboring to construct new views of Judaism, Christian theologians have been hard at work attempting to create theologies of Christian-Jewish dialogue. The most innovative of these have gone beyond the positions articulated by the church statements. This was to be expected, since individuals are always freer than institutions to explore new territory. I will briefly examine three of the most interesting of these new Christian evaluations of Judaism.

Paul van Buren

Paul van Buren devoted more than twenty years of fruitful labor to constructing a new theological understanding of the relationship between Christianity and Judaism.[34] For him the failure of the church's early hope for the Parousia led to a dehistoricizing of that hope. Christianity de-emphasized its future expectation, abandoned history, theologically speaking, and took refuge in an otherworldly view of the triumph of Christ's resurrection. This leap from history into mysticism was a profoundly un-Jewish one that served to sever the church from its Jewish roots and from the Jewish community and faith. But van Buren insists that the church must now recognize the common heritage of messianic expectation and divine calling that unites it with the Jewish people. Jews and Christians together are Israel, the people of God. They must come to know and understand each other.

A crucial result of this process will be the Christian acknowledgment that Jesus was not and is not the Messiah of Jewish expectation.[35] What Jesus accomplished was the possibility of world redemption as the conveyor of the God of Israel and God's commandments to the gentiles. Jesus, like many of his fellow Jews, expected the coming of God's reign. Thus Christians and Jews today share that ultimate hope. Christ was Judaism's great gift to the nations. If today most Jews and Christians see Jewry as having rejected Christ, it is because they are reading back into Jesus' day the second-century Jewish rejection of mistaken Christian claims that Jesus was the Jewish Messiah. Now Jews and Christians must come to see Jesus as "given" by the Jews to the nations who, through him, can now enter the covenant between God and Israel. There is no question of Jews becoming Christians. Rather, as Christians, gentiles can join Jewry as a new branch of Israel. And this new Christian branch is called to imitate Jesus in his love for and service to the Jewish people.

Van Buren poses some very interesting issues. It is indeed to be hoped that recognition of the Jewish roots of the Christian faith and of the Jewish partner in the dialogue can lead Christianity back to its early world-redemptive self-understanding. And his view that both Jesus and the Jewish "no" to Christianity were gifts to the nations, inspired by God, would lead Christians away from their puzzlement or anger at Jewry's supposed "rejection of Christ."

In fact, van Buren, the Christian, endorses Jewry's nonacceptance of Jesus as Messiah on the grounds that the Nazarene did not fulfill the messianic hopes of Israel's biblical and postbiblical texts. But here he oversimplifies a complex issue. At the time of Jesus there was no single religion called "Judaism." The Jewish people were divided into a variety of groups and sub-groups, some of which considered their particular community to be the one and only legitimate "Israel." As there was no "mainstream" Judaism, there was no single messianic expectation. Some expected a human Messiah of David's line, a king who would bring victory over the Romans, political independence to Israel, and an era of peace and justice to the world (Psalms of Solomon 17:21–33). Others expected a heavenly figure, preexistent and eternal, who would come with clouds and angels to judge and redeem Israel and the whole creation (Dan. 7; 1 Enoch 37–71). Others expected two Messiahs, one royal, one priestly, with the Aaronic anointed taking precedence (Dead Sea Scroll: the Zadokite Document 12:22–23, 13:20–22, 14:18–19, etc.; Dan. 9:25–26). One group spoke of a Messiah who dies before the last judgment (4 Ezra 7:29). Others spoke of a suffering innocent (Wisd. of Sol. 2–5). And many expected direct divine intervention into history without any Messiah figure at all.

All of these expectations were expressed in texts produced by various Jewish sects. None of them can be considered more or less legitimate than any other. Among these sects was the Nazarene or Christian group. As one of the many Judaisms of the first century, they had the same right as the others to develop their own theory of the Messiah. It does not have to meet any one standard of Jewish "correctness," since, at the time, no such standard existed. Today, Christians look to the future for the vindication of their faith in Jesus as Messiah. Jews look in the same direction for the fulfillment of their messianic hopes. Until one or the other hope is realized, it is futile for us to argue over which expectation is accurate. We await the same events. We differ as to the personage who will bring them about. Time will tell. Until then "we are partners in waiting," both united and divided by our shared but differing expectations. For the present—and probably long into the future—Jesus remains the expected Messiah of Christianity. Neither the Jews nor the Jewish-Christian dialogue can or should ask Christians to abandon that hope any more than Christians should insist that Jews adopt it. Neither van Buren nor other Christian theologians should ask their coreligionists to give up this or other elements of traditional Christian faith. Careful definitions are called for, but the age-old formulas will remain, shorn of their negative implications.

A. Roy Eckardt

A. Roy Eckardt was one of the great pioneers of the Christian-Jewish dialogue. Before Paul van Buren, he saw the Jewish "no" to Christianity as an expression of fidelity to God.[36] It was the divine will that the Jewish people remain distinct. But, against van Buren's inclusive Jewish-Christian definition of Israel, Eckardt sees only Jewry as holding that title. Like van Buren, he sees one covenant uniting Israel and the church, but in a creative relationship in which each one's role is distinct. Like Rosenzweig (and Will Herberg after him),[37] Eckardt sees Israel as guarding its uniqueness, looking inward and cultivating its own life while the church does its work out among the nations. Each has a revelation of equal value, but he seems to be saying that there is ultimately one revelation that has been given twice, once to Jews and then two millennia later to the nations. Thus the church misunderstands its own role when it tries to speak of itself as the fulfillment or replacement of Judaism. It is, rather, the result of the breaking open of the covenant to include gentiles. That is all it is. And that should be enough. Now Christians share in the promises of Israel's God.

Remarkably, during the 1970s and 1980s Eckardt did not see these promises pointed to by the resurrection. In fact, in these years he worked his way to the unique position (for a Christian) of denying the resurrection entirely. As a theologian of the Jewish-Christian dialogue Eckardt could find no way to affirm this traditional claim of the church without insult to Jews and Judaism. For him, during those years, the proclamation of Jesus' resurrection, whether physical or spiritual, expressed a Christian triumphalism and a repudiation of Judaism. If God has raised Jesus from the dead and the Jews deny this, then they are found to be in opposition to God and God's definitive redemptive act. If Christianity is correct in its claim, then the Jews are simply wrong, and the resurrection represents God's final "no" to them and their faith. For Eckardt, that divine "no" to Jews and Judaism leads directly from the empty tomb to the fires of Auschwitz. It was to avoid this path that Eckardt dispensed with the resurrection altogether. In a later work he quotes his own words of the 1970s:

> The man from Galilee sleeps now. He sleeps with all the other Jewish dead, with all the distraught and scattered dead of the murder camps. . . . But Jesus of Nazareth shall be raised. So too the young Hungarian children of Auschwitz shall be raised. Once upon a coming time they shall laugh and play . . . "for the earth shall be full of the knowledge of the Lord as the waters cover the sea." (Isa. 11:9)[38]

In the late 1980s Eckardt began to reconsider this position. In *Reclaiming the Jesus of History*, he develops a nontriumphalist, nonsupersessionist way of proclaiming the resurrection at least in "an extrabodily or spiritual" sense.[39] Here he stresses the Jewishness of the doctrine and sees it as a point of contact between Judaism and Christianity. In fact it represents the continuity and interrelatedness of the two faiths. He sees Christ's future as bound up with the future of Israel.[40] Rather than a repudiation of Judaism, the resurrection can be seen as a vindication of Jesus the Jew, an affirmation of the ongoing life of Israel, and the promise of the future resurrection of all of God's people.

And so Eckardt ultimately resurrected the Christian doctrine of resurrection. He came to repudiate his earlier denial of this central Christian affirmation. I well remember an exchange I had with him at the meeting of the National Christian-Jewish Workshop in Pittsburgh in 1992. I had read a paper, "Toward Total Dialogue: Taking the Next Step in Jewish-Christian Dialogue," and the question period was under way. Roy Eckardt raised his hand and asked for my view of the resurrection. I replied: "Following the death of Jesus his followers continued to have experience of him in his bodily form. I have no reason to doubt the authenticity of that experience." As I recall, he reacted quite negatively to that response. If at the time he was in the process of revising his earlier denial of the resurrection, it is difficult to see why he found my reply so unsatisfactory. Did he want me, a Jew, to deny the truth of this Christian affirmation? Was I affirming more than he, a Christian, was at that time willing to assert?

But Jews do not ask Christians in the dialogue to give up core doctrines. How would Jews respond if Christians who have problems with Zionism demanded that Jews give up the theological claim that God has given us the land of Israel? Some Christians have, in fact, made that demand of Jewish dialogue partners. The Jews have responded properly that the divine bestowal of the Holy Land is a core doctrine of Israelite faith that cannot be given up for the sake of the dialogue or to suit anyone's preferences. The gift of land is a "given" of Jewish religious experience, and Jewish theology must reflect that experience if it is to remain authentic. Israelites may decide to give up some of the land because the same God who gave the land also commands us to be "pursuers of peace." But the land is ours to give.

Similarly, the incarnation and resurrection are essential experiences of Christian faith. In Christ the transcendent God comes down to earth as, in the gift of land to God's people, the Holy One acts in the world and its history. These doctrines are parallel concretizations of the divine activity crucial to the respective faiths. Eckardt was right in concluding that he had gone too far. There are many ways of understanding the resurrection, but its total abandonment would be fatal to Christianity. Jews must view with alarm all such attempts to dismantle our sister faith. There can be no dialogue if one of the partners decides to self-destruct.

At the same time, I have problems with Eckardt's Rosenzweig-like acceptance of an inward-looking Judaism that leaves activity among the nations of the world to the church. The Jewish people has its own historic dynamic, its own active redemptive work to do in the ethical, social, political, and spiritual life of the world. It will not abandon the world, "the theater of God's glory," to another. It is, of course, more than willing to share it.

Clark M. Williamson

With his 1993 book, *A Guest in the House of Israel: Post-Holocaust Church Theology*, Clark M. Williamson took his place among leading Christian theologians of the dialogue.[41] His book is a comprehensive and well-balanced review of Christian theological claims illuminated by the fires of the Holocaust that some of those claims helped to ignite. While he does not hold that Christian anti-Jewish doctrines provided sufficient conditions for the destruction of European Jewry, he does believe that the church's teaching of contempt for all things Jewish did lay the necessary groundwork for the catastrophe. And even today, fifty years and more after the tragic events, the church has failed to eliminate from its regular worship expressions of anti-Jewish bias. He comments sadly on the "explanatory" prefaces often read before lectionary scripture selections at Sunday services. References to the "Jews'" alleged hatred of Jesus and opposition to his good works are still to be found in such prefaces, which poison minds against the Jewish neighbor and reinforce age-old prejudices.

He is correct in this, but he might also have mentioned the lectionary readings themselves. They too need to be dealt with. This is especially true as regards Holy Week readings. Is it really necessary to repeat the established cycle of readings year in and year out that requires the public pronouncement of slander against an entire people? If the churches in their official statements of the past forty years have rejected the notion that "the Jews" were responsible for Jesus' passion, why are New Testament selections still read in worship services that repeat the old canards? Can all priests and ministers be counted on to explain to their congregations the conditions of Jewish-Christian rivalry in the late first century that produced these distorted statements? Would it not be preferable to choose readings with an eye to avoiding passages that are unjust and untrue?

I recall one weekday during Holy Week on which a Catholic priest of my acquaintance had asked me to meet with him in his office to discuss a Passover Seder that I was to conduct at his church. He had just stressed to me that he did not want a watered-down version of the service, but desired that his people be exposed to the full Seder service read from the Haggadah "just as Jews do it in their homes." At that point he looked at his watch and said that he had to go into the church to offer the noon Mass. I accompanied him and sat through the beautiful liturgy, delighted to be there, until they reached the Scripture readings of the day. I was horrified to hear selections from John painting "the Jews" in the most negative terms. Following the Mass we returned to his office, where he began once more to insist on the authentic Jewishness of the upcoming Seder, going so far as to suggest the exclusive use of kosher food.

At that point I interrupted him to mention what seemed to me to be a blatant contradiction. This good man, so friendly to Jews and eager to educate his flock in the Jewish faith, had just read New Testament selections intensely hostile to "the Jews" as a group. As I spoke, I could see that he was genuinely stunned. All this had never occurred to him. He truly had never thought about it. After a moment of thinking about it, he assured me that there was no danger of any of his congregation absorbing anti-Jewish attitudes from the readings, since no one paid attention to them anyway. Needless to say, I was not reassured. If his flock paid so little attention to what they heard in church, then why did he expect them to learn anything from the Seder we were planning? When I suggested that words did have consequences and that he might have chosen other readings, he responded that he was not free to do so but was obliged to read the selections ordained for that day.

As a frequent visitor to church services, I have run into this situation many times. Too many lectionary passages present Jews as the villains of the Christian story and contain accusations that have been repudiated by most mainstream churches. As things stand today, any Jews attending Holy Week services will be made to feel intensely uncomfortable. But Christians of good will should also be made uncomfortable by this anachronistic situation. The church has a real problem here, and she must deal with it. Williamson is correct in his insistence that all the high-minded denominational statements will come to nothing if the worship of the churches is not reformed to reflect the new attitudes. Reform of the lectionary should be the church's next priority in the dialogue.

Williamson notes that changes have been made in liturgical readings to avoid offending or degrading women, but little has been done to remove readings offensive to Jews. It is true that liturgy usually represents the most reactionary tendencies in religious life. Worshipers become wedded to traditional formulas and terms of speech and are much less willing to allow changes than theologians have been. But the present situation, in which lectionary readings at times contradict official church positions, ought really to be corrected. If church leaders are determined to do this, the laity will follow.

In nonliturgical areas of its life the church has made great strides in moving away from traditional anti-Jewish attitudes. Mainline denominations no longer hold that Jews had to be rejected by God so that gentiles could be elected or that Jews misunderstand the promises of their own Scriptures. The *adversus Judaeus* tradition that Williamson calls the "sickness at the heart of Christianity" is on the way out, more so, perhaps, than Williamson recognizes. He calls on Christians to take Jews seriously as a living people and faith. His view is that Paul was the last Christian theologian to do so until the twentieth century. He may be right. This, of course, makes all the more remarkable the recent changes in Christian attitudes.

Williamson's call for a new post-Holocaust Christian theology is not issued primarily to benefit Jews but to achieve a new authentic existence for Christianity and Christian believers. No Christian theological statement is credible if it cannot be made in the shadow of Auschwitz. Faith must be expressed today as discipleship, not as ideology, with its rigid, lapidary pronouncements. He calls for the development of a new Judaized form of Christianity, devoted to world redemption, to acting as a light to the nations and to the realization—the concrete this-worldly realization—of God's reign on earth.

In speaking at churches and teaching classes in their adult Sunday schools, I have often been challenged by well-meaning, friendly people who have great difficulty overcoming the notion they have been taught all their lives that Judaism is carnal and worldly while Christianity is spiritual and altogether on a higher plain. By a "re-Judaizing" of Christianity, Williamson seems to have in mind a rejection of such shallow distinctions and the adoption by Christians of the Jewish view that feeding the hungry, housing the homeless, and clothing the naked are as much religious responsibilities— are just as "spiritual"—as are questions of grace and salvation. The Jesus of the parables of the last judgment (Matt. 25) would agree, of course, but somewhere, somehow the church began making bogus distinctions between spiritual and physical needs that have little to do with lived human experience. Williamson is calling for a Christian return to the more holistic Judaic view of the total human person. If redemption has nothing to do with social justice and the elevation of the quality of life lived in human community, then it means little to this Christian theologian. Jews can only applaud this view. Of course, so would many Christians who are much more committed to religion-inspired social action in the world than Williamson seems to realize.

In his zeal to reform his own faith, Williamson sees great benefit coming to the church from close cooperation and conversation with Jews. But like many Christian lovers of Israel, he seems not to consider that this new interfaith closeness can also benefit Jews and Judaism. I do not mean that it will make Christian mistreatment of Jews less likely, although that is certainly the case. What I am suggesting is that Judaism, as much as Christianity, needs to hear "the voice of the other" that can put it back in touch with the best in itself. Williamson states that "Jews never lose sight of the fact that God's people are called to be a light to the nations,"[42] and that Christians can be reminded by faithful Israel that this universal calling to world service also belongs to the church.

But here he surely idealizes Jewry, as so many Judeophiles so often do. The fact is that too often, Jews, individually and collectively, do forget their witness to the world. We grow complacent and self-satisfied. Our worship becomes routinized and uninspiring. We think of ourselves as a defensive ethnic minority rather than as a divinely commissioned witness people. The sad fact is that too many Jews have never thought of our people as a "light to the nations" but have lived in a self-imposed mental ghetto with little concern for those beyond the walls. The particularism of Jewish life has too often overwhelmed the universalism that calls us to the task of world redemption. Williamson and other Christian friends must avoid comparing Christianity at its worst to Judaism at its best.

We Jews need close contact with Christians to help us rediscover that outward-thrusting missionary zeal that invigorates a faith community. This is not to say that either community should be engaged in proselytization. Mission today means an active life of service to all of God's children in every area of human need, from bodily succor to moral uplift to cultural elevation. The "us-against-them" mentality to which all particular communities are subject must give way to an "us-for-them" commitment to world service. Christians and Jews can teach each other, can learn from each other, and can bolster each other to achieve levels of world-redemptive activity that they might never reach on their own. Christian theologians ought not be afraid to suggest that Judaism will benefit as much from close contact with Christianity as the latter will from contact with the former. Any dialogue worthy of the name must move in both directions.

Williamson believes that all Christian theology must now be done in conversation with Jews. All traditional propositions and beliefs must be recast in the light of the Holocaust. This is fine so long as it is understood that while interpretations may change, essential doctrines cannot be discarded without destroying Christianity itself. This theologian seems to recognize that and does not suggest a dismantling of the central propositions of his faith. It is the exclusivism of Christianity, its failure to make room for the other, rather than its positive doctrines, that must change. Williamson points to the Jewish tradition of response and commentary, which finds new ways of reading traditional beliefs. The adoption of this practice as regards Christian attitudes toward Jews and Judaism will give new life to Christianity by freeing it from the false premises of the past, even if those premises were grounded in New Testament texts. Since the days of the early church the anti-Jewish polemic has been the negative side of the Christian message. It can be left behind without threatening in any way the positive Christian message. The purification of that message from this pollution will, in fact, strengthen and renew the church and its teaching.

Some will resist new interpretations of Scripture, but others will observe that only once a canon is closed can it truly be open to liberating new readings that keep it relevant to every age. For example, Christians have usually read John 14:6, "I am the way and the truth and the life; no one comes to the Father but by me," to mean that only those professing Jesus Christ as savior can reach God. Following an address to a Methodist audience, I was challenged by one of my listeners with that quote. Much to my questioner's amazement, I said that I agreed with it. "Then why don't you become a Christian?" he asked. I replied that there was more than one way to interpret the verse in question. I chose to read it to say that no one comes to God except through the kind of life Jesus led, the life of service to humanity, of devotion to God and self-sacrifice in the cause of world redemption. A Jew could and should live such a life as well as a Christian.

Read in this manner, the words attributed to Jesus become a compelling call to the self-transcending religious life rather than a threat to anyone who is not in "our" theological camp. Interpreted thus, a saying long read as an "us-against-them" pronouncement becomes an "us-for-them" call to world service. Pluralism replaces exclusivism, and the verse is liberated to reflect the true spirit of Jesus of Nazareth. Those who resist such new humane readings and cling to the old divisive interpretations do so out of hardness of heart and their own need to rejoice that they are "not like other men" (Luke 18:11).

I well recall a conversation I had with my mentor and teacher, the brilliant theologian Gabriel Vahanian, as we walked across the campus of Syracuse University. I expressed my anxiety that an essay I had just written would be frowned upon by "traditional" Jewish readers. He stopped, grabbed my arm, looked into my eyes, and said with intense conviction, "You don't honor a tradition by endlessly repeating it. You honor a tradition by marching forward in its name." He said this to me more than thirty years ago. His words were liberating, and I have never forgotten them.

Williamson is marching forward in Christianity's name. He does not hesitate to call the church's former understanding of Jews and Judaism radically defective.[43] God calls the church into a new life together with Jews. Christians must try to understand Jews as Jews understand themselves. All stereotypes must be left behind. The truth is that "the church shares in Israel's election without superseding it."[44] Church statements of the past three decades have recognized this by asserting that God's covenant with Israel is eternal, by rejecting the "teaching of contempt," and by calling for a halt to proselytizing Jews. Williamson adds that the age-old "mission to the Jews" must be replaced by a Christian commitment of service to the Jews, the people of Christ, who have suffered so grievously at the hands of the followers of Christ.

Williamson paraphrases Karl Barth in calling Christians "guests in the house of Israel." Gentiles are grafted on to the stock that is God's people. Their inclusion renews and broadens the covenant, but it can do so only if the original covenant between God and Israel remains living and healthy. I would add that Christianity, which has long proclaimed itself to be the fulfillment of Judaism, is so, but only in a limited sense. It does partially fulfill the divine promise to Abraham that in his election all the peoples of the world would be blessed. Through Christianity many peoples of the world have come to know Israel's God as their own. Once Christians come to see themselves as extending the reach of the covenant community (and Jews allow themselves to see Christians in this way), both Christians and Jews will be freed to work side by side as partners rather than rivals.

Perhaps Williamson's most powerful argument is based on his view of divine grace. He directs this argument at his fellow Christians who still cling to the notion that in electing gentiles as a new people of God through Christ, God rejected the people Israel because they failed to accept Christ. This view contradicts an essential claim of Christianity that God showers all people with unmerited divine love in an act of pure grace. Deuteronomy proclaims that God chose Israel not because she was more numerous than other peoples (or more powerful or more virtuous) but simply and sublimely because God loves Israel—an act of pure, undeserved grace. Israel was a tribe of sinners—as all people are sinners—when God chose her. Israel remains a people of sinners—as all people remain sinners. If Israel is beloved of God—if Israel is a redeemed people—she remains a nation of redeemed sinners. Nothing Israel can do can separate her from her God and God's infinite love. The covenant is not conditional. A Jew may obey its requirements or disobey, but he cannot escape his loving, demanding God.

Elie Wiesel once came to speak at Montclair State University, where I teach. After Wiesel's talk, a man in the audience asked him if he believed in God after all he had gone through in the Holocaust. After a long pause, Wiesel responded: "A Jew is sometimes for God, and a Jew is sometimes against God, but a Jew is never without God." The covenant is binding. An individual Jew can only be faithful or unfaithful because the covenant that he chooses to obey or disobey is ever present and, from God's side, unbreakable.

Williamson points out that God's covenant with gentile Christians is likewise a covenant of grace. After all, only sinners need to be redeemed; only sinners *can* be redeemed. Nonsinners would not need redemption. So God's love for humanity through Christ is poured out on an undeserving race of sinners who continue to sin even as they are redeemed. If God would break the covenant with Israel because of Israel's sin, then God would break the covenant with the church due to its sin. How could Christians continue to trust in God's grace to them, if God abandoned prior grace toward Israel?

The traditional Christian teaching on the rejection of Israel is theologically oxymoronic, according to Williamson. If God chose Israel by grace and then cast her off because she did not perform the "good work" of accepting Christ, then the "old covenant" was one of works, not grace. And so is the "new covenant," since, according to this theory, Christians would be elected to it due to their performance of the "good work" of accepting Christ that Jews failed to perform. But if the "new covenant" is one of works, not grace, then it can be repudiated by God at any time due to the ongoing sinfulness to which all Christians admit. Such a conclusion would declare Christianity to be based upon the same "works righteousness" that Christians have unjustly accused Jews of practicing.

But, in fact, the Hebrew Scriptures declare God's choice of Israel to be an election by divine grace, God's unmerited love for this people. The New Testament declares God's love to be poured out on the gentiles through Christ as an expression of the same grace. Either both claims are true or both are false. Christians cannot, without ludicrous self-contradiction, affirm that election of the church meant rejection of Israel or that God in any way or under any conditions would reject "the people whom he foreknew" (Rom. 11:2). If God would or could do this, then God would be proved to be a liar (God forbid), the whole doctrine of election by grace would come crashing down and both our religions along with it. Thus Williamson demonstrates that Christians cannot hold to their traditional "divine rejection of Israel" theory without contradicting the logic of their own faith. This argument is a significant contribution to the theology of the dialogue.

It seems to me that there is another self-contradiction in the age-old *adversus Judaeus* tradition. Christians have at times pointed to the tribulations of Jewish history—the dispersal and suffering of the Jews—as proof of divine disfavor. Persecution of Jews was seen as the just deserts of a people who had at best rejected Christ or at worst killed him. But it never occurred to these same Christians to view the suffering and death of Jesus as proof of divine displeasure. On the contrary, the passion of Christ, his rejection and persecution, were seen as proofs of his election to a world-redemptive task, the necessary conditions of his ultimate vindication and elevation to the divine realm. Why was suffering in the case of the Jews seen as proof of rejection, while suffering in the case of Christ was seen as proof of election? Similar evidence was used in the two cases to arrive at two contradictory conclusions. There is no logic here, only hatred—hatred of a kind that the churches now realize contradicts everything Christianity claims to represent.

In his excellent discussion of Jesus' respective roles for Christians and for Jews, Williamson points out that Jesus called Jews back to their God. He challenged them to be better Jews, more devoted servants of the Lord and of God's peoples—all peoples, as shown in the parable of the Good Samaritan. So he called Israel to something old—very old—their covenant with the Holy One. On the other hand, Jesus (through Paul) called gentiles to something radically new. He called them away from pagan gods and abominable practices into a newly expanded covenant with Israel's God, now revealed as their God as well. And if God called (and calls) gentiles into the covenant via Christ, he also calls them (at the same time and with the same voice) into communion with Israel, the original people of the covenant. Jesus may not be the Messiah *of* Israel (as defined by rabbinic Judaism), but he may be seen as the Messiah *from* Israel who (defined according to the new categories of Nazarene Judaism, later called Christianity) opens the covenant to gentiles as gentiles (that is, they do not have to become Jews to partake in it).

Christians have long claimed to be bound to the God of Israel through Christ. What they have denied is that, in the same redemptive act, they are bound forever to the Israel of God in fellowship and mutual service. Jews, of course, have also denied this connection. And here, for once, Williamson does have a suggestion for Jews. He holds "that Jews can acknowledge that for Christians Jesus has become the way in which they find Israel's God."[45] Of course Jews can do this. Many Jewish authorities, both classic and contemporary, have said as much. I discuss some of them in this work. And Christians must at last see that in becoming more dedicated to Judaism, Jews are acting as Jesus once summoned them to act.

Jesus never called Jews to a belief in him as Messiah. Nowhere in the synoptic Gospels does he make any such public claim. If he made no such claim to the Jewish masses, they can hardly be said to have "rejected" him as Messiah. He was viewed variously as prophet or rabbi or wise man. The wisdom he dispensed to Israel was similar to that of the great Hillel, and a number of his Jewish hearers responded positively to his words, recommitting themselves to their God and to lives of humane service. Today Jews must come to understand that the constant focus on Christ in Christian worship and practice is not a distraction from or alternative to focus on God, any more than is Jewish emphasis on Torah and the story of the people Israel. For Christians, Christ and church are concretizations of the Word of God; for Jews, the same concretization is achieved through Torah and Israel. We have spent so long working diligently and deliberately at misunderstanding each other in order to justify ourselves. Can we not now turn that same energy to the urgent task of trying, at long last, to listen to each other toward the end of mutual regard, respect, and understanding?

Affirming the Claims of the Other: A Personal Jewish Response

For nearly 2,000 years there was little or no movement in the theological evaluations Judaism and Christianity offered of each other. At best Christians saw Judaism as incomplete Christianity, while Jews saw Christianity as adulterated Judaism. At worst Jews were seen as deicides and Christians as idolators who lived without moral law. The teaching of contempt held sway among Christians, while Jews often felt disdain for all things "goyish." In the age of interfaith dialogue this is all in a process of radical change. Our two religions, having failed for so long to deal in any positive fashion with the other, are discovering that other anew and, as an unexpected result of this effort, are rediscovering long-neglected aspects of themselves. The question now before us is of how far we can go in affirming the other and modifying our own claims. How far can we go without compromising the uniqueness and integrity of our own faith commitments and systems of thought?

I remarked earlier that the dialogue ought not to require either participant faith to dismantle itself or to deny age-old core beliefs. We have inherited symbols, concepts, and creeds that tell us who we are and how we fit into the divine scheme of things. Where these positions are positive, affirming our self-conceptions and our views of God's work, we alter them at our peril. Christians who reject all use of the term "Messiah" to designate Jesus' identity or who deny the resurrection as part of the essential kerygma of the church may well be going too far. There is much room for reinterpretation, but outright dismissal of core concepts and of the time-honored words expressing them will leave us with a form of Christianity few will recognize. Similarly, Jews who deny the election of Israel or who reject the category of revelation itself may be dismissing what makes Judaism Jewish and makes religion religious. Again, new ways of understanding these teachings should be explored, but outright rejection does violence to the inherited structures of faith.

But if this is true of positive doctrines, it is not true with regard to negative attitudes. One can affirm the identity of Jesus and his resurrection without holding that all who do not are damned. One can believe in the chosenness of Israel and God's revelation to this people without claiming that God can make only one choice or communicate with only one nation. In other words, we ought to reaffirm our positive traditional attitudes while reexamining the negative attitudes that we believed to flow from them. Why should the church's self-conception as the new Israel invalidate the claims of the first Israel? Why does God's revelation through Torah to Israel deny the possibility of God's revelation through Christ to the nations? I see no reason why Christianity cannot continue to affirm all its positive doctrines even as it strips them of their negative aspects. Every "yes" of Christian faith can be affirmed without the corresponding "no" to Judaism that has for too long poisoned the relationship between these two sister communities. I will say no more about this here but will focus on drawing the outlines of the similar project confronted by Jewish theology in the context of the dialogue.

Great progress has been made in the last forty years—so great, in fact, that we are now prepared to take the next step in mutual understanding. That step must be one in which we truly attempt to see the other as closely as possible to how she sees herself. This means for Jews that we move beyond constructing Jewish conceptions of Jesus, even the most positive ones, and try to confront Christian claims about him as we actually hear them from Christians. As Jews, we cannot and should not see Jesus through the eyes of Christian faith, but we can try to understand that faith in the light of our own. As Abraham Joshua Heschel has said, the prerequisite for attempting to understand another's text is commitment to our own. We must start where we are with our own text-based self-understanding and then move out—if our text permits—to evaluate the text of "the other."

Buber believed that Jews cannot comment on Christian doctrines or evaluate Christian history at all. I disagree. What he said might be true of Buddhist doctrine or Shinto history, but a special relationship exists between Judaism and Christianity that permits us to comment, each on the other. We share a core text and core concepts. We both acknowledge that we worship the same God. We believe in revelation in history and in redemption at history's end. And we both begin with Abraham.

God called Abraham to bring blessing to all people. Judaism and Christianity begin with that commission. Today Jews can hardly escape the recognition that the vast majority of those who worship Israel's God are gentiles. These people have been drawn into the covenant—have received the blessing given to Abraham—through the spread of Christianity. We must see this development as part of the divine plan first laid out in God's call to the patriarch to bring blessing to the world's peoples. Otherwise we must view the spiritual history of Christianity as a gigantic mistake or apostasy from God's design. How can we do this in the face of the fulfillment of the prophet's words, "From the rising of the sun to its going down my name is great among the nations" (Mal. 1:11)?

This means that Jews, faithful to their own tradition, can, through the text of that tradition, come to see Christianity as a means of extending their core conceptions into the wider world. This has been recognized since Judah Halevi and Moses Maimonides. Why should it be so difficult to say it now? In its own way Judaism is also engaged in the world, blessing every society in which Jews dwell as moral, ethical, and spiritual catalysts. But to deny that Christianity has brought our God to the nations is to deny the fulfillment— the partial fulfillment at least—of our own Abrahamic commission. Recognition of Christianity's redemptive work does not require Judaism to follow Rosenzweig and retire from the realm of history. There is room here for two (and more) and work enough for all. We *can* evaluate Christianity's spread across the world, despite Buber's refusal to do so. We can do it because it has happened in accordance with categories and expressions found in our own texts. To be sure, no one could have predicted the manner in which all this has happened, but such divine surprises often occur. Jesus, who may have thought of himself as a reformer and prophet to his own people and whose followers thought of him as Messiah, has turned out to be (through his interpreters) the Jewish envoy to the nations of the world. At least that is what he is from the Jewish perspective.

But Jews need not leave it at that. Once we affirm, as I believe we must, that Jesus is the means by which Israel's God has chosen to come to the gentiles, then we are obliged to ask the following question: if God has acted to break open the covenant to include the other peoples of the world, and God has done this through Christianity, is it appropriate for us to continue to consider Christianity to be composed of false doctrines? Is it necessary for us to say "no" to Christian claims as they affect the non-Jewish world? Our "no" was a response to the Christian insistence that we abandon the post God has assigned to us and the Torah God has given us, and accept the claims of Christianity. Now one church after another is moving away from such demands, having accepted the ongoing validity of Judaism and discovered in Jewry's endurance through the ages the will and purposes of God. This changed situation leaves us free to do what we could never do before. While continuing to say "no" to any remaining Christian attempts to "win us for Christ," we can endorse the "yes" given by others to the Christian message. We can even attempt a reevaluation of the contents of that message in the light of our own texts.

What are the central propositions of the Christian faith? I would suggest the following:

1. The incarnation of God in Jesus.
2. The vicarious sacrifice of Jesus for the sins of the world.
3. The resurrection of Jesus from the dead.

While these propositions do not speak to Judaism, they have spoken most eloquently to the nations and have, in fact, provided the symbol system for conveying the knowledge of Israel's God to the world. However, these claims are more than symbols for most Christians. They refer to "religious events" by means of which untold millions have been brought close to God.

However, "religious events" are not identical with ordinary historical events. In historical events all the terms are finite ones, limited to categories of time and space. But the "religious events" found in the Bible tell of the breaking of the infinite into the finite, the eternal into time. In such occurrences, there is always an irreducible element of objective uncertainty, which has the paradoxical result of intensifying the subjective certainty—the faith— of the religious believer. He believes passionately in events that he realizes can never be proved objectively. In this sense, "religious events" are real and true, but quite different from the time-and-space-bound "facts" of ordinary history. These distinctions are crucial. They are discussed more extensively in chapter 8, "Truth and Fact in Religious Narrative."

My question is whether Jews, faithful to Israel's Torah, can find in our sacred text, first, a way better to understand these Christian affirmations and, second, a way to deal with them in a positive manner. I believe that, *while we cannot affirm the truth of these propositions, we need no longer insist on their falsity.* We cannot affirm their truth because that can only be done from the standpoint of Christian faith, a standpoint we do not share. Nevertheless, we need no longer insist on their falsity, because their message is not now being used by mainstream churches to undermine our faith and because the logic of our view that the divine hand guides Christianity as well as Judaism leads us to entertain the possibility of their being true. If God has chosen to open the covenant to include the nations and has done so through Jesus as interpreted by Paul and others, then God may have accomplished this by means of the events claimed by Christianity to have taken place. The accounts of these events sound strange to Jewish ears at first hearing, but by examining our own Scriptures we may find that they are not as alien as we might have thought.

_ 1. *Incarnation.* While almost certainly not an element of the teaching of Jesus, rabbi and prophet of Galilee, the affirmation that God or God's "Word" took human form in the Nazarene became central to the Christian kerygma after Jesus' death. The vast majority of Jews at the time who knew of Jesus rejected this claim, probably because they found no particular reason to accept it. Jesus may have been a notable rabbi; he may even have been a prophet, as many Jews apparently believed (Mark 8:22; Matt. 21:6), but there was simply no evidence for a claim of divinity. To Jews today the claim that God took on human form may seem utterly incredible, but the Torah may tell a different story. Genesis 3:8 tells us of "the Lord God walking in the garden in the cool of day"; Genesis 18:1 states that "the Lord appeared to him [Abraham]" in human form. This is not a vision. God, together with angelic companions, eats real food during this encounter. Genesis 32:24 reports that "jacob was left alone; and a man wrestled with him." He concludes, "I have seen God face to face." Exodus 24:9–11 states, "Then Moses and Aaron, Nadab, and Abihu, and seventy of the elders of Israel went up [to Sinai], and they saw the God of Israel; and there was under his feet as it were a pavement of sapphire . . . [and] they beheld God."

For Jewish believers, then, the thought may come to mind that, if God can take human form in a series of accounts put forward in one's own sacred texts, one would be unjustified in dismissing out of hand the possibility that the same God might act in a similar fashion in accounts put forward in another text revered as sacred by a closely related tradition.

Beyond this we cannot and need not venture. What is proclaimed in the Christian doctrine of incarnation (in its several variations) is certainly not the same message we find in the Torah, nor are the accounts cited above central to Judaism in the way the "Christ event" is to Christianity. We do not claim that what is described in the Hebrew Scriptures is exactly the phenomenon at the heart of Christian faith. The appearances of God in human form referred to above are not identical to the Christian account of God's or God's Word's being conceived, born, and living and dying as a man. However, the simi-larities between Jewish and Christian accounts should lead Jews away from precipitous denial of the possibility of the latter. Again, I wish to emphasize that, whatever we make of the Christian claim, it can have no impact on our belief or practice. If it happened, it happened for the sake of the gentile mission of the church.

2. *Vicarious atonement*. This interpretation of Jesus' death as an atonement for the sins of the world seems strange and foreign to Jews who believe that the problem of sin had already been dealt with in the Torah. Its text, together with later authoritative commentaries, outlines what is for us the proper path of life, the means of repentance, and the forgiveness of sins. As stated previously, the gentiles could have come to Torah by conversion to Judaism. Some did just that, and some among them continue to do so, but most have sought the forgiveness of Israel's God through another mediator— in Christian language, "Christ crucified." The vicarious sacrifice of Jesus for humanity's sins may seem strange to Jews, but it comes out of a Christian reinterpretation of verses in Hebrew Scripture, including the familiar words of Isaiah 53. We need only reproduce verses 4 through 6:

> Surely he has borne our griefs
>   and carried our sorrows;
> yet we esteemed him stricken,
>   smitten by God, and afflicted.
> But he was wounded for our
>   transgressions,
> he was bruised for our iniquities;
> upon him was the chastisement
>   that made us whole,
> and with his stripes we are healed.
> All we like sheep have gone astray;
> we have turned every one to his
>   own way;
> and the Lord has laid on him
>   the iniquity of us all.

This suffering servant of God, whether interpreted as a single exemplary Israelite or as the collective individual, the people Israel, is part of Jewish tradition and Jewish faith. Most of us will read these lines as a poignant description of Israel's redemptive suffering through history, sometimes for the misdeeds of others (4 Macc. 1:11, 17:21, 18:4). We can continue to maintain this interpretation that has such power for us as we contemplate our people's tragic and glorious story. At the same time, and because of this self-understanding, we can also comprehend what Christians mean in holding that these verses present for them a vivid picture of the atoning work of Jesus.

Once again, while it seems strange to us that one man should play this role for the nations, believing what we do about the meaning of these lines, we need not feel obliged to dismiss the Christian interpretation as inauthentic. Their view may not work for us; it may, in fact, be redundant for those who have been granted a prior and eternally efficacious means of pardon. Nevertheless, the nations have found in it the means of grace provided to them by Israel's God. We have no reason to deny its validity for them or to greet the news of it with anything but rejoicing.

Israel has suffered so often in its life of service to the Holy One and to humanity. Surely, we can recognize this redemptive pattern as it reappears in the Jesus story. In Chagall's great painting *The White Crucifixion*, the artist superimposes the icon of the crucified Christ, loins wrapped in a white and blue Jewish prayer shawl, over a background of images of pogroms, burning synagogues, and fleeing Jews—a fitting parallel, indeed, and one in which Jewish and Christian elements reinforce and illuminate each other.

3. *Resurrection*. Once again, we must observe that most Jews of the time saw no reason to accept the proclamation that Jesus had been raised from the dead. All those who reported seeing the risen Christ were already part of his following. The New Testament text seems to be telling us that the resurrected Christ was clearly visible, but only to those who looked with eyes of Christian faith. Paul was perhaps the exception, but he had a vision, a religious experience quite different from the resurrection appearances described elsewhere. True, he lists it together with them as one of a series of apparitions, but his description of what he saw reveals the special nature of his experience. Visions are certainly valid for those who have them, but, by their very nature, they cannot demonstrate their validity for others not privy to them.

The important thing to remember is that the majority of Jews could not have rejected the news of Jesus' resurrection because they found the very idea of it preposterous. Resurrection of the body was a Jewish doctrine. It had been affirmed by the Pharisees for many years as part of their apocalyptic hope. Late scriptural and intertestamental books refer to it (Dan. 12:2; 2 Macc. 7:9, 11, 14, 23, 29). As far as we know, only the Sadducees explicitly denied its possibility. What most Jews rejected for lack of evidence was not the possibility, even the ultimate certainty, of physical resurrection but the claim that the man Jesus had, in fact, already been raised.

Today, there is no more reason for Jews to accept as true the news of Jesus' resurrection than there was then. However, faced with this claim, and affirming as we now must the validity of the church's outreach from Israel to the nations, we Jews can no longer dismiss the Easter faith out of hand. If such a thing took place far in advance of our apocalyptic expectations, it neither speaks to us directly nor threatens us in any way. It does, as its proclamation intends, astonish us that such a thing could occur in the ordinary course of time. But that is the way of miracles or of claimed miracles; they are astonishing. If this particular claim has come to be accepted by the nations as the ultimate demonstration of the truth of the other two Christian proclamations discussed earlier, so be it. Why should this trouble us? We need not share the resurrection faith (except insofar as we already do in our eschatological hope) in order for us to take satisfaction in its acceptance by those who so desperately need to hear it. In this proclamation the nations have come to know what we already knew, the faithfulness of God who has raised Israel from death to life time and time again.

Conclusions

My question in this chapter has been: How far can Jews and Christians go in affirming the faith of the other? I have attempted to answer this question from both the Jewish and Christian sides. It is my view that the dialogue does not and should not ask either faith tradition to give up any of its *positive* doctrines. Judaism and Christianity should not be expected to become spiritual or doctrinal amputees as the price of full sharing with each other. On the contrary, the dialogue can lead each to reaffirm core convictions, but now understood in a wider context. We can make room for each other in God's larger plan of salvation without diminishing ourselves. What we must be willing to do is to reevaluate our *negative* convictions. In altering our views of the other we recognize that both Judaism and Christianity have crucial roles to play in sacred history.

Several church statements have affirmed that while Christianity needs Judaism for its self-understanding, Judaism can fully define itself without reference to Christianity. Not true! Since Christianity has been a conveyer of the word of Israel's God to the nations, it is today impossible for Jews to understand their role as inheritors of the commission given to Abraham while blinding themselves to the work among the nations of the church that shares that commission and that inheritance. To do so would be for God's first elect people to miss the comprehensive nature and universal scope of God's project. It is of the essence of the Jewish calling in the world to develop a new and positive appraisal of the church and of Christian faith. And, as John Pawlikowski and Paul van Buren have suggested, it is also time for us to construct a view of Jesus that reflects his unique role in opening the covenant to include the gentile world.

How far can Jews and Christians go? Far enough to embrace and affirm each other and even to recognize the possible truth of the other's doctrinal claims. This must be a mutual process of opening to the other while continuing to be oneself. We are called to self-transcendence and self-affirmation together. In our time this is God's most urgent call to individuals, nations, and faith communities.

5

The Forty Years' Peace

Christian Churches Reevaluate Judaism

Catholic Statements on the Jews and Judaism from *Nostra Aetate* to the New Catechism

It is a depressing fact that until the issuance of the Declaration on the Relationship of the Church to Non-Christian Religions (*Nostra Aetate*, no. 4) on October 28, 1965, the whole Roman Catholic approach to the Jewish people and their faith could be summed up in Jules Isaac's term the "teaching of contempt." For nearly two millennia the church had viewed the people and religion of Israel as at best spiritually blind and at worst guilty of the singular crime of deicide. Never before in human history had a people been branded as killers of God or been incorporated into another's mythos as the cosmic enemies of all that is true and good. The picture of Jews and Judaism painted by church fathers and reflected in church councils was so extreme and so unique in its malevolence that Christian people could only conclude that no level of persecution was so cruel that it could not be visited on this reprobate people rejected by God and marginalized by Christian civilization. Were not the crucifiers of the Lord also poisoners of wells, murderers of children, and followers of their "father the devil" (John 8:44)? Is it possible that the church did not envision the profound impact such teachings were to have on the popular imagination or the ghastly consequences for the Jews of Europe? The question is worthy of debate if only because the same church that created this horror fantasy vision of Jews often intervened to protect Jews from annihilation at the hands of mobs inflamed by those very images.

The issue of the level of church awareness of the cause and effect relationship between anti-Jewish propaganda and anti-Jewish violence is one for historians to debate. What is clear today is that the church now understands that she must accept blame for the creation and perpetuation of anti-Jewish attitudes that issued in the unprecedented horror of the Nazi Holocaust of 1942–45. It is this realization of the consequences of such teaching that has led to the extraordinary efforts by church authorities to change course utterly in their approach to the whole question. The church, confronted with the Holocaust, has responded with a ringing proclamation of "Never again!" and has undertaken to alter its teachings and attitudes accordingly.

Since 1965 the Roman Catholic Church has issued three official statements on the Jews and Judaism (in 1965, 1974, and 1985). Added to these are numerous statements by the pope and documents issued by local Catholic sources (individual bishops, dioceses, and archdioceses). All of these must be examined to produce a picture of the progress made over the decades, as well as the initial breakthrough in 1965. We will see that progress is not always steady, that unofficial statements are often more innovative than official declarations, and that there is still much difference of opinion within the church regarding how far to go in affirming the full validity of contemporary Judaism as what the church would call "a path of salvation." In this overview we will also discuss the new Catechism of the Catholic Church (1994) as it incorporates or does not incorporate the changes in Catholic teaching regarding the Jews and Judaism.

In all these statements and declarations many issues are addressed. We will mention them in passing, but we are here concerned with one in particular. Does the church today view contemporary Judaism as having a divinely ordained mission in the world, and, if so, does it regard Jews as acting in fidelity to God and God's calling by remaining Jews rather than joining the church? Only if we can answer "yes" to these questions would we be justified in responding by developing a new Jewish attitude toward Christianity.

Nostra Aetate (1965), Ecumenical Council, Vatican II

The declaration, which "recalls the spiritual bond linking the people of the new covenant with Abraham's stock," sees Christians as included in Abraham's call to be a blessing to all peoples and declares that the church "draws sustenance from the root of that good olive tree onto which have been grafted the wild olive branches of the Gentiles" (Rom. 11:17–24).[1] It is significant that this last statement is made in the present tense. The church today "draws sustenance" from Israel. The spiritual indebtedness is not only a thing of the past. Israel, as people of God, is of the present as well. The declaration goes on to state that "the Jews still remain most dear to God because of the fathers, for He does not repent the gifts He makes nor the calls He issues" (Rom. 11:28–29). The statement recommends "mutual understanding and respect" and "brotherly dialogues." While the church is the "new people of God," the Jews should not be presented as repudiated or cursed by God.

What is being implied is that there are today two "peoples of God," Jews and Christians, or root and branch of a single people of God. The addition of the gentile branch apparently did not dispossess the original root. How could it, given the logic of the metaphor? For if the root dies, so does the branch. Certainly any clearheaded understanding of Christianity must hold that the validity of that faith depends on the prior validity of Judaism. The question has always been whether that validity of the earlier faith persists once the newer faith has come. The traditional Christian answer had been "no"; the Jews are rejected, cast out, and repudiated by God and their faith displaced by another. Vatican II changed all that. But problems remain. The Jews are still spoken of as "dear to God because of their fathers." These are the patriarchs beloved of God long before the Christ event. To speak thus implies that what the Jews did while that event was being played out and what they have been doing since is not the reason God loves them. And indeed the declaration notes that "Jerusalem did not recognize the time of its visitation" (Luke 19:44). Most Jews did not respond positively to the gospel, many opposed it, and some "pressed for Jesus' death." Despite all this, God still loves this people whom God foreknew. If Jewry did not recognize its own Messiah, then it has been living for two millennia on a misunderstanding and has, to that extent, been acting in a manner that could hardly be pleasing to God.

But there are other ways to see and evaluate Israel's "no" to Jesus as Messiah and to the claims of the church. In Romans 11 Paul holds that "through their [Israel's] trespass salvation has come to the Gentiles" (v. 11). Israel's "no" led Paul to carry the gospel to the gentiles and was therefore part of God's redemptive plan. But this declaration does not make this argument, nor is there any evidence that its framers had thought that far into the issue. There is no hint here of what Israel's present mission in the world might be, or even that she has one in a "postresurrection" world. Israel exists today as a still beloved people of God, heirs of the patriarchs but also of those who did not recognize Jesus. The picture is a mixed one, free of bitterness or generalized blame ("what happened in His passion cannot be blamed upon all the

Jews then living, without distinction, nor upon the Jews of today"), but still very much of a first step, although a giant one, away from the horror images of the past. The good seeds had been sown.

Guidelines and Suggestions for Implementing the Conciliar Declaration *Nostra Aetate* (No. 4), January 1975

This document, signed by Cardinal Willebrands, president of the Commission for the Catholic Church's Religious Relations with the Jews, is largely practical rather than theological but does contain significant theological advances over Vatican II.[2] In fact, while *Nostra Aetate*, read from today's perspective, seems partial, hesitant, even grudging in tone, the Guidelines of 1975 appear even today as a creative, innovative statement, moving far beyond both the spirit and the content of the document it purports simply to implement. Most significantly, it is the first Catholic statement that calls Christians to try to see Jews as they see themselves, a move that is the key to all true human encounter, including interfaith dialogue.

In the Guidelines' preamble the clear statement is finally made that it was the Holocaust that moved the church to open this new chapter in its relations with the Jews. It goes on to recognize as causative of that catastrophe the fact that due to an ever-deepening mutual alienation, "Christian and Jew hardly knew each other," leading to 2,000 years of "mutual ignorance and frequent confrontation." The tone is one of deep sorrow and genuine regret, if not outright penance. All forms of antisemitism are repudiated as in *Nostra Aetate*, but here Christians are called upon to "strive to acquire a better knowledge of the basic components of the religious tradition of Judaism; they must strive to learn by what essential traits the Jews define themselves in the light of their own religious experience." This is truly a new insight and a crucial one. Judaism is seen as a worthwhile, living religious tradition that Christians should study as eager learners. The text goes on to ask Catholics to respect the faith and religious convictions of Jews.

But now the statement confronts the issue of dialogue with the Jews and struggles honestly with what must be for Christians a deep dilemma: "In virtue of her divine mission, and her very nature, the Church must preach Jesus Christ to the world. Lest the witness of Catholics to Jesus Christ should give offense to Jews, they must take care to live and spread their Christian faith while maintaining the strictest respect for religious liberty." Here we see the first articulation of a Catholic attempt to come to terms with two seemingly contradictory demands of its contemporary faith: the first to preach

Christ to all peoples, the second to respect the faith of Israel, which does not accept Jesus as Messiah. Is Christianity capable of saying, or will she ever be capable of saying, that God has made an earlier and permanently efficacious agreement (covenant) with Israel that is fully sufficient to bring Jews to what Christians call "salvation"? If Judaism is still valid after Jesus as it was before, then is not this the obvious conclusion? If not for salvation, then for what is it valid? If Jews must become Christians, then Judaism must not be valid. But if it is, why should Jews convert? And if they should not, why preach Christ to them even in a noncoercive manner and in accordance with principles of religious liberty? Clearly Christianity is caught in a dilemma here, and an honest one.

Do Jews have an eternally valid covenant relationship with God prior to, and still operative after, the Christ event? Jews would like Christians to see things just this way. At least two Protestant Church statements seem to reflect such thinking, but this is a very hard path for Christians to walk, to deny the universality of the work of Christ; and the Roman Catholic Church is, as yet, not ready to walk it. So, like most of the churches in the dialogue, the Catholic Church continues to consider it her duty to attempt to spread the faith to all peoples (presumably including Jews) while, at the same time, engaging in an exchange premised on full mutual respect for the religious views of the other. There may be a way out of this dilemma, but as of 1974 the church had not found it.

Nevertheless, a new note is struck in the Guidelines. Catholics "will likewise strive to understand the difficulties which arise for the Jewish soul, rightly imbued with an extremely high, pure notion of the divine transcendence, when faced with the mystery of the incarnate Word." This remarkably human attempt at a sympathetic understanding of the Jewish position is typical of the Guidelines and evidences a new openness toward the other without which true dialogue is impossible.

In the section on liturgy the Guidelines state what *Nostra Aetate* had not regarding the nature of contemporary Jewish religious life: "The idea of a living community in the service of God, and in the service of men for the love of God, such as is realized in the liturgy, is just as characteristic of the Jewish liturgy as it is of the Christian one." The language of equivalency, of full equality of the communities before God, the observation that they see themselves as doing the same thing in serving God and humanity and expressing this in their active prayer lives, is most welcome. This realization that the other is doing in his own way what I am doing in mine, and that his way is not so different from mine, is a simple yet profound insight necessary for mutual understanding. But then the very next paragraph strikes a seemingly self-contradictory note. It states that elements of the Old Testament retain their own "perpetual value," which "has not been canceled by the later interpretation of the New Testament," but then goes on to insist that "the New Testament brings out the full meaning of the Old."

Does this mean that the Hebrew Scriptures are incomplete without the Christian "fulfillment"? If so, no Jew could endorse this view. But there is one sense in which Jews might agree. If the Hebrew Scriptures are of "perpetual value" but still need the New Testament, might this mean that the former tells of God's eternal covenant with Israel, while the latter opens that covenant to all the nations, thus fulfilling (at least in part) the commission to Abraham to bring the blessing of the knowledge of the one God to all? From Maimonides to Rosenzweig, and in the present work, a number of Jewish theologians have endorsed just such a theory. Read in this light, the statements of this paragraph are not contradictory, but are complementary, as are the respective roles of Judaism and Christianity in God's divine plan of redemption.

The next paragraph is interesting for the new understanding it expresses of the traditional Christian "promise-fulfillment" model of the two covenants. It pledges to stress the continuity of "our faith with that of the earlier Covenant, in the perspective of the promises." Note the use of "earlier" rather than "old" covenant, an attempt to avoid any suggestion of the first covenant's being over and done with. The text goes on to say, "We believe that those promises were fulfilled with the first coming of Christ. But it is none the less true that we still await their perfect fulfillment in his glorious return at the end of time."

Thus both Judaism and Christianity are in need of fulfillment in the future. Both contain promises still outstanding. Note that the text says, "we believe" regarding the first coming of Christ. This manner of speech avoids proclaiming that Jesus fulfilled "Old Testament" promises but states, rather, that Christians believe that he did. And so they do, basing that conclusion on a belief-based interpretation. For this is what Christianity and Judaism both are: two interpretations of a single ancient Israelite text (or collection of texts) now called the Hebrew Scriptures or Old Testament. In the first century of the present era a number of Jewish sects flourished, each with its own faith-based reading of the texts available to them and many with their own messianic expectations. These expectations varied greatly and are discussed elsewhere in this work. But of all these schools of thought, only two survived the Jewish revolt and Roman conquest of 64–70 c.e. The Nazarene movement and the Pharisee movement emerged and grew into Christianity and rabbinic Judaism. Both began as sects of Judaism, and each cherished its own messianic vision. Why should they be expected to agree? One is no more legitimate than the other, but they are different. Only the ultimate messianic advent will settle the matter. The Guidelines are correct in pointing to that fulfillment for which both communities wait in faith and hope. They wait each in the place they have been assigned by God. Is it too much to hold that the One who has called them both to that hopeful waiting may be pleased to see that at long last both communities have come to realize that neither of them waits alone?

An important footnote to this section on liturgy deals with the use of the term "the Jews" in the Gospel of John. Pastors are called upon to educate their parishioners to understand that these texts refer to certain adversaries of Jesus, not the Jewish people as a whole (which would, of course, include Jesus himself and all his disciples). This point is only preliminary. Churches must do much more than they are doing even now to edit their lectionaries to avoid occasions of the sin of antisemitism, especially in Lenten and Holy Week readings. If a pastor is not prepared, year after year, to explain to his people how to interpret John in non-anti-Jewish ways, then the fourth Gospel should be dropped from public reading. This issue is too serious to be sidestepped. Words have consequences.

In the section on teaching and education, the Guidelines once again point out that Judaism is a living tradition, not a relic of the past: "The history of Judaism did not end with the destruction of Jerusalem, but rather went on to develop a religious tradition." So far, so good, but the text continues: "And, although we believe that the importance and meaning of that tradition were deeply affected by the coming of Christ, it is still nonetheless rich in religious values." What can this mean? The use of "still nonetheless" seems to suggest that the Jewish tradition is valuable despite Jesus' coming. In this context, saying that it is "still nonetheless rich in religious values" sounds like condescension and "damning with faint praise."

Of course Christians believe that the meaning of Jewish tradition was deeply affected by Jesus' appearance. I agree. The covenant now comes to the world at large. But why should this diminish the "importance" of Judaism if God's covenant with the Jews is ongoing? Yes, there is now a larger context of revelation to the nations within which Judaism must carry on its witness. Yes, Judaism now has a partner in the redemptive work, but to work side by side with a related redemptive community is not diminishing to either party. As each nourishes and encourages the other, both are strengthened. Is this not what the dialogue is all about? Why, then, this unseemly note of triumphalism, which strikes a sour chord in this otherwise exemplary document?

But, despite this, the Guidelines represent a tremendous advance beyond *Nostra Aetate*, which was, of course, a tremendous advance over all that had gone before.

Notes on the Correct Way to Present the Jews and Judaism in
Preaching and Catechesis in the Roman Catholic Church (June
1985)

Issued by the Vatican Commission for Religious Relations with the Jews, this
statement represents both an advance and a retreat from earlier positions.[3]
Among the more positive points we find:

> Because of the unique relations that exist between Christianity and
> Judaism, "linked together at the very level of their identity" (John
> Paul II, 6th March, 1982), relations "founded on the design of the
> God of the Covenant" (ibid.), the Jews and Judaism should not oc-
> cupy an occasional and marginal place in our catechesis: their pres-
> ence there is essential and should be organically integrated.

This point is crucial. Christian-Jewish relations are not comparable to those
between the church and other world religions. They cannot be swallowed up
in the wider, but less deep, encounter with the other faiths. The two biblical
faiths are truly sisters, twins, though not identical twins, who cannot understand themselves without the other. Both founded by the One God, they exist
in covenant relationship with the Holy One. What each thinks of the other is
crucial to each one's own self-evaluation.

The statement goes on to call Christians to examine "the faith and religious life of the Jewish people as they are professed and practiced still today."
Judaism is called "a still living reality closely related to the Church." Christians
must recognize the "permanent reality of the Jewish people." In the last section
(II:25) of the statement it is pointed out that the Diaspora life of post-70 C.E.
Jewish communities must be viewed as a worldwide witness, "often heroic," of
fidelity to God so as to proclaim God before all peoples. Israel's permanence is
"a sign to be interpreted within God's design." Israel is eternally a chosen
people with "a continuous spiritual fecundity." All this is very positive and
spells out for the first time the meaning of Israel's life in the world as witness
to and proclaimer of the One God and the divine plan of redemption, for the
consummation of which both Israel and the church pray daily.

But in section I:7 another note is struck. It is as if the authors, alarmed at
possible misreadings of earlier statements, pull back into an exclusivist stance
that seems to run counter to parts of the Notes referred to previously:

> 7. In virtue of her divine mission, the Church, which is to be the all-
> embracing means of salvation in which alone the fullness of the

means of salvation can be obtained...must of her nature proclaim Jesus Christ to the world.... Church and Judaism cannot then be seen as two parallel ways of salvation and the Church must witness to Christ as the Redeemer for all.

The plain meaning of these lines is that there is only one way to God. Christians are on that way; Jews are not. But if this is what is meant, why the dialogue? And why are Christians advised to observe Jews at prayer and learn more about the riches of Judaism's ongoing "spiritual fecundity"? As far as I can see, the Notes offer no explanation of these apparent contradictions. In praising the ongoing "heroic" witness to God of the Jews and in affirming the eternal covenant in force between God and this clearly non-Christian people, the Notes seem pluralistic in tone. But in section I:7 the assertions seem to be exclusivistic, "outside the Church, no salvation." The Notes make no attempt to reconcile these contradictory statements. We will have to look elsewhere to find an answer.

The Text of the Seventh General Audience Talk of John Paul II, the Vatican (May 31, 1995)

If we read the Notes in the light of this address by the pope, we find that the earlier statement is neither *exclusivist* (You must be a Christian—or Catholic—to be saved) nor *pluralist* (There are a number of ways of salvation). The position of the church is *inclusivist*. Selections from the pope's talk follow:

> [As to] the problem of the salvation of those who do not visibly belong to the Church.... The gift of salvation cannot be limited to those who explicitly believe in Christ and have entered the Church. Since salvation is open to all, it must be made concretely available to all.... many people do not have the opportunity to come to know or accept the Gospel.... frequently they have been brought up in other religious traditions.... What I have said above, however, does not justify the relativistic position of those who maintain that a way of salvation can be found in any religion, even independently of faith in Christ the Redeemer, and that interreligious dialogue must be based on this ambiguous idea.... The way of salvation always passes through Christ.... For those too who through no fault of their own do not know Christ and are not recognized as Christians, the divine plan has provided a way of salvation.... In the heart of every man of good will grace is active invisibly.... The Holy Spirit offers to all the pos-

sibility of being made partners, in a way known to God, in the paschal mystery. . . . Divine grace is granted to them by virtue of Christ's redeeming sacrifice, without external membership in the Church. . . . They do not know the church and sometimes even outwardly reject her. . . . Belonging to the Church, the Mystical Body of Christ, however implicitly and indeed mysteriously, is an essential condition for salvation.

This position has been called the doctrine of the "anonymous Christian." Others speak of the "baptism of desire." It is a way for the church to hold both that Christ is necessary for salvation and that the two-thirds of the world's population who are not Christian are still eligible for that salvation. Christ died for all, yet one does not need explicitly to acknowledge this in order to benefit from his sacrifice. All people of goodwill who act according to conscience are in some mysterious way already in the church, already part of the mystical body of Christ, though they do not know it. This would be especially true of Jews, who share so much common tradition with Christians and who are already covenanted with the One True God.

I have presented this approach to Jewish audiences, reading to them the words of the pope quoted above. Most of them react with amazement that in the eyes of the church they are already in some sense within the Catholic fold. Some giggle in amusement at what seems to them to be an obvious absurdity at odds with all the facts of their lived experience. It is, after all, no small thing to tell a kashrut-observing, Sabbath-keeping, holiday-celebrating synagogue member that he is somehow a Christian. Some become incensed at another religious body's presuming to define their lives and their standing before God. But when I remind them of how the church has viewed them in times past, they usually agree that this is a big improvement. If the only way the church can justify its abandonment of the mission to the Jews is to take the inclusivist position that Jews are, in fact, already in the church in some invisible sense, so be it.

Jews will always have trouble taking such a claim seriously. They know in their deepest being that they are Jews, not Christians, but this is a Christian, not a Jewish theory, and one that, in fact, hinges on Jews not accepting it. And we must remember that there are Jews who view Christianity as the Judaism of the gentiles. Is it any more bizarre for Catholics to view Judaism as a sort of Christianity for the Jews? It would be far preferable if each party to the dialogue would truly allow the other to define herself. If we impose identities on the other foreign to her lived experience, there is no dialogue, only a mutual monologue in which little genuine understanding takes place. The church says it desires true dialogue, but in this crucial particular it falls short.

However, we must recognize the difficulty under which the church labors. The New Testament does contain passages that seem to speak of one salvation for all. There are others (the Great Commission in Matthew is discussed elsewhere in this work) that can be read as calling for baptism for everyone except Jews. But the church has never read them that way. It may be, then, that the inclusivist position is as far as the church can go. We would prefer a pluralistic solution of multiple revelations of God, covenants sealed with different groups at different times. Jews, then, relate to God through the patriarchal/Sinai covenant, while Christians come to the same God through the renewed and widened covenant in Christ. If the first covenant is truly still in force, and, through the church, gentiles are grafted in, why insist on this retroactive imposition of Christ back into an earlier tradition? Why? Because Christian tradition has always insisted on it, and the church is not yet ready to depart from that long-established approach. Perhaps she has gone as far as she can go. Perhaps not.

The Notes also follow Christian tradition in another particular. In section IV:21:C reference is made to "the sad fact that the majority of the Jewish people and its authorities did not believe in Jesus." But if this fact is "sad," then the logic of the Gospels is somewhat skewed. *Nostra Aetate* pointed to the New Testament passages that report that "authorities of the Jews and those who followed their lead pressed for the death of Christ" (John 19:6). Presumably these are the same "authorities" who, "sadly," did not believe in Jesus. But suppose they had believed in him? If the High Priest had not had Jesus arrested and brought to Pilate, would Jesus have been crucified? And, if not, would the salvation proclaimed by the church now be available? If the answer to both questions is "no," then why is the disbelief of the authorities, necessary for humankind's salvation, "sad"? Can the church continue to have it both ways? Paul explains the "hardening" of Israel as presenting the opportunity for the conversion of the gentiles (Rom. 9–11), hardly a "sad" outcome.

The question also presents itself of what exactly, or even generally, the Jews were supposed to have believed about Jesus. According to Peter at Cesarea Philippi, many Jews viewed Jesus as a prophet (Mk. 8:27–30). Since, according to the synoptics, he had made no public statements regarding his messianic status, people could hardly be blamed for not recognizing it. Absent such a claim, the title of prophet was the highest available to Jewry at the time. But, in a larger sense, all the preceding is pointless speculation. In both the Guidelines and the Notes the church declares itself prepared to deal with and accept the results of the biblical criticism of the past century. In dealing with John and his hostile references to "the Jews," both documents point out that these passages were written long after the earthly life of Jesus and reflect the bitter rivalry of the church and rabbinic Judaism then taking shape. They have little to do with conditions at the time of Jesus.

During his lifetime only 20 percent of world Jewry lived in Palestine. Of these, only a small number could have heard of Jesus in that age lacking mass communications. An even smaller number were in any position to come to a conclusion regarding who he was. Now, if the church can recognize all this, why does it persist in its official statements in repeating judgments from the synoptic Gospels that are without historical foundation? The fact is that Jesus, whatever claims he made or did not make, was never presented to the Jewish population as a whole for "acceptance" or "rejection" during his lifetime. When he was presented in a later generation, it was as the incarnation of the divine Word or at least as one whose supernatural powers implied a divine status. Most Jews did not accept this claim simply because there was insufficient evidence for them to do so. That remains the case at the present time.

Today the church is beginning to think of Jews not in terms of what they do not believe but in terms of what they do believe. The people Israel are the faithful of God, witnessing in their convictions, in their conduct, in their very existence to the faithfulness of God. They are a people created and called by God to proclaim God's holiness, to keep God's laws and to build God's kingdom on earth. This has been said by the church with eloquence over the last four decades and more. Why muddy the waters with laments over the "sad" fact that Jews are not Christians? Things are as God has ordained them to be. It is to be hoped that such antiquated thinking will be left behind as the church proceeds on the road toward a total dialogue of mutual respect and acceptance. Meanwhile, we see in these contradictions evidence of the internal struggle within the church and within individual framers of these documents, a struggle between exciting new advances in thought and the age-old tendency to fall back into obsolete formulas.

Additional Documents

Most of the local documents drafted by Catholic Church bodies on the Jews and Judaism reflect the three universal Church statements discussed earlier. But some do carry the dialogue further with new insights and departures of thought.

One such study paper, titled "The Mission and Witness of the Church," was prepared by Professor Tommaso Federici and presented at the sixth meeting of the Liaison Committee between the Roman Catholic Church and the International Jewish Committee for Interreligious Consultations, held in Venice in 1977. Here Christian mission to Jews is redefined: "The mission of the Church to Israel consists . . . in a Christian life lived in total fidelity to the One God and his revealed Word, so that Jews and Christians emulate each other in their turning to God . . . and this is the universal salvation of the Jews and all peoples." If this is Christian missionary activity, who could object to it? Jews and Christians are both witness peoples, inspiring each other and hoping to win the world for the God they both honor and worship. The paper goes on to speak of "Israel's important fundamental work" of honoring God's name in the world. The statement continues: "it is the faithful Jews, who 'sanctify the divine name' in the world, living in justice and holiness and causing the divine gifts to bear fruit, who are a true witness to the whole world." No Jew could have said it with greater eloquence or clarity.

Mention must be made of the statement by Cardinal Etchegaray of Marseilles at the plenary session of the Synod of Bishops on Reconciliation, meeting in Rome in October 1983. Here the Cardinal likens the church and the Jews to two sons (of God) who in the history of salvation must share the divine inheritance. Neither of the two sons can gain possession of the entire inheritance; each one is for the other, without jealousy, a witness to the gratuitousness of the Father's mercy. This is a felicitous picture of partnership and brotherly mutuality in the service of God entirely appropriate to the Jewish-Christian witness in the world. The rejection of triumphalism is especially welcome.

The most advanced Catholic thinking on the Christian-Jewish relationship is to be found in the paper entitled "Basic Theological Issues of the Jewish-Christian Dialogue," produced by the Workshop on Jews and Christians, Central Committee of Roman Catholics in Germany (1979). I will summarize a few of this document's important theological points as follows:

Each side must take the contemporaneousness of the other in full
   seriousness.
Both sides must recognize that each has something crucial to say to
   the other.
Each party must listen fully to and be open to influence from the other.
Christians must fully accept the dignity and election of the Jews of today.
Jews must seek to understand the faith of Christians as a fulfillment
   of God's commission to Abraham to be father of many peoples.
Jewish partners in dialogue must recognize that "God caused some-
   thing to happen in Christianity" which concerns Jews.

Jews and Christians are "fundamentally prohibited" to seek to convert the other, "to move the other to become disloyal to the call of God which he has received."

This document courageously attempts to prescribe proper dialogical conduct for both parties and ventures into the most exciting area of the dialogue by establishing a basis for a Jewish theology of Christianity and a Christian theology of Judaism.

I would offer the following Jewish response. It is no good for Jews to claim that Judaism, as intrinsic to and temporally prior to Christianity, has much to say to its daughter faith, while Christianity is extraneous to, subsequent to, and thus without impact on, Judaism. First of all, this formulation is historically incorrect. Both Christianity and rabbinic Judaism arose in the years following the Temple's destruction. In the wake of that great overthrow, two forms of Judaism emerged out of the multiplicity of pre-70 c.e. Jewish sects. Yes, Pharisaic Judaism predated rabbinic Judaism and influenced it, but it also predated Christianity and influenced it, to a lesser degree. Judaism as we know it and Christianity are two interpretations of ancient Israelite faith. They are sisters, and like it or not, they grew up together in the same household of their common Parent. Having reached maturity, it is time to put aside childish jealousy and recognize our common origins and common goals. How can Christianity hope to understand itself without taking into account its beginnings and the life-giving Israelite roots that nourish it still and that caution it to resist triumphalism and to remember that the divine reign is still a distant hope and largely unrealized in the world. Judaism speaks to the church of holy community, of justice as a stern but necessary component of the coming kingdom, and of the unfinished work that lies ahead.

And how can Judaism ignore the entirely new context in which it must now work in the world? Christianity has spread worship of Israel's God "to the far isles," has, in fact, opened the covenant so that God's grace may flow out to all peoples. Christianity reminds Judaism of the universal mission of Abraham's seed, counsels Judaism to resist religious chauvinism, politicization of its self-conception, and soulless nationalism. The two peoples called and commissioned by God need one another desperately to cultivate the best in their respective callings while resisting the worst distortions of their self-identities. Each community, each theological system acts iconoclastically on the other. They keep each other honest and together "make straight the way of the Messiah." Here is the boundless promise of the flowering relationship between the two peoples of God, a promise toward which the present dialogue is leading us.

The Catechism of the Catholic Church (1994)

As one might expect from such a document, the new Catechism has nothing of novelty to say on the question before us. It is conservative and cautious in tone and often falls back on traditional formulations that are less than helpful. Frequently its approach to Jews and Judaism is confused, if not self-contradictory. The oft-repeated model for the Jewish-Christian relationship is that of promise and fulfillment. While Israel is the root for the gentile branches (60), its scriptures are "obscure" until the passion opens them fully to our understanding (112). The Old Testament (never revoked) is not voided by the New (123), but is to be read as a prefiguration of the latter (128). God's love for the people Israel is "everlasting" (220), but "a hardening" has come upon them that will be overcome by their "inclusion" in the Messiah's (Christ's) work in future (674). Jews are among those who have "not yet received the Gospel" (839) and who wait with Christians for the Messiah's advent, but in a waiting that is, in the Jews' case, complicated by their "misunderstanding Christ Jesus" (840). While Christians are urged to familiarize themselves with Jewish liturgy and self-understanding (1096), they must remember that the "Old Law" is imperfect, showing what is to be done but powerless to impart the strength to do it. It is a law of bondage that cannot remove sin and yet a teacher that endures forever (1963). In his life and death Jesus took upon himself the Law's fulfillment (577, 578). In studying Jesus' trial and death Christians must seek to understand the position of the Sanhedrin (591), remember that quite a few Pharisees believed in Jesus, and recognize the historic complexities of the trial (the "manipulated crowd," the ignorance of who Jesus was, etc.). Jesus was reserved about messianic self-designation because the general view was of a political Messiah (439). He was the Messiah, but not of the kind expected. A new disclosure of the meaning of the term is at hand in Jesus and his self-sacrificial redemptive role (440).

In all these points we are presented in the Catechism with the tired old conception of Judaism as the preparation for Christianity with no mention of what Israel, while still "beloved of God," might be doing in the modern world. This document contains nothing of the exciting new breakthroughs of thought regarding the two sisterly communities both witnessing to God and laboring for the coming of God's reign. Old themes of Jewry's misunderstandings are struck in the same document that asks Christians to try to see the Jewish point of view regarding Jesus and how Israel would have had trouble accepting a newly defined messianic pattern. The Catechism is disappointing, but such official teaching documents are usually conservative. There is no return to pre–Vatican II thoughts regarding Jews, but one gets the feeling that what is being conceded to Judaism is being conceded grudgingly and often gracelessly.

If we compare this official document of the Church Universal with papal statements and those of the cardinals we have examined, we may conclude that we must look to the latter two for innovative thoughts on the Jews and Judaism. A consensus document such as a catechism is not likely to break new ground on this or any theological issue. The new exchange between Jews and Catholics will evolve slowly, sometimes seeming to take two steps forward and one step back. The pace is slow and sometimes unsteady, but the process is irreversible.

Protestant Churches Reevaluate Judaism

In 1948 the First Assembly of the World Council of Churches (WCC), meeting in Amsterdam, Holland, took note of the extermination of 6 million Jews only three years prior to the time of its meeting. Declaring that no people had suffered more bitterly from the "disorder of man" than the Jewish people and proclaiming their special solidarity with the Jews, they denounced as a "sin against God and man" all forms of antisemitism. The Assembly went on to announce to the remaining Jews of the world, "The Messiah for whom you wait has come. The promise has been fulfilled by the coming of Jesus Christ." It called for a renewed effort to convert Jews to Christianity and to provide for this purpose ministers specially educated and literature specially prepared to win the Jewish people for Christ.[4]

Twenty years later, in 1968, the WCC issued a statement calling for "rethinking the place of Jews in the history of salvation." In it they recognized as stereotyped ways Christians had thought about Jews up to that point and noted that, in the last twenty years, churches as well as individual Christians had come to rethink their relationship to the Jews. They noted that by God's grace Jews,

> have preserved in their faith truths and insights into [God's] revelation which we have tended to forget. . . . By their very existence . . . they make it manifest that God has not abandoned them. In this way they are a living and visible sign of God's faithfulness to men, an indication that [God] also upholds those who do not find it possible to recognize him in his Son. We believe that in the future also God in his faithfulness will not abandon the Jewish people, but that his

promise and calling will ultimately prevail so as to bring them to their salvation.[5]

The text then expresses hope for the final inclusion of Israel among the worshipers of Christ.

This 1968 statement goes on to report a split in the ranks of its framers. Some still believed that "to speak of the continued election of the Jewish people alongside the church is inadmissible. It is the church alone, they say, that is, theologically speaking, the continuation of Israel as the people of God." Others had "come to believe that they (the Jews) are still Israel, i.e. that they are God's elect people. These would stress that after Christ the one people of God is broken asunder, one part being the church which accepts Christ, the other part Israel outside the Church ... " This latter view leads to a rejection of "missionary witness" and its replacement by "ecumenical engagement," presumably another word for interfaith dialogue. In this engagement, the statement concludes, the church expects "a real enrichment of its faith."

Nine years later, in 1977, in a report to the WCC, the drafters reported on widespread dialogue meetings with Jews. They went on to denounce the Holocaust as physical genocide against Jews and the Inquisition as spiritual genocide. They called for further study on "how Jews and Christians are jointly, yet distinctly, participating in God's mission to His creation." Among issues recommended for further study was "what assurances can Christians give Jewish dialogue partners against proselytizing of Jews?"[6]

Another WCC study of the same year declared as "nothing short of a miracle" the reconstruction of Jewish life following the Holocaust. Calling for a review of the issue of proselytism, the study declared that dialogue "demands respect at a deeper level and acceptance of the integrity of the faith of the other." Rejecting the idea that the church has replaced Israel as the people of God, the WCC held that the gentile Christian community had now been included in that people of God together with the Jews who continue in that role.[7]

Also in 1977 a WCC Consultation on the Church and the Jewish People meeting in Jerusalem proclaimed:

Some of us believe that we have to bear witness also to the Jews; some among us are convinced, however, that Jews are faithful and obedient to God even though they do not accept Jesus Christ as Lord and Savior. Many maintain that as a separate and specific people the Jews are an instrument of God with a specific God-given task and, as such, a sign of God's faithfulness to all humankind on the way to ultimate redemption.[8]

In 1982 a WCC statement reported once again a difference of opinion among its members regarding the question of mission, some still hoping to convert Jews, others believing "that a mission to the Jews is not part of authentic Christian witness, since the Jewish people finds its fulfillment in faithfulness to God's covenant of old."[9]

Another church statement reporting a similar division of opinion on the meaning of witness to Jews was issued by the American Lutheran Church in 1979. Other churches have affirmed that Jews and Christians together make up the people of God, thus, by implication abandoning all active efforts at converting Jews. So reads the statement of the Belgian Protestant Council (1967) and that of the Mennonite European Regional Conference, the Netherlands (1977). A church statement explicitly rejecting missionary activity directed at Jews was issued by the General Conference of the United Methodist Church (1972), whose declaration on interreligious dialogue stated that "[interfaith] conversations need not and should not require either Jews or Christians to sacrifice their convictions. . . . In such dialogues, an aim of religious . . . conversion, or of proselytizing, cannot be condoned." An even broader statement rejecting conversionary activity was issued by the Synod of the Protestant Church of the Rhineland (1980): "the church may not express its witness toward the Jewish people as it does its mission to the peoples of the world." Finally, the Texas Conference of Churches (1982) issued the most plainspoken of all such church statements, titled "Dialogue: A Contemporary Alternative to Proselytization." It states, "jews and Christians share a common calling as God's covenanted people. . . . [The] most appropriate posture between Christians and Jews today is one of dialogue. . . . We dedicate ourselves to . . . avoidance of any conversionary intent or proselytism in the relationship."[10]

A Jewish Response

It seems to me that in these varied statements there can be discerned three stages in the churches' progressive acknowledgment of a post-Easter role for Judaism in God's plan of salvation. All reject the traditional Christian reading of Paul's Letter to the Galatians that with the coming of Christ the Jews were cast out as was Ishmael when Isaac came on the scene. The 1948 statement of the WCC affirms the ongoing divine love for the Jews and insists that special Christian attention be given to their plight as victims of Christian indifference and/or persecution. The result of this loving attention will be a new conversionary effort to reveal to Israel "its own Messiah." The Jewish role in the postresurrection world is a crucial one; it is to acknowledge Christ as quickly as possible so as to speed the work of universal salvation. This is clearly a predialogic position that sees no value whatever in the continued existence of Judaism. Needless to say, this is a view profoundly offensive to Jews. What is new is that it is now equally offensive to Christian participants in the dialogue.

The next step in Christian affirmation of the Jewish role in redemption is that of Paul's Letter to the Romans, chapters 9 through 11. The continued existence of the Jewish faith and people in today's world is divinely willed and ordained. It is to be viewed either as an impenetrable mystery (Why would God arrange for Judaism and Christianity to exist side by side? But God does!), or as a means of educating the church in areas of divine truth she may have overlooked. Jews can remind the Christians of the communal dimension of religious life or of the need of the "creed" to be validated by the "deed" or of the as yet unredeemed state of the world, and so on. But this is purely a temporary stage in the long-range plan of redemption. The Jews, still beloved of God, still the chosen people (along with Christians newly ingrafted) follow a religion of great value. However, this is not a permanent condition. Ultimately, though not now—with the messianic advent, one supposes—the Jews will in their turn be ingrafted into the Christian covenant, or the Christian fulfillment of their covenant. Thus the question of conversion is put off indefinitely but not forgotten.

This view is, from the Jewish perspective, much preferable to the former one. Christians accept the validity and value of Jewish faith. They even seek to learn from it. And, most important, they leave Jews alone as regards attempts at conversion. The Torah-centered way of life is acknowledged as providing Jews a rich and a true relationship to God. However, this view also attributes to Christianity an ultimacy it denies to Judaism and is thus at the theoretical level less than satisfactory to most Jews.

The third step in the development of a new Christian evaluation of Judaism rejects both contemporary missionary activity and also the expectation that Jews will and must ultimately recognize Christ as their Messiah or savior. While affirming the necessary salvific role for Christ in the lives of Christians, it recognizes, by implication at least, that God has provided another means of salvation for Jews, presumably Torah. If this were not the case, Christians would be spiritually and ethically irresponsible in abandoning hope for Jewish acceptance of Christ. In this understanding there is affirmed equal standing for Judaism and Christianity as means of salvation. Here dialogue is between redemptive partners with no superiority or exclusive ultimacy claimed by either. The last three church statements referred to seem to reflect this view. It is clear that this position is the one most Jews would like to see Christians adopt.

As I have said, the three positions outlined in this chapter are acceptable to Jews in varying degrees, the first one, of course, not at all. Jews would be most comfortable if Christians were to adopt the third alternative, the one already endorsed by the United Methodists, the Texas churches, and the Church of the Rhineland. But is this Jewish preference sufficient reason for the church to change its longtime insistence on the immediate or future conversion of the Jews? Some, such as the Southern Baptist Convention, in its controversial resolution of summer 1996, will insist that it is sufficient to renounce and denounce all forms of antisemitism, to embrace the Jewish people lovingly and pledge to defend their human rights. It is another thing entirely to agree to refrain from proclaiming to them the most precious possession of the Christian and the world, the love of God as definitively and fully revealed in Christ and his sacrifice for sin on the cross. To withhold this "good news" from Jews would be a spiritual crime against the Jewish people, Christ's own "according to the flesh."

Now many Christians in the dialogue will respond that these Baptists and others like them are still stuck in the position of the WCC back in 1948. They will hold, with the Jews, that God has established with Israel a prior and eternally valid means of salvation in the Torah. Therefore, to refrain from preaching the gospel to Jews is not an act of indifference to their eternal fate but an act of respect for their Torah and for the God who revealed it. But others will reply that the gospel was originally brought "to the Jew first and also to the Greek" (Rom. 1:16). If Paul sought the conversion of Israel, so must contemporary Christians. To do other than this would be to deny the universal scope of Christ's work and to reject an essential requirement of Scripture.

But the fact is that Christian Scriptures have more than one thing to say about the need to convert Jews. And the message is far from consistent. The word in Galatians is radically different from that in Romans 9 through 11. In fact, one might well hold that what we have seen in the last forty years of dialogue is a crucial movement of Christian thinking from Galatians to Romans. Now all Christians in the dialogue agree that the first covenant is eternal, therefore, not abrogated by the second. But all do not agree that this means that the Jews do not finally have to convert at the "end of days." For Christ is the ultimate fulfillment of Israel's covenant. Thus the decision of many churches to refrain from conversionary efforts in this epoch of world history does not necessarily entail the abandonment of their hope that eventually "all Israel will be saved" through Christ (Rom. 11:26). Until that distant date Israel will continue in its own path either for mysterious reasons known only to God or to enrich humanity and the church with its own Jewish insights and modes of spirituality.

Now, there is a certain inescapable Christian logic to this position. For, if Christ is indeed the Messiah—not evidenced by his first coming perhaps (save to those who see him through the eyes of Christian faith)—but surely to be demonstrated conclusively by his glorious Second Coming, then, when he comes, surely Jews, seeing this, will need no Christian prodding to recognize him and "join up." (The corresponding belief among Jews would be that when it turns out that the Messiah is not Jesus after all, Christians will drop their claims and become one with Jewry.)

But this Christian theory, logical as it may be, establishes a permanent inequality between Judaism and Christianity, attributing ultimate truth only to the latter. Many in the dialogue will find this less than satisfactory. It is undeniable that this theory is based upon a reading of *some* Christian Scriptures. Some scholars would, of course, read Galatians and Romans differently. The former is directed to gentiles, not Jews, and outlines only the attitude that gentiles, not Jews, should adopt toward the Jewish Law. The latter does not say that Israel will have to recognize Christ, but only that "all Israel will be saved"; this leaves room for Israel to be saved through Torah or, perhaps, by a final revelation of God's redemption beyond both Torah and Christ.[11] This is all quite interesting, but I must admit to skepticism regarding this new pluralist reading of Paul. It seems to me that we must acknowledge his hopes for Israel's ultimate acceptance of Christ as universal savior, for Jews as well as for everyone else.

Where does this leave us? If Paul really does hope for and expect Israel's inclusion in the Christian consensus, then do we have to rest content with the move from Galatians to Romans? Is this as far as the church can be expected to go? But I said earlier that Christian scriptural passages do not agree on this issue. Surely Paul's attitudes in Romans 9 through 11 are far different from those in Galatians. Perhaps the church can come to recognize the ultimate equal standing of the revelations in Torah and in Christ (equal, not the same) by shifting its attention to another Scripture that, as Gospel, takes precedence over Paul's epistles.

Almost all scholars agree on one thing, that Jesus never baptized anyone.[12] He preached, he taught, he healed—but he never baptized. Why not? If we follow Matthew in this, Jesus preached and had his disciples preach "only to the lost sheep of the house of Israel" (Matt. 15–24). In fact, in another passage he instructed the disciples that, in their mission of healing and preaching, they were to "go nowhere among the gentiles" (Matt. 10:5). Except for the Canaanite woman (Matt. 15:22–28) and the Gadarene demoniac (Matt.

8:28–34), Matthew's Jesus preached to and healed only Jews. Other Gospels disagree, of course, but if they are correct and Jesus did include gentiles in his earthly mission, then why was there such a fuss in Acts when Peter preached to the gentile Cornelius (Acts 11:1–18), and why, in his own defense, did Peter not say to the Jerusalem church leaders who objected, "Jesus preached to gentiles; why shouldn't I?" It seems to me, therefore, that Matthew is correct that Jesus restricted his work to calling Israel to reform and repentance before the coming of the Reign of God. He did not baptize because, having been born Jews, those among whom he worked were in no need of what was for Matthew a ceremony of rebirth into an expanded Israel. It is true that Matthew's John the Baptist understood baptism differently, but Jesus' view was quite otherwise, as we shall see.

Now, after a career of earthly witness as outlined by Matthew, Jesus was crucified and then raised from the dead. He appeared three times to his disciples as the risen Christ. The third appearance, known as the "great commission," is remarkable, since it expresses the conviction of Matthew's branch of the church that the resurrected Christ gave his disciples instructions quite at odds with his words to them during his earthly sojourn. First of all he told them to go "to all nations [kal goyim] baptizing them in the name of the Father and of the Son and of the Holy Spirit" (Matt. 28:19). He thus reverses his policy of "Jews only" and commands a ritual (baptism) that he himself had never performed. If Matthew's earthly Jesus saw himself as a preacher, teacher, and healer to his own people, Matthew's risen Christ saw himself as the proclaimer of proto-trinitarian truth to the gentiles. When a Jew says kal goyim, he almost invariably excludes Israel from the reference. "The nations" means the others, the gentiles. Those nations would have to be baptized, born again, precisely because they were gentiles, not born Israelites. He did not baptize during his own career because his audience was made up of born Jews, and thus did not require this symbolic rebirth into Israel.

If they did not require it then, why should Christians assume that they require it now? If the Father, Son, and Holy Spirit formula was not part of Jesus' message to Jews, why should it be part of the church's message to them now? Baptism and the now fully developed trinitarian theory is for gentiles, not Jews. The radical differences between Jesus' message for Jews (in Matthew) and the proclamation of the risen Christ for gentiles (baptism and proto-trinitarian formula) opens the way for today's church to direct its message exclusively to gentiles while recognizing that the life of Torah is God's will for Jews now and in the future. In this recognition the church will be following the lead of its master.

6

Engaging Two Contemporary Theologians of the Dialogue

Irving Greenberg

I first met Rabbi Irving Greenberg on October 31, 1983, when he delivered an address as part of a lecture series at Montclair State College sponsored by our Department of Philosophy and Religion. The subject of the series was Jewish-Christian religious dialogue. The speakers were Dr. Alice Eckardt, Dr. Greenberg, my colleague, Dr. Eva Fleischner, and I. I listened carefully to Dr. Greenberg's remarks as he shared with the audience his current thoughts on issues he had been addressing in print since 1967, just as the impact of the 1965 Second Vatican Council was beginning to be felt.

Back in 1967 he had written that the central messages of Judaism and Christianity were the same: humanity is not alone, God loves all people, evil will one day be overcome.[1] He drew a parallel between the Exodus event and the Christ event as liberating the followers of the respective faiths and pointed to other similarities rarely if ever recognized by his fellow Orthodox Jews. (I still recall the utter bewilderment of the Orthodox rabbi who was my Hebrew tutor during my undergraduate years at Syracuse University when I asked him to recognize the simple and obvious truth that what Christians did in church was comparable to what we did in synagogue.)

Among Orthodox rabbis, Dr. Greenberg was and is unusual to the point of uniqueness. In his writing of 1967, he also lamented the supersessionist theology of Christianity, which held that the rise of the new faith meant the rejection and replacement of the old (Judaism), as confirmed, in Christian eyes, by the destruction of the Jerusalem Temple. As the new covenant spread among gentiles, a "Jewish problem" began to emerge in the Christian imagination. Now that the full truth of Christ had come (demonstrated by the resurrection) there was no further need for Jews in the divine salvific plan. What was to be done about the Jews and Judaism that stubbornly insisted on going on in defiance of the universal claims of the church? The conflict of the two covenants could be solved by denying that Judaism was a living religion and converting, degrading, or murdering the Jews.

Jews responded with their own stereotyped conceptions of Christians and Christianity but were in no position to implement their hostility. Christians were. The result was the history of persecution culminating in the Holocaust. And it was that final catastrophe that led to the "new encounter" between the faiths. In the aftermath of Auschwitz, Christians have come to the full, chilling recognition of what the hatred in the heart of their religion of love had ultimately wrought. This realization, and the determination to repent and to right this great wrong, wrote Greenberg, is a sign of contemporary Christianity's spiritual health.

The "new encounter" of the two faiths celebrates life after the apotheosis of death in the Shoah. Stimulated also by the rebirth of Israel as a nation, Christians now recognize Jewry as a vital, living community and Judaism as a vibrant faith. Both faiths are called to see in each other valuable insights that can enrich their own religious lives. Each is encouraged by the other to live its life of witness to God for all humanity, free of the exclusivist poison of the past. The age of rivalry is done; now the two faith communities are free to give up mutual distortions of the other and work together in service to the God they both worship. This hopeful, affirmative vision was only an outline in 1967, but Greenberg filled it out in subsequent writings as the dialogue moved forward.

In 1979 Greenberg, focusing on the covenant as a central theme, pointed out that Christianity, growing in the bosom of Judaism, sees itself as an unfolding of the earlier covenant and a fulfillment of its promises.[2] For him, the covenant relationship between God and humanity must be open to the future, revealing new events and dimensions of "covenant living." Christians are convinced that Christ's life was an "authentic revelation." While his unexpected early death might have led his followers to view him as a false Messiah, instead they saw it as a "new revelation of the character of messianic salvation." Although Jews did not and do not share this view, for Greenberg this Christian determination to reaffirm the promise of salvation in the face of death and disaster was "deeply Jewish in its logic."

Meanwhile, Jews reacted in a similar fashion to the destruction of the Temple. Instead of giving up and dying out, Jewry concluded that a new avenue of salvation (rabbinic Judaism) had been opened by the destruction of the old. At the time, neither group was able to see this parallel, now so insightfully pointed out by Greenberg. Christians saw Jews as rejected by God; Jews saw Christians as idolaters.

Not until Vatican II did the church open to a positive view of Jews as still the people of God and Judaism as a living, valid faith. This new recognition by Christians should stimulate Jews to recognize Christianity's contributions to world redemption and to give up negative images of Christians and gentiles developed as a response to persecution. Both faiths must surrender claims of exclusivism and triumphalism and rediscover the universal image of God in all humanity.

Greenberg becomes more specific at this point. He calls Christians to support the empowerment of the long-powerless Jews that is the meaning of Israel's rebirth as a nation. This rebirth is the life-affirming response to the kingdom of death that was the Holocaust. It was an unprecedented act of redemption that was called for by the unprecedented horror of the Shoah. Greenberg recognizes the threat of idolatry inherent in "a secular state with a religious message." But Zion reborn is still for him a divine revelation, even if flawed and partial. Greenberg insists that both Jews and Christians accept the Holocaust/Zion events as revelatory. From the Holocaust we learn the ghastly consequences of holding the other in contempt. From Zion reborn, we learn that new acts of redemption are ever possible in ongoing, salvation history. Christians are called to rid their religion of hate and to recognize their responsibility to substitute love of Jews and support for the Jewish state for age-old anti-Jewish patterns of thought. Jews, in turn, will now be free to consider the "possibility" that Christianity is a broadening of God's covenant with Israel to call gentiles to God.

As the years passed, Greenberg continued to fill in and fill out his vision of a new, mutually affirming relationship between the two faiths. In 1986 he published his controversial essay, "The Relationship of Judaism and Christianity: Toward a New Organic Model."[3] It was this lecture, I believe, I heard that night in October 1983. It had not yet been published and bore another title having to do with the post-Holocaust period. But whether he delivered it that night or at another meeting shortly thereafter, I recall differing with some of his central points. However, this was not the first time I had disagreed with Greenberg's ideas.

In his 1979 essay, discussed earlier, Greenberg had insisted that Christians show their repentance for past anti-Jewish sins by active support for the

State of Israel. But I have a problem with such a requirement. I do not believe that he appreciates the distinctions that exist in many non-Jewish minds between religion and politics. For liberal Christians, those most likely to feel the guilt of the Holocaust, the separation of religion and state is something of a secular dogma. This is also true for Jewish liberals, with the sole exception of their support for the Jewish State of Israel. Here it is the Christians who are far more consistent than the Jews. They do not believe that their hostility to certain Israeli policies, or even to the very idea of a religious state, suggests an anti-Jewish attitude. Is it appropriate for Jews, devoted to Israel, to demand as proof of freedom from antisemitism that Christian friends endorse Israeli policies or self-conceptions to which they have what they consider valid moral objections? Greenberg recognizes (in passing) the danger of idolatry in mixing politics and religion, the danger of making an earthly state the absolute reality rather than God. But he seems not to grasp the significance of the point he has just made.

Here is the dilemma: just at the moment when Christendom was shaken by the revelation of the Holocaust and reeling from the other horrors of the Second World War . . . just as Europe came to confront the dead-end reality of the nationalism that had twice in one century turned the continent into a field of slaughter . . . just as nationalism was being repudiated by most of the war's participants and political power was falling from the church's grasp . . . at that very moment the people Israel reentered political history, formed a nation, gained territory, and created a powerful army. And here is a state defined as a homeland for a single group precisely at a time when multiculturalism and pluralism were beginning to sweep Europe and America. The majority of Jews may view Israel's rebirth as a divine revelation, but can we really expect that all Christians will agree?

Of course, many will and have. But, paradoxically, those who do are fundamentalist and evangelical Christians who would also be delighted if we all converted to Christianity, abandoning our Judaism. They mean us no harm in this desire; they do not realize that what they would take from us is our most precious possession, our living relationship through Torah with Israel's God, the Holy One who has placed us at this post and has sustained us as God's covenant partners from generation to generation. So, too, do our liberal friends mean us no harm. They affirm the ongoing validity of our faith but question the appropriateness of a religious state—even a democratic one—in the twenty-first century. The problem is far more complicated than Greenberg recognizes. We Jews must find some way to explain to liberal Christians that Judaism with Auschwitz but without Zion reborn would be like Christianity with the crucifixion but without the resurrection. Impossible! In addressing this problem, Jews and Christians must both wrestle with complex issues raised by the interaction of theology and history. Jews must also think much more deeply before we attempt to set up "tests" for evaluating Christian attitudes. And political tests of religious attitudes are always problematic. We—or Christians or both of us—may be caught up in a confusion of political and religious categories that at the least requires a careful and precise analysis of a kind that has not yet been attempted.

In the same essay, Greenberg had written that the Catholic Church, while recognizing the value of the ongoing Jewish tradition, had hedged this acknowledgment by stating that the importance and meaning of Jewish tradition had been "deeply affected by the coming of Christ."[4] But why does Greenberg consider this "hedging"? Is it not obviously true that the Christ event, which opened the covenant between God and Israel to include the gentiles, *did* deeply affect the importance and meaning of the Jewish tradition? If the Jesus movement brought knowledge of Israel's God to billions of human beings beyond the boundaries of Jewry, is this not a major event in Jewish as well as world history? Is it not a partial fulfillment of God's commission to Abraham to bring a blessing to all peoples?

Greenberg suggested this as a "possibility" at this stage of his writing. But, if he really believes this, how could such a development not have a profound impact on Jews and Judaism and the mission of Israel as a witness people? Here as elsewhere Greenberg states what sounds like a breakthrough position—or at least the "possibility" of it—but then pulls back rather than explore the newly opened line of thought, following it to its logical conclusion. In many ways Greenberg is a brave man, venturing where no other contemporary Orthodox rabbi has dared to go. Yet he is also very cautious and at times hesitant to stray too far from his roots. Considering the harsh criticism he has received from that quarter, all this is understandable.

In his 1986 essay, he opens many very promising lines of thought. While stating that he could never say with Martin Buber that Jesus is "my great brother" (why not, I wonder?), he still admires the "daring and power" of the affirmation. He warns against Jewish approval of Christianity that is offered only if we shape Christianity to fit Jewish patterns of thought. And he goes on to suggest that Jews be open to the categories of Christian self-understanding. Can a Jew take seriously the possibilities of incarnation, resurrection, and other Christian claims? But having asked this crucial question, he fails to follow up with possible answers or even serious discussion. Instead he states that what is needed is "a model that would allow both sides to respect the full nature of the other in all its faith claims." How right he is, and how difficult such a model would be to construct. And, it must be said, how far from such a model is what follows in his essay.

He proceeds with a skillful and accurate sketch of how Christians and Jews misconstrued each other. He notes that Jews, seeing the ongoing unredeemed state of the world long after the Christ event, concluded that Jesus was a false Messiah. And now Greenberg begins to construct what is perhaps his most well-known argument. He calls for a new Jewish evaluation of Jesus not as a *false Messiah* but as a *failed Messiah*. He immediately explains that this is no criticism. For Jews "worldly success is no criterion of validity." Abraham failed: he did not convert the world to monotheism. Moses failed: he did not free the slaves internally from their slave mentality, nor did he bring them or himself into the Land of Promise. Jeremiah failed: no one listened to him, and Jerusalem was destroyed. And Jesus failed: he did not bring on the redemption of the world. False Messiahs have false aims or false principles. Jesus' aims were the right ones, as were his principles. Even Christianity recognizes his failure in its hope for the "second coming," at which time Jesus will bring to fruition the world redemption he failed to achieve at his first appearance.

Is this the model that would allow both sides to respect the other in all its faith claims? Does Greenberg really think that Christians will recognize their savior in any definition that includes the word "failed"? Should they? Can the one whom billions look to as the human face of divinity be viewed as a failure of any kind?

I find much to differ with in this argument. First of all, if Jesus is a failed Messiah, then there must have been a single Jewish definition of Messiah extant at his time. But, as I point out in chapter 2, "The Question of the Messiah," there were as many messianic conceptions abroad in first-century Judaism as there were authors or groups that produced texts containing messianic expectations. The term was in the public domain, available for any sectarian movement to attach to their particular conception of a redeemer figure. And often the term was not even used, although imaginative portraits of liberator-redeemer figures abounded. They were called by many names. Of these sectarian groups, one was the Nazarene fellowship which gathered around Jesus and which, following his death, constructed a radical new definition of "Messiah" reflecting the pattern of his life. For them the Messiah was the one who preached and taught and healed, drove out demons to demonstrate the coming power of the emerging divine reign, and then put the capstone of martyrdom on his career of witness by suffering, dying, and rising from the dead for the redemption of the world.

This is what Christians call the "messianic pattern" of Jesus' life outlined in the Gospels. Such a pattern was unknown outside of Christian circles at the time of its development. But it has gone on to convert much of the world. Is this once-new "messianic pattern" any more or less valid than the dozen or so others floating about first-century Palestine? What came to be accepted as the rabbinic movement's notion of the Messiah was the one most Jews adopted in the second century. But if Jesus did not reflect that definition, it merely means that he fit another. There is no question of "failure" here. Even the Christian explanation of the Second Coming that reflects the "One Like a Son of Man" vision of Daniel 7 is far more supernaturalized than the expectations of a human king of David's line pictured in earlier messianic prophecies. Thus the very assumptions on which the judgment of Jesus as a failed Messiah is constructed are false, based on an oversimplification of a complex and varied field of messianic speculation.

If we seek a positive Jewish view of Jesus, one is readily available. It is one that Christians will find to be true as far as it goes ... yet incomplete. That is inevitable. If we Jews were to adopt a conception of Jesus that is both true and complete as judged by Christianity, we would have become Christians ourselves, which is, of course, not our intention. We seek a positive *Jewish* view of Jesus, not one of the many Christian views ranging from low to high christology.

The Jewish view I have in mind is not that Jesus was a false Messiah or a failed Messiah or any kind of Messiah at all. Jesus was, rather, the one sent by Israel's God to bring gentiles into the covenant that until then had connected the Holy One exclusively with the people Israel. The vehicle of that connection was Torah and membership in the chosen people. Now through Jesus—or, rather, through Paul and other interpreters who understood the true purpose of God in sending Jesus—membership in the people Israel was opened to the nations. Henceforth Israel, Jewish root and Christian branch, entered a new stage of its life under an expanded covenant open to all peoples.

This definition of who Jesus was is compatible with both Judaism and Christianity (although the latter group will add to it), and it is true. It is true because it reveals (in whole or in part) who Jesus actually *was*. How do we know this? We know it because we know what Jesus *did*. He brought Israel's God to the nations (via Paul's work and that of other missionaries). What else he was or did is up to Christians to work out. And we Jews have no reason to quarrel with any conclusions they reach as long as they concern the salvation of gentiles, leaving Jews to continue to live out our life of sanctification and covenant partnership along ancient lines established for us by the Holy One.

The theory that Jesus (or, more properly, his interpreters) opened the covenant to include the nations is not merely an interpretation of the call of Abraham and his seed to bring blessing to all the world. We may also see it as a fulfillment of a number of biblical prophecies. Of course, the prophets who spoke the original words had no idea of Jesus or Christianity. But they did look forward to a day when gentiles would join themselves to the people Israel and to Israel's God. Now, if some Jewish theologians of the dialogue have come to view Christians as a grafted-on branch of Israel (as Paul put it), then we are free to develop the view that these ancient prophecies have already come to pass in the spread of the worship of Israel's God to the nations via Christianity.

Deutero-Isaiah is the great, though not the only, prophet to foretell the future conversion of the pagans to (a version of) Israel's religion. In chapter 49:1–6 Israel is the "light to the nations" through whom the Lord's salvation will reach to the ends of the earth. And what is that light? Undoubtedly the proclamation of the universal monarchy of God to which all peoples must submit. "Turn to me and be saved, all the ends of the earth" (Is. 45:22). "To me every knee shall bow, every tongue shall swear" (Is. 45:23). There are at least another half dozen similar prophecies in Isaiah. The prophet Zephaniah has a similar vision of gentile conversion in chapter 2, verse 11: "to him [the God of Israel] will bow down, each in its place, all the lands of the nations." This suggests that the gentiles will not have to come to the holy land to join its inhabitants, but "each in its place," in whatever ethnic community the people are found, will join Israel in its worship of the one God. In modern parlance, gentiles do not become Jews when they come to God, but they do become Israelites. Habakkuk, too, sees a future day when, as he sublimely states, "the earth will be filled with the knowledge of the glory of the Lord as the waters cover the sea" (Hab. 2:14).[5]

With these and many other prophecies telling of the conversion of gentiles to Israel's faith, and with so many Christian theologians (Monica Hellwig, Paul van Buren, A. Roy Eckardt, J. Coos Schoneveld, Clark Williamson, et al.) seeing the Christ event as the opening of the covenant to all peoples, why does Rabbi Greenberg, who agrees with this position, need to go further and state an additional theory (Jesus as failed Messiah) certain to be off-putting to our Christian dialogue partners? We were hardly pleased to hear Christians in predialogue days declare the history and faith of Israel to have been a failure. Let us not return this noncompliment in kind.

Greenberg usually strives to be fair to both faiths as he analyzes them. He frequently points out that there is enough divine love for all and enough redemptive work for at least two holy communities. But in this essay he breaks his pattern of evenhandedness to hold that, in one respect at least, Judaism is superior to Christianity. He points out that Judaism (or ancient Israelite faith) is a good deal older than Christianity. If we trace it back to Abraham, it is 1,800 years older. From Moses' time onward it was a sacramental faith. The people, an ignorant peasantry, brought their offerings to a priestly caste who, in a shrine structure open only to the priestly elite, sacrificed on the people's behalf to a God "high and lifted up," "enthroned above the cherubim." With the destruction of the Temple, Judaism emerged in its rabbinic phase. In this postsacramental, more participatory epoch, people came to be more and more active partners in the covenant. God, in turn, became more hidden, intervening less and less, leaving rabbis and sages to interpret God's mysterious will. Education was necessary so the people could read the sacred books, join in synagogue worship, and apply the commandments to their daily lives. The human role grew apace.

Meanwhile, Christianity moved in the opposite direction. In Jesus, God was not hidden but visible for the first time. Christianity was a new sacramentalism, perhaps more continuous with the biblical Israelite faith than was rabbinic Judaism with its central stress on human deeds. This is a very interesting analysis. Judaism was in its second stage while Christianity, much younger, was still in its sacramental first epoch. Although Greenberg does say that perhaps this was more suitable to the gentiles at the stage they had reached at the time, he also says, "I personally consider the rabbinic to be a more mature mode of religion."[6] Too bad. Usually he stresses how much we have to learn from each other. One can only regret this momentary fall into "one-upmanship." And he does not explain why one form of religion is more "mature" than another. If maturity is measured by the expanded human role in the faith, then we must tread cautiously. In atheism the human role is 100 percent. Perhaps we need another measure.

But even with our eyes fully open to the idolatrous possibilities in the theory that we are entering a world of "humanity come of age," we must see in Greenberg's three-stage theory of religious development an insightful analysis of our spiritual history. First comes the sacramental stage, then the rabbinic, then, after Auschwitz, the dawn of "holy secularity," at which point the human person truly comes into his own, taking fuller responsibility for the building of the kingdom as evidenced by the rebirth of Israel as a nation.

The only problem with this interesting model is that it places Christianity one rung lower than Judaism, since the former remains at the first stage while Judaism moves on to the second. We must question the accuracy of this picture of Christian history because it seems to ignore the Protestant Reformation, which was about (among other things) overthrowing the sacramental system and empowering the laity to participate in the body of Christ which is the church. Thus much of the Christian world already entered the second stage hundreds of years ago. Now Greenberg calls on Jews to enter the third stage and Christians to enter the second. But when he characterizes this third epoch of widened human responsibility, he seems really to be calling both Jews and Christians to enter the third stage together. Corrected in this way, we can still find great value in his theory of spiritual epochs shorn of the one-upmanship that, it seems to me, is inappropriate to the interfaith dialogue.

In the first year of the current century Dr. Greenberg published an essay, "Judaism and Christianity: Covenants of Redemption."[7] It is a comprehensive and intellectually rich expression of his recent views, as well as a recapitulation of his thought over thirty three years. I find myself in agreement with its overall thrust and with many of its themes, which are similar to those I have been developing since the 1980s. But let me mention three of them in particular. I disagree with the first, am puzzled by the second, and am pleased to see him articulate the third.

In this essay I am sorry to see him return to his argument of 1989 that Jesus is a "failed Messiah." I explained earlier why I find this position to be inaccurate and a nonstarter in the dialogue with Christianity. It wrongly assumes the existence of one standard Jewish conception of "Messiah" at the time of Jesus; it also wrongly assumes that if God sent Jesus, it must have been his mission to effect the immediate consummation of the eschatological hopes of Israel. While it is true that Jesus preached that "the Kingdom of God is at hand" (Mk. 1:15) and predicted that "this generation will not pass away until all these things [the glorious coming of the Son of Man] take place" (Mk. 13:30), we must look beyond Jesus' own expectations to discover what God had in mind in sending him. God has a way of doing what God pleases even if those involved fail to see the whole picture. Here we may utilize John Pawlikowski's view of the progressive, developing nature of christology to grasp the whole divine plan. Contrary to all expectation, Jesus suffered and died horribly. Did he anticipate such an earthly end? This is unclear. The passion predictions in the Gospels may be genuine, or they may be the product of the evangelists' further meditation on the matter after the fact.

But following Jesus' death, his followers continued to have direct experience of his living presence. Such experiences always contain an irreducible element of objective uncertainty. However, the subjective reality of the experience is indubitable. The disciples underwent ghastly suffering and death testifying to the truth of their experience. Deeper Christian pondering of all this led to the emergence of a new messianic pattern of a life lived, laid down, and taken up again for the sake of human redemption. That this powerful conception went on to spread across much of the world, drawing people afar off into the circle of those worshiping Israel's God, testifies to its truth, a truth designed for the conversion of the gentiles.

This, of course, is a truth added to yet echoing the original and eternal truth revealed in the creation, calling, and salvation history of the original Israel. It represents an expansion of the covenant to include all peoples. I am a committed Jew, faithful to the Hebrew Scriptures' sacred narrative and bound by the immutable truths and laws of conduct revealed by the Holy One to my people. But I can also see in the Christian story a further expression of the divine will, this time for the non-Jewish world. Thus I can in no way view the unfolding of the consequences of Jesus' life as a failure in any sense whatever. This is the stuff of world redemption pointed to from the first moment of divine revelation to Abraham at the time of Israel's birth as God's original redemptive agent on earth.

I am puzzled by another issue Greenberg raises. Or, perhaps, it is he who is puzzled or, at least, undecided. In this essay, he seems to agree with Maimonides that some Christian teachings are simply "wrong."[8] He expresses the hope that "the growing Christian emphasis on Jesus as the path to God rather than on Jesus as God Incarnate may yet win out."[9] Clearly he would hope that John Pawlikowski's incarnational christology, discussed later in this chapter, would yield to the lower christology of a strictly human Jesus. He goes on to insist that "erroneous doctrines do not necessarily delegitimize the faith that incorporates them."[10] But I wonder why he feels called upon to consider a doctrine as false rather than as a variation on the theme of the earthly concretization of God's redemptive plan. Our Hebrew Scriptures present similar concretizations in the election of the people Israel and the gift of the Promised Land. On this subject I recommend Michael Wyshogrod's book *The Body of Faith: Judaism as Corporeal Election*. Judaism does not carry this theme from concretization all the way to incarnation, as does Christianity. But it is, in differing measure, common to both of them.

But strangely, in his next paragraph, Greenberg seems to change his mind. What was on the previous page an "erroneous doctrine" becomes a possible truth. Greenberg tell us, "One can hardly rule out the option [of incarnation of God in Jesus] totally, particularly if it was intended for gentiles and not for Jews."[11] Here I think he is right on target. I have been writing the same thing since 1995. But it is far from certain what his position actually is. I may be wrong in reading it as inconsistent, but that is how it seems to me. It is understandable that an Orthodox rabbi would proceed with extreme caution in these unfamiliar waters.

One recalls the case of Jonathan Sacks, chief rabbi of the British commonwealth, who, in the first edition of his fine book, *The Dignity of Difference*, suggested that God has inspired religions other than Judaism.[12] The Orthodox rabbis of Britain raised such a hue and cry in response to what is surely an obvious truth that Rabbi Sacks was forced to delete the passage in all future editions of the book. Thus, Greenberg's hesitancy is understandable. Still, one hopes for greater clarity in the future.

Finally, I was delighted to find in the last paragraph of this essay the welcome statement that "Christians may be deemed to be members of the people Israel."[13] When, in the 1980s, I spoke and wrote about "Jewish Israelites and Christian Israelites" as two branches of one people (I would say today "stock and branch"), I received some furious criticism from a number of rabbis. That Rabbi Greenberg now feels free to state this still-controversial formulation is a welcome development and a demonstration of the forward-thrusting dynamism of the ongoing dialogue.

From the 1990s to the early years of the twenty-first century, Greenberg has continued to develop and refine his views along lines not dissimilar to my own thinking. Both of us have published a number of essays in the venerable *Journal of Ecumenical Studies*. And, although he stresses history more than I do, while I focus more than he does on details of theology, we seem to be heading in a similar direction. I believe that my emphasis is greater than his on the similarities and parallels between the two faiths, but we agree that there is truth in both of them, that they need each other (and the insights of other faiths) to become truer still (more complete), and that they must labor cooperatively, side by side, for the realization of the divine reign that is their shared hope and goal.

John Pawlikowski

I have known the Reverend John Pawlikowski for some twenty-five years, having interacted with him at meetings of Jewish and Christian theologians where we were both speakers or panelists. In fact, it was something he said to me that moved me to write a series of articles and finally this book. While assuring me that, whatever the Jewish response, Christian theologians would continue to develop their new positive theologies of Judaism, he yearned for some Jewish theological reevaluation of Christianity that would encourage the process. He went on to express the hope that Jewish religious thinkers might find some way to allow our faith to open itself to enrichment by the life and teachings of Jesus and from the Christian tradition.

And so, in the 1980s I began to develop my arguments for the Jewish-Christian dialogue to move "from mutual respect to mutual influence." The sticking point for many Jews was the word "mutual." It was obvious to them, and to a growing number of Christians, that Christianity could not under-stand itself without taking into account the Jewish context out of which it arose and in which Jesus developed his thoughts. Judaism's temporal priority and the fact that all the categories of Christian religious thought were mod-ifications or new formulations of Jewish ideas made the truth of Judaism the necessary foundation upon which Christian truths had been constructed.

However, many Jews (and Christians) did not see that Judaism's self-understanding was incomplete if it did not take into account the opening of its covenant to the world, represented by the figure of Jesus as he was presented to the gentiles by Paul and other early church missionary theologians. It has been said that "truth is in the context." The Christianization of the world in which the vast majority of Jews lived and practiced their faith inevitably af-fected that faith in fundamental ways, for better or worse. Along with crucial liturgical and sociopolitical changes resulting from this new reality, theolog-ically Jews must recognize that to witness for Israel's God in a world that, in its own way, already believes in that God is a far different task than to do so in a pagan environment.

What is the nature of Judaism's witness in a Christian environment? Is it to show forth the reliability of God's promises just by continuing to exist as a vital religious community? Is it to deny by that same continued existence the universal claims of the church? Is it to influence the dominant faith to keep its theological feet on the firm soil of this world rather than drift off into an otherworldly realm of abstract contemplation? Is it to guard the purity of biblical monotheism against pagan and syncretistic tendencies in the church? Is it to keep alive the reality of holy community and collective world re-demption against the atomistic individualism into which the church might otherwise fall? All these roles and more reveal how Judaism can influence and has influenced its sister faith.

But the influence also moves in the opposite direction. What does Chris-tianity have to teach Judaism? Since the theological differences in the two faiths are always a matter of emphasis rather than of conflicting ideas, Chris-tianity is in a position to call Judaism to awareness of themes within the Jewish faith that may have been neglected, often in an attempt to avoid ideas adopted and stressed by Christianity. Now that we no longer need to define ourselves over against each other, our dialogue with Christianity can put us back in touch with our own individual spirituality, with the more mystical aspects of our faith, with a deepened understanding of human sin and of God's forgiving grace. Christian universalism can help us fight the ethnic chauvinism, narrow nationalism, and negative views of the other that always threaten to distort Judaism. By opening the covenant to include all people,

Christianity partially fulfills the universal call at the heart of God's commission to Abraham. Jewry does not exist for its own sake but to do God's work of redeeming all the world. Opening ourselves to the influence of ideas that lie at the very center of Christian self-understanding will ultimately open us to ourselves and our own faith tradition in new and enriching ways yet to be fully realized. The influence is—must be—mutual. We Jews, as well as Christians, must not be afraid but must welcome this as we grow together and learn from each other.

In the winter 1990–91 issue of the *National Dialogue Newsletter* (sadly, now defunct), edited and published by the late, beloved Frank H. Brennan Jr., I wrote an article entitled "Toward Total Dialogue," growing out of an essay I had written for the fall 1989 issue of the *Journal of Ecumenical Studies* (entitled "Jews and Christians: Taking the Next Step"). In both pieces I called for a full, unrestricted dialogue open to mutual influence with no issues, no matter how delicate, left off the table. In the same issue, and in two more to follow, thirteen leading theologians of the dialogue responded, and I responded to their responses. Among the respondents were the Reverend James L. Heft, Dr. Franklin Sherman, Dr. Isaac Rottenberg, the Reverend Edward H. Flannery, Rabbi A. James Rudin, Dr. David Bossman, Dr. Paul Mojzes, Dr. Robert Everett, Rabbi Irving Greenberg, and the Reverend John T. Pawlikowski. What a feast for the mind and spirit! It was dialogue at its best, with everyone learning from everyone else. The contributions of Greenberg and Pawlikowski were especially rich and thought-provoking.

In his response Fr. Pawlikowski expressed satisfaction that he found in my essay a Jewish response to his earlier statement that "it is time that organized Jewry began to think seriously about Christianity as a complementary religious tradition." He expressed understanding that the history of Christian anti-Jewish attitudes and the resulting persecution made it "difficult [for Jews] to initiate a search for religious values in Christianity." He agreed with my point that, without such a search, Judaism could become "overly sectarian," that Jesus' life and mission was an important moment in Jewish, as well as world, history, and that the Jesus movement saw itself as a reform movement within the Jewish community.

Fr. Pawlikowski called on me to develop my arguments further, to pay more attention to the scars left by the Holocaust, the damage done by the continuing efforts of some Christians to convert Jews, and the need to include discussion of these issues and of Israel's rebirth in any "total dialogue." I hope I have responded in these pages to some of these suggestions.

Pawlikowski has been, since Vatican II, a major theological voice from the Catholic side of the dialogue. His profound feeling for Jewish suffering and deep understanding of Jewish faith entitled him to call for a Jewish response to the Christian initiatives of the past forty years. He is also, perhaps, the leading chronicler of the dialogue, reviewing and summarizing skillfully the positions of dozens of dialogue thinkers. And, of course, he has developed his own arguments in his many essays, books, and lectures.

I have never had a chance to review and comment on his still-developing theology of the dialogue, and I do so here with deep appreciation for his insightful contributions over many years.

Pawlikowski has always insisted that a Christian theology of the dialogue not be held separate from Christian theology itself. There can be no question of parallel theological pursuits here. Dialogue theology must be one with the church's deepest reflection on itself. He stresses the impact of the Catholic theology of Judaism on core christology. The church's encounter with Jewish theology and with the Jewish thought of the Second Temple period—particularly with Pharisaism—has had a permanent and profound impact on his own christology that lies at the heart of his Christian faith.

Together with many Christian theologians of the dialogue (Paul van Buren, Clark Williamson, A. Roy Eckardt, et al.), Pawlikowski does not see Jesus as the Jewish Messiah or as fulfilling Old Testament prophecies. Not only did Jesus not do so, but the claim that he did reduces Judaism to a mere prolegomenon to Christianity with no function or place in the world after the Christ event. But if not the Messiah, then who was Jesus? This question draws Pawlikowski into an in-depth analysis of the Pharisee movement of the Second Temple period. He holds that these lay leaders developed a Judaism quite different from what had gone before. "Pharisaism signaled a profound theological reorientation among the Jewish people in their basic understanding of the God-humanity relationship."[14]

God, who had heretofore been seen as restricted to an interaction with patriarchs, prophets, kings, and priests, now reached out to every Jew in a new intimate relationship. Class distinctions, at least in the area of religion, ceased to exist. This democratizing movement within Judaism elevated the individual to a new level. Rabbinic leaders (educated laymen) held forth in the synagogues that stood in every village and town. All could come together to pray and speak directly to God, the divine parent of each person and of the community. Table fellowship meals celebrated the new equality of all members of the people and, crucially, individual salvation—resurrection—was promised to the faithful. Of course, this was a future promise; all the righteous would be raised at once as a community. No single person could enter life eternal in advance of the eschaton. Thus this was an individualism-within-community.

Jesus' words and the example of his life must be seen within this context. He shared the Pharisees' outlook, but, crucially to Christianity, he carried their insights farther than ever they did. At this point we should note that Pawlikowski is building an argument over and against those dialogue theologians who see Christianity as no more than Judaism for the gentiles. Paul van Buren, A. Roy Eckhardt, Clark Williamson, and others hold that Jesus' role was to open the covenant to the nations and to bring them the knowledge of God Jews already possessed. There is one eternal Israelite covenant, established by God with Abraham, ratified with Isaac and Jacob, reconfirmed at Sinai, renewed periodically by Joshua, Josiah, Ezra, and others, and opened by Jesus to include all the world. Jesus does not add to it, he universalizes it.

Now, I see few problems with this "single-covenant" position. But I am a Jew. It is clear that many Christians would insist on a more profound, complex, and unique role for the one they call Lord and savior. Pawlikowski is among them. He leans toward a "double covenant" theology that insists on Christianity's introduction of new elements—or, at least, new emphases— which add substantially to Jewish religious thought.

For Pawlikowski, Jesus built on the Pharisee recognition of the individual-in-community and went beyond it to stress "a personal bonding with the Father"[15] more radical than their conception. He insisted on the absolute value and dignity of every individual. In so doing he seemed to devalue the Jewish community as a core concept. His choice of what the Pharisees considered "bad company" indicated his total overthrow of all distinctions of rank and education, and his radical call to love one's enemies must have been seen as a threat to the Jewish people's sense of solidarity in the face of surrounding foes.

It seems to me that if Pawlikowski is right in this last point (in which he follows Israeli scholar David Flusser), it was Jesus' stress on the individual, rather than the group, that freed him to speak of loving the enemy. On the other hand, is not the book of Jonah an extended parable on the "love your enemies" theme? And so this message actually appeared in Israelite Scripture long before Jesus. Pawlikowski goes on to point to what he considers to be other "unique" Jesus teachings. Jesus stressed "the actual presence of the reign of God in his activities and person in a way that emphasized that the messianic reconciliation between God and humanity had in fact already begun. For the Pharisees such reconciliation lay entirely in the future."[16] Jesus also forgave sins, something no rabbi then or now would venture to do. This was truly revolutionary. In short, Jesus stretched Pharisee ideas and principles to their ultimate limit.[17] According to Pawlikowski, the insights of Pharisaism "seeded" the Jesus movement, but Jesus took a giant step beyond them. I agree that Jesus was unique in his readiness to forgive sins, but I cannot agree with Pawlikowski on the issue of the kingdom. More on this later.

This leads us beyond the question of what Jesus taught to the question of who Jesus was. Having rejected the fulfillment christology of Jesus as expected Messiah and refusing to be content with Jesus as merely the opener of the covenant to gentiles, Pawlikowski approaches the core issue of Jesus' unique identity.

First of all, he notes that the synoptic Gospels (Matthew, Mark, and Luke) never conflate Jesus with God. The distinction always remains. But christology is progressive in the New Testament and in the development of Christian thought. Early Christian liturgy carried the popular view of Jesus beyond the relatively low christologies of the synoptics. Gradually the term "God" began to be used for Son as well as Father. In later New Testament writings also, the Gospel and letters of the Johannine tradition and the later letters attributed to Paul, the divinity of Jesus is stressed. This begins, in fact, with some of the letters actually written by Paul. For Pawlikowski it is this "incarnational christology" that expresses the truth of Jesus' identity and role—a truth, not incidentally, that can be held by Christians without any denigration of Judaism, unlike the messianic fulfillment christology, which relegates Judaism to a strictly pre-Jesus existence.

What this incarnational theology reveals is the humanity of God as well as the divinity of Jesus. The identity must move in both directions. This implies that every human person "is somehow divine, that he or she somehow shares the constitutive nature of God."[18] Christ is the symbol for this interpenetration of the divine and the human. The preamble to John's Gospel, with its proclamation that the word that became flesh in Jesus was in God from the beginning (John 1:1), insists that humanity was always in God; the appearance of Jesus manifested this eternal truth to all.

One can only catch one's breath at the audacity of this theological tour de force. It would seem not just that "God became man so that man might become God," but rather that God always was human, and from its creation, the human was divine. If this is the meaning of the Christ event, the message is stunning indeed. Pawlikowski insists that this new message in no way denigrates Judaism, which also stresses the divine dignity of the human person, but does not carry the theme as far as Christianity.

In my opinion, he is correct. Every theme he has mentioned as found in Jesus' preaching and church christology is also found in Judaism. This is certainly true in the case of the relationship between the human and the divine. The Hebrew Scriptures begin with the creation of humanity in the image of God. If humans are the image of the divine, then the divine is the image of the human. I would read these verses existentially to mean that to be in the image of an imageless God (no statues or pictures are permitted of the God of Israel) is to be imageless. Both God and humans are unnamable, indefinable, and irreducible to any image. "I shall be what I shall be" (Ex. 4:14) is the nameless name of humans as well as God.

Abraham's debate with God over the fate of Sodom reverses the usual categories of God as the conscience of humans. Here the human becomes the conscience of God, challenging God's humanlike temptation to use power unrestricted by full justice. Who is God here? Who is human?

And Jacob's wrestling match. Who are the participants? Is Jacob struggling with himself? Yes. With another man? Yes. With God? Yes. But in the course of the encounter, Jacob becomes Israel—"Yisra-El," "God wrestler." "El"—God—is now part of the name of the human. One cannot invoke the human without invoking the divine reality. The truly human being includes divinity in her very essence as the divine will forever show forth God's humanity.

Pawlikowski is right; this theme of the relationship of the divine and the human is Jewish (and so is that of the divine-human *interpenetration* as found in the Jacob wrestling match, although Pawlikowski denies this). But it does seem that there is a difference in degree between Jewish and Christian expressions of this luminous, astonishing idea. For Judaism God and humanity are inseparable. In the beginning God, world, and the human; there is no precreation theo-biography in the Torah. God and the human appear in the same first chapter of the story. But inseparable as they are, they remain distinct, even in the Jacob/Israel story, where they come closest to complete identification.

In Christianity, however, God and the human are both inseparable and, in Christ at least, indistinguishable (nondistinct). Does this also hold true for humanity at large? Pawlikowski stresses that Christ was unique in his oneness with the Father, and yet Pawlikowski goes on to include all persons in this human-divine blending. I find his views here to be a bit murky. He needs to spell out what he means. And reading this as a Jew, I must caution him. He seems to want it both ways. In one sense humanity is divine; in another it is distinct from God. We must remember the tempting words spoken in Eden, "you shall be as gods" (Gen. 3:5), and we must remember who spoke those words.

I deeply respect Pawlikowski's theory of who Jesus was and what he symbolized, but at day's end, I must cast my lot with the Pharisees and pull back from the precipice. Martin Buber wrote and sounded like a mystic, but he was not. And why did he always deny being so? Because he sought an

"I-Thou relationship" with the Holy One, not an ultimate union. To him the true mysticism that seeks oneness with God in loss of self through a final divine/human blending was a form of human presumption. I will not join him in that charge but simply say that, like my fellow Jews, I will rest content with a union of purpose and will with the Eternal One while always remembering as Abraham did, even as he acted as God's conscience, that "I...am but dust and ashes" (Gen. 18:27).

Pawlikowski, like Greenberg—regrettably, I think—finds it necessary to state that his religion is superior to that of the dialogue partner:

> I am professing my belief that on this point [the interpenetration of the divine and the human] Christianity has moved beyond the pale of Judaism and done this correctly.... Saying this does not fundamentally invalidate the Jewish covenant nor reduce Judaism to total inferiority vis-à-vis Christianity. It is only, but importantly, to say that I remain convinced that Christianity has the more developed understanding in this regard, an understanding I deem vital for resolving important aspects of the human condition, and that is why I choose to remain a believing Christian rather than converting to Judaism.[19]

No one could be more polite or respectful of Judaism than John Pawlikowski. But I wonder why he feels the need to say that "Christianity has the more developed understanding in this regard." Meanwhile, Irving Greenberg, who expresses profound regard for Christianity, feels the same need to say that, at least in its rabbinic period, Judaism was "a more mature mode of religion."

"More developed"—"more mature." They seem to cancel each other out. Why must we think in these terms? And, Pawlikowski adds, if he were to think otherwise, he would covert to Judaism! Well, France has a more beautiful capital city than America, it has better food and wine, its language is far more melodious. Does all this mean that I, a loyal American, should consider becoming a French citizen? On Mother's Day I send flowers to my mother, not anyone else's. Does that mean that my mother is the best mother in the world? (Of course, she is!) But if I found out that somewhere, someone else's mother was in some respect better than mine, would I send the flowers to her or petition her to adopt me?

True pluralism calls me to value the truth in all faiths, rather than arrange them in hierarchical order. "I am a Hebrew; and I fear the Lord, the God of Heaven who made the sea and the dry land" (Jon. 1:9). This is the post to which the Holy One has called me. My dialogue partner is a Christian and could make similar declarations. Let that be sufficient.

I am not persuaded by Pawlikowski's statement (he offers no argument) that "Jesus' sense of the presence of the kingdom [of God is]...the most distinctive aspect of his teaching."[20] Apparently the Jewish New Testament scholar Amy-Jill Levine has led him to this conclusion. Greenberg, too, states that, while the kingdom of God is an important minor theme in Judaism, in Jesus' teaching it is central.[21]

I agree that "the kingdom of God is at hand" (Mark 1:15) is the essential proclamation of Jesus. My objection is to any suggestion that this message makes Jesus unique. It seems to me that the kingdom theology was also essential to ancient Israelite faith and to later Judaism. My doctoral dissertation (Syracuse University, 1977) was entitled "The Kingdom of God in Jewish Theology: Myth, History and Creation." It traced the central Israelite-Jewish concepts of the kingdom and God as king from the Hebrew Scriptures, through the Middle Ages, to the present. At times Israel as kingdom was conceived historically (the period of the Davidic kings, the Maccabee monarchy, and the present-day Israelite state), at times, mythically (Israel as the people ruled by an invisible divine monarch and thus the nonpolitical kingdom of the divine king, as in the tribal confederacy, the Babylonian exile and the later world diaspora). The Sabbath, too, is to be experienced as "Kingdom Present" the title of an essay on the Sabbath I published some years ago.[22]

Thus, unless I have been laboring under a misapprehension all these years, Israelites have always conceived of themselves as dwelling in God's kingdom. That is what it means to be a Jew, subject to the king's law, rule, and revelation. The Pharisees understood the Sabbath and the people Israel as the kingdom of God in time and space, respectively. They also understood that in the future, the kingdom would shine forth undimmed in a new and powerful manifestation.

If Pawlikowski, Levine, and Greenberg are correct that Jesus taught that full flowering of the kingdom was present at hand, then the Nazarene was indeed conflating present and future senses of the term in a unique way. But is this so? Even Jesus distinguished between "realized eschatology" ("the kingdom of God is in the midst of you"; Lk.17:21) and apocalyptic eschatology (the kingdom is yet to come; Mk. 13:30). There certainly is a notable urgency in Jesus' preaching about the kingdom, but we should beware of exaggerating the alleged uniqueness of this element of his message. The kingdom of God has been a central and important concept in Israelite thought—including "kingdom present"—throughout, I believe, the history of our faith.

If Pawlikowski and Levine are claiming that the presence of the kingdom is an idea *uniquely* stressed by Jesus, or Greenberg is stating that the kingdom of God is only a minor theme in Judaism, I must strongly disagree. Nearly half a century ago, Old Testament scholar Sigmund Mowinckel made what to me is a convincing case for the centrality of the kingdom of God in Hebrew religious experience.[23] He focused on the Psalms, a number of which he titled "enthronement psalms," as hymns composed for and chanted at the great, central feast of the Lord's annual enthronement as king of Israel and the universe. Psalms 47, 93, 95, 96, 97, 98, and 99 belong to this classification.

Mowinckel demonstrated that the enthronement of God was a major motif of the New Year, Atonement, Tabernacles, tripartite Harvest-Renewal festival celebrated every autumn in Jerusalem. In the Israelite mythos God had been king of the world since creation, had become king of Israel at the establishment of the nation, and would be recognized as universal ruler at the glorious consummation of history. These and many other psalms refer clearly to all these aspects of God's kingship. The annual festival gave cultic expression to the mythos.

Eventually the theme of God as king of Israel and the world became focused in the liturgy of the New Year (Rosh Hashanah). And there we find it today in the "kingdom verses" recited as a central feature of the New Year service, incorporating nine biblical passages referring to or proclaiming joyously the kingship of the Lord. And these verses are not at all restricted to the enthronement psalms; they are drawn from Torah and prophets as well, and they testify to the absolute centrality of the concepts of the kingdom of God and God as king in Israel's faith.

And, as noted earlier, the focus was not only on God's having become king at the creation (kingdom past) or being proclaimed king at the culmination of history (kingdom future). No, God is hailed as king now (kingdom present). All Israel assembled to witness God's reenthronement every year at the great autumn festival proclaiming God's continuing present and eternal rule over Israel and the world, which are, respectively, God's micro-kingdom and macro-kingdom. If Jesus made this proclamation of the presence and coming of God's kingdom the centerpiece of his message—and I agree that he did—he was articulating with his usual power and eloquence the central proclamation of Israelite faith.

And, as it was in antiquity, so it remains. It is no exaggeration to say that dozens of times every day of his life, a pious, observant Jew proclaims, "Blessed are you, Lord our God, *king* of the universe." This is the essential form of Jewish prayer. It expresses the intense, immediate consciousness of the Jewish believer that God is king, and Israel and the whole world constitute God's kingdom, past, present, and future.

More than a century ago, Christian scholar Adolf Harnack, searching for a unique element in Jesus' teaching to distinguish him from his Jewish contemporaries, came up with the "higher righteousness," actually suggesting that Judaism was concerned with external conduct while Jesus was singular in teaching that motivation counted. One "must do right rightly," that is, for the right motive (selfless love). More recently some have suggested that in calling God "Abba," Jesus was addressing God as father in an intimate sense unknown to Judaism, which saw the Holy One as a distant monarch. Both these positions have been revealed as erroneous or at least as vast exaggerations. Once liberal Christian theologians no longer felt comfortable with strictly supernatural explanations of Jesus' uniqueness, they believed they had to come up with unique elements of his message to contrast it with Judaism in order to prove that, if he was not unique in his person, he was in his teaching.

The search for such singular aspects in Jesus' message will continue. As a Jew I am content to see him as an eloquent spokesman for a progressive form of Judaism, unburdened by legal minutiae and focused on its moral and spiritual essence. He was, of course, also a powerful proclaimer of Israel's long-established theology of the reign of God, both present and to come. And, indirectly, through his interpreters, this rabbi and prophet, who rarely, if ever, preached to non-Jews, became the occasion for the opening of the Israelite covenant to the nations. That is enough to place him among the great spiritual benefactors of humanity. But I certainly understand the desire of Christian thinkers to stress Jesus' uniqueness in one or another aspect of his message or identity. So be it. But this search should not be pursued by minimizing or passing over central themes of the faith of ancient Israel or contemporary Judaism.

Both our traditions offer riches to the world. Yet both are partial and incomplete. We are finite servants of the Infinite One who has graciously called us to be the upbuilders of God's kingdom, a kingdom already present in the people Israel, Jewish stock and Christian branch, yet a kingdom still to come in all its fullness. Let us work together for its realization, side by side, with all hints of rivalry left behind. Irving Greenberg and John Pawlikowski are two of the most productive laborers in the Lord's vineyard.

7

Into Another Intensity

Christian-Jewish Dialogue Moves Forward

Since the Second Vatican Council of 1962–65, a revolution has taken place in the views of most Christian denominations toward Jews and Judaism. Until that time Christians had seen the Jewish people and faith largely through the twin lenses of triumphalism and supersessionism. According to this view, Judaism was a used-up, virtually dead religion of the past, the Jews having given up their place as God's people to a new people of God (the church) who replaced them in the divine plan of salvation. All this happened when the Jews rejected Jesus and were, in turn, rejected by God, an event manifest to all with the destruction of the Temple in 70 c.e. This was the generally held Christian belief.

To Jews, of course, it was obviously a false belief. "The Jews" could not have "accepted "or "rejected" Jesus during his lifetime, since only 20 percent of Jews lived in the Jewish homeland, and only a small percentage of them would have had the opportunity to meet or even hear of Jesus. What had ended in 70 c.e. was not Judaism but merely one of its components, the Temple sacrificial system of the Sadducees. In fact this passing of the Temple worship led to the triumph of the rabbinic Judaism that had been developing out of Pharisaic thought in the shadow of the Temple system. Only with the Temple's destruction could the synagogue, the rabbi, the religion of Torah, prayer, and good deeds come into its own.

It was not until long after Jesus' death that large numbers of Jews heard for the first time of Jesus Christ, the God-man of Christian theology. Jewish religious leaders were busily reinterpreting Israelite faith to fit post-Temple conditions, but they could find no way or see any reason to incorporate into their faith the concept of Christ which had been developed by the Christian movement. This was true for several reasons. First of all, Jesus had not accomplished what rabbinic Judaism expected the Messiah to do. The Jesus movement had been one of the many Jewish messianisms of the first century c.e., neither more nor less legitimate than any other; but by the second century the rabbinic concept of the royal Messiah who gathers, liberates, and rules the nation had become mainstream. Second, the church presenting Jesus to the world was now a largely gentile institution; and third, the very notion of a God-man struck Jews as pagan, as did many of the ideas that became fundamental church teachings. And yet these Christians, so many of whom were gentiles, were claiming to be "the new and true Israel." Here was a situation in which Jews and Christians would inevitably be led into violent conflict. We are just now emerging from that period of conflict nearly 2,000 years later.

That began to happen with Vatican II. Many are familiar with the scores of statements reevaluating Jews and Judaism issued since 1965 by virtually every mainstream Protestant Church, as well as the three official documents on the Jews produced by the Roman Catholic Church, expanded by a number of statements by the pope and various episcopal commissions.[1] I have evaluated these statements in earlier essays and in chapter 5 of this work.[2] It seems to me that the key acknowledgment in all these statements on the Christian side of the dialogue is that *the church did not replace the Jews* with the coming of Jesus. These statements all agree that in the following 2,000 years, Jews continued to be faithful to their God and developed new and vibrant expressions of belief and practice. Jews remain a people eternally covenanted with God. Today the Roman Catholic Church as well as all mainstream Protestant churches recognize this.

For the Jewish side, the key to successful dialogue must be the recognition that through Jesus, *Christians joined Jews* in the worship of the God of Israel. Another way of putting this is that, through Jesus and his interpreters, the covenant established between God and Israel was opened to include gentiles, thus widening the meaning of *Israel* to embrace all who followed the one true God. Now, nearly 2,000 years after the initial mutual misunderstandings, Jews and Christians are at last in a position to realize what they could not have seen earlier: that Jews and Christians are, in truth, root and branch of the same ongoing covenant and that each is the fruit of divine revelation in which the one God has broken into history to reveal God's truths to two distinct but closely related communities.

For the first 2,000 years of its history, Israel was one and alone in its devotion to God and God's revealed truth. For the second 2,000 years, Israel has had two branches. Today Jewish Israelites and Christian Israelites worship the same God, using somewhat different but intimately related symbol systems. For Jews, the people Israel is *the collective individual* called by God to lead the world to redemption, to reconciliation with its Creator. Born of a miracle birth (Isaac, born to the aged Sarah and Abraham), the people Israel labors and suffers for the Kingdom of God it is called to build. Given up for dead again and again, Israel rises to new life to take up once more the work of healing a broken world.

For Christians, Jesus, born of a miracle birth, labors and suffers for the Kingdom. He too heals the sick of the world and witnesses to the presence of God. As the *single individual*, the *exemplary Israelite*, he recapitulates the history of Israel in his own life. As Israel bears the word of God (Torah) in its midst, so Jesus bears it within him. And he too suffers, dies, and returns to life. Once one realizes that what the collective individual redeemer (Israel) accomplishes in Judaism, the single individual redeemer (Jesus) does in Christianity, one is freed, as it were, to see the full power of the parallels existing between the two faiths. And one is also led to conclude that both are of God. It is with this conclusion in mind that I tend to evaluate developments in the Jewish-Christian dialogue, an ongoing encounter that I hope is moving toward the realizations outlined above.

Progress toward this end is in some ways easier for Christians. True, they will have to recognize that Judaism did not end with the coming of Jesus. For this they will be required to move beyond their own tradition to concern themselves with a religious heritage that for two millennia has paralleled their own. But since what Christians call the Old Testament has been incorporated into the authoritative text of the church (the Holy Bible), in an important way, key concepts, events, and hopes of the Hebrew Scriptures are already interior to Christian tradition. The Christian Scriptures speak in the language and represent the concepts of the earlier Hebrew text. In short, the New Testament makes, and could make, no sense without the Old. It would have no validity without the prior validity of the Hebrew Scriptures. Christians hear and read about ancient Israel every Sunday in church. They certainly recognize the connection between the Jewish family living down the street from them and the ancients they read about in their Bibles. They are in a good position to come to new realizations about that family's continuing fidelity to the Hebrew Scriptures and to the God revealed therein.

But for the Jews, a new understanding of Christians and Christianity will take them entirely beyond the parameters of their rabbinic faith and the biblical sources out of which it grew. Jews will never encounter the term "Christianity" in their biblical or rabbinic studies. The temporal priority of ancient Israel's faith and the perceived isolation of rabbinic Judaism from Christianity make the Jewish encounter with this other faith something new the minute it gets beneath the anecdotal surface level. The general Jewish view has been that Judaism has no need of Christianity for its own self-understanding. But that view ignores the ongoing influence of the surrounding Christian culture in the midst of which Judaism lived and developed its practice and thought, sometimes in imitation of the dominant faith, sometimes in contrast to it. It is also true that if Christianity parallels Judaism's work of witnessing to the world and building the Kingdom, Jews are no longer alone in their labors. Christians now work beside us to advance God's reign. A change in exterior context inevitably brings about a change in interior self-understanding. Today, in order to understand ourselves and our calling as Jews, we must look around us and see how Christian activity in the world has affected our task. That process of Jewish reevaluation of Christianity has begun.

Prior to 1965, some Jewish theologians had written of Jesus and, less frequently, of Christianity with sympathy and understanding. Notably, Martin Buber spoke of Jesus as "my great brother,"[3] and Franz Rosenzweig developed a comprehensive theory of the related roles of Judaism (the divine flame) and Christianity (the flame's rays of light) in God's plan to enlighten the world.[4] Since 1965 a number of Jewish thinkers have attempted to respond to the new Christian overtures with their own evaluations of the churches' recently more open spirit.[5] But it was not until 2000 that a group of Jewish religious thinkers produced a comprehensive statement expressing a Jewish view of the Christian faith. This statement was sponsored by the Institute of Jewish and Christian Studies of Baltimore, Maryland, a twenty-year-old group of concerned Jewish and Christian scholars, clergy, and laypeople committed to advancing understanding between the two faiths. The institute supports a wide variety of educational programs, including radio broadcasts, student essay contests, seminars, and conferences.

"Dabru Emet"

Presented as a "thoughtful Jewish response" to the dramatic shift in Christian attitudes toward Jews and Judaism, the statement "Dabru Emet" (Speak the Truth)[6] listed a series of eight points, some obvious, some quite new:

1) Jews and Christians worship the same God; 2) Jews and Christians seek authority from the same book—the Bible; 3) Christians can respect the claim of the Jewish people on the land of Israel; 4) Jews and Christians respect the moral principles of the Torah; 5) Nazism was not a Christian phenomenon; 6) The...differences between Jews and Christians will not be settled until God redeems the entire world....[Meanwhile,] *Jews can respect Christians' faithfulness to their revelation just as we expect Christians to respect our faithfulness to our revelation* [italics mine]. Neither Jews nor Christians should be pressed into affirming the teachings of the other community;[7] 7) A new relationship between Jews and Christians will not weaken Jewish practice...nor create a false blending of Judaism and Christianity. We respect Christianity as a faith that originated within Judaism....We do not see it as an extension of Judaism; 8) Jews and Christians must work together for justice and peace."[8]

For me the most important points are 1, 6, and 7. Certainly Jews and Christians worship the same God, although they have not always recognized this. While the church long ago rejected Marcion and adopted the text of the Old Testament, Christians continued to see the God of Hebrew Scripture as a "wrathful" figure as opposed to their "God of love." And Jews, reacting to the Christomonism of some Christians, concluded that the church worshiped a man rather than God. But greater familiarity with each other's texts and liturgy has led both sides to look more deeply into the complexities of the other faith. The same God is certainly the subject of both. The symbol systems are somewhat different, the styles of thought and worship as well, but Christians recognize that the God of Jesus and the church is also the God of Israel.

What is the Jewish position on these questions? In the first point of "Dabru Emet," we find that "through Christianity, hundreds of millions of people have entered into relationships with the God of Israel."[9] So the God of Christianity is Israel's God. Jews "rejoice" that the covenant has been opened to include non-Jews. It is suggested that this may, in fact, be the work that Jesus or his interpreters were sent to do. If not the Messiah according to rabbinic expectations, Jesus was an indirect agent of world salvation, since the knowledge of God has come to the nations through his church. We can see this as a partial fulfillment of Abraham's divine commission to bring blessings to all the peoples of the world (God called Abraham, out of whom came the people Israel, out of whom came Jesus, through whose interpreters came the church, from which came the knowledge of God for the peoples of the world). Judaism and Christianity are therefore two ways of relating to the one God.

Does this mean we should see them as two human paths to God, or as two divine paths to humanity? What is at stake here is the all-important issue of revelation. The question is whether we Jews can see Christianity as a revealed religion. No Jewish authority since Rabban Gamaliel, the great first-century Pharisee, has taken that view, and even he raised it as a possibility, not a conclusion. Of course, Gamaliel's alleged view that Christianity may be "of God" (Acts 5:33–39) is reported in the New Testament and may be somewhat tendentious. Many would dismiss it as Christian propaganda. If he said it, he was certainly the most open-minded character in the New Testament, the only one prepared to consider the possibility of more than one religious truth. But, while the authenticity of the Gamaliel quote remains unproved, in "Dabru Emet's" sixth point we hear an echo of its willingness to entertain the truth claims of the religious "other." In this statement we seem to find a contemporary Jewish affirmation of the view that both Judaism and Christianity are products of genuine revelation.

Here we read: "Jews can respect Christians' faithfulness to their revelation just as we expect Christians to respect our faithfulness to our revelation."[10] This is, I believe, the first time this crucial issue has been met head-on by Jewish theologians and formulated in a positive manner. The text is clear; Christians as well as Jews have received a divine revelation, an in-breaking into history by God—the one God, the God of Israel—who is also revealed through the life, words, and deeds of Jesus. It is this that constitutes the revelation to which Christians are faithful. It is called here a *revelation*, not an earthly symbol system or a humanly created religion.

Now Christians have always held that ancient Israelite faith was of God and that it originated in historical communications (revelations) from God containing information about the world, instruction in the divine plan, and ethical and moral laws to live by. And, of course, Christians believe that God has broken into history yet again to reveal truth in and through Jesus. Are the authors of "Dabru Emet" agreeing with this latter claim? It would appear so. It is significant that in this statement the word "revelation" is used of Christianity by Jewish religious thinkers for the first time. This is an important breakthrough that in no way diminishes Judaism. Rather, it affirms what thoughtful Jews must have long suspected. The God of all humanity could not have restricted divine religious concerns to one tiny group of people. If the Creator loves all humanity, providing sun and rain, the earth and its beauties, food and water for all, how could we imagine that God is indifferent to the spiritual well-being of everyone but the Jews? Surely God would speak to more than these. If some 2 billion people worship the God of Israel as revealed through Jewish scriptures *and* in Jesus, can we view it as some kind of accident, or is it part of the same divine plan initiated through Abraham? ("In you shall all the nations of the world be blessed"; Gen. 12:3). "Dabru Emet" is suggesting the latter explanation in stating clearly that Christianity is a revealed religion. This makes "Dabru Emet" unique and a major advance on the Jewish side of the dialogue.

I find myself in some disagreement with the formulations in the seventh point of the statement: "We respect Christianity as a faith that originated within Judaism....We do not see it as an extension of Judaism." There is something unsatisfactory about the way this has been put. Might it not be preferable to see *both* Christianity and rabbinic Judaism as *extensions of ancient Israelite faith?* There were once others. Essenes, Sadducees, Zealots, and other groups that produced the richly varied intertestamental books were all expressions of Israelite faith, all "Judaisms" of the period between the testaments. Two of those Judaisms, the followers of Jesus, sometimes called the Nazarene movement, and the Pharisees survived the Roman wars. The first fed into early Christianity; the second developed into rabbinic Judaism. Both were grounded in their particular interpretations of the Hebrew Scriptures; both eventually added new sacred writings through which they read the commonly inherited text. It would be futile to attempt to determine which of these movements reflects the faith of ancient Israel more closely or exactly. Both differ greatly from ancient Israelite practice. Would Moses be any more at home in a modern synagogue than in a church? Both Jews and Christians have produced—or been guided by God to—new things. Which is newer, which is older, which is more biblical? Such attempts at legitimizing ourselves at the expense of the other are unworthy of either people of God. Each of us feels that we are extensions of the faith of the Hebrew Scriptures. And so we are, although we have each "extended" that tradition in unique though related ways.

"Dabru Emet" is a significant accomplishment, a worthy response to the many Christian statements on Judaism that cried out for Jewish acknowledgment and reaction. Once the church had affirmed the ongoing validity of the Jewish covenant in the 2,000 years since the Christ event, conditions were right for Jews to affirm the validity of God's later covenant with the nations through Christianity. Neither of these moves was easy for either party. Monotheistic religions tend to make universal claims. We both still make such claims, but not in the exclusivist way we once did. We have learned that it is possible to affirm the truth of one's own faith tradition without having to devalue or deny the truth claims of the other faith. This is especially true of Judaism and Christianity, sister faiths, both daughters of an ancient Israelite mother and joined in common memory and shared hope.

"A Sacred Obligation"

In September 2002, in response to "Dabru Emet," the Christian Scholars Group on Christian-Jewish Relations issued its ten-point statement: "A Sacred Obligation: Rethinking Christian Faith in Relation to Judaism and the Jewish People."[11] The Scholars Group has existed since its establishment in 1969 by the Faith and Order Commission of the National Council of Churches. Currently it is partnered with the Center for Christian-Jewish Learning of Boston College. It is made up of leading Protestant, Catholic, and Orthodox scholars and holds regular meetings devoted to various aspects of Jewish-Christian relations. The following are the statement's ten headings:

1. God's covenant with the Jewish people endures forever.
2. Jesus of Nazareth lived and died as a faithful Jew.
3. Ancient rivalries must not define Christian-Jewish relations today.
4. Judaism is a living faith, enriched by many centuries of development.
5. The Bible both connects and separates Jews and Christians.
6. Affirming God's enduring covenant with the Jewish people has consequences for Christian understandings of salvation.
7. Christians should not target Jews for conversion.
8. Christian worship that teaches contempt for Judaism dishonors God.
9. We affirm the importance of the land of Israel for the life of the Jewish people;
10. Christians should work with Jews for the healing of the world.[12]

This statement is important because it states explicitly and in one place a number of ideas only hinted at in prior church pronouncements. The Scholars Group, aware of the delicacy and complexity of these issues, deliberately chose direct and unequivocal language so that its views would not be seen as ambiguous by later interpreters.

In the first point, they reject supersessionism absolutely. "God does not revoke divine promises. . . . God is in covenant with both Jews and Christians." They affirm "the abiding validity of Judaism."[13] This is the key move for Christians in the dialogue. Without it all theological conversation must cease. Jews will not long continue to talk with people who refuse to see their faith as valid or, indeed, as a living reality. Of course, Christians who see Judaism as a fossil will, for their part, have little interest in the dialogue.

As discussed earlier in this book, the point that "God does not revoke divine promises" has been developed elsewhere by Clark Williamson, one of the signers of "A Sacred Obligation." His argument is that if God would break what the Torah had described as an *eternal* covenant with Israel, due, presumably, to Israelites' sins, what would keep God from breaking the eternal covenant with the church whose members are also guilty of sin. Seen in this light, the traditional Christian supersessionist theory that Israel once possessed but later lost its covenant relationship with God would call into question the reliability of all of God's promises and undermine the Christian's certainty of "standing on" those very promises. Here is another reason, one centered on Christian self-conception, for moving beyond all supersessionist theories.

The third point, regarding past Jewish-Christian rivalries, focuses on the anti-Jewish passages in the New Testament. It asks the churches to recognize what scholars have known for a century and a half: that these confrontational passages reflect the mutual hostility between rabbinic and Nazarene Judaism (proto-Christianity) of the late first century. Vying with each other for the title of "true Israel," the parties engaged in fierce mutual name-calling. Some passages in the Gospels reflect this conflict within the Jewish community. These anti-Jewish passages should not guide Christians today any more than Jews should cling to ancient rabbinic denunciations of early Christianity. Once again, if only we would let the implications of Gamaliel's words in Acts guide us, we could break down our exclusivist prejudices and affirm the truth of both traditions.

The fourth point expands on the first. Freed from its ties to the ancient Temple worship, rabbinic Judaism came into its own. Both Jeremiah and Jesus had recognized the inadequacy of the Temple cult to express the higher spiritual aspirations of Israel's faith. Prophetic faith had grown up as one alternative, then the prayer life of the synagogue, then the religion of Jesus and that of the rabbis. It took the Roman legions to finally sweep the Temple away and to open the way for rabbinic Judaism and Christianity. Both stressed prayer, repentance, and righteousness with God's grace ever-present to make up for our failures in achieving the last of these. Through Torah and this new Judaism, Jews have lived out their faith for two millennia. Through Christ and church, Christians have lived theirs. In each case, this history reveals the divine hand. Neither faith can understand itself without understanding the role of the other in God's plan.

The sixth point returns to this issue, demonstrating how the realization of the ongoing life of Jewry and Judaism is crucial to Christianity's self-understanding. This may be the most radical point of this statement and the one that will prove to be the most controversial. It must be quoted in full:

6. Affirming God's enduring covenant with the Jewish people has consequences for Christian understanding of salvation.

Christians meet God's saving power in the person of Jesus Christ and believe that this power is available to all people in him. Christians have therefore taught for centuries that salvation is available only through Jesus Christ. With their recent realization that God's covenant with the Jewish people is eternal, Christians can now recognize in the Jewish tradition the redemptive power of God at work. If Jews, who do not share our faith in Christ, are in a saving covenant with God, then Christians need new ways of understanding the universal significance of Christ.[14]

This is a very complex issue and a fascinating one. On the one hand, Christians have long believed that salvation is available to all the peoples of the world through Jesus Christ and only through him. On the other, many Christians have now come to realize that God's covenant with the Jews is eternal and still salvific after Jesus as it was before. What, then, of the universal claim of salvation only through Christ? Can these two views be reconciled? This statement holds only that "Christians need new ways of understanding the universal significance of Christ." It does not suggest what those ways may be. However, significantly, it does not say that Christians should give up the claim of "the universal significance of Christ," only that they need to rethink it. What might that rethinking look like?

Evangelical Protestants (according to polls, 46 percent of our American population) will resist such a rethinking. For them, every individual must consciously accept the salvation offered by Christ and recognize Jesus as personal savior. But there are other possibilities.

It has been said in Catholic statements (one by the pope himself) that, while Jesus is the necessary vehicle of salvation for all, one need not recognize this to benefit from his saving act on the cross.[15] Christ died for all. He opens heaven to all who live according to conscience and do their utmost to adhere to the moral law. They may never have heard of Jesus or may even be hostile to him because of their upbringing. But if they try to be good people according to their best lights, they can be saved through Christ. Jews will, of course, find this view strange, but, according to its universalist logic, if they are good Jews, they too will be saved by Christ.

Interestingly, this rather benevolent (if somewhat condescending) approach is sometimes coupled with a denial of the view stated in "A Sacred Obligation" that the Jewish covenant is or ever was salvific. It is Christ and Christ alone who saves both in Old Testament times and today. The Catholic "inclusivist" theory can be held together with the ancient story that the Patriarchs and heroes of the Hebrew Scriptures were not, in fact, saved until the coming of Jesus and his descent into Limbo on Holy Saturday. This account illustrates the belief that Jesus' salvific act was retroactive and that even the earlier generations were saved by the eternal work of Christ. Again, Jews would find all this alien to their self-understanding. But this is a theory for Christians, not Jews. It offers them a way to maintain the universal applicability of Christ's self-sacrifice without condemning to Hell people who never heard of Jesus or, having heard, fail to accept him due to non-Christian upbringing. Certainly, in terms of our concept of God as loving and righteous, this theory (inclusivism) is a great improvement over the exclusivist version of salvation only for those who accept Christ as personal savior.

Liberal Protestants, like Catholics, have sought to overcome exclusivism. Christ's death and resurrection were for all, not just Christian believers. Most broadly conceived, this would be expressed in a formula something like that used by a former pastor of the First Presbyterian Church on lower Fifth Avenue in New York. At lunch one day, I asked him to be absolutely honest with his Jewish dining companion. Did he or did he not believe that salvation was available only through Christ? He put down his fork and thought deeply for a few minutes before answering. "Yes," he replied, "salvation is of and through Christ. By Christ I mean the Word of God. That Word is spoken to me through Jesus of Nazareth, the Word made flesh. It is spoken to you through Torah and your membership in the Israel of God." I replied that, in my view, he and all Christians are Israelites (God wrestlers), members of the Christian branch of Israel. His view seemed to complement mine from the Christian perspective. Jewish Israelites are a people who are collectively the enfleshment of Torah, the Word of God, as is Christ in the New Testament. This is surely "inclusivism" in its most comprehensive expression. And since this theory identifies Christ as the Word of God operative in Judaism as well as in Jesus, this is an inclusivism that is, in practical effect, pluralism

If one were to go beyond this view, one would arrive at a full-blown self-conscious pluralism. Some liberal Christian thinkers have gone there already. John Hick[16] and Paul Knitter[17] come to mind. But they differ in crucial ways. For Hick, religions are humanly created symbol systems a number of which can get one to God, or the "Real," as he prefers to call it. Any one of them—or all of them—is true if they produce virtuous people. This is truth seen not in terms of a religion's being an accurate reflection of the divine reality but as producing a desired end. Religions are like diets. A diet aims at producing a slim and healthy person. Any number of diets work—as long as you follow them. Religions seek to produce virtuous and God-fearing people. Many of them work and are thus "true" in this functional sense. For Hick, God reveals only God's reality, God's existence itself. All the rest of religion is human. The problem with this version of pluralism is that it seems alien to the lived experience of the believer in the pew who is convinced that the content of his faith is divinely revealed. Of course, in presenting this view, Hick is writing as a philosopher of religion, not as a theologian analyzing the truth claims of a particular creedal system. If theologians let themselves get too far from the religious experience of their fellow believers, they may be doing philosophy of religion, but not theology, which must be based on the living tradition of a particular faith as experienced by its members.

Paul Knitter has, in my view, a theory of pluralism more responsive to the demands of theology. He holds that religions are not human paths to God, but divine revelations to human beings. In other words, revelation has a complex content. More than just God's existence is revealed. A varied message is given by God to God's people, including doctrines, ethics, mytho-historical accounts, and theological truths. And he reverses the direction of all this content. It is not a human production enlarged and flung out at the heavens, but a divine revelation that comes to us from God. His theory is pluralistic because he holds that God sends different revelations to different people at different points in history. Thus Judaism is the revelation of God's message and purpose to the Jews, and Christianity is a revelation of God to the gentiles. Both are true; both are of God.

From what I have already written, it should be obvious that I think he is right on target. Without revelation, there can be no religion. Without revelation, we are left with a one-way road from the human to God. This is what I would call spirituality, an expression of the human capacity for self-transcendence. But for what I mean by religion, one must hear the voice of the God who says, "thou shalt" and "thou shalt not." That voice will be heard by different people, at different times, in different ways, and one hearing need not cancel out the others. In Jewish terms, God did choose Israel as God's elect people; but who says God can make only one choice?

It appears that the authors of "A Sacred Obligation" probably have some formulation in mind short of full-blown pluralism, perhaps a variation on the Presbyterian minister's inclusive formula, which is indeed a "new way of understanding the universal significance of Christ."

The seventh point is important. Sensitive Christians of many denominations have come to understand how insulting it is to Jews to urge them to give up the faith that defines and expresses their relationship to God. The Catholic Church long ago dismantled its Office for the Conversion of the Jews. Its aim is now partnership with Jews in healing the world (the tenth point in this statement), rather than conversion. Pope John Paul II has declared that the very existence of Jews today as a flourishing religious community demonstrates this people's fidelity to God and God's fidelity to them. Fifty years ago a pope would have said it proved how stubborn and stiff-necked the sons and daughters of Jacob were in their refusal to accept Jesus. Quite a change!

Christians had long considered Judaism an "incomplete Christianity." But if we properly understand ourselves, *both* Jews and Christians are incomplete. We both await the complete knowledge that will come with the unfolding of the Kingdom. We are "partners in waiting." There will come a day when "all will worship God with one voice." Until then we Jews and Christians who await the Messiah differ as to his identity and as to whether he has been here before. But is this difference a fatal one? Hardly. It gives us so much of importance to discuss while we are waiting and laboring for the redemption.

In Julius Caesar (5.1), Brutus says his farewell to Cassius:

> O that a man might know
> The end of this day's business, ere it come:
> But it sufficeth that the day will end,
> And then the end is known.

Let it suffice us that this human day will end and at last we shall look upon the face of King Messiah. Then we shall know him even as he knows us. For now, we wait and we work, faithful to the truths that have been revealed to us in this dispensation.

The eighth point brings up a crucial issue which I have discussed at some length earlier in this work and which should surely be the next step for churches in dialogue with Jews: lectionary reform. As noted previously, passages in the New Testament express the Christian side of the late first-century and early second-century hostility between proto-rabbinic Jews and early Christians. John's indiscriminate use of the terms "Jew" or "the Jews" could better be rendered in the lectionary to say what he really meant. Terms like "Jesus' opponents" or "the authorities" or "the crowd" would convey the meaning of the text more faithfully. There are some passages that probably should not be read publicly at all, at least without explanation by the clergy on hand. Since this cannot usually be counted on, some sections, certainly some read during Holy Week, should be changed for less inflammatory and more accurate readings. It should be possible "to tell the old, old story," focusing on "Jesus and his love," rather than hate for or anger toward anyone, especially a whole people, the one from whom Jesus came.

Overall, "A Sacred Obligation" is a splendid and comprehensive statement, a landmark of reconciliation in the history of the new relationship between Jews and Christians. It is a worthy response to "Dabru Emet."

"Reflections on Covenant and Mission"

In August 2002, "Reflections on Covenant and Mission" was issued by the delegates of the Bishops' Committee for Ecumenical and Interreligious Affairs (Roman Catholic) and the National Council of Synagogues (Conservative and Reform Jews). These two groups of clergypersons were established some twenty years ago by their respective churches and synagogues and have been meeting twice a year since then to discuss issues in the ongoing dialogue between the faiths. "Reflections" was a joint statement but not a shared one. Each faith produced a separate reflection on covenant and mission. It must be said that what the two sides produced is strangely unbalanced, even unrelated. The Catholic statement deals extensively with Jews and questions of mission to Jews, while the Jewish statements hardly mentions Christians and says nothing at all about Christian theology or religious claims and beliefs. There is one passing reference to the fact that Jews await the Messiah while Christians await the Second Coming. This is pointed to as a significant difference. That's it for reflections on Christian religious thought. Following this, the Jewish statement elaborates on common social action Jews and Christians can undertake to make a better world. Earlier there is offered an excellent survey of Jewish faith developed historically via the scriptural story of Israel. As a Jewish document it is fine as far as it goes, but as part of a joint statement issued together with Christians, it is woefully lacking. It says nothing of interest about Christianity. It offers no new insights on the Catholic faith of those producing the twin statement. Indeed, it all but ignores the other participant as a religious community.

Perhaps the problem was the subject matter: covenant and mission. Catholics cannot address the topic of mission without speaking of Jews, whom they have been trying to convert for nearly 2,000 years. For Jews, mission has not entailed converting others for nearly as long a time. It has to do with building the Kingdom of God in the human community in a moral and ethical sense. Jews have realized for many centuries that you do not have to be Jewish to be moral. Indeed, the statement quotes Jewish tradition that "the righteous of all nations have a share in the world to come."[18] Why, then, try to make them Jews? Jews are to live morally and witness to the universal moral law to all peoples. It is morality, not Judaism, that all people must accept. Since Jews have not seen their mission as conversionary for some seventeen centuries, there was no need in this statement to do more than renounce such activity once in passing.

Still one feels that a great opportunity was lost here to raise the question of whether Christianity is a covenantal faith, and if so, whether it is an ex-

INTO ANOTHER INTENSITY 179

tension of Israel's covenant or a distinct new covenant. The Jewish participants took the easy path. They fell back on the usual practice of speaking of
God's love for all peoples and the equality of all human souls (Jewish and non-
Jewish) before God. This is the easy path because it is taken to avoid discussing Christianity and Christians as such. So the question of whether
Christianity is of divine origin, or merely a human product, is avoided, as are
the work, mission, and teachings of Christianity beyond social action in the
world. True, the call to engage in joint social and political activities with
Christians would probably not have been part of a Jewish statement fifty years
ago. But too many Jewish statements are stuck at that point. "Dabru Emet"
was the groundbreaking exception. One would have thought that after its
appearance, there could be no going back. But here we are, two years later,
back at the old social action stand.

Another explanation for this theological reticence may be that this statement was written by synagogue groups, the Conservative and Reform Movements. "Dabru Emet" was issued by a group of theologians who did not have
to answer to boards of rabbis or lay organizations. The fact is that no official
branch of Judaism has ever issued a statement on Christianity. The United
Synagogue of Conservative Judaism has addressed the question of God's
dealing with non-Jews in the general terms of the old seven Noahide laws that
outline the moral rules all peoples must follow. This discussion is found in
"Emet ve-Emunah" (Truth and Faith),[19] issued by the United Synagogue
some years ago. In fact, the present statement falls back on the Noahide laws.
But these laws are for gentiles in general. Never are Christianity or Christians
as such dealt with in terms of their religious claims and beliefs. This is utterly
inadequate as part of a joint Christian-Jewish statement today.

For their part, the Catholic participants speak directly and in an admirably
progressive spirit to issues of vital concern to Jews. Their statement recapitulates earlier Catholic statements and restates essential points in a refresh-
ingly direct fashion. And they go further, taking a step into what one of its
framers has called "*de facto* pluralism." They speak of Jews as "the present-day
people of the covenant concluded with Moses. . . . partners in a covenant of
eternal love which was never revoked"[20] They note that Catholic belief in the
permanence of the Jewish people's covenant with God has led them to a "new
positive regard for the post-biblical or rabbinic Jewish tradition."[21] They call
upon Catholics to note the continuing fecundity of Judaism and to observe it
to help their own self-understanding as Catholics. Past persecution of Jews
is denounced, Jewish survival is seen as part of "God's design,"[22] and rabbinic Judaism seen as being "of God."[23] This has never been said so strongly
before.

These Catholic authors go on to redefine evangelization in new ways. The church must evangelize. This means that it must work for world liberation from evil. This evil includes religious bigotry. Thus interfaith dialogue is part of evangelization, and it must be "devoid of any intention whatsoever to invite the dialogue partner to baptism."[24] They go on to speak of Christianity's unique relationship with Judaism: both share the Hebrew Scriptures, the hope for the coming Kingdom of God, and the obligation to prepare the world for its advent. Thus the church "shares a central and defining task with the Jewish people."[25] The statement notes the sad history of forced conversion of Jews and points to the passing away decades ago of the Catholic Church's Office for the Conversion of the Jews. Indeed, missionary activities "are not appropriately directed at Jews."[26] This is because "mission...refers to the conversion from false gods...to the true and one God....Jews...[already] believe in the true and one God."[27]

Developing this thought, the statement goes on to quote Cardinal Walter Kasper, president of the Pontifical Commission for the Religious Relations with the Jews. His words, first articulated in May 2001, are repeated here as expressing the views of this bishops' committee: "God's Grace, which is the grace of Jesus Christ according to our faith, is available to all. Therefore, the church believes that Judaism, as the faithful response of the Jewish people to God's irrevocable covenant, is salvific for them, because God is faithful to his promises."[28]

Now this statement is not official Church policy, which continues to be the inclusivism discussed earlier. With this in mind, I invite the reader to look again at Cardinal Kasper's statement. The question is whether the cardinal is expressing the official inclusivist view or a new pluralist perspective. If the latter is the case, he is saying that it is "God's grace" that saves. For Christians, that grace takes the form of "the grace of Jesus Christ," but for Jews it is found in "God's irrevocable covenant," which is equally salvific for them. It is not Christ who saves "even Jews," but divine grace that saves all through both Christ and Judaism. This is true religious pluralism. But if we read the cardinal's statement in an inclusivist manner, then God's grace is always "the grace of Jesus Christ," which for Jews is expressed through "God's irrevocable covenant." According to a clarification issued by Dr. Phillip A. Cunningham,[29] one of the framers of "Reflections on Covenant and Mission," both "Reflections" and Cardinal Kasper's statement in their "twin affirmations of Israel's ongoing covenantal life and of the universality of Christ are closer to what might be called a 'de facto pluralism.'" This position, while seeming self-contradictory to Jews, enables Catholics to affirm both the salvific power of Judaism and the presence of Christ as mediator of salvation to all. As I read it,

Cardinal Kaspar's statement is sufficiently ambiguous to give rise to some very stimulating discussions and debates among theologians of the dialogue. As I have said, pluralism is not the official view of the church; it may never be. But as I read Cardinal Kasper's statement, it could indicate a development in Catholic thinking that may yet bear fruit. Meanwhile, even Catholic inclusivism is opposed by some in the church. Indeed, the cover story of *America* magazine in fall of 2002 dealt with the problems created for Christianity by the bishops' statement. In this article, Cardinal Avery Dulles denounced the bishops' statement and invoked old supersessionist ideas.[30] Appealing to the New Testament's Letter to the Hebrews, with its relentless supersessionist message, Dulles, as if awakening from a theological slumber of nearly four decades, seemed unaware of his church's current position on Jews and Judaism. For him there can be no question of the salvific power of the divine covenant with the Jews, since that covenant was superseded and replaced by Christ and Christianity 2,000 years ago. Three leading Catholic participants in the dialogue (including Dr. Cunningham) responded to the cardinal's statement, pointing out that biblical literalism is foreign to a church that believes in the ongoing interpretation of Scripture by its Magisterium.[31] The dispute will continue over an issue that is, to me, one of the most pressing and fascinating in the dialogue.

"Reflections" goes on to quote then-Cardinal Joseph Ratzinger (later to become Pope Benedict XVI): "God's providence . . . has obviously given Israel a particular mission in this 'time of the Gentiles.' "[32] Thus the church's mission "no longer included the wish to absorb the Jewish faith into Christianity and so end the distinctive witness of Jews to God in human history."[33] As the statement nears its close, it proclaims once more that "Jews already dwell in a saving covenant with God" and so must not be subjected to conversionary efforts. To those who would cite the "great commission" of the resurrected Christ to convert the world (Matt. 28:19), the authors note that Jesus on this occasion commanded his disciples to go to "all nations" (*kal goyim*), meaning to gentile nations, not to Jews. They are on firm ground here, as I and others have written. When Jews spoke (or speak) of *goyim*, they mean peoples other than Jews. It is true that during his life, Jesus called Jews, but he called them to be better Jews; he could hardly have been calling them to become Christians.

One could read many seemingly exclusivist New Testament passages in an inclusivist or even pluralist manner. When Jesus says, "No one comes to the father except through me," we might interpret this to refer to living the kind of self-sacrificial life he led, not to a need to confess him as savior. Alternately, one might read it as Rosenzweig did, to refer to gentiles who are far from the Father and must come via Jesus. It could not refer to Jews who are already with the Father. They must work on the relationship they have, but they are already where the gentile convert to Christianity wants to be.

This statement—at least its Catholic half—is an extraordinary expression of the new sprit of openness toward Jews and Judaism animating the Catholic Church and the mainstream churches of the Protestant world. There are still many holdouts who interpret their faith in exclusivist ways. But even they must acknowledge that there are other ways to be faithful Christians, ways that do not entail denying the validity of the Jewish faith whose patterns of thought and practice are so similar to theirs.

Likewise, there are Jews who still resist looking around them and seeing that they are no longer alone in building the Kingdom. The God of Israel is the God of all humankind. God would not leave the whole world, outside of some 15 million chosen, without spiritual direction. If God has chosen (as God apparently has done) to open the covenant to include the gentiles—and if God has done this through Jesus and his interpreters—why should we Jews not rejoice as we see the nations come to know the God we cherish above all else? The words of the psalmist are being fulfilled: "From the rising of the sun to its going down, the name of the Lord shall be praised" (Ps. 113:3).

8

Truth and Fact in Religious Narrative

Interfaith dialogue as I envision it goes much further than mutual respect. Ultimately mutual influence is the goal. Given the pluralist theory of multiple revelations I have presented in this work, such cross-fertilization between faiths would be inevitable. If the divine revelations that established each religious community are, necessarily, finite, then the valid but limited revelation that gave rise to one faith would be no more or less "true" than that which brought another into being. Since each is a finite revelation of the one infinite God—as each must be, since we, the recipients, are finite, thus incapable of receiving an infinite message—then the other faith may have received another finite disclosure of truth. In dialogue, each of us can come to learn and be enlarged by the truth cherished by the other group but hitherto unknown to us. Where one faith is strong, the other may be weak; thus, by sharing our insights with each other, we all grow closer to a fuller understanding of the purposes of the infinite God.

In dialogue we all grow together, learning from and teaching our brothers and sisters of all faith communities. As pointed out earlier in this work, the truth claims of each of the faiths to bear a revealed message can only be evaluated in terms of their ethical and spiritual fruits. "By their fruits you shall know them" (Matt. 7:15–16). All of them must lead their adherents to self-transcending lives of respect for the dignity of all people, reverence for all forms of life, for the earth itself, and for the divine source of all things. Pluralists will consider all such faiths to be "true" in this performative sense. But while all these "true" faiths will adhere to shared ethical and spiritual standards, their truth claims must be further examined.

Traditionally all religions have claimed to be true in that their descriptions of the divine are accurate depictions of the way God "really" is in heaven. But, since human epistemological capacity is not adequate to "know" the state of the transcendent reality in question, pluralists discard this "correspondence theory" of religious truth as indemonstrable, indeterminable, and thus irrelevant. If I were to say that it is raining outside, the truth of my words would be easily demonstrable. I would simply walk to the window, extend my arm outside, and make a conclusion based on whether water was falling on my hand from the sky. But how do I test the truth claims for statements about a heavenly reality beyond all possible earthly experience? And how do we deal with the earthly claims of the religious narratives? In what sense does a Jew accept the truth of the miraculous stories in the Hebrew Scriptures or a Christian affirm the equally "supernatural" accounts in the New Testament?

First of all we must ask if, from a religious point of view, the natural-supernatural distinction is necessary or helpful. More than 200 years ago liberal theologian Friedrich Schleiermacher (1768–1834), rejecting the traditional understanding of "miracle," redefined the word to mean any event originating in God.[1] Now, as seen through the eyes of faith, every so-called natural event can ultimately be traced back to God. There may be a long line of intermediate causes between the happening and the ultimate divine source, but God is always the necessary first cause. Thus, the daily flowing of the Red Sea is as "miraculous" as the division of that body of water at the command of Moses. Actually it was the command of God that split the sea and put it there in the first place. How does the former event differ from the latter? It differs in frequency. The sea split only once; it flows on over the centuries. Schleiermacher concludes that "miracle" is simply a religious person's term for a so-called natural event.

Taking the argument one step further, it becomes clear that the "natural-supernatural" distinction is only needed by people who have given up, in a religious sense, on nature. That is, they are unable to find evidence of God's hand in the "ordinary" events of daily life. They are blind to the miraculousness of the everyday. Could it be that the miracle stories in the Bible are meant to point us to a view of reality in which there is no supernatural realm because there is nothing that we should define as natural? All is God's creation, "the theater of God's glory." The spacious firmament and every blade of grass cry out together, "the hand that made us is divine." In the world and the words of the Bible, there is no concept or term for nature. In fact, one might view the Bible as an extended polemic against the concept of nature. Nothing is natural; all is divine creation.

Nature or creation: the difference between these two terms reflects a vast gulf between two worldviews. Dr. George Brantl, the founder and first chairman of the Department of Philosophy and Religion at Montclair State University, used to say that the difference between the nonreligious person and the religious one is this: the nonreligious person stands in the midst of a field of daisies and says without affect or enthusiasm, "Look, daisies." The religious person stands amid the same flowers and exclaims with joy and rapture, "Look! Daisies!" One sees "mere" nature and dismisses it; the other is dazzled by the glories of the radiant creation. He stands before the miracle—the miracle that is in the eye of the religious beholder.

Logically, of course, if one views the world as "nature," one looks into it to discover its source; if one sees the world as "creation," one looks beyond it to find its cause. "Nature" implies no reality beyond itself; "creation" points to—requires—a Creator in the very definition of the term. The latter conception is self-transcending—like the religious person himself; the former is not. In the Gospel of Thomas, Jesus is asked where the Kingdom of God may be found. He replies: "The Kingdom of the Father is spread out upon the earth, but men do not see it" (Thomas 113). The Jews are told in their popular lore to be prepared for every newborn baby to be the Messiah. Every birth is a miracle birth, not just that of Adam's son, which causes his mother Eve to exclaim, "I have gotten a man with the help of the Lord" (Gen. 4:1). Every birth requires divine aid. The story of the miracle birth of Isaac to the hundred-year-old Abraham and the ninety-year-old Sarah is surely an account of a miracle, but one that is no more miraculous than the astounding conduct of sperm and egg that gives rise to every new human life.

Are we to label as "miraculous" only the rare aberrations or irregularities within a reality we otherwise label as "mere" nature? Or are we to call a miracle only an event that occurs at just the right time to benefit or save us? Is Jewish survival over all the centuries a miracle? To believing Jews, of course it is. Others would disagree. And what about the rebirth of Zion after 2,000 years of exile? Again, the miraculousness would depend on one's larger worldview.

The issue of miracles, of how the Holy One acts in the world to guide history and of how we perceive the divine hand, is one of the great issues of theology. Jews and Christians struggle with such questions in their respective traditions of thought. The problem takes on a new dimension if we examine it in the context of interfaith dialogue. If our traditions have difficulty deciding how to define or evaluate the miraculous claims in our own faiths, how then are we to evaluate the miracle stories of the other's narrative?

Each faith tradition presents its worldview in a book or, more commonly, a library of books, such as the Bible. These books are written by many human authors, but the faithful believe them to be, in some sense, divinely inspired. But on what basis does a Jew accept as binding the thirty-nine books of the Hebrew Scriptures and the many subsequent commentaries, while rejecting other books that are similar in tone and message such as the New Testament? On what basis does a Christian accept the Hebrew Scriptures minus the Jewish commentaries, but *plus* the New Testament? What leads a Mormon to accept both the Hebrew Scriptures and the New Testament plus the Book of Mormon, the Pearl of Great Price and Doctrine and Covenants? And on what basis does a Muslim reject the accounts in Hebrew Scriptures and New Testament while adopting their characters and presenting their stories in altered (or, as claimed, in "original") form in the Qur'an? From some imagined "objective" exterior point of observation, such choices appear totally arbitrary. One views as sacred the books one has been raised to see in such terms. And usually, one dismisses as nonbinding on oneself the writings of other traditions. In fact a believer in one religion frequently holds all others— together with their texts—to be false. Again, such decisions appear, to the outside observer, to be quite baseless in logic. And so they are.

Logic has nothing to do with such choices. Religious people are deeply involved with the sacred as revealed in their particular traditions. Their take on such matters is profoundly subjective. Søren Kierkegaard compares them to lovers.[2] In fact they are lovers of God. As expressed by the prophets, Israelite faith is a love relationship between Israel and God. Can a believer, prodded by a nonbelieving critic, really consider the possibility that his God is unreal or that there is another God he might just as easily have come to love? Suppose one were to say to an earthly lover of an earthly beloved, that, had he not visited the theater that night or not gone for that walk on that particular street, he might never have met his beloved, would have met and fallen in love with another, and might today be married to a different person? If he could seriously ponder this possibility, accepting the arbitrariness or chance character of his love relationship, he would cease to be a lover. As a lover, all he knows is "this is my beloved."[3] On this he takes his stand; in this love he lives his life. The same is true for a religious believer. He, too, is a lover, but his beloved is no earthly wife or sweetheart. He is in love with the Holy One of Israel—or Christ—or Allah.

The prophets present the relationship as one between a divine father and a human child, Israel (Isaiah, Jeremiah), or as between a divine husband and human wife, Israel (Hosea, Jeremiah). The Song of Songs is interpreted by the rabbis as a love song between two lovers, Israel and her divine beloved. So, the religious lover lives in the profound subjective depths of his love for his beloved creator, sustainer, and redeemer. He "feels" in his bones and "knows" in his heart that his tradition's texts testify to the true nature of the object of his love. But while this conviction of truth is surely properly identified as "feeling," in what sense is it "knowledge," properly so called?

Clearly it is not. As we said earlier, its truth claims are nondemonstrable. How can one measure the "truth" of a religious claim? I know that I am sitting in this chair with this pen in my hand. I can demonstrate that. All the terms of my claim are measurable in finite, physical ways. In other words, the correspondence theory of truth is operative here. My words about the chair and the pen are true because they correspond to physical facts that are observable and testable. But religious claims are quite different. The sentence "I know that I am sitting here" uses the word "know" far differently than does the phrase "I know that my redeemer liveth." What is the difference? We have already observed that one claim is demonstrable while the other is not. And yet, is it not strange that when people choose to live or die for a truth, it is always a nondemonstrable truth they choose? Duty, honor, country, love, the good—God. People do not live their lives or give their lives for chairs and fountain pens. Logical certainty or physical obviousness have little to do with the world of subjective truths we human beings inhabit. The truths we live and die for are not the trivial facts of the visible world. All facts are not truths. I lift up the water glass; a fact, hardly a truth. God loves me; a truth, but is it a fact? All truths may not be facts.

The situation seems to be as Kierkegaard pictured it. Those realities that seem to be most objectively uncertain are believed in with the most intense subjective certainty. So it is with religious truth. Faith is the passionate relationship of the individual to the truth of his life. That religious truth is an infinite truth; it is God. The religious person believes passionately in that truth. Her belief is, by definition, subjective. It is not knowledge. It cannot be demonstrated to correspond to any objective fact. This is because all the terms of the religious relationship of the human person and God are not finite, earthly terms. God is infinite. Religious faith is the relationship of a finite being to an infinite being. The faith expresses the coming together of the infinite and the finite, what T. S. Eliot has called "the intersection of the timeless with time."[4] There is, and always must be, an irreducible element of uncertainty regarding the object of faith, the infinite pole of the relationship. But, paradoxically, this necessary objective uncertainty serves to intensify the subjective certainty of the believer. Thus faith is a passionate subjective certainty regarding an objective uncertainty. But this is not an intellectual relationship. It cannot be, because it is not knowledge. It is a love relationship between the finite lover and the infinite beloved, which is itself a passionate response to the feeling of the human lover who is involved that he is loved by God. And so God is really not an object at all but the divine subject in the light of whose love I see myself.

The atheist does not understand the paradox of faith, the subjective grasping of an objective uncertainty. The atheist says that since God is objectively uncertain, as God surely is, therefore he will not believe subjectively. On the other hand, the fundamentalist concludes that, since she believes with such intense subjective certainty, surely God must be objectively demonstrable, God must be provable. Both miss the point. If the atheist had his way, the ultimate human self-transcendence would be disallowed, and no meaning would be available to us beyond this earthly time-bound context. The result would be a shrunken, spiritually impoverished conception of the human that would cast into doubt all firm ethical standards and crush all human spirituality. Without these, what is left of the human? As for the fundamentalist, she would destroy that which she seeks to secure. To pretend that faith reveals absolute, objective knowledge is to claim an exclusive grasp of truth that dismisses the religious claims of all others. That way lies the road to endless religious wars based in a narrow sectarianism that would plunge humanity back into a pre-enlightenment darkness in which every person felt obliged by his truth to wipe out all those holding different views. This is the approach of today's Islamist fanatics.

What is needed is a "grown-up" existential conception of religious truth based on the lived experience of the believer. The Scriptures give us examples of such mature religious relationships. The story of Jacob's wrestling match will point us in the right direction:

> And Jacob was left alone; and a man wrestled with him until the breaking of the day. When the man saw that he did not prevail against Jacob, he touched the hollow of his thigh; and Jacob's thigh was put out of joint as he wrestled with him. Then he said, "Let me go, for the day is breaking." But Jacob said, "I will not let you go, unless you bless me." And he said to him, "What is your name?" And he said, "Jacob." Then he said, "Your name shall no longer be called Jacob, but Israel, for you have striven with God and with men, and have prevailed. "Then," Jacob asked him, "tell me, I pray, your name." But he said, "Why is it that you ask my name?" And there he blessed him. So Jacob called the name of the place Peniel, saying, "For I have seen God face to face, and yet my life is preserved." The sun rose upon him as he passed Penuel, limping because of his thigh. (Gen. 32: 24–31)

This luminous story offers us a profound and complex account of the intense relationship that is the religious life. It is appropriate that it is expressed through the metaphor of a desperate wrestling match. We think we know who Jacob is; but who is his wrestling partner/antagonist? We are told that "Jacob was left alone." Thus on some basic level he is wrestling with himself, confronting his own depth as all must do in true religious experience. As Heidegger might say, we must "unhide Being," in this case, our own Being. In this encounter with ultimacy, there can be no masks, no pretense. Without total honesty before God and before ourselves, no religious encounter worthy of the name can take place. In the religious experience we confront our true selves.

But the story goes on to say that Jacob was met by another—"a man"— who engaged him in combat. For it is also true that in the religious encounter we meet and interact with the human community. How we are with others *is* how we are with God. Deuteronomy tells us to "love the lord your God" (Deut. 6:5), but Leviticus adds, "love your neighbor as yourself" (Lev. 19:18). Jesus, rabbi and prophet of Galilee, agrees and combines the two commands (Mk. 12:30–31). On this crucial twofold definition of religion-in-action Judaism and Christianity are one. The Kingdom of God is indeed to be found in the midst of the human community. It is there, together with our brothers and sisters, that we must work out our salvation and seek the meaning of our lives. And the "man" will wrestle with him "until the breaking of the day." We may interpret this to mean that at the conclusion of this drama, the light of understanding will arise and Jacob will come to see what the experience was all about.

Neither pugilistic partner can prevail over the other. The struggle is evenly matched. There is a balance of forces here. This is not a contest in which the human will be defeated. But the "other" does wound Jacob. His thigh is wrenched and injured. There is a price for challenging the ultimate. We bear the marks of such an encounter forever. We are never the same afterward. But who has the upper hand here? Again this match is evenly balanced. Jacob is injured, but he holds fast to the "other," refusing to let him go unless he is given a blessing. And a blessing is what he receives. His name is changed to Israel (Yisra-El), "God wrestler." And why? Because he is wrestling with God and man—or with "God *or* man." Read the former way—God *and* man—the religious encounter is, once more, seen as involving confrontation with both the divine and the human; read the second way—God *or* man—the uncertainty of the other's identity is stressed. Jacob is not told who his partner/ antagonist is. It is God *or* man; *he* must decide. He alone can determine the meaning of this struggle, which is an ongoing one for the religious individual as it is for the collective individual that is Israel. Thus there is the irreducible uncertainty of which I wrote earlier regarding the identity of the one with whom we contend in the life of religious striving.

And yet we, the subject in the encounter, receive a new identity as a result of the struggle. It is a struggle for ourselves, a drama of self-discovery in which we find that the truly human being is the self-transcending person who meets, grasps, and contends with ultimacy—who wrestles with God. Human life can only achieve its highest meaning by confronting the highest.

Israel, having revealed his name, and received a new one, now demands to know the name of the other. Like all of us, he cries out to know who it is who holds him fast, calling forth all his power and will. "Tell me, I pray, your name." I would translate the Hebrew response as: "How can you ask such a question?" Jacob has asked the unanswerable question. The ultimate cannot be reduced to a name. Later in Israel's ongoing story Moses will ask the same question at the burning bush. He, too, will receive a response, but surely not an answer. "I shall be what I shall be" (Exod. 3:14). The ultimate is pure possibility, open-ended and irreducible to any finite categories. As Moses will learn later, "Man shall not see me and live" (Exod. 34:20). Moses had asked to see "God's ways," and his request had been granted. We finite beings can receive God's partial self-revelation in human terms we can comprehend: "merciful and gracious, slow to anger and abounding in steadfast love and faithfulness" (Exod. 34:6). But we cannot see the divine face, the infinite reality that finite humans cannot absorb—again, the irreducible uncertainty of the reality of the divine.

The mysterious other refuses to reveal his name or essence to Israel. Yet he immediately blesses him for having asked the question that cannot be answered. Is this the inescapable human lot—as finite creatures to beg and plead for certainty about the infinite? We yearn to know that what we feel and believe is really so. We try to cajole God into an indubitable self-revelation. But God will not be tempted to remove the objective uncertainty and thus destroy the possibility of faith. It is as if God hides behind the clouds and reacts to our plea that God prove to us that God is what and who we believe God to be by responding, "No, no, no, that's cheating. *You* must decide. But I bless you for asking the question I will always decline to answer . . . for your own good."

Having concluded the wrestling match, Israel renames the site of the encounter Penei-El, "face of God." He has followed the other's counsel and has decided himself on the meaning of the experience and the identity of the one who would not tell his name. It was God—and from now on the face of God will shine forth for Israel from every hill and valley, from every tree and bush. It is all the face of God, reflecting indirectly the divine glory.

And now comes the "breaking of the day" referred to earlier. Nothing in the story is static; nothing remains the same. Jacob, world, and God all change and grow in this redemptive struggle. Israel now lives in the light of a new understanding of the human: he now knows himself as the God-wrestler—a new understanding of the world: it is now for him the "face of God" (Penei-El)—and a new understanding of God: the one who engages, challenges, and embraces the human in an ongoing relationship of infinite striving and spiritual exertion. Israel will limp for the rest of his life so as never to forget that "the way of man is not in himself" (Jer. 10:23). He leans on another who is his strength and his high tower.

Friedrich Schleiermacher defined religion as feeling rather than knowing.[5] Søren Kierkegaard developed this line of thought, intensifying that feeling until it became in his reckoning an "infinite passion." Schleiermacher's rejection of an intellectual definition of faith as knowledge became, for Kierkegaard, the conviction that what the religious person believes in with all his subjective passion was forever objectively uncertain.[6] It seems to me that these experiential conceptions of religion can be helpful in dealing with the issue of religious narrative, our own and that of the religious other. I have touched on this question earlier in this work but never developed it.

If we were to claim that the Hebrew Scriptures with their wondrous stories were all factual accounts of reality, the question of their truth would be asked in terms of what we have called the "correspondence theory." But I have suggested that fact and truth are not always the same thing. However, they are always closely related and, in common life, usually inseparable. There is no "fact" that is not clothed with "meaning." The meaning is the "truth" of the fact, its significance for me. Students often ask me how I came to be a professor of religious studies. I am certainly willing to give them a "true" answer to their question. But every time I respond, my story comes out differently.

Sometimes I tell them of a religious experience I had when I was five years old. I remember it well and can describe it in detail. More often I speak of a wonderful book my mother gave me a year or two later. It was a large picture book titled *The Little Island*. Similar brightly painted scenes appeared on every page. They were views of a small island in the midst of the sea: a grassy meadow, a copse of trees, an outcropping of rock. One day a picnicking party arrives in a sailboat. With them is a black cat with enormous eyes and a tiny protruding tongue. The cat explores the island and inaugurates a conversation with it. He taunts the little island for being isolated, cut off from the land by the surrounding sea. The island replies that deep down "in the hidden places" under the sea, the island is rooted in the earth and is thus part of the whole. The cat refuses to believe this, and so the island suggests that he ask a fish:

> So the kitten caught a fish.
> "Answer me this or I'll eat you up,"
> said the kitten.
> "How is an Island a part of the land?"
> "Come with me," said the fish,
> "down into the dark secret places
> of the sea and I will show you."
> "I can't swim," said the cat.
> "Show me another way or I'll eat you up."
> "Then you must take it on faith
> what I tell you," said the fish.
> "What's that?" said the cat—"Faith."
> "To believe what I tell you
> about what you don't know," said the fish.
> And the fish told the kitten
> how all land is one land
> under the sea.
> The cat's eyes were shining
> with the secret of it.
> And because he loved secrets he believed.
> And he let the fish go.[7]

The secret is of the "one" in and behind the "many," the revelation of that primal unity, that transcendent reality which "runs through and holds together" all the elements of our experience.[8] Was this moment of insight the stimulus for my career in theology? Or was it some other encounter or a combination of many? Can there be one "true" answer to such a question? Are we in a position to "know" why we do what we do? Can I account for my motivations of the last hour, much less those that shaped my personal or professional life? So every time the question of what brought me to where I am is asked, a different answer can honestly be given. But perhaps the answer is only an honest one if I realize as I give it that it is merely the "official story" of the moment. It is no more "factual" than a dozen others might be. But it is "true." It expresses the truth of my experience as I grasp it at this moment. The whole truth, if such there be, is in one of those "secret places" of which the fish spoke. Like the cat's, our eyes too shine with wonder at the mystery—"the great deep"—hidden within ourselves and, indeed, within all reality. That sense of wonder leads us to exclaim, "Look! Daisies!" and to cry out with

Jacob, "Surely the Lord is in this place; and I did not realize it.... How awesome is this place! This is none other than the dwelling place of God, and this [realization] is the gate of heaven" (Gen. 28:16–17).

Every fact is clothed with meaning—wrapped so tightly that the covering has fused with what it covers. If they were ever separable, they surely are not now. The story of the cat and the fish is one I tell to make sense of my life, by mapping out the way I have come. What really happened way back then—who can know? Who needs to know? The story—the experience I reenact every time I tell it—is true in the deepest sense of the term. It helps to reveal myself to myself—to tell me who I am in the context of the great mystery of being to which it points.

So it is with the stories we find in the Scriptures' luminous pages. They are true stories, but we must analyze what we mean by "truth" in this case. On one extreme of interpretation we have the fundamentalists who insist that these accounts are factual. I am sitting in this chair; Elijah was swept up into heaven in a whirlwind, attended by a chariot of fire (2 Kings 3:11). Of course, fundamentalists never realize that literalism is itself a form of interpretation, one form among many. They insist on the six-day creation of the world—six twenty-four hour days. Why? Because the Bible says "day." But a biography of our first president might also include the sentence "In Washington's day, men wore powdered wigs." Would any intelligent reader conclude from this that Washington lived for only one day?

The more serious problem with the insistence on biblical literalism is that it distracts the reader from the main point of the story at hand. For example, the marvelous book of Jonah is famous for entirely the wrong reason. If one gets tangled up in debates over whether the prophet was actually swallowed by a "great fish" and how he could have had the presence of mind to compose a hymn while in the fish's belly, one misses the sublime point of the story. Together with the book of Ruth, the tale was probably composed to refute the racialist and nationalist definitions of Jewish identity developed by Ezra and Nehemiah during the period of their administration of Judah (ca. 450–400 B.C.E.). The message of Jonah is "love your enemies," even the hated Assyrians who had conquered northern Israel and carried its population into exile. The last lines of the story tell of God's attempt to explain to the Jewish prophet that the Holy One cares for all people—not just Jews—and desires that all repent and live righteous lives. Could any lesson be more central to true religion? But that message of universal religious humanism is usually missed by readers who prefer magic to morality and therefore focus on the miraculous account of the fish with the big appetite. Many of Scripture's most profound lessons are missed this way.

Fundamentalists, in current debates over evolution, often declare that we must take literally the "biblical account" of creation. But they seem to be totally unaware that there is more than one such account in the Bible. The book of Genesis opens with the six-day story (Gen. 1:1–24a). It is attributed by biblical scholars to the Priestly author of the Torah (ca. 550 B.C.E.) and tells of a sequence of events quite different from that found in the one-day account of creation found in the next story (Gen. 2:4b–25) of Adam and Eve, attributed to the "J" author (ca. 950–850 B.C.E.). Which are we to take literally, since they differ in crucial details? And what about the third creation narrative that appears in fragments in Isaiah 51:5 and Psalms 74 and 89, telling of the creation of the world from the broken body of a cosmic primal dragon of watery chaos? Here the God of Israel is given credit for creative acts attributed in the Babylonian epic *Enumah Elish* to Marduk, king of the earlier civilization's divine pantheon. So, which account are we to take literally? And, if we add John 1:1–5 as a fourth creation account, the problem is compounded even further.

Of course the very fact that our Israelite ancestors included the first three in their holy texts indicates that they could not have taken any one of them as literal fact. How did they understand these tales? Perhaps the Greeks can help us here. In Plato's *Timaeaus*, Socrates recounts his story of creation: the eternal intelligible realm of the Forms and how the Creator imposed these Forms on the equally eternal but chaotic world of undifferentiated matter, thus bringing into being the orderly world of formed matter that exists today. A fine story! Note that when asked by one of his listeners whether this account was meant to be taken as literal fact or, rather, as "a likely story," Socrates chooses the latter designation.

So it must be with all such narratives, including those in our holy texts. The fundamentalist insistence on literal facticity reveals that the one so insisting shares with the atheist a definition of truth as fact that concludes that if one cannot know if an event happened as recounted in the story, the story has no value and should be discarded as "false." For them the correspondence theory of truth is the only one worthy of the name.

The approach usually presented as an alternative to literalism is the metaphorical reading of sacred texts. Guided by this type of interpretation, one would read the Scripture as one would any work of poetry or, perhaps, a good novel. Are such literary works "true" or "false"? Are these categories appropriate to the analysis of poems and novels? I once found myself at a luncheon seated next to a woman who, in the course of conversation, asked me what I was teaching that semester. I answered that I was teaching a seminar on the poetry of T. S. Eliot. She responded, "Ah, poetry. I took a poetry course in college. But I never understood it. The teacher kept asking 'What does the poet mean?'" "Yes," I responded, "he might well ask that question." "Well," she said, "I kept answering that he means exactly what he says." At that point I asked her to consider the opening line of Alfred Noyes's poem "The Highwayman." I recited: "The road was a ribbon of moonlight." I paused and asked her, "*Was* the road a ribbon of moonlight?" She thought for a moment before bursting out with, "No, not literally!" "You see," I replied, "the poet did not mean what he said; he meant what he meant. It's a metaphor— true, but not literal fact." She assured me that she had learned more in our five-minute interaction than she had in that semester-long poetry class.

But will religious believers in large numbers ever come to accept a met- aphorical reading of their sacred texts? If theologians focus exclusively on this type of interpretation, we may find ourselves at too great a distance from the traditions we claim to represent. Elsewhere in this work I stress the impor- tance of pluralist theologians' acceptance of revelation as the source of our traditions for the same reason. We dare not deny bedrock convictions that have long characterized our faiths. Of course, the bottom line of textual in- terpretation is always the discussion of what the story means. Whether we take it literally or symbolically, the meaning beneath the surface is always the ultimate issue. However, must we ask the followers of our faith traditions to dismiss the question of whether the events related in the story ever happened.

Even Philo of Alexandria, the first-century father of the allegorical inter- pretation of Scripture, never stated directly that the events recounted in the biblical stories had not taken place. In his commentary on Genesis, for ex- ample, he held that in the Eden mythos Adam represented the intellect, Eve the body, and the serpent and his proffered fruit, the temptations of the physical world. But, as stated earlier, he never concluded that the story was *only* an allegory and that Adam and Eve never existed. It is not necessary for us to go further than Philo in our wrestling with the "truth" of the text. While stressing the lived meaning as the crucial aspect of the biblical stories, we can still leave open the possibility that the events recorded *may* have taken place. The issue is forever in suspense due to the irreducible objective uncertainty of faith.

Again we look to Kierkegaard's definition of faith—subjective certainty about an objective uncertainty—and apply it to the texts before us. I can be reasonably certain about an account of current events close to me in time and space because they are made up of elements that are all finite and physical— "I just drove to the university in my car." However, the biblical stories contain elements of the eternal and infinite reality as it impinges upon the time- bound and finite environment in which we live. As such, there is—as in faith itself—always that irreducible element of objective uncertainty regarding accounts in which the divine intersects with the earthly.

The central symbols of our Jewish and Christian traditions represent the crucial meeting of the two spheres. The Shield of David is made up of two intersecting triangles, one pointing down from heaven, the other pointing up from earth. They meet as interpenetrating signs of divine and human self-transcendence. The figure formed by their meeting is rightly called by Franz Rosenzweig "the star of redemption." The same can be said of the intersecting vertical and horizontal axes of the Christian cross, representing the meeting of the divine and the human realms. God reaches beyond God's own self and there is the human; humans reach beyond themselves and there is God. In Judaism and Christianity God reaches toward us and we toward God. The resulting divine-human encounter *is* the religious experience that is expressed in the respective symbols of the two faiths.

Let us go back to the Jacob wrestling account. The change of name speaks eloquently of the mutual self-transcendence of the divine and the human. Jacob's name is now Israel—Yisra-El, God-wrestler. This is the name of the fully human being, he who reaches beyond himself to touch the ultimate, the finite one who understands herself as participating in the infinite. Likewise, the name of God is inextricably attached to that of the human; El (God) is forever an element of the name of the human Yisra-El. Here God and the human meet and penetrate each other. The meaning of human life is God; the meaning of God's life is the human. The human name (Yisra-El) requires the divine; the divine name (El) is part of the human.

This mutual self-transcendence is what the Bible stories are all about. It is their meaning. They are believed in by the faithful as accounts of actual events. If meaning clothes all fact or, as in the Jacob wrestling account, penetrates and becomes one with it, how can we deny the presence of the Holy One in daily life, even in the most extraordinary ways? And so we may be led by faith to affirm that the Scriptures speak of actual events—eternal truths expressed in real human experiences—to which we may subjectively commit ourselves while always acknowledging their objective uncertainty. These events are real; they are true; they *may* be fact. Like Jacob, we wrestle with uncertainty. No guarantees, no assurances are given. We cry out for certainty. God refuses to be drawn out by our pleas. *We* must decide. *We* must determine the meaning of our own experiences. Like Jacob we may conclude, "I have seen God."

Clearly, this approach to our own tradition's sacred stories can just as well be employed in our reading of the texts of other traditions. We read our stories with the eye of faith we may not use in looking at other traditions. But if their

stories are similar to our own, we may conclude that, while objectively uncertain (as are ours) the other's tales may also express truths that can enlighten our own subjectivity—and they *may* point to actual events. Thus, by
thinking deeply about what our own faith means to us and how we Jews are to
evaluate the truth claims of our sacred stories, we may come to recognize that
those of other faiths—certainly Christians—struggle as we do and with accounts remarkably similar to those we cherish. Religion lived at this depth
may prove to be a force that can urge each of us to gain wisdom from the
similar religious experience of the other who is much closer to us than we
might have thought. This recognition of shared religious experience and of
the truth of similar sacred stories is one of the great discoveries of the Jewish-
Christian dialogue.

9

Bringing the Dialogue Home

This chapter will deal with some of my experiences over the past several decades of trying to bring the Jewish-Christian dialogue into the lives of believers of both faiths. Since Vatican II, the new meeting of Jews and Christians has been slowly creeping down to the grass roots. In my teaching, preaching, and involvement in interfaith projects I have tried to encourage this process.

I will cover some of these activities without discussing my regular professional work of teaching religion courses at my university. I want to focus on what can take place out in the community to deepen and enhance the understanding between Christians and Jews. While I am a professor of religious studies and a writer in this field, I am also a citizen of my town, a member of a number of synagogues, and a seeker of better interreligious relations in the daily lives of people of every faith, race, and calling. I offer the activities of which I will write as examples of what can be done to further the vital work of religious reconciliation in which we are all involved.

Teaching the New Testament in Synagogue Classes: A Unique Experiment

In 1982, Christmas Eve fell on a Friday evening, the start of the Jewish Sabbath. I had been teaching adult education classes at Congregation Shomrei Emunah of Montclair, New Jersey, since the mid-1970s and had been devoting much thought to the theological relation-ships between Judaism and Christianity for much longer than that. After finishing the studies for my doctorate at the Department of Religious Studies at Syracuse University, I had joined the faculty of the Department of Philo-sophy and Religion at Montclair State College (now Montclair State Uni-versity) in autumn of 1973. Shortly thereafter I joined Montclair's Conservative Congregation Shomrei Emunah and founded its adult education program.

As might be expected, the classes focused on Jewish Scriptures, theology, and history. As director of adult education, I had no higher academic author-ities to answer to. Thus I was free to design the courses exactly as I wished, taking as much or as little time as I needed to cover the topics I chose. A course originally scheduled to last one semester on a selected book of the Bible could be extended over several semesters if I needed the extra time to cover the material to my satisfaction. It was a professor's dream come true. Subjects, scheduling, and course requirements were all up to me. I was very happy with the situation.

And so, apparently, were the congregants. Some twenty to twenty-five students signed up and attended every Sunday morning for ten-week se-mesters in fall and spring. They were eager to gain deeper knowledge of the Jewish faith, its beliefs and practices, its texts and observances. I began with a comprehensive overview entitled "The History of the Jews from Mesopotamia to Montclair." Originally conceived as a two-semester course, it went on for six semesters (three years) and was followed by Bible and theology offerings.

Then came that Sabbath eve/Christmas Eve of 1982. Struck by the co-incidence of the holidays, I approached my rabbi and proposed that I deliver a sermon that evening entitled "Jesus the Jew: A Reappraisal."[1] He agreed that it would be an interesting experiment. The day arrived; I delivered the sermon at the Friday evening service. The congregants responded with great interest. Attendance was high, and the people stayed long into the night for a question-and-answer session and discussion. They had never heard of such a thing at a synagogue, and they were eager to ask all the questions they had stored up on Jesus in his Jewish setting, as well as in his Christian context. We discussed Jesus as a first-century rabbi, perhaps a Pharisee of the liberal wing of the movement; Jesus as a prophetic spokesman for the God of Israel, seeking to call Jews back from an emphasis on ritual and man-made custom to the spir-itual and ethical essence of the faith; Jesus as a popular preacher/healer/ teacher among the people who threatened the entrenched power of the Temple's Sadducee elite and the Roman occupiers.

I proposed reappropriating Jesus as a proto-Conservative Jew who (like the current Conservative branch of Judaism) recognized the authority of Jewish

Law while distinguishing between biblical essentials and later human accretions. His willingness to reform the tradition without violating it and his stress on human need rather than abstract legal absolutes made his approach familiar and attractive to modern theologically liberal Jews. I concluded by stating, "Just because others viewed Jesus as more than human is no reason for us to view him as less than Jewish." The congregation responded with enthusiasm and with an eagerness to hear more.

Having succeeded with this attempt to bring the Jewish-Christian dialogue to the grassroots level, I began to think of ways to carry this effort forward. It occurred to me that, since we had our adult education classes already in place with a well-attended weekly program, this would be the ideal vehicle for continuing education in interfaith dialogue. And so we began what I believe to be a unique experiment in synagogue-based adult Jewish education: a program that included, together with traditional Jewish offerings, courses in Christian Scripture and theology, as well as in the history of the relationship between Jewish and Christian communities. I started with Christian Scripture, covering the synoptic Gospels, the book of Acts, and the letters of Paul. Other courses followed. Student interest remained strong. Usually fifteen to twenty students took the courses. At a few points I had to add extra courses for those who could not attend on Sunday mornings.

The Doctors' Class on Paul

A study group made up of Jewish physicians in the community contacted me with a request that I teach a series of classes on the letters of Paul. They had tried to read them on their own but were having trouble without a guide. (This, of course, is just what a teacher loves to hear.) It proved to be a fascinating experience with highly intelligent, articulate students, so well educated in their medical field and so eager to learn about an area of thought of which they knew nothing.

The doctors were deeply impressed with the brilliance of Paul's original formulations. I presented Paul's theology as containing Jewish elements but in an entirely new arrangement, as if the great thinker had turned Judaism on its head. While Judaism holds that righteousness leads to salvation, Paul believes the opposite. For him, first one is saved by an act of divine grace—an unmerited gift from God. Once one accepts this gift, one is "born again," having allowed God in Christ to enter one's being, displacing ego as the motivating force of one's actions. Now one can say with Paul, "Not I live, but Christ liveth in me" (Gal. 2:20). This is salvation. Righteous deeds will now issue from the saved sinner who is motivated by Christ within, living his selfless life over again, as it were, in and through the newly redeemed "babe in Christ."

At this point the students took exception to what Paul seemed to claim. They could not agree that anyone could be so thoroughly "reborn" that all moral struggle was ended. They would not accept Paul's statement that "not I live but Christ liveth in me." They suggested that Paul should have said, "not I live alone, but Christ also lives in me." This would acknowledge that, while God strengthens and fights for the religious individual, that person's tendency to backslide into sin is also ever present. The students preferred Judaism's theory of the good inclination and the bad inclination always contending within the human person, with no once-for-all solution available. Of course, Paul himself slips into this more Jewish position. Why else would he feel the need to advise newly "saved" followers of Jesus to stay on the straight path? If they were not still capable of sin, such advice would scarcely be necessary. Here as elsewhere he is far from consistent.

The doctors also had little patience with Paul's insistence that if one is circumcised, thus putting oneself under the authority of the Jewish law—and then one fails to keep all of its commandments—the law becomes a curse rather than a blessing. As practicing Jews, they knew that, regardless of the biblical quote Paul cites out of context (Deut. 27:26), this view is a distortion of Judaism. Our faith assumes that we will fall short of the law's demands. That is why we have Yom Kippur as well as the prayers of repentance that are part of our daily liturgy. Judaism has never taught that one could earn salvation by good deeds alone. Sin is real. And so God's forgiveness is always needed. My students were correct on this point. Paul's presentation of Judaism as an unforgiving, absolutist legal system is not a fair description of the true teaching of our faith.

Of course, Paul would say that the Jews are correct that righteousness leads to salvation. Their error is in thinking that this righteousness is a human possibility. No, according to Paul, it is Christ's righteousness on the cross—the only truly selfless deed ever performed—that is salvific. We are saved by our faith, our acceptance of this divine righteousness as a gift that God, through grace, counts as *our* righteousness. When we accept the gift, Christ enters us and purifies our motivation, making it possible for the first time for us to act righteously. Thus Christ's divine righteousness, accepted through human faith, leads to human righteousness. The doctors were amazed at this inversion of Jewish thinking. The categories are the same, but the order of things is reversed.

Unlike Paul, Judaism does not hold a view of original sin that renders human beings incapable of righteousness. For Judaism sin is what we do; for

Paul sin is what we *are*. We can stop doing what we do; we cannot stop being what we are. Adam sinned. The result, according to Judaism, was that we, his descendants, got into the habit of sin. This habit can be broken, or at least fought, with the guidance of Torah. Judaism and Paul agree that an act of divine grace is needed, but for us the act is far less radical than it is for Paul. God's unmerited gift of Torah to Israel, a divine act of grace, assumes that human beings, even after Adam's sin, are capable of righteous conduct, even righteous motivation, if guided properly by the Law of God. After all, God appeals to Cain's righteousness to lead him to emulate his brother. God points out that Cain has free choice regarding his brother. It is true that Cain fails to act righteously, but his freedom is assumed. His sin was not necessary. And remember that Noah is called "a righteous man." And he is saved.

But other verses in the Bible could be quoted to support Paul's position. In Romans 3:10 he quotes Psalm 14:2–3, which states that God, looking down upon humankind, sees that "They have all gone astray, they are all alike corrupt; there is none that does good, no, not one." For us sin is inevitable, but for Paul, it is necessary.

In teaching Paul to a class of Jewish laymen, my purpose was not to demonstrate Judaism's superiority but to educate them in the thought of a great theologian and to illustrate the fascinating differences between Judaism and Pauline Christianity. They were amazed to discover that this theory of human depravity, seemingly so alien to Judaism, can find support in a number of ancient Jewish texts. It is true that many more biblical verses speak of the possibility of human righteousness than deny it, but Paul's thought is hardly foreign to Judaism. The differences are really a matter of emphasis.

The students were also intrigued to discover another example of how Paul reverses the order of Jewish concepts. Judaism holds that good deeds, as they are performed, filter inward, as it were, purifying the motivation of the doer of the deeds. The very structure of our basic form of prayer indicates this. "Blessed are you, Lord our God, King of the universe, who makes us holy through your commandments and commands us" to perform such and such a commandment. This prayer is recited before fulfilling a divine command. But look at its claim. It holds that through the deed in question, the deed we perform as we are commanded, we are made holy. The righteous act purifies the motivation; the external deed makes holy the inner life.

Don't worry about your motivation for doing a good deed. Just do it! You will find that as you become accustomed to acting righteously, your motivation will be purified ("Purify our hearts to serve thee in truth").[2] Again, don't worry about why you perform the good deed, whether you do it for the sake of the good or to make yourself feel righteous. After all, it is natural that a good person will feel good if he does good. A bad person feels good when he does evil. Surely we would not expect a good person to feel *bad* because he has done good. If we wait for an absolutely pure, selfless motivation before doing good, we will never get around to the deed but will obsess endlessly about the purity of our motives. Judaism teaches us to do the deed. In time we will, as it were, internalize its goodness, thus purifying our motivation.

Paul, on the other hand, holds that first the heart must be made pure by the in-breaking of Christ. Only then can the deeds issuing from a human being be truly good. For him, the purified motive purifies the deed. For Judaism it is the other way around. The good deed eventually purifies the motive. What else can we mean by the prayer: "Make us holy through your commandments"? Here is another instance where Judaism and Pauline Christianity seem to be the reverse of each other. Yet there is truth in both theories. They are two takes on the relationship between motive and act. Perhaps we need both of them to grasp the great complexities of these psychological/ethical issues. The students plunged eagerly into these debates, and both they and their teacher emerged the wiser.

Back to the Sunday Classes

Meanwhile, the Sunday morning students were continuing to wrestle with issues raised in the Gospels. With whom did they sympathize: with Jesus or his opponents among the Pharisees or the Sadducees? Is the Gospels' "description" of the Pharisees accurate? After all, today's rabbinic Judaism is the heir of Pharisaic thought. Was Jesus correct in relaxing the ritual laws (Sabbath observance and perhaps kosher requirements) while strengthening moral laws (preaching against divorce or lustful ogling of women)? What about his celibacy and poverty or his focus on the individual rather than on the people Israel? Is this latter issue a fundamental distinction between Judaism and Christianity? Does Christianity have much to teach us about individual spirituality? How many Jews will go into a synagogue to pray alone? Is this a practice we should try to develop, inspired by the many Christians who do this? On the other hand, how many Christians have the strong sense of religious community so common among Jews? Should Christians try to develop a consciousness of being a spiritual family similar to the Jews? We concluded that Jews and Christians have much to teach each other for the mutual enrichment of both communities.

We searched in these classes for Jewish patterns of thought expressed in the Gospels as well as for Hellenistic ideas that, in Christianity, combined with Hebraic traditions. Judaism often attempted to weed out alien influences; Christianity spread across the world because it accepted and baptized such foreign ideas. This brought up the whole question of our responsibility to the entire human race, our relationships to the outside world. Abraham was called to be a blessing to all the peoples of the world (Gen. 12:3). Judaism and Christianity have both tried to obey that divine commission, each in its own way. One is a witness people; the other is a missionary people. How do these two patterns of conduct relate to each other and to the larger project of world redemption of which both peoples are a part? Stimulated by this question, the class went on to wrestle with ways in which each faith influences and, in a sense, "fills out" the other.

Can Judaism, with its continued waiting for the Messiah, protect Christianity against spiritual triumphalism born of the assumption that the world is already redeemed? Does Christianity need the "not yet" aspects of Jewish thought to prevent it from sinking into a religious complacency and accommodation with the world? Likewise, students asked, does Judaism need Christianity to fend off its tendency toward spiritual self-ghettoization? The mission of Israel is world redemption. Jews seek not to make the world Jewish but to lead it to a universal morality often referred to as the Kingdom of God. At times Judaism has forgotten this and turned inward. But the world-embracing mission of the church can inspire us to remember that we too are a world-redeeming people called to proclaim the One God and the ultimate triumph of righteousness. In short, here too, we need each other to become fully what we are.

All these and many more issues have been dealt with in these ongoing courses. For me the theological issues are the most interesting, but for many of the students the history shared by the two faiths has been of central concern. And we have covered this often painful subject in depth. From its beginnings, Christianity has been deeply ambivalent toward its Jewish origins. It was always understood that the validity of Christian faith rested on the validity of prior Jewish claims. The story of the life of Jesus in the Gospels is written so as to repeat and recapitulate the story of the people Israel in Jewish Scriptures. But if the ancient Israelites are viewed with reverence in the New Testament, the Jewish contemporaries of Jesus are often viewed with hostility or contempt.

While Jews are painfully aware of the anti-Jewish polemics of sections of the New Testament and of much of the Christian tradition, they are not aware of the hostility of Jewish authorities to the nascent Nazarene movement of the first century. The Temple's Sadducee priesthood opposed Jesus and his early followers—and the Pharisees joined in once the antinomian views of Paul became mainstream within the church. They saw this new Jewish sect of Nazarenes as a heretical movement within the Israelite faith, while the Jews who followed Jesus saw themselves as the new and true Israel. Mutual hostility was inevitable.

The challenge for my classes was not to decide who was most to blame but to understand what had happened and resolve to be part of a new irenic solution to this age-old problem. Hans Kung has said that there can be no peace in the world until there is peace between the religions. My students came to realize that they could become actors in the great drama of mutual reconciliation that is the Jewish-Christian dialogue. This is a work of supreme significance for all of us. If Judaism and Christianity can be reconciled, then other religions that have not shared 2,000 years of mutual hostility can also be. This is the hope of the world.

A Congregant Objects

I would be dishonest if I did not report that a few in my synagogue were disturbed by our educational experiment. One day during the penitential season known as the Days of Awe (between Rosh Hashanah and Yom Kippur), I received a memorable telephone call. The Days of Awe are set aside for reconciliation. Before we approach God on Yom Kippur for forgiveness of our sins of the past year, we are commanded to apologize to anyone we have harmed over the twelve months since last Yom Kippur. This is not easy. We are to write or telephone or meet with those from whom we must ask forgiveness. So it was that during this period, about ten years after I began the Jewish-Christian courses, the phone rang. It was a prominent member of the congregation who was calling to apologize. I responded that I knew of nothing for which he had to ask my forgiveness. He told me that he had been enraged by what he took to be my propagandizing for Christianity in the synagogue. Viewing Christians as enemies and persecutors of the Jews, he had been denouncing me as an agent of the "Jews for Jesus" to anyone who would listen. However, having spoken with many of those who had taken the courses, he now understood that my intentions were far different from what he thought them to be. He apologized.

This was a learning experience for me. It brought home how the issue for Jews is not Christian theology and certainly not Jesus or Paul, but rather the history of persecution which has caused Jews to distrust Christians so deeply. Such Jewish attitudes are all too understandable; it will take a long time before suspicions fade away. That is, of course, one of the goals of the dialogue.

The Interfaith Committee of Essex

Opportunities have arisen beyond my home congregation to bring the Jewish-Christian conversation down to the grassroots level. For a number of years in the 1980s, a local group of Jews and Christians entitled the Interfaith Committee of Essex sponsored a series of public forums at synagogues and churches in Essex County, New Jersey. The committee was founded by a local Christian clergyman and his Jewish wife. The leadership eventually passed to my colleague at the Department of Philosophy and Religion at Montclair State, Dr. Eva Fleischner, and to me. The meetings were educational opportunities for laypeople of both faiths to come together, hear a lecture or an interfaith panel, or engage in a general discussion of a wide variety of issues. We discussed Jewish and Christian approaches to the nature of the divine, God's activities in the world, ethics, spirituality, suffering, mission, witness, "faith versus works," Jesus, Holocaust, Zionism, religious exclusivism, and pluralism. We covered all these issues and a great many more and spent some delightful and stimulating evenings together. I always tried to move the discussions beyond the "we believe this, you believe that" stage. Most dialogues end there. But true dialogue must open each side to possible influence by the "other." What do we have to learn from the other faith? Do they see something we may have missed? Only by opening ourselves to such questions can we begin to move beyond each faith's illusions of self-sufficiency. Only then can dialogue become an experience of in-depth learning and growth.

After a number of years of these meetings, a problem emerged. We noticed that the same people kept attending and few others seemed interested. When others did come, they were often fundamentalists who were opposed to the very idea of there being more than one way to truth. Eventually the project petered out. We were either preaching to the already convinced or locking horns with the unconvincible. This is not to say that such projects should not be undertaken in other communities. For as long as they last, lectures or discussion evenings shared between a number of churches and synagogues can be quite helpful in educating the congregants in the faiths of their neighbors. Lectures and panel discussions followed by open question periods can be particularly enlightening. Interest may run out eventually, but the effort is still more than worthwhile.

Interfaith Thanksgiving Services

Similarly, joint worship services of churches and synagogues at Thanksgiving can be very worthwhile. Of all aspects of religious life, liturgy is the most conservative and the last to change. Today it seems to me that lectionary reform is the next step for Christian churches engaged in interfaith dialogue. Public Scripture readings that attack or denigrate the religious "other" (in this case Judaism) have no place in the liturgies of those churches seeking reconciliation with Jews. This becomes a major problem during Holy Week services. However, this issue obviously does not come up at Thanksgiving. This is the ideal holiday for shared Jewish-Christian worship. Of course, one must be careful to avoid giving offense with hymns or readings that cannot be sung or said by all worshipers.

Some years ago I was approached by a committee from a number of churches and synagogues in and around Montclair, New Jersey. They came to see me as the chairman of the Montclair State University Department of Philosophy and Religion. This was a committee formed to create that year's multifaith Thanksgiving service. The service had run into trouble in the two previous years. Two years earlier it had been held in an African American church. Before a congregation, half of which was African American, the guest preacher, a rabbi, began his sermon by reminding his listeners that their ancestors had journeyed to America to be free! The next Thanksgiving, at a church service where about 20 percent of the mixed congregation was Jewish, the choir began the service with a hymn entitled "Just One Look at Jesus and Your Soul Will Be Healed." Clearly something had to be done. They had come to me, a teacher of both Judaism and Christianity, to see if I could create a Thanksgiving service that would say something but would offend nobody. I was delighted to have the opportunity.

I love Thanksgiving, which combines three of my great enthusiasms: God, country, and good food. For forty years I have attended the oldest interfaith Thanksgiving service in America. Started in the 1930s by three New York congregations—Central Synagogue, Christ Church Methodist, and the Park Avenue Presbyterian Church—it was originally conceived as a protest against rising antisemitism in Europe. With that experience behind me, I put together a service including the grand old hymns of the day—all Protestant but nonchristological—added Bible readings from both Testaments (Jesus can certainly be quoted in this context), and included prayers offered "in the Lord's name," which, of course, could be interpreted however the individual worshiper chose.

I was so eager not to divide the congregation that I did not include the president's Thanksgiving proclamation lest that offend members of the other political party. Instead I inserted the original Thanksgiving proclamation of Governor Bradford of Plymouth Colony. Who could object to that? The preacher of the day was carefully chosen and was briefed beforehand. ("Offend no groups present. If you must offend individuals, be sure to offend all of them equally.") All went smoothly at what turned out to be a successful evening of fellowship and shared worship. Such community interfaith events are splendid opportunities for celebrating our common convictions in the embracing spirit of American respect for all faiths.

Teaching Church Classes

Over the years I have been invited to teach Scripture classes at a number of churches. From an African American Baptist church in Newark, New Jersey, where the pious ladies would march in holding their Bibles before them like "the shield of faith" (Eph. 6:16), to a progressive Episcopal church and a more traditional Lutheran church in Charleston, South Carolina, I have had the pleasure of teaching Scripture to eager adult students. The very fact that I am a Jew teaching classes in a Christian church speaks for itself. We have much to say to each other about the common texts that both unite and divide us. Our entire dialogue rests on that text. We share the words of the Hebrew Scriptures (Old Testament or First Testament, as you wish) but differ as to its interpretation. It is those differences that offer us all the rich possibilities for profound engagement and exchange of ideas that characterize the dialogue at its best.

But, I believe, we Jews and Christians also share the New Testament, albeit in a more complex way. As a collection of books and letters written almost exclusively by Jews, the Christian Scriptures tell us much about a crucial, paradigm-shifting period of Jewish and human history. The world of the New Testament is one of rabbis and synagogues, of Torah interpreters, and of Jewish yearning for the fulfillment of Israel's hopes. If one of those Torah interpreters became the central figure of a new faith founded by Jews who developed a variant reading of Jewish tradition, should not we Jews find the accounts of all this as fascinating as do gentiles? This is our history. It is surely not inappropriate for Jews to teach this very Jewish story. Of course, I bring a Jewish perspective to these classes, but I also explain the various Christian analyses of the texts to the mostly Christian students. My task is, as always, to look at the reading from every side. What, I ask, does this passage mean to us as Jews, as Christians, and as human beings? It is wondrous how a class exploring alternate readings of the same text can open and illuminate the mind and heart, leading students to value differences of interpretation rather than scorn or fear them. This is what Jews and Christian can do for each other through shared Bible study.

Guest Sermons in Churches

On many a Sunday morning I have had the pleasure of preaching in a number of Christian churches. One Christmas, representatives of a Baptist church that was between ministers asked me to preach the Christmas morning sermon. I explained to the church leaders that I was a believing, practicing Jew (kosher, Sabbath-observing, and synagogue-going), but they were not to be dissuaded. And since I had already preached a Christmas sermon in a synagogue, I saw no reason why I should not do so in a church.

I took as my text a theme of Meister Eckhart, the fourteenth-century Catholic mystic and heretic (heresies are often the most exciting expressions of religions): "The Eternal Birth." It focused on what I take to be the theme of Christmas: the birth of God in man, the breaking of the infinite into the finite, "the intersection of the timeless with time" (T. S. Eliot). I sought to use the particular elements of the story (the holy family, the Christ child, the shepherds, the manger) as symbols that express what the story is trying to tell us of the relationship between the divine and the human. In doing this, we render the symbols transparent. We see through them to the universal truth toward which they point, a truth equally available to Jews, Christians, and all seekers of the Infinite Life.

The sermon must have been successful. At the next meeting of the church elders, someone suggested that the church offer me the position of part-time minister!

I have delivered other sermons in the churches of many denominations in which I have explored themes common to Jews and Christians or have analyzed our disagreements. So often our differences are not a matter of our beliefs, but of the symbols we use to express those beliefs. Religions are symbol systems, revealed, I believe, by God to many communities. We can view those symbols either as opaque or as transparent. Considered as opaque, the symbols become one with what they symbolize. They express ultimate truth in such a direct way that the believer must view as false all other religions, since they are made up of different symbols and images. But if we understand the symbols of our faith to be transparent, we see them as our particular, finite ways of conceiving of an infinite reality that is beyond them all. We are thus able to see through our own symbols to a universal truth. We understand that other faiths are also expressions of that truth, though imaged forth via different symbol systems. Every religion can be understood as either opaque or transparent. It seems to me that those who view the symbols as transparent can more easily be open to the truths of faiths other than their own. This does not mean that the symbols are interchangeable in the lived experience of believers. We all feel most comfortable with the language and metaphors of our own faith.

Although there are some prayers directed to Jesus in which I do not join, I have no problem participating, where I can, in Christian worship. That is because I believe that the God of Israel sent Jesus and his interpreters for the purpose of opening God's covenant with Israel to include non-Jews. While my Christian neighbors in the pews around me are thanking God for sending Christ to save them, I am thanking God for sending Jesus, my ethnic and religious brother, to save them too. Not to save *me*, but *them*. Of course God is the savior of us all, but he saves me through his Word in Torah and his Jewish people (Israel, Jewish stock), while he saves them through his Word in Jesus and the church (Israel, Christian branch). What Jesus came to teach was, I believe, already known to Jews: "You shall love the Lord your God with all your heart, and with all your soul, and with your all mind, and with all your strength" (Mk. 12:30; Deut. 6:5); "You shall love your neighbor as yourself" (Mk. 12:31; Lev. 19:18).

But gentiles did not know this. Jesus taught them. He taught us too, but he taught us to be better children of Israel while he, as interpreted by Paul, taught them how to *become* children of Israel by adoption through faith and a virtual birth ceremony. This is baptism, a necessity for gentiles who desire to enter the people Israel (Christian branch), but a redundancy for Jews who are already natural members by birth of the same people (Jewish stock). For me the truth of Judaism does not negate the truth of Christianity. Both were revealed by the same God, but at different times to different peoples. I try to witness to the shared truth of both faiths when speaking before Jewish and Christian audiences and congregations. From people's reactions, it would appear that, at long last, many are ready to hear this message.

It seems to me that inviting Jewish guest preachers to speak at churches and Christian guest preachers to address synagogue congregations is a splendid way to build mutual trust and acceptance. To be effective, the speaker would have to be familiar with both traditions but would not necessarily have to be a clergyperson or professor of religion. We should all be open to hearing heartfelt statements of faith from those of other traditions as long as they respect our beliefs and have absolutely no hidden proselytizing agendas.

Conclusions

It is crucial that the religious dialogue move beyond the elite leadership of the faiths and become better known by the laity. This new openness is too important a phenomenon to be restricted to a tiny minority. Believers must be encouraged to leave fear and parochialism behind as they open themselves and their beliefs to influence by the other. Perhaps that other tradition possesses insights ours may have missed. Every revelation of the Infinite One must, of necessity, be partial, that is, finite. This is not because God is finite but because we are. Our religious culture will inevitably be enriched by contact with the other—and that other, by contact with us. As stated earlier, religion-in-action is both self-affirmation and self-transcendence. This is as true for the group as it is for the individual.

Scripture tells us that God is "enthroned above the praises of Israel" (Ps. 22:3). Therefore, religiously considered, all of us are finite bearers of the Infinite Life of God. We come closer to that Infinite Life when we realize that we are not alone. Others bear it with us.

10

Does Politics Trump Theology?

The Israeli-Palestinian Dispute Invades the Jewish-Christian Dialogue

A Short Review of the Dialogue

We are privileged to live in an age unprecedented in the history of Judaism and Christianity. In the forty-plus years since the Second Vatican Council, Christians and Jews have moved from mutual hostility into an extended period of dialogue and growing friendship.

In my plenary address to the Mid-Atlantic American Academy of Religion meeting in Baltimore in 1996, I asked the following question regarding Judaism and Christianity: "Can siblings grow beyond rivalry?" Today the answer is clear. Yes, even ancient historical and theological foes can come to see themselves as sister faiths growing out of a common ancient Israelite root—no longer rivals, but partners in the all-embracing work of healing a broken world.

The Roman Catholic Church took the lead in the work of reconciliation. The Vatican Council declared that Jews are still the people of God, tied to the Lord in an eternal covenant. That covenant was not abrogated by their failure to respond positively to the "Christ event." One by one, mainline Protestant churches followed the Catholic lead. Anglicans, Lutherans, Methodists, Presbyterians, the United Church of Christ (UCC), and other mainstream churches penned resolutions declaring that dialogue, not proselytizing, must now characterize the churches' interaction with Jews and Judaism. Do these liberal Christians still preach the conversion of Jews? Not actively. Of course, if a Jew desires conversion, he is welcomed—but such a step is not seen by these Christians as necessary for salvation.

Why not? Different churches took different positions on this all-important question. Some took the "inclusivist" position. Christ died for all and is the *one way* to salvation. However, a person can be saved by Christ without being aware of the cross or even having heard of Jesus. If one lives one's life with integrity, following one's conscience and seeking to serve the good and live virtuously, one can benefit, all unknowingly, from Christ's saving work. Virtuous Jews and others need not become Christians to be saved by Christ. This is "inclusivism." Righteous non-Christians are included among the saved.

Some individual Christian theologians and some churches went further and ventured into theological "pluralism." Christ is not *the* one way, but is *one* way among other paths to salvation. Christ for Christians, Torah for Jews, presumably other paths for other religions, all of them established by God—a plurality of life-giving revelations to humanity.

This pluralist view is difficult for many Christians. There is something about messianism—and Christianity is a powerful messianism—that is, by its very nature, universal in its claims. Jews certainly believe that when the Messiah comes he will come for everyone, not just Jews. Can Christians be expected to say that Jesus, their Messiah, came only for Christians or, even more peculiarly, for everyone except Jews? So inclusivism is more widespread among liberal Christians than is true pluralism. But according to both views, Jews are fine where they are. They need not convert to Christianity to live in covenant relationship with God.

Of course, for the evangelical and fundamentalist churches, neither inclusivism nor pluralism is acceptable. Since to be saved, one must declare Jesus Christ to be one's "Lord and Savior," only baptism can open the way to salvation. This position—"exclusivism"—is the bedrock of the missionary thrust of these churches and has kept large denominations like the Southern Baptists out of the Jewish-Christian theological dialogue. Jews, for their part, can hardly be expected to engage in theological discussion with those who view their faith as invalid since the Christ event.

But the Roman Catholic Church and the liberal Protestant churches have recognized the ongoing validity of the Jewish faith. They have even advised their adherents to visit synagogue services and Passover Seders to witness and learn from the vibrant, living faith of Israel. The late Pope John Paul II declared to a visiting Jewish delegation that the ongoing existence of Jews and Judaism proclaimed to the world two great truths: Israel's faithfulness to God and God's faithfulness to Israel. Christian churches participating in the dialogue all agree to this. If not a missionary faith, Judaism is a *witness* faith called to proclaim God's oneness, God's rule over humanity, God's universal moral laws, fidelity to divine promises, and love for Israel and for all of humankind. Progressive Christians see Jews much as Jews see themselves: as upbuilders of the Kingdom of God and, as such, partners in this work with their Christian fellow believers.

Until now, I have been discussing the Christian side of this dialogue—how Christians have altered their view of Jews and Judaism. But what about the Jews? How have *they* altered their view of Christianity and its adherents? While in one way fundamental change is harder for Jews than for Christians, in another it is easier. Judaism has never viewed itself as the one true way of life for all peoples. In the eighth century B.C.E. the prophet Micah declared: "For all the people walk each in the name of its god, but we will walk in the name of the Lord our God forever and ever" (Mic. 4:5). Other people need not become Jews. Judaism is the faith of the people Israel. Others have other ways. Later the *Tosefta*, a rabbinic text of the second century C.E., laid out seven universal moral precepts revealed to the sons of Noah (non-Jews) by which all human beings could live lives acceptable to God. And, of course, the Talmud famously declares that "the righteous of all nations have a share in the world to come."[1] Thus while Judaism demands fidelity to a universal ethic, it accepts and has always accepted a fundamental religious pluralism.

But if Judaism is more open to pluralism than is Christianity, it is less able to deal with one specific religious "other": Christianity. It is one thing to say that God covenanted with humanity in general (the sons of Noah) long before creating Israel. It is quite another to acknowledge that, after 2,000 years of Israelite faith, God has revealed Christianity. Why has this been so hard for Jews? Perhaps because of the exclusivism that characterized Christianity until 40 years ago and certainly because of Christianity's record of abusing Jews and denouncing Judaism. The sad fact is that many Jews do not fully trust Christians. They are not convinced that the inheritors of a tradition that, in its texts and its conduct, has maligned and mistreated their people and their faith for centuries have really reformed. It will take more than 40 years to undo 2,000.

And so, while church after church has expressed new, positive attitudes toward Jews and Judaism, not one synagogue branch—Reform, Reconstructionist, Conservative, or Orthodox—has ever issued a statement on *Christianity* specifically. Each has spoken of gentiles in positive ways, but not of Christians as such. The memory of Christian persecution is still too fresh to allow for sufficient agreement among Jews to produce any official synagogue statements on Christianity.

However, as discussed in chapter 7, in the year 2000, a group of Jewish theologians, writing as individuals, did produce a historic document, "Dabru

Emet" (Speak the Truth), containing many positive views on Christianity. Most significantly, they suggested that, like Judaism, Christianity is the result of a divine revelation from the same God who revealed the Jewish faith to the people Israel. This statement was eventually signed by hundreds of rabbis, theologians, and laypersons, indicating how eager many Jews were to respond positively to the many friendly statements by the churches affirming the eternal truth of Judaism. A group of leading Christian theologians soon responded to "Dabru Emet" with their own statement on Judaism, "A Sacred Obligation." And so the Jewish-Christian dialogue, surely one of the most important developments in the history of both faiths, moved forward.

But, in the summer of 2004, in an example of how politics can threaten to derail theology, a new element was introduced into the relationship between the faiths. Through actions of the Presbyterian Church (U.S.A.), the Israeli-Palestinian conflict invaded what had previously been primarily a religious discussion. This is not to say that the Middle East conflict had not been mentioned earlier. But now it appeared to be taking center stage. It was probably inevitable that this would happen. After all, the Israel-Palestine struggle is continually in the news, and one of the parties is often called the "Jewish state." In fact, Zionism had already been touched on in the dialogue; many of the official statements issued by the churches regarding Judaism had included the recognition of the tie between the Jews and the land of Israel.

Often those Christian statements seemed awkwardly worded. They recognized the importance of the land to contemporary Jews but added that this recognition should in no way be seen as a denial of the rights of the Palestinian people. One got the impression from reading these formulations that the Jewish dialogue partner had insisted on this reference to the land of Israel while the Christian side had added the reference to the Palestinians so as not to be co-opted by the Zionist agenda. Before proceeding to an examination of the events of 2004, it would be well to consider the Presbyterian document of 1987, which lays out in detail the church's new understanding of its relationship to Jews and Judaism.

The "Theological Understanding" of 1987

In 1987 the Presbyterian Church (U.S.A.) issued "A Theological Understanding of the Relationship between Christians and Jews." This statement is among the most progressive ever produced by a national church body. Recognizing that "theology is never done in a vacuum," that "the age of 'Christendom' has passed," and that our age is increasingly "global" and "pluralistic," the Presbyterians set out to fashion a new understanding of their relationship with Jews and Judaism. They affirmed the "Word of God, given in covenant to the Jewish people, made flesh in Jesus Christ, and ever renewed in the work of the Holy Spirit among us." It is significant that early in the statement, a note of caution is struck: "Things said by Christians in North America about the relationships of Christians and Jews will be heard by Christians in the Middle East, where there are painful conflicts affecting the entire region." Later references are made to "the rights of the Palestinian people to self-determination" and "our Arab Christian brothers and sisters in the Middle East. We have listened to the anguish of the Palestinians, and we have heard their cry."

Even before 1987 the Presbyterians had issued statements supporting the rights of both Israelis and Palestinians to live in freedom and peace in two states side by side. And they were well aware that statements of Jewish-Christian amity could be interpreted by Arab Christians, especially Palestinians, as endorsements of general or specific Israeli government policies. The Presbyterians realized they were walking a tightrope and tried to find balance by noting later in the 1987 statement: "The State of Israel is a geopolitical entity and is not to be validated theologically." It was important for them to state clearly that, in Middle East matters, politics and theology were two very different categories. The Presbyterians pointed out that they are not Christian Zionists who see modern Israel as the fulfillment of biblical promises. In making this sharp distinction, they were also putting themselves at odds with many, perhaps most, Jews who also view the State of Israel through the eyes of faith.

Having distinguished theology from politics early in their 1987 statement, the Presbyterians went on to develop a seven-affirmation policy on Jews and Judaism that continues to be the basis of their interaction with Jews.

Affirmation 1 confirms "that the living God whom Christians worship is the same God who is worshipped and served by Jews ... the Triune Lord of all." As it stands, this sentence is not an expression of religious pluralism. It suggests that while God surely addressed ancient Israel, that revelation was not as full as the revelation through Christ of the triune nature of the deity. If the statement had said that *Christians* understand the God who revealed himself to Israel as "triune," then the radical unity of the Israelite conception of God would have been granted an equal truth claim. Both trinitarian and unitarian conceptions, whether viewed as divine revelations or human ideas, would point beyond themselves to the infinite God, beyond all such finite images. But the statement deliberately refers to "the Triune Lord of *all*" (italics mine), which suggests a superior truth status for the trinitarian conception.

However, a few paragraphs later, in the explanation of Affirmation 1, the section closes with a summary referring to the discussion of the triune God and the redemption of all through Christ: "This is the way in which Christians affirm the reality of the one God who is sovereign over all." Now, *this* sentence is much more open to pluralistic interpretation. God is one. Jews and Christians agree on that. Beyond that we part over the role of Jesus and the trinitarian conception. But these are both elements of the Christian understanding of a reality beyond all human conception. The difference between this and the earlier sentence seems to me to be crucial. Is *our* conception of the ultimate God the one true conception, reflecting the way God really is . . . or is our conception one truth among others—valid for us, who are willing to recognize as valid the conceptions developed by others?

How can a truth be true for me or my group, while making no absolute claims on others? As we have seen, Søren Kierkegaard, perhaps the most sophisticated theologian since Paul, held faith to be a subjective certainty about an objective uncertainty.[2] Paradoxically the irreducible objective uncertainty of the object of faith serves to intensify the subjective certainty of the believer. His faith is held with a passionate intensity, in T. S. Eliot's words, "costing not less than everything."[3] But he knows that his passionate belief reveals nothing that can be proved objectively. Such faith—whether Christian or Jewish—does not require objective certainty to be what it is. In fact, objective certainty would destroy it by making its object an object of knowledge, not faith. In faith, it is subjective passion that is required . . . a subjective passion that, since it is subjective, must make room for the subjective passions of others. Thus a Christian would find in her subjective passion for Christ and the Trinity a profound bond with the Jew who, with equal passion, affirms Torah, Israel, and the radical unity of the divine. Kierkegaard gets us out of our dilemma, but such a complex and sophisticated theology is hardly likely to find its way into a denominational statement of the kind we are examining.

In Affirmation 2 of this statement the Presbyterians chose a benign Christian view of their relationship with Judaism over a malevolent one. Both views have found expression in the history of Christian thought. The positive view holds that, as Paul stated in Romans (11:17–24), Christians have been engrafted into the people of God (Israel). The negative view is that of supersessionism, which holds that Christians have *replaced* Jews as the people of God. The Presbyterians now realize that Christian inclusion into the saving plan of God did not mean Jewish exclusion. God is faithful to his promises to "the people whom He foreknew" (Rom. 11:2).

The statement confronts with admirable honesty an ongoing problem for the church. If the covenant established by God with Israel through Abraham,

Isaac, Jacob, and Moses at Sinai is irrevocable and eternal, then Jewish conversion to Christianity would be a theological redundancy. If, as Paul said, a
Jew is a natural-born child of God, while a Christian is an adopted child, why
would one who is already his parent's child by birth insist that his natural
parent adopt him? Such adoption would be necessary for an orphan (in this
case, a gentile) but not for one who is already a born child of the parent in
question. Thus, Presbyterians who reject supersessionism and affirm the
permanence of God's covenant with Israel would have no reason to hope for
the baptism of Jews.

On the other hand, if all are sinners, condemned to ultimate death unless
saved by Christ, then Jews would need baptism along with gentiles. Unless, of
course, Christ's blood bought universal salvation for all from original sin regardless of whether a given individual consciously accepted the proffered
salvation. This is the "inclusivist" position. But here it all gets increasingly
complicated. If, according to inclusivism, all are saved even if they do not
respond with faith in Christ crucified, still they must live lives of fidelity to
conscience and to the good as each person conceives it. But there's the rub. If
all are sinners by nature, how can anyone live according to his conscience or
the good?

Recognizing this, Paul made salvation dependent not on flawed human
works but on the perfect work of Christ on the cross. Thus, the belief in the
necessity of the cross is based on the prior belief in original sin. This is
precisely the sin from which we cannot free ourselves. This type of sin, according to Paul, is not a matter of *what we do* but of *what we are*. We can stop
doing what we do; we cannot stop being what we are, at least not on our own.
So another must provide the righteousness needed for salvation. All of this, as
stated earlier, rests on one's belief in original sin. A student of mine, a believing Jew, was once asked by his deeply concerned evangelical Christian
girlfriend, "Who will die for your sins?" Amazed by the question, he burst out,
"No one, I hope!"

But for Presbyterians this is a real problem. How can God will both the
continued existence of the Jewish people and faith at the same time that God
desires all to come to Christ? In Affirmation 2, the statement holds that "the
continued existence of the Jewish people and of the church as communities
elected by God is . . . a 'mystery.' We do not claim to fathom this mystery . . . at
the same time we can never forget that we stand in a covenant established by
Jesus Christ . . . that requires us to call all women and men to faith in Jesus
Christ. We ponder the work of God."

They may well ponder how they can hold two contradictory positions.
Some Presbyterians have reconciled them by holding that God's covenant

with Israel was with the people, not with the faith known as Judaism. Some hold that if Jews enter the church they remain Jews but now possess a fuller understanding of God's redemptive plan. Presbyterians who believe this support "Jews for Jesus" and other groups seeking to bring Jews to belief in Christ. This, they say, would not make them Christians, but fulfilled Jews. Other Presbyterians oppose church support of such efforts as contradicting their belief in the eternal validity of Israel's covenant. The denomination remains divided on this issue, but major stress remains on talking and working with Jews, rather than seeking their conversion.

Affirmation 3 states "that both the church and the Jewish people are elected by God for witness to the world." They are bound "together in a unique relationship for the sake of God's love for the world. We testify to this election, but we cannot explain it." They cannot explain it because they are, as discussed earlier, still trying to hold together their ancient belief in the universality of Christ's salvific work and their new recognition of the eternal validity of God's covenant with Israel.

Affirmation 4 continues to examine the dilemma, holding that "the reign of God is attested both by the continuing existence of the Jewish people and by the church's proclamation of the gospel of Jesus Christ. Hence, when speaking with Jews about matters of faith, we must always acknowledge that Jews are already in a covenantal relationship with God." This is exactly what Jews have been insisting on for 2,000 years.

The statement goes on to affirm and celebrate the miracle of Jewish survival. The intention prompting it was, doubtless, entirely benevolent. But it ventures into deep and murky waters. It notes that "by ordinary human reckoning," the Jews should have disappeared from history long ago. Not so! Under ordinary historical conditions, there would be hundreds of millions of Jews in the world today. It is due to mass slaughter, relentless persecution, and the resulting conversions to Christianity that there are today fewer than 15 million Jews in the world. The framers of this statement ought to ponder these facts rather than view as miraculous the survival of the remnant of Israel. Under conditions created by Christians seeking to make life all but unlivable for a people they declared to be deicides, it may indeed be miraculous that any Jews survived, but let us be clear as to why a miracle might have been needed to save this people. Christian hatred and persecution of Jews amounted to an illness that afflicted a whole civilization. It had nothing to do with "ordinary human reckoning."

The rest of this affirmation acknowledges that Christians have tried to uproot Judaism by baptizing all Jews. It calls for Christians to stop and take a new look at the Jewish people.... Such reappraisal cannot avoid the issue of evangelism.... [This] often implies a negative judgment on Jewish faith.... On the other hand, Christians are commissioned to witness to the whole world about the good news of Christ's atoning work for both Jew and Gentile. Difficulty arises when we acknowledge that the same Scripture which proclaims that atonement... [also] clearly states that Jews are already in a covenant relationship with God.... For Christians there is no easy answer to this matter.

But is this problem really so insoluble? Christians have departed from the words of Scripture on many occasions. Jesus said, "Call no man your father on earth" (Matt. 23:9), yet Catholic clergy, both Roman and Anglo, are called "father" by the faithful. Paul said, "Let women be silent in church" (1 Cor. 14:34), yet women clergypersons hold forth from the pulpits of many Christian denominations. Jesus said in Mark (10:1–12) that divorce was forbidden, yet it is permitted by most Christian churches. And, of course, same-sex unions are now being debated in many denominations where they are not already permitted.

With all these changes taking place, is it really too much for Jews to expect that Christians will at long last leave them alone and stop trying to take from them their relationship with the living God of Israel, the God of our fathers and of our mothers? Of course in the last forty years, many churches, including the Presbyterian, have ceased their efforts to convert us. But we must appeal to those within these denominations who have not yet got the message, to come to terms with the reality of a vibrant Jewish community of faith that has no intention of abandoning the post to which God has assigned them. Despite these problems with the issue of evangelization, the authors of this statement conclude that "dialogue is the appropriate form of faithful conversations between Christians and Jews. Dialogue is not a cover for proselytism."

In Affirmation 5, the statement acknowledges "the church's long and deep complicity in the proliferation of anti-Jewish attitudes and actions through the 'teaching of contempt' for the Jews." It goes on to repudiate all such teaching and attitudes. Significantly, the framers include anti-Jewish passages in the New Testament. Such passages, they say, should never be read in worship services without proper explanation by the clergy. I would suggest that such passages be either retranslated to reflect what is truly meant or deleted completely from the lectionary. If the church concludes that it must continue to read publicly verses such as John 6:41–42 and 20:19, let it adjust the translation to avoid anti-Jewish sentiment, as well as to express more clearly what is meant. For example, John 6:41–42, which is now translated, "The Jews then murmured at him, because he said, 'I am the bread which came down from heaven.' They said, 'Is not this Jesus, the son of Joseph, whose father and mother we know? How does he now say, "I have come down from heaven?"'" The skepticism of the people here is not due to the fact that they are Jews. So, of course, is Jesus. It is, rather, the result of their having known Jesus since his birth. That is why these neighbors of his are not impressed with the supernatural claim he is now making. Thus the meaning of the passage would be more clearly expressed if the speakers were described as "townsfolk" rather than as Jews. Likewise in John 20:19: "On the evening of that day, the first day of the week, the doors being shut where the disciples were, for fear of the Jews, Jesus came and stood among them." All those in the room are Jews, as is Jesus. It makes no sense to describe them as fearing "the Jews" as such. Substitute the word "authorities" for "Jews," and the passage both makes sense and is freed of its anti-Jewish bias.

The two changes suggested here have, in fact, already been made in the lectionary readings at St. Stephen's Episcopal Church, Charleston, South Carolina, where I teach Bible classes in the summer. I pointed out the problem to my adult Bible students and to the rector. They agreed that the changes had to be made. The rector immediately authorized the two substitutions I recommended, and he is prepared to make others so as to eliminate anti-semitism from public Scripture readings at St. Stephen's. It seems to me that there is no reason that clergy of goodwill could not do the same elsewhere. Of course, in the Roman Catholic Church, the hierarchical structure would require that the decisions be made higher up than at the congregational level. However, if some churches are unwilling to make such changes, it would be better to remove these and similar readings from the public lectionary, since it cannot be expected that the clergy present will have the education or concern needed to explain the unfortunate verses as they now stand.

Affirmation 5 also includes a crucial admission that the negative attitude fostered by the church "was a major ingredient that made possible the monstrous policy of annihilation of Jews by Nazi Germany." The section concludes, "We pledge, God helping us, never again to participate in, contribute to, or (in so far as we are able) to allow the persecution or denigration of Jews or the belittling of Judaism." Who could doubt the sincerity of such powerful, moving words? Such expressions led Jews in the dialogue to look upon the Presbyterian Church (U.S.A.) as a true and reliable friend in time of trouble.

Affirmation 6 deals once again with the issue of "God's promise of land along with the obligations of that promise to the people Israel." With these words the church is bearing witness to Jews that, while it affirms the tie of Israelites to the land of Israel, it will also hold the people accountable for their stewardship over that promised land. The statement quotes an earlier paper issued in 1985 by the Church of Scotland: "The Hebrew Prophets made clear to the people of their own day...that those in possession of 'land' have a responsibility and obligation to the disadvantaged, the oppressed and the 'strangers in their gates.' God's justice, unlike ours, is consistently in favor of the powerless (Psalm 103:6)...we confess our complicity in the loss of land by Palestinians...[who] cry for justice as the dispossessed."

With such words, the church seeks to play the role of prophet in the complex Israel-Palestine dispute. The problem, of course, is that the prophets were not outsiders to the societies they addressed, but Israelites criticizing their own people. Can non-Jews today play such a role? If they attempt to do so, they must be extremely careful to be evenhanded, in this case, recognizing that there were in 1948 hundreds of thousands of "dispossessed" on *both* sides of the conflict. Jews left Arab lands, sometimes under duress, at the same time that Arabs fled from Jewish territories, some of them also under duress. There is enough blame for *both* sides to be called to account. With this statement the Presbyterian Church (U.S.A.) was proclaiming its intention as of 1987 to keep a concerned eye on the doings in the Middle East. We may also find here an early indication of a tendency to favor the Palestinian "underdog."

The final affirmation, Affirmation 7, proclaims, in a felicitous phrase, that Jews and Christians are "partners in waiting" for the Messianic Advent and the Kingdom of Peace and Justice yet to come. While waiting we must work together, two communities commonly elected to strive for social justice, for peace among peoples, for recognition of the holy, and for cultural excellence, all in service to humanity as witnesses to all of God's people.

The Resolution of 2004

The "Theological Understanding" of 1987 provided the ultimate word in Presbyterian understanding of Jews and Judaism until 2004. On July 2 of that year the General Assembly of the church passed a resolution to investigate divestment of the church's $8 billion portfolio in companies doing business with Israel, particularly those aiding in the occupation of the West Bank. Added to this resolution was a call to consider a boycott of Israeli products and a denunciation of the separation fence between Israeli and Palestinian territories. The resolution noted that much of the fence was, in fact, being constructed on the Palestinian side of the 1967 border.

Responses were quick in coming from every side. Buoyed by their church's consideration of joining the Arab boycott of Israel, a radical group of church members traveled to Lebanon and met with leaders of the now infamous Hezbollah, a violent, Iran-sponsored group, dedicated to Israel's destruction and prominent on the U.S. government list of terrorist organizations. Hezbollah was responsible for the 1983 bombing of the Beirut barracks of the U.S. Marine mission that murdered 241 American servicemen, as well as a long series of suicide bombings of innocent Israeli civilians. Its kidnapping of Israeli soldiers was to trigger the war of summer 2006. Embarrassed, the church quickly disavowed those who initiated and attended the meeting.

From the other side, Jewish groups and individuals involved in the Presbyterian-Jewish dialogue reacted with dismay and a profound sense of betrayal. As indicated previously, the Presbyterian Church had long been a leader in the dialogue, having issued some of the most far-reaching statements disavowing proselytizing and recognizing the eternal validity of the Jewish faith and the Jewish covenant with God. It seemed to Jews that people they had viewed as friends had turned on them, joining the enemies of the embattled Jewish state. The fact that polls indicated that only 28 percent of Presbyterian laypeople supported the resolution mattered little. The actions by the church leaders had rekindled among Jews the age-old doubts about Christian sincerity.

The following autumn, the Episcopal Church followed the Presbyterians, voting in convention assembled to engage in a yearlong examination of possible divestment. It also called for the fence to come down. The United Church of Christ followed some months later, threatening to divest and denouncing the fence. In this it was backed by the World Council of Churches. The Evangelical Lutheran Church was soon heard from. It did not suggest divestment, but it did call for the fence to come down, Israeli checkpoints to be closed, and the West Bank Israeli settlements to be abandoned.

Jews were shocked by what they saw as a treacherous attack by churches that had been their closest dialogue partners. Ironically, as the crisis deepened, other churches that had always avoided the theological dialogue with Jews flocked to Israel's defense. Christian Zionist groups made up of evangelical and fundamentalist churches spoke out. The International Christian Embassy in Jerusalem and the Christian Chamber of Commerce in the same city called for increased church investments in Israel. These "Christian Right" groups cautioned fellow Christians against joining the enemies of the Jewish state. Declaring that God had given Israel to the Israelites, they warned that to attempt to delegitimize Israel or to turn on the embattled state in its hour of need was tantamount to opposing God's will as expressed in Scripture.

Israel was delighted to receive this support at a difficult time. The problem, of course, was that it was precisely these pro-Israel churches that denied the eternal validity of the Jewish faith. According to their theology, since the coming of Christ, it was the Christian churches that held the keys to salvation—and Jews wishing to be saved needed baptism and conversion. Still, they held with Paul that "God has not forsaken his people which he fore-knew"(Rom. 11:2). So the Jews—even in theological error—are still the beloved people of God entitled to God's gift of the land though destined for ultimate inclusion into the new Israel of the church.

Jews found themselves in a peculiar position. Those who were our political allies seemed to be our religious antagonists, while those who were our religious allies seemed to be our political antagonists. Of course, some Jews said that this situation was not unique or surprising at all. It proves, they said, that Jews have no true allies among Christians and must go it alone in a world where antisemitism of one sort or another is always lurking in the Christian mind. Since I cannot agree with this grim conclusion, I will attempt another understanding of what is going on here.

First of all, it seems to me that philosemitism, not antisemitism, may be at work among liberal Christians. Perhaps they hold Israel to a higher standard of conduct because they expect more of the people of the covenant. One recalls the anguished cry of the disillusioned young Israeli assassin, reluctantly engaged in hunting down Palestinian terrorists in the film *Munich*: "But we're supposed to be the righteous ones, aren't we?" Why else would the liberal churches single out Israel for criticism while saying little about the murderous forces arrayed against the state or the many more pressing issues of human rights abuses around the world? Perhaps they expect better of us who are "supposed to be the righteous ones."

The problem is that it is easy to be righteous when one has no power to be otherwise. The powerless pre-Constantine Christians were pacifists, devoted to the selfless teachings of their master. That changed overnight with the Christian assumption of Roman imperial power. Jews, too, were largely powerless to affect their own condition until, after 2,000 years of exile, they re-entered history as a political-military force.

Now what? Recent history has taught us that without a state and an army Jews end up in gas chambers and ovens. But *with* those accoutrements of worldly power, where do we end up? Do we become "like the nations," invested in defending self-interest, incapable of self-transcendence, we who are "supposed to be the righteous ones"?

This is an agonizing, heartrending dilemma, and one we have yet to face fully. Perhaps our Christian dialogue partners have seen the problem before we have. How have Jewish political nationalism and military power impacted the Jewish religious and ethical witness? Christians are asking this and related questions. Is it not time that we begin to notice the problem and ask similar questions of our own? This is our dilemma more than theirs. Since the rebirth of Zion in 1948, we Jews have presented ourselves to the world in two capacities: as a witness people of faith and as a political nation armed to the teeth. Do not these capacities clash? Must they clash? What can we do to rescue our spiritual calling from being crushed under the weight of new political necessities? At the same time, Arabs must ask if the churches find less fault with them because they expect less of them. The racialist implications of this possibility are disturbing.

But let us consider another approach. Perhaps the problem is that Christians tend to see distinctions where Jews do not. For example, the division of body and soul in the constitution of the human person means much more to Christians than to Jews. Judaism was already an ancient religion when this Greek dualism entered Jewish thought. Early Israelite faith made no such distinction: the human person was seen as a unity. The concept of "God versus Satan" was similarly a late development in Israelite faith, which had been content to see the misuse of human free will as the source of evil until Judaism came into contact with dualistic Zoroastrianism.

Trinitarism itself, a distinction of three persons within the one God, was never acceptable to Judaism. And how many times, while addressing Christian audiences, have I been asked questions about Judaism's failure to make a radical distinction, as Christianity does, between the carnal and the spiritual? Christianity is much more involved in drawing sharp distinctions than is our faith. Thus it seems strange to Christians that religious, non-Israeli Jews should object to Christian criticism of the political policies of the Israeli government. In their minds, they are in no way being critical of the Jewish people or faith.

But Jews feel in their marrow a profound sense of identification with all other Jews. Even more than a religious faith or a political entity, Jews feel themselves to be a family—a family often under threat from outside. Jews see the twentieth century as made up of two great historical events: the Holocaust and the rebirth of Zion. These can no more be separated from each other than can the Christian events of Good Friday and Easter Sunday. Death and resurrection is a theme common to both faiths. Steven Spielberg's *Schindler's List* and Mel Gibson's *The Passion of the Christ* were, respectively, Jewish and Christian films about the same theme: the death and resurrection of the son of God. In the Jewish Scriptures, Israel is often called "the son of God"; in the New Testament it is Jesus who bears this title. Israel is the collective individual begotten by God to redeem the world; Jesus is the single individual divinely begotten for the same purpose. One goes from Auschwitz to Zion-reborn in three years, the other from the cross to new life in three days. The mystical implications of this last parallel are deeply ponderable.

Without the rebirth of Israel, Jews would be left with the Holocaust. For Jews everywhere, if Israel loses, Auschwitz wins. We do not make the distinction Christians do, in this case at least, between religion and politics. We tend to see Christian attacks on Israeli policy as assaults on our family. And when many Jews experience such attacks, they are led to reflect that, if it had not been for Christian persecution of Jews in Europe, there might not have been the need to gather the Jews in a tiny country that, while being a beloved ancient homeland, is also located in what is perhaps the most dangerous neighborhood in the world. Given Christian conduct toward Jews for 2,000 years, Jews feel that the descendants of the persecutors should have the grace now to avoid criticizing their longtime victims.

Yes, Jews still see Israel as a victim. Little Israel, 5.5 million Jews, surrounded by hundreds of millions of murderous enemies. Liberal Christians, of course, see things differently. They see unjust policies. They see oppression of an underdog by a relatively powerful, nuclear-armed state, and they react as liberals react. When the Jews were the underdogs, liberal Christians were deeply sympathetic. Now the Palestinians have taken that role. They see Israel as the Goliath to the Palestinians' David. All has changed. Dialogue with liberal Jewish Americans is one thing. They agree with liberal Christians on most social and political issues. But nationalistic, power-wielding Israelis are quite different, and Christian liberals are much less sympathetic. This is a distinction Jews do not see or accept—hence the misunderstanding. Since one aim of true dialogue is for each participant to strive to see his dialogue partner as that partner sees himself, it is time for Christians and Jews who value the ongoing conversation to grasp fully this radical divergence of perceptions and include it among the topics to be discussed.

Meanwhile, the conservative churches love victors as liberals love victims. They admire a self-made man and a self-made nation—a scrappy little country of fighters determined to defend their rights and, incidentally, closely allied with America in its fight first against Communism and now against terrorism. Perhaps there is another political issue at work here. It may be that liberal Christians are impatient with Israel because its government seems to be on such close terms with the American administration and its foreign policies.

There is another possible explanation for the conduct of these churches. There are influential Arab Presbyterians, Lutherans, UCC members, and

Episcopalians who have pressed their churches to pass resolutions criticizing Israeli policy. For example, the Reverend Munib A. Younan, bishop of the Evangelical Lutheran Church in Jordan and the Holy Land, has been an outspoken advocate of anti-Israel positions at church assemblies in America. Canon Naim Ateek, a Palestinian Anglican clergyman, is influential in some Episcopal circles. He challenges Israel's right to exist and speaks in highly charged terms of "Israel's crucifixion system," referring to Israel's leaders as "modern-day Herods" overseeing another "slaughter of the innocents." Several anti-Israel resolutions have referred to information fed to the churches by the Sabeel Ecumenical Liberation Theological Center of Jerusalem, a source of much one-sided opinion on Israeli-Palestinian issues. The Reverend Mitri Raheb, Lutheran from Bethlehem, is another anti-Israel spokesperson influencing some church opinion. These men and groups have been active in the movement to blame only Israel for the Middle East dilemma.

Clearly the churches are torn over this issue. They desire ongoing interaction with Jews, yet they are influenced by Arab Christians to find fault with Israel. The churches feel solidarity with Palestinian members of their own denominations and fear an exodus of Christians from the ongoing violence on the West Bank. It is not clear, however, whether Israeli withdrawal from the West Bank would bring peace or deepening chaos. Consider the fate of Gaza, which, once free of Israelis, became a chaotic war zone of rival Palestinian gangs. What would be the fate of Christians in a West Bank in the throes of a civil war between Hamas and Fatah?

The National Assembly of 2006

The divestment resolution of 2004 and the subsequent fierce debate over Middle East policy revealed a deep fault line between the Presbyterians' desire for friendly relations with one once-persecuted minority and their yearning to express solidarity with another minority they perceived as currently being mistreated. As some in the church see it, the oppressed have, tragically, become the oppressors. Deeply conscious of two injustices—one perpetrated by Christians against Jews for centuries, and another they saw as being brought about by Israeli government policies toward Palestinians—the Presbyterians were caught in an agonizing dilemma of conscience. But, in consultation with Jewish dialogue partners, they did find a way out, at least temporarily.

In the two years following the 2004 resolution, interaction between Presbyterians and Jews increased and deepened dramatically. Small conversation groups sprang up across the country, bringing together local church and synagogue members alarmed by the threatened rift and eager to discuss the issues. Sometimes one or two meetings took place between representatives of the respective congregations; sometimes an ongoing series of monthly gatherings was added to the regular schedule of congregational events of the churches and synagogues involved. During the same period, mixed delegations of Jewish and Presbyterian leaders visited Israel and the Palestinian territories to observe conditions and interview locals on many sides of the complex issues that continue to vex the region. Over a two-year period, a more balanced Presbyterian view of the ongoing conflict emerged.

Through reflections and frank discussion among themselves and with Jewish counterparts, a crisis that seemed at first to threaten the future of the dialogue ultimately led to more profound understanding between the two groups. The good will that had grown out of the forty years of talking and sharing enabled the parties to come through a difficult period and emerge together reconfirmed in their cordial relationship.

In June 2006, the Presbyterian Church (U.S.A.) met once again for its biannual national assembly. By a vote of 483 to 28, the delegates revised the resolution of 2004. The lopsided vote reflected the sentiments of grassroots Presbyterian laypersons who had been objecting to the earlier divestment resolution since its adoption two years earlier. They had been made deeply uneasy at the prospect of their church's seeming to join the decades-old Arab boycott of Israel. Overturning the earlier one-sided resolution, the delegates of 2006 voted to invest Presbyterian funds in both Israel and Palestinian territories "only in peaceful pursuits." Gone were the calls of 2004 to divest exclusively from companies doing business with Israel. Mark Pelavin, director of interreligious affairs of the Union for Reform Judaism, an observer at the 2006 assembly, was quoted by the Associated Press as calling the revised resolutions "a critical step toward removing an ugly stain on the church's history of fighting for peace and justice." He was certainly expressing the views of the vast majority of Jews who see Israel as the aggrieved party in the conflict. They never did understand how the Presbyterians could have considered their earlier pro-Palestinian position as continuous with their long-standing policies of promoting "peace and justice."

The crisis in the dialogue may have been overcome, but one suspects that the basic differences remain. The resolution went on to proclaim that, while a sovereign state (meaning Israel) has the right to protect its borders, the present location of Israel's security fence "illegally encroaches into Palestinian territory." Of course Israel does not see it that way. To the Israeli government, the "Palestinian territories" are, in fact, "disputed territories," the boundaries of which remain to be defined. We will hear much, much more of this crucial clash of perceptions in coming years. The resolution of 2006 also called for an end of terror against both Israelis and Palestinians. The whole package was adopted to the enthusiastic applause of the delegates assembled.

Other Protestant churches have also decided not to divest in companies doing business with Israel. Following consideration and debate, the United Church of Christ, the Episcopal Church, and the Evangelical Lutheran Church have all voted not to divest. Clearly they value the dialogue over the opportunity to inject themselves into a complex situation in which there is blame enough for all parties. One-sided resolutions will not bring Middle East peace, but they could destroy the crucial ongoing Jewish-Christian dialogue so successfully begun.

Jews are gratified over these developments yet still puzzled by the denunciations of the security fence by all these churches. Surely, say Jews, the critics must realize that the fence is the most effective measure for defending Israeli civilians against suicide bombings. One might well hold that it should be built on the Israeli side of the green line, but without *any* fence, mad bombers could walk from Palestinian towns and villages into Israeli population centers in as little as fifteen minutes. What country would fail to protect its citizens from such dangers if it had the means to do so? The fence is no long-term solution, but in the short term it appears to be invaluable. Suicide bombings within Israel have almost completely stopped. The churches should make clear that they understand this, while the Israelis should understand that the present route of some sections of the fence will, if not changed, continue to provoke criticism.

And so the issue of the Israeli-Palestinian conflict remains a pressing one. It will continue to be so. But those of us deeply engaged in the Jewish-Christian dialogue must do what we can to keep such questions from destroying one of the most hopeful developments in Western religious history in the last 2,000 years.

II

Toward a Pluralist Theology of Judaism

This work has been concerned with constructing a Jewish theology of Christianity. Such a project can only be undertaken by those willing to move beyond the notion that religious truth is restricted to only one faith tradition. But the openness to a wider truth that underlies that move must eventually—and sooner rather than later—lead us beyond the Jewish-Christian dialogue to a consideration of other religions: to Islam, the third of the Abrahamic faiths, and beyond, to religions outside this tripartite tradition. Thus the underlying assumptions of the Jewish-Christian dialogue must open the participants to a full multifaith pluralism. This is the next step in our spiritual and intellectual journey. It is not the major burden of this study. It still lies before us in all its fullness and richness. But it is implied by what has been said here. In this final chapter I will outline the structure of a possible pluralist theology of Judaism so as to hint at the great promise of universal religious understanding and the hope for human fellowship that lies before us.

From its inception, Israelite faith has been characterized by a balance between particularist and universalist themes. Abraham was called to be the father of a "great nation," centered in a particular holy land. But the ultimate meaning of that nation's life was a universal one: "In you shall all the peoples of the earth be blessed" (Gen. 12:3). In different ages of its history, Israel has stressed one or the other of these aspects of its divine commission. Today, as we search for an understanding of Judaism appropriate to the contemporary world, we must revisit these ancient categories of thought, interpreting them in new and enlightened ways. Conceived narrowly, Jewish particularism could lead us to conclude that God is interested exclusively in one "chosen people," while remaining indifferent to the rest of humanity. Similarly considered, the universal theme of Israel's bringing blessing to all peoples could be seen as a call for Jews to attempt to impose their faith on the whole world. But, if we adopt, as we must, a broad pluralistic interpretation of the particular and the universal in Jewish tradition, we arrive at a liberating vision that will enable Judaism to live in a productive and mutually enriching relationship with its sister faiths around the world. Interpreted in the pluralist spirit, Jewish particularism tells us that Judaism is the faith of the Jewish people and has no mission to convert the world to its own religious laws and practices. Similarly, the universal stress of our faith calls us to search out the image of God in all human persons, to practice reverence for all life, for all being, and to seek to make real the justice and love of God throughout God's world.

Pluralism shows us the way to this higher vision. A responsible contemporary Judaism must develop its self-conception in the context of the global consciousness that is affecting religion as well as all other aspects of world culture. We must deal with and evaluate the truths revealed to others, as well as those we have had revealed to us. We must determine whether any of our own claims must be given up in a pluralistic world. And we must decide what our role is to be in the new global environment as we continue to strive to live up to our divine calling to be a blessing to all the world's peoples.

Judaism Affirms Pluralism

Judaism is a faith that already contains elements of pluralism, for while Judaism views itself as the true faith of the Jewish people, it does not insist on a world in which everyone is Jewish. "For all people will walk every one in the name of his god, and we will walk in the name of the Lord, our God, forever and ever" (Mic. 4:5). Judaism gladly accepts converts, but would-be converts are always told that they need not become Jews in order to live lives acceptable to God. The specific belief system and laws of conduct Judaism has developed are incumbent upon Jews only. What is universal in Judaism are certain ethical principles that are true for all peoples.

The *Tosefta*, a second-century rabbinic text, contains a universal moral code based on God's words to Noah's offspring following the flood. There were, of course, no Jews at Noah's time. The teaching was given for the guidance of all peoples. Its seven rules prohibit blasphemy, idolatry, murder, theft, sexual abominations, and cruelty to animals. It requires all people to establish courts of law to govern their societies. Non-Jews can live lives pleasing to God by obeying these seven precepts. The requirements for a full Jewish life are much more stringent. One source lists 613 commandments given to Jews. Now, later Jewish sources may set much higher standards for gentile conduct than these seven rudimentary laws, but the principle has not changed. There are two basic categories of revelation: one for gentiles, one for Jews. Both are genuine revelations from God. Both are true. That is why Judaism does not actively seek out converts. Any religion that leads its adherents to live moral lives is, to that extent, "true." Thus conversion to Judaism, while possible, is not necessary. Judaism believes in a universal ethic but not a universal theology. While holding that there is one God, Jews expect that different peoples will conceive of divinity in widely differing ways.

Revelation Is Real but Partial

This pluralist tendency, present in Judaism since biblical times, must now be developed further as we engage in full dialogue with those of other faiths. As we do so, we expect other religious communities to do the same. We are especially gratified to see Christianity moving in this direction.

There is no question that pluralism of some sort is exactly what Jews would like Christians to adopt. We hold that our covenant with God is eternal, unaffected (as regards the conduct and faith of Israel) by the coming of Jesus of Nazareth. Pluralists will recognize and respect our faith, in its own integrity, not subsumed under some larger Christian conception (inclusivism) or rejected as invalid since Calvary (exclusivism).

But, while Jews welcome such views, there is a problem with some pluralist interpretations of the world's religions. What is the origin of the world's faiths? Are all the great religions worthy of equal respect as noble products of elevated human imagination? Do communities of people develop religious systems in their attempts to conceive of what John Hick has called the "Real," the ultimate ineffable "isness" beyond all human conception?[1] Surely, this view is true in part. But it ignores the divine role in the establishment of religion.

Does any religion understand itself in exclusively human terms? Certainly, none of the Western religions does. Judaism, Christianity, and Islam are founded on *revelation*. This is not some out-of-the-way, trivial, or easily ignored claim; it is of the essence of these religions. It is among their central convictions. Judaism does not see itself as the product of a group of people who project their concept of God onto the void—or even the "Real." The faith of Israel stands or falls on the conviction that the God of Israel, who is the Lord and Monarch of the Universe, has elected this people to be God's witness in the world. Israel is to proclaim God's sovereignty, keep God's laws, and advance God's reign on this earth.

The moral, ethical, and spiritual message Israel brings to a sometimes receptive, sometimes resisting world is the content of the revelation it has received from the Holy One. For not only does God reveal the divine existence to Israel, God also reveals commands, propositions, and goals. In short, revelation has a *content*; this content is found in Scripture and is filtered through human responses down through the ages. Of course, it is human beings who hear the divine voice as they are able, and it is human language in which that voice is expressed. I am not propounding a biblical fundamentalism or denying the human element in the revelatory process. Tradition tells us that "the Torah speaks in the language of humanity."[2] But, at the same time, those humans who have received and passed on in human words the Word of God have been acutely aware that what they were transmitting, they had received. God's Word is not identical with the human words that express it, but it is borne aloft by them as they struggle to articulate the divine message. Religions based on revelation give up that self-understanding at their peril. Religious persons know that they are "addressed" by God, and they feel called upon to respond.

Whether the command is "Thou shalt not murder" or "Honor the Sabbath day," whether they consider the election of Israel or the gift of the holy land, religious Jews feel in the very fiber of their being the summons of their God. The central command is "Hear, O Israel!" Israelites know themselves to be the object of God's attention, concern, and command. They understand themselves as being understood by God; they see themselves as being seen by God. They stand before God, and they know before whom they stand. This is the very essence of Jewish self-understanding. For believing Jews, their religion is not a human projection but the result of an original divine outreach to humanity. The God of the Bible is a God who reaches down to touch human creatures and make them subjects of God's earthly kingdom.

Some pluralists assert that Jews and members of other religious communities are only accidentally adherents of this or that faith. Essentially they are seekers of meaning and fellow travelers on the spiritual high road to the "Real." But for believers their identity as Jewish or Christian or Muslim is no accident of time or place. Jews know that they were chosen by God as Israelites at Sinai, long before their individual births. Thus, from the perspective of Judaism, there is no such thing as a purely "cultural Jew" or "ethnic Jew."

All Jews are Jews religiously even if they do not practice their religion. They are Jews religiously because they have been chosen and commissioned by Israel's God to be among God's witnesses on this earth. " 'You are my witnesses,' says the Lord" (Is.10:12). They may be good witnesses or poor ones, but they are witnesses nevertheless. What they do or do not do reflects upon the people Israel and its Heavenly Monarch. Even the frenzied energy with which some Godless Jews proclaim their alienation from their people and its God, the Jewish apostate's frequent leadership of groups and movements devoted to removing God-consciousness from ever greater areas of human life, attest to the power of God's call. Jews hear that call in their very marrow, and they respond with humble obedience or with energetic defiance. One only attempts to silence a voice that one has heard.

This compelling sense of being commanded by God and of being shaped and defined by that command is missing in much of the pluralists' writing on religion. It is, of course, correct that no faith tradition and certainly no individual can know God entirely as God is. No revelation can exhaust the inexhaustible. "You cannot see my face; for no one can see me and live" (Exod. 33:20), says the Lord. And yet God goes on to describe aspects of the divine life to Moses: "The Lord, the Lord, a God merciful and gracious, slow to anger, and abounding in steadfast love and faithfulness" (Exod. 34:6). All of these terms are, to be sure, relational. They describe not the divine essence but God in interaction with humanity. God is merciful—to whom?—to us! God abounds in steadfast love—for whom?—for us! All that we can say of God—can know of God—is revealed in the life God deigns to share with us, the creatures whom God loves. The divine totality is, of course, hidden from finite human beings. But that does not mean that we can know nothing of God or that all that we can know is a human projection. God is not wholly unknowable because God has chosen to reveal some aspects of the divine self to us. We only know of God what God has told us. This is not human speculation but divine self-disclosure.

Revelation's content goes beyond commands and goals for human life. We dare to believe that the God of the universe has in some humanly unspeakable way invited us into the very divine life, has shared it with us insofar as we are capable of understanding it. What has been revealed may be only the tiniest fraction of the divine totality, but it is, nevertheless, as real a part of that totality as the inconceivably greater part that remains hidden.

This is what revealed religions claim, and those who call themselves theologians of these religions dare not dismiss these claims. If they do, they cease to represent the traditions they are attempting to articulate in new and creative ways. Theologians interpret the claims of their respective faiths. They may conceive them in radical formulations. But they may not simply ignore them any more than they may reject them outright. If they do, they become philosophers of religion engaged in freelance theorizing, making their way through belief systems, accepting or discarding traditional doctrines as they will. But if they choose this path, they have ceased to be theologians, properly so called.

Theology is not conducted in a vacuum or from some allegedly objective perch in the middle of the air. Theology must be grounded in a living faith tradition. To be part of a tradition does not mean that one must endlessly repeat the affirmations of one's forebears. It means, rather, that one must march forward in their name. But the steps one takes in this progressive journey must be along a path that is continuous with the one laid out by those who came before. Tradition is never a dead letter; it is a dynamic, growing reality. But new insights must emerge from the living fabric and deal with the categories of thought and experience that have given it its unique character and definition. Revelation need not be conceived as a literal voice from heaven. Nor need one identify the Word of God precisely with the human words that bear it aloft. But to give up the sense of being addressed by a power beyond the human is to give up too much.

Revelation Is Both Partial and Universal

Can one be a pluralist while holding to the truth of the revealed nature of one's own faith? Certainly, as long as one makes room for revelation beyond the bounds of one's own group's experience. Jews are in possession of the word of truth through revelation, but that is not to say that theirs is the final word. Other traditions have an equal right to claim their own word of truth. We cannot judge their claims in advance. But we are called by our universal Creator to listen and evaluate and, perhaps, learn something new. It may well be that the God revealed to Israel has revealed other truths to other peoples through other means. We Jews know from the revelation given to us that the power of revelation is so great, its breadth so wide, that we dare not restrict it to a single word. We are called upon to proclaim with conviction and eloquence the truth that has been revealed to us, while listening to the equally impassioned (and perhaps equally valid) truths others claim to have had revealed to them. This is not simplistic relativism or unreflective universalism. It is an affirmation of the reality of a truth communicated by God combined with a humble admission that we may not be in possession of all of it. In fact, if we are limited human beings, we cannot possess a truth that, in its fullness, is in God alone. By definition, the finite cannot absorb the infinite.

Religious pluralists need give up none of their positive claims or traditional beliefs about what they have received. Only one claim must be surrendered: the single negative claim that there is truth to be found in no faith save our own. This pernicious attitude toward the religious other has been the source of the all too real negative tradition in religion, the dark side of the light of faith. Pluralist theologians can affirm a religion that is recognizable to the people in the pews while calling on them to transcend self-satisfied and self-congratulatory attitudes that contradict their own faith in a just and loving God who would not abandon most of the human race to darkness.

Judaism Avoids Exclusivism

Certainly Jewish pluralists must affirm the truth of what God has said to us while opening ourselves to the possible truth of others' claims. Such a theory of multiple revelations would be compatible with the views of pluralist Paul F. Knitter.[3] Jews would, in fact, be more open to this approach than would many Christians. Theoretically, at least, Judaism has been more tolerant of other faiths than has Christianity. The history of Jewish bigotry has been real enough, but it has told of a Judaism that has been intolerant primarily of deviations within the Jewish fold. Jewish authorities persecuted Christian sectarians as long as they claimed to be Jews, especially when they claimed to be the only true Israel (people of God). As it gradually became clear in the second century that the Nazarene or Christian sect of Judaism had become a new gentile-dominated religion—no internal threat to more traditional forms of Judaism—active opposition by Jewish authorities faded. Nasty remarks and negative evaluations of Christianity continued to be heard, but less and less frequently and with declining intensity. Jews simply assumed that gentiles would believe strange things and took little interest. There were internal Jewish heresies to combat and sufficient opportunities to express negative impulses within the community.

Christianity, on the other hand, with its missionizing zeal, became obsessed with the Jewish other who refused to recognize the divinity of the Christian Messiah to whom Judaism had given birth. In time Christian negative attitudes would be directed at Muslims and others, but the Jews were always the most unbearable other for their sister faith whose universal claims seemed to be mocked by continued Jewish existence. How could the God revealed in Christ, the "universal savior," also will the continued existence of Jewry and Judaism? The monistic view fashioned by the church to deal with Jews became the model for Christian dealings with all other faiths. Henceforth, for Christians, the world would be divided between those already in the fold and those not yet brought to the one universal truth. Jews were seen as enemies of that truth and were consequently subjected to savage persecution by Christian authorities.

Jews, however, while assuming that their truth was incalculably fuller and richer than that granted to others, still recognized that God had spoken to and about gentiles through those ancient universal ethical rules revealed to the sons of Noah. They never claimed that Israel alone had heard the word of God. No matter how rudimentary and partial God's message to the gentiles had been, still it was a genuine divine communication. This view, as unsatisfactory as it may be in this age of dialogue, did prevent Jews from claiming the kind of revelatory exclusivism insisted on by Christians. Not only did Jews recognize that non-Jews could live by revealed ethical law, but they were also willing to see such a life as salvific for the religious other. "The righteous of all nations have a share in the world to come."[4] What was missing was any willingness to entertain the possibility that Israel's God may have revealed more to gentiles than the Noahide laws. Christianity was never seen as having a divine source. Christians would be judged by God strictly in Noahide terms, as would all gentiles. While no true Jewish theological evaluation of Christianity was attempted, nevertheless, as gentiles, Christians and others could exist outside of Israel while remaining in touch with Israel's God who was always conceived as the God of all humanity. This is pluralism of a very rudimentary kind, but in proposing that God had spoken and continues to speak to non-Jews, it prevented Judaism from adopting a harsh exclusivism or a muddled inclusivism.

A Jewish Pluralism

If all this is true, then Jews will have fewer problems than will Christians in accepting a pluralist theory of multiple revelations. We already recognize that God revealed to humanity guidelines for ethical life prior to the creation of the people Israel. And since Jewish tradition has continued to apply these standards to gentile societies, we know that the revelations to Israel in no way superseded or invalidated the earlier more general revelation. Here the Jewish view of the continued applicability of the Noahide laws stands in contrast to the traditional Christian position regarding the pre-Christian revelations to

Israel. Of course all Christians recognize that the present validity of the New Covenant rests upon the prior validity of the Old. But it was usually assumed (following Paul's reasoning in Galatians rather than in Romans) that, with the coming of the new dispensation, the old had passed away. In contrast, Israel never held a similar view of the Noahide laws. They remained as valid for gentiles after the creation and election of Israel as they had been before. They continue to offer minimum standards of conduct for gentile societies.

Thus Judaism subscribes to a "double-revelation" theory, which can now be expanded into a multiple revelation theory as we examine and attempt to evaluate the claims of other faith communities in all their particularism. Unlike Christians, who will have to think for the first time of another possible revelation (or revelations) existing side by side with Christianity, Jews have that thought structure already in place. But we now must apply it in ways we never have before, dealing for the first time with the specific claims of other faiths and their followers rather than simply lumping them all together as "gentiles." Is it possible that the God who addressed the pre-Israelite world in Noah's day has also addressed the non-Israelite world with new revelations? This question cannot be answered a priori. But if we examine each of the great world faiths and find that they lead their followers to elevated lives of spiritual striving, ethical sensitivity, and moral conduct, we must conclude that there is truth in them. And if their adherents claim that that truth has been received by them through divine disclosure through revelation, what reason would we have to dispute that claim? A pluralist theology of multiple revelations seems best suited to compassing the world's faiths, trying to see them as closely as possible to the way they see themselves.

Conclusions

At the beginning of the Israelite tradition, God calls Abraham with these words: "Get you out of your land and of your father's house" (Gen. 12:1). Get you out! Get out of where you are and go to where you can be. This is a call to self-transcendence at the very beginning of the story of Israel and of the Western religious tradition. Get out of where you are, out into a wilderness, out into trackless desert. Abraham does not know where he is going; he goes by faith, and God says: "I will make you a great nation." Now this cannot mean a great nation in terms of numbers—the Jews are a tiny people—but a great nation in that Israel bears a great message into the world. Now Christians and Muslims are together more than 3 billion strong. If Christians and Muslims take it into their heads to think that they are the only bearers of truth, they are narrow-minded and egocentric; but if we Jews, with at most 15 million people, insist that we are the only bearers of truth, not only are we narrow and egocentric, we are indulging in a kind of theological madness. Can we seriously entertain the notion that God, having created the 6 billion people now living on this earth, is concerned with the religious welfare of only 15 million? One is led to ask why God bothered to create the rest of them. But this question is ludicrous, as are the exclusivist assumptions on which it is based.

The God who is the loving parent of all people must have provided divine guidance to many cultures and societies in an effort to make the heavenly will known to all. Naturally such words of revelation would be spoken to many peoples in many tongues, terms, and symbol systems. Pluralism would seem to be the theory best suited to account for the wondrous variety of religions flourishing in the world. But what kind of pluralism are we talking about? There are many kinds. There is a plurality of pluralisms. I tend to do pluralism from the inside out, not the outside in. Rather than beginning with pluralist assumptions, I search for elements in our Jewish texts and traditions that are self-transcendent, that lead us inevitably beyond Judaism, out into the world of our sister faiths.

And there we find Christianity with which we share a book; then Islam with which we share a foundation of law and radical monotheism. And then beyond, to all the faiths with which we share a commitment to live the life of the spirit and to respect the dignity of every human being. Pluralist principles require self-transcendence and oppose egocentricity, whether it be an egocentricity of the individual or of the group. Religion in practice is, I think, both self-affirmation and self-transcendence. It calls the self to proclaim the truth it has received, but also to reach beyond the self, whether that self be individual or collective. We must take into account the religious beliefs and practices of others. It has been said that what people have in common is their uniqueness. There is no one theology for all. Every group's theology must recognize and make room for the theologies of others.

But, paradoxically, opposition to any universal theology seems to assume the upholding of a universal ethic. If there is no universally applicable ethic, how are we to distinguish between true religion and false religion, between the divine and the demonic? I accept the pluralist principle that a religion is "true" not because it accords with the true nature of God as God actually is (for who can know the divine nature in its totality?), but because that religion has the power to produce virtuous people. To say this we must hold to a standard of virtue that applies to everyone. So, if we are going to be safely relativist about theology, we must be universal in our ethics.

Jewish tradition teaches us to say in our prayers, "I am but dust and ashes, yet the world was created for my sake."[5] We humans are finite creatures, limited in every way, except perhaps for our yearning, our yearning for the infinite. And this too leads us into pluralism, because our finite theories of the divine cannot compass the infinite divine itself, and yet we yearn to do so. Limited beings that we are, we turn to each other, and to each other's traditions to fill out what our particular visions lack.

Someone has said that all theology is local. In pluralist terms all theories of the divine are restricted by time and place, by language and historical experience. But if we allow these theories to meet, to talk to each other, to enrich each other, then the local begins to expand, ever growing, ever widening, until the vision of a new and wider world may emerge. With that vision, and bearing with us the wisdom we have gained from absorbing the teachings of other traditions, we may go back into our own communities to right wrongs, to smash the idols that isolated communities inevitably carve out for themselves from their fears and their need for ego gratification.

Religious exclusivism is nothing more than corporate egoism of creed and community. Pluralism must include a humane prophetic witness, which will enable us to deal with our fellow beings of different faiths as well as with our own people, valuing distinctions of culture and belief rather than condemning or denigrating them. Pluralism offers us new structures of thought designed to do just that. How radically new are these structures? They are as new as the indefinite article in speech is unlike the definite article. Instead of being *the* chosen people, my people begin to see themselves as *a* chosen people. Instead of *the* true church, Christians come to see themselves as *a* true church. Nothing has changed in my devotion to my tradition. Yet everything has changed because the world in which my tradition functions is recognized as filled with chosen peoples and true churches.

In other words, they are "chosen" and "true" in that they are communities that see themselves as chosen to seek out the truth. What a breath of fresh air all this represents! A new vision inspired by the infinite and the eternal to which we seek to draw near. In a world darkened by human self-isolation, by fear and distrust growing out of that isolation and ignorance of the other—the other who is in every case our brother and our sister—in the midst of that darkness pluralists say in the words that Jewish Scripture attributes to divinity itself, "Let there be light!"

There is a famous story in the Midrash, the ancient Jewish collection of legends, about Abraham and the idols. Abraham's father, says the story, was a manufacturer of idols. One day he went out, leaving little Abraham in the idol shop to watch the statues. Abraham had at that moment a revelation of the true God, and he took a club and smashed all the idols except the biggest one, and put the club in the hands of the largest statue. His father came home and said, "What happened here?! All my statues are smashed!" Abraham answered, "Well, they had a fight, and the biggest one killed all the others." His father replied, "What do you mean they had a fight? They are only statues." "Ah," replied Abraham, "then why do you worship them?"[6]

There are idols of thought as well as idols of stone. John Calvin said that the human mind is a factory for the production of idols. And what is true for individuals is true for our religious communities; it is often the communities that produce the idols. Each faith community, I think, generates a particular kind of idolatry unique to it. Catholicism produces "ecclesiolatry," the worship of the church as an institution, rather than God. Protestants have their own form of idolatry. Karl Barth was speaking to a group of Protestants when he said, "You congratulate yourselves because you have no pope; but you have made the Bible into a paper pope." So Protestants produce "scriptolatry"— their version of idolatry, the absolutizing of the biblical text. We Jews produce our own kind of idolatry, which is "ethnolatry"—the absolutizing of Jewish peoplehood, rather than of God, to whom our people are called to witness.

What is idolatry? It is to put any earthly things in place of God. To put anything finite in place of the infinite. To put anything time-bound in place of the eternal—a church, a book, a people. But God can also be an idol, if we mean by God only a human conception. Now we have to have human conceptions of God. If God is to impinge on our lives, we must have such human conceptions, because we are human beings and we can have no other conceptions. And God must impinge on our lives if we are to call ourselves religious. I am a Jew. I worship the God of Israel. But that God can become an idol if I stop with it and imagine that I possess all of God. The idol is always opaque; the idol is always limited. However, that same conception of God can become a genuine revelation of God if we allow it to become transparent. True self-transcendent religion understands that the Holy One, the Ein Sof, the God beyond god, the Desert of the Godhead, the No-Thing, the Thou that cannot become an it, the Light Invisible is shining through the symbols and images revealed in our respective traditions.

Now what do I mean by revelation? How are these ideas revelations of God? Is revelation a truth that comes from God, or does it come from the human self? Well, it is both. It must be both because the human, according to the Scriptures, is created in the divine image. But what does that mean? In Judaism there can be no images of God; there can be no pictures of God. These are forbidden. I think they are forbidden because, as I wrote in chapter 1, there already is a divine image and we are it. But surely we are not the image of God in a physical sense. God is imageless, and yet we are in the image of God. Thus humans are fashioned in the image of an imageless God. In Judaism the God who is imageless is also unnamable. We are forbidden to write or even to say the divine name. And yet we Jews know what that name means—God is called "The One who Shall Be" (Exod. 3:14), in other words, the endlessly self-transcendent. That is the nameless name of the Eternal One.

If God is unnamable, indefinable, and irreducible to any image or any definition, then so are we, since we are earthly images of God. The human person is always more than any definition can name, always more. The higher religion should be an iconoclastic smashing of all the idols, of all the images that claim to be the totality of God, as well as images created of the human by the various disciplines that we have at all our universities.

Are we social beings? Sociologists say yes. They are right, but we are more. Are we sexual beings? Freudians say yes. They are right, but we are more. Are we economic beings? Marxists say yes. They are right, but we are more. Are we political beings? Yes, the political scientists are right, but we are more. It is the "more" that makes us human, as it is the "more" that makes God, God.

Alfred, Lord Tennyson put it well in his poem "In Memoriam":

> Our little systems have their day;
> They have their day and cease to be.
> They are but broken lights of thee,
> And thou, O Lord, art more than they...

Revelation is the breaking of the infinite into the finite to reveal to the finite the infinite life that was already there but in such a way that the finite was unaware of it. This is the infinite life within us, the *nefesh*, or soul. It is a reflection of the infinite life without, the *ruach*, the spirit of God. Revelation makes clear to us that this inner soul is the mirror of the universal spirit, that the infinite macrocosm is reflected in the finite/infinite microcosm. Thus we are introduced to our true nature by the revelation of God who is "more distant than stars yet nearer than the eye."[7]

One path to pluralism is to view all conceptions of God as merely human constructs. But this is only a partial truth. There must be something human in them or human beings could not receive them. But this is just the point. These concepts of God are received, not generated by people. If we insist that positive images of God are human creations and only human creations, we are denying the core experience of religious believers. That experience is of receiving a revelation of at least a part of the divine reality. Without revelation there can be no religion. Without revelation we are left with a form of human spirituality or self-transcendence that is crucial to religion but not sufficient. There must also be a breaking in from beyond the human, a communication from the divine. If theologians do not take this central experience of faith into account, or even deny it, then they will end up speaking for no one and speaking to no one. Our formulations are only valid if they reflect the lived experience of believers.

But it will be objected that the different revelations claimed by the various traditions sometimes contradict one another. How, then, could one divine reality be the source of them all? But why should God not use the varied languages and symbol systems of the world's peoples to reveal divine truths? Each age, each culture yearns to hear the voice of revelation anew. This is true even within a single faith in which a strong ongoing tradition still remains open to new insights from its transcendent source. If it does not cultivate such openness, it will soon cease to be a dynamic, living faith. Some examples may be of help here.

Jewish tradition insists that we never refer to "the God of Abraham, Isaac and Jacob." No, we must always refer to the Eternal as "the God of Abraham, the God of Isaac, and the God of Jacob." We must do this to remind ourselves that the Holy One is revealed to each new generation in new ways, ways that may be very unlike prior revelations. This does not mean that God changes in the divine essence or totality, whatever that may be. Rather, it means that people and circumstances change, and so the divine messages must change so as to speak to those who need to hear them in the situations in which they find themselves. None of these revelations contains the totality of the divine. How could a finite message to finite human beings compass the infinite reality of God? Yet each message is true as a partial revelation of the One who, as infinite divine totality, is forever hidden from us.

In the "Hymn of Glory," chanted in the Orthodox synagogue at the end of the Sabbath morning service, God is described as imaged forth in many apparitions recorded in the Bible:

> I have not seen thee, yet I tell thy praise,
> Nor known thee, yet I image forth thy ways.
>> For by thy seers' and servants' mystic speech
>> Thou didst thy sov'ran splendor darkly teach,
> And from the grandeur of thy work they drew
> The measure of thine inner greatness too.
>> They told of thee, but not as thou must be,
>> Since from thy work they tried to body thee.

To countless visions did their pictures run,
Behold through all the visions thou art one.
 In thee old age and youth at once were drawn,
 The grey of eld, the flowing locks of dawn,
The ancient judge, the youthful warrior,
The man of battles, terrible in war,
 The helmet of salvation on his head,
 And by his hand and arm the triumph led,
His head all shining with the dew of light,
His locks all dripping with the drops of night....
 His head is like pure gold; his forehead's flame
 Is graven glory of his holy name.
And with that lovely diadem 'tis graced,
The coronal his people there have placed.
 His hair as on the head of youth is twined,
 In wealth of raven curls it flows behind....
Ruddy in red apparel, bright he glows
When he from treading Edom's wine-press goes....[8]

The hymn declares that, beneath all these images, God is One, and One who is revealed to God's children as they are able to receive the image that bears the message. To one seer God appears as a youth, to another, an "ancient of days," to a third, a judge, to a fourth, a warrior. And what of the greatest seer of all who saw in one encounter a burning bush, in another a cloud of smoke and, in a third, the back of a human figure? Did any of these sages doubt that it was the same One who was revealed in all these widely varied epiphanies? These images, all part of the Jewish tradition, have no more in common with each other than they do with apparitions of God found in the religious traditions of the East. Varied appearances do not necessarily imply varied sources. If this is true within one tradition, why should it not be true of the many traditions through which God speaks to humanity? To ask which of these appearances is "truest" is clearly to ask the wrong question. To hold that they are too different from each other to arise from a single source is to jump to the wrong conclusion. All come from God. They may seem contradictory, but all are partial but real experiences of an outreach from the divine to the human.

In his First Letter to the Corinthians, Paul speaks of himself as having become "all things to all people so that by all means some might be saved" (9:22). With the Greeks he became like a Greek, with the Jews like a Jew. What he wrote to the Galatians was the virtual opposite of what he wrote to the Corinthians. Imagine the chaos that would have ensued if he had mixed up the letters and sent them to the wrong communities! Was Paul contradicting himself? No. He told each group what it needed to hear. Why cannot God do the same thing?

I offer the three examples here to support the proposition that God has revealed different truths to different peoples at different times and places. All of them are partial truths designed to guide each group according to their needs. If this view can provide the basis for a pluralist theory of revelation, then pluralism need not deny the truth of revelation as it is experienced in the actual religious life of believers.

True pluralism calls on all the higher religions to recognize the power of revelation in the others. In other words, they come to see the religious other to be of God. God reveals and discloses. God introduces selves to themselves and to each other in all the great religious traditions. I start with Judaism, but from that perspective, Christianity is just here, just at the ends of my fingers, and just beyond is Islam and then the other great faiths.

But if revelations of the divine and the human are also to be found in Buddhism and Hinduism and Jainism and Sikhism and Taoism, et cetera, et cetera, then all faiths are true that lead us from egocentricity to participation in the infinite life with all its ethical and spiritual blessings. The important thing is not to know Moses or Jesus or Buddha; the important thing rather is to know what Moses and Jesus and Buddha knew, and that is available to us in the contemporary world in new ways. Aided by modern communications and global consciousness, we can learn what each of our traditions has to teach us to enrich our lives. When that happens, what those great sages knew is seen not just as human constructs in the earthbound sense. They lead us from what we merely are to what we really are: human participants in the divine life in which "we live and move and have our being" (Acts 17:28).

Notes

INTRODUCTION

1. Talmud: Pirke Avot, chap. 1:14.

CHAPTER ONE

1. T. S. Eliot, "Choruses from the Rock," in *T. S. Eliot: The Complete Poems and Plays* (New York: Harcourt Brace, 1980), p. 111.

2. Søren Kierkegaard, *Philosophical Fragments,* in *A Kierkegaard Anthology,* ed. Robert Bretall (Princeton, NJ: Princeton University Press, 1972), p. 169.

3. James Joyce, *Ulysses* (New York: Modern Library, 1961), p. 37.

4. Talmud: Sanhedrin 4;5.

5. Talmud: Sanhedrin 56b, Tosefta.

6. Talmud: Pirke Avot, chap. 1:3.

7. Augustine, *City of God,* book XIV, chap. 13, trans. Gerald G. Walsh et al., (New York: Doubleday, 1958), p. 308.

8. *Mahzor for Rosh Hashanah and Yom Kippur,* ed. Jules Harlow (New York: Rabbinical Assembly, 1972) p. 413.

9. Augustine, *Confessions,* book XI, trans. Edward B. Pusey (New York: Modern Library, 1949) pp. 243–69.

10. Poem LIX: "When they come back, if blossoms do." See Emily Dickinson, *The Poems of Emily Dickinson,* ed. Martha Dickinson Bianchi and Alfred Leete Hampson (New York: Little, Brown, 1939), p. 311.

11. Jean-Paul Sartre, *Being and Nothingness,* trans. Hazel E. Barnes (New York: Philosophical Library, 1956).

12. *Catechism of the Catholic Church* (New York: Libreria Editrice Vaticana Catholic Book Publishing, 1994), Article 405.

13. Ibid., Article 407.

14. Ibid., Article 411.

15. *Mahzor for Rosh Hashanah and Yom Kippur*, ed. Jules Harlow (New York: Rabbinical Assembly, 1972), p. 243.

16. Roger Haight, *Jesus, Symbol of God* (Maryknoll, NY: Orbis Books, 1999), pp. 155–78.

CHAPTER TWO

1. Luke Timothy Johnson, *The Real Jesus: The Misguided Quest for the Historical Jesus and the Truth of the Traditional Gospels* (San Francisco: Harper, 1997).

2. A number of helpful collections of messianic texts are available to the interested reader, including Raphael Patai, *The Messiah Texts* (Detroit, MI: Wayne State University Press, 1979); and Jacob Neusner, William S. Green, and Ernest Frerichs, eds., *Judaisms and Their Messiahs at the Turn of the Christian Era* (New York: Cambridge University Press, 1987). The first Princeton Symposium on Judaism and Christian origins produced a valuable volume of essays: James H. Charlesworth, ed., *The Messiah: Developments in Earliest Judaism and Christianity* (Minneapolis, MN: Fortress Press, 1992).

3. "Hail to the Lord's Anointed" (Advent hymn), James Montgomery, 1821.

CHAPTER THREE

1. Moshe Halbertal, "One Possessed of Religion: Religious Tolerance in the Teachings of the Me'iri," *Edah Journal* 1:1 (Marheshvan, 57–61): 2.

2. Jacob Katz, *Exclusiveness and Tolerance: Jewish-Gentile Relations in Medieval and Modern Times* (New York: Schocken Books, 1962), p. 116.

3. Ha Me'iri, *Beit Ha-Behirah* on Avodah Zarah 20a, p. 46.

4. Moses Maimonides, *Hilkhot Melakhim*, 11.

5. Moses Maimonides, *Commentary on the Mishnah: Avodah Zarah*, 1.3.

6. Augustine, *The City of God*, book 4, chap. 34; book 18, chap. 46, trans. Henry Bettenson (London: Penguin, 1972), pp. 177, 827–28.

7. Philo of Alexandria, *Embassy to Gaius*, trans. F. H. Colson (New York: Loeb Library, 1943), vol. 10, pp. 3–187.

8. Talmud; Avodah Zarah.

9. Ha Me'iri, *Beit Ha-Behirah, Ta'nit*, ed. A. Sofer p. 97.

10. Halbertal, "One Possessed of Religion," p. 7, fn. 16.

11. Ibid., p. 9.

12. Ibid.

13. Ha Me'iri, *Beit Ha Behirah*, on Shabbat, p. 615.

14. Talmud: Pirke Avot, chap. 2:1.

15. Alexander Altmann, *Moses Mendelssohn* (Alabama: University of Alabama Press, 1973), p. 249.

16. Ibid.

17. Eva Jospe, ed., *Moses Mendelssohn: Selections from His Writings* (New York: Viking Press, 1975), pp. 134–35.

18. Moses Maimonides, *Mishneh Torah: Laws of Kings*, 8:11.

19. This appeared in a footnote to Mendelssohn's letter to Christian theologian Johann Caspar Lavater. The footnotes appear in M. Sammuel, *Memoirs of Moses Mendelssohn*, 2nd ed. (London, 1827), pp. 148–49. Cited in the essay is "Mendelssohn's Religious Perspective of Non-Jews," by Zvi Jonathan Kaplan in *Journal of Ecumenical Studies* vol. 41, nos. 3–4 (Summer–Fall 2004).

20. Kaplan, "Mendelssohn's Religious Perspectives," p. 2.

21. David Sorkin, *Moses Mendelssohn and the Religious Enlightenment* (Berkeley: University of California Press, 1996), p. 84.

22. Moses Mendelssohn, *Jerusalem*, trans. Allen Arkush (Waltham, MA: Brandeis University Press, 1983), pp. 89–90.

23. Michael Wyschogrod, *The Body of Faith: Judaism as Corporeal Election* (New York: Seabury Press, 1983), p. 64.

24. Søren Kierkegaard, *Philosophical Fragments*, in *A Kierkegaard Anthology*, ed. Robert Bretall (Princeton, NJ: Princeton University Press, 1946), pp. 164–74.

25. Elijah Benamozegh, *Israel and Humanity*, trans. Maxwell Luria (New York: Paulist Press, 1995).

26. Moses Maimonides, *Mishneh Torah: Hilkhot Malakhim*, 10.10.

27. Benamozegh, *Israel and Humanity*, pp. 237–59.

28. Ibid., p. 246.

29. Ibid., pp. 260–80.

30. Ibid., p. 239.

31. Ibid.

32. Ibid., pp. 50–52.

33. Ibid., p. 51.

CHAPTER FOUR

1. Franz Rosenzweig, letter to Rudolph Ehrenburg, in *Jewish Perspectives on Christianity*, ed. Fritz Rothschild (New York: Continuum, 1996), p. 169.

2. T. S. Eliot, *The Family Reunion*, in *The Complete Poems and Plays* (New York: Harcourt, Brace and World, 1962), p. 275.

3. Franz Rosenzweig, letter to Rudolph Ehrenburg, Nov. 1, 1913, Rothschild, *Jewish Perspectives on Christianity*, p. 170.

4. Franz Rosenzweig, letter to Rudolph Ehrenburg, Nov. 4, 1913, in Rothschild, *Jewish Perspectives on Christianity*, p. 173.

5. Franz Rosenzweig, letter to Eugen Rosenstock-Huessy, Nov. 7, 1916, in *Judaism Despite Christianity*, ed. Eugen Rosenstock-Huessy (New York: Schocken Books, 1969), p. 133.

6. Franz Rosenzweig, *The Star of Redemption* (New York: Holt Rinehart and Winston, 1971), p. 337.

7. Franz Rosenzweig, letter to Rudolph Ehrenburg, Nov. 1, 1913, in Rothschild, *Jewish Perspectives on Christianity*, p. 171.

8. Franz Rosenzweig, *Star of Redemption*, p. 396.

9. Franz Rosenzweig, letter to Rudolph Ehrenburg, Nov. 1, 1913, p. 172.

10. "Romantic Religion," selections from Leo Baeck, *Judaism and Christianity: Essays*, translated with an introduction by Walter Kaufman (New York: Jewish Publication Society, 1970); Leo Baeck, "Judaism in the Church," in *Hebrew Union College Annual 2* (Cincinnati, OH: Hebrew Union College, 1925), pp. 125–44.

11. Martin Buber, "The Two Foci of the Jewish Soul," in *Israel and the World: Essays in a Time of Crisis* (New York, Schocken Books, 1963), p. 35.

12. Martin Buber, "Church, State, Nation, Jewry," in Rothschild, *Jewish Perspectives on Christianity*, p. 133.

13. Ibid., p. 135.

14. Ibid.

15. Ibid.

16. Ibid., p. 136.

17. Ibid.

18. Ibid., p. 142.

19. Talmud: Sanhedrin 8b.

20. Rothschild, *Jewish Perspectives on Christianity*, p. 140.

21. Martin Buber, *Two Types of Faith*, trans. Norman P. Goldhawk (New York: Harper Torchbook, 1961), pp. 12–13.

22. Ibid., p. 26.

23. Ibid., pp. 173–74.

24. James Parkes, *Jesus, Paul and the Jews* (London: SCM, 1936); Parkes, *Judaism and Christianity* (Chicago: University of Chicago Press, 1948); Parkes, *The Foundations of Judaism and Christianity* (London: Vallentine, Mitchell, 1954). In these and other works, this pioneer of the Christian-Jewish dialogue discussed the theological differences and similarities of the two faiths.

25. Abraham Joshua Heschel, "Protestant Renewal: A Jewish View," *Christian Century*, December 4, 1963, pp. 1501–4.

26. Ibid.

27. Ibid.

28. Ibid.

29. Abraham Joshua Heschel, "No Religion Is an Island," in *No Religion Is an Island: Abraham Joshua Heschel and Interreligious Dialogue*, ed. Harold Kasimow and Byron L. Sherwin (Maryknoll, NY: Orbis Books, 1991), p. 10.

30. Ibid., p. 12.

31. Ibid., p. 16.

32. Ibid., p. 17.

33. Ibid., p. 19

34. Paul M. van Buren, *A Theology of the Jewish Christian Reality*, 3 vols. (San Francisco, Harper and Row, 1980, 1983, 1988). In these works van Buren has developed the most thoroughgoing Christian theological understanding of Judaism yet produced.

35. Ibid., 2:349–50

36. Eckardt has produced more than half a dozen groundbreaking works in which he has focused on Jewish-Christian issues. From *Elder and Younger Brothers: The Encounter of Jews and Christians* (New York: Scribner's,1967) to *Reclaiming the Jesus of History* (Minneapolis, MN: Fortress Press, 1992), his contribution to the dialogue has been invaluable.

37. Will Herberg, "Judaism and Christianity," *Journal of Bible and Religion* 21 (April 1953). Herberg was an open and creative thinker, not widely recognized but with much of interest to say about the relationship of the two faiths.

38. Eckardt, *Reclaiming the Jesus of History*, p. 211.

39. Ibid., p. 215.

40. Ibid., p. 214.

41. Clark M. Williamson, *A Guest in the House of Israel: Post-Holocaust Church Theology* (Louisville, KY: Westminster/John Knox Press, 1993).

42. Ibid., p. 13.

43. Ibid., pp. 233–45.

44. Ibid., p. 37.

45. Ibid., p. 43.

CHAPTER FIVE

1. Helga Croner, comp., *Stepping Stones to Further Jewish-Christian Relations: An Unabridged Collection of Christian Documents* (New York: Stimulus Books, 1977), pp. 1–2.

2. Ibid., pp. 11–16.

3. Helga Croner, ed. and comp., *More Stepping Stones to Jewish-Christian Relations: An Unabridged Collection of Christian Documents, 1975–1983* (New York: Stimulus Books, 1985), pp. 220–32.

4. Croner, *Stepping Stones*, pp. 69–71.

5. Ibid., pp. 73–85.

6. Croner, *More Stepping Stones*, pp. 157–59.

7. Ibid., pp. 160–64.

8. Ibid., pp. 165–66.

9. Ibid., pp. 167–74.

10. All the church statements referred to in this paragraph are to be found in *More Stepping Stones*.

11. Krister Stendahl, *Paul among Jews and Gentiles* (Philadelphia: Fortress Press, 1976), pp. 4–5.

12. John P. Meier holds open the possibility that Jesus did baptize. I find his case unconvincing. See John P. Meier, *A Marginal Jew*, vol. 2, *Mentor, Message and Miracles* (New York: Doubleday, 1994).

CHAPTER SIX

1. Irving Greenberg, "The New Encounter of Judaism and Christianity," *Barat Review* 3, no. 2 (1996): 113–25; reprinted in Irving Greenberg, *For the Sake of Heaven and Earth: The New Encounter between Judaism and Christianity* (Philadelphia: Jewish Publication Society, 2004).

2. Irving Greenberg, "New Revelations and New Patterns in the Relationship of Judaism and Christianity," *Journal of Ecumenical Studies* vol. 6 (1979): 249–267; reprinted in Greenberg, *For the Sake of Heaven and Earth*, pp. 124–44.

3. Irving Greenberg, "The Relationship of Judaism and Christianity: Toward a New Organic Model," in *Twenty Years of Jewish/Catholic Relations*, ed. Eugene Fisher, James Rudin, and Marc Tanenbaum (New York: Paulist Press, 1986), pp. 191–211; reprinted in Greenberg, *For the Sake of Heaven and Earth*, pp. 145–61.

4. Greenberg, *For the Sake of Heaven and Earth*, p. 129.

5. J. Lindblom was the Old Testament scholar who stressed this theme in the postexilic prophets. J. Lindblom, *Prophecy in Ancient Israel* (Philadelphia: Fortress Press, 1962), pp. 399–403.

6. Greenberg, *For the Sake of Heaven and Earth*, p. 156.

7. Irving Greenberg "Judaism and Christianity: Covenants of Redemption," in *Christianity in Jewish Terms*, ed. Tikva Frymer-Kensky et al. (Boulder, CO: Westview Press, 2000); reprinted in Greenberg, *For the Sake of Heaven and Earth*, pp. 213–34.

8. Ibid., p. 232.

9. Ibid.

10. Ibid.

11. Ibid., p. 233.

12. Jonathan Sacks, *The Dignity of Difference* (London: Continuum, 2002).

13. Greenberg, *For the Sake of Heaven and Earth*, p. 233.

14. John T. Pawlikowski, "Christology, Anti-Semitism, and Christian-Jewish Bonding," in *Reconstructing Christian Theology*, ed. Rebecca S. Chopp and Mark Lewis Taylor (Minneapolis, MN: Fortress Press, 1994), p. 259.

15. Ibid., p. 260.

16. Ibid., p. 261.

17. John Pawlikowski, *Christ in the Light of Christian-Jewish Dialogue* (Eugene, OR: Winf and Stock, 2001), p. 104.

18. Ibid., p. 115.

19. John Pawlikowski, *Jesus and the Theology of Israel* (Wilmington, DE: Michael Glazier, 1989), p. 84.

20. John Pawlikowski, "Christology and the Jewish-Christian Dialogue: A Personal Theological Journey" (unpublished paper).

21. Greenberg, *For the Sake of Heaven and Earth*, p. 182.

22. Michael S. Kogan "Kingdom Present," in *A Shabbat Reader: Universe of Cosmic Joy*, ed. Dov Peretz Elkins (New York: UAHC Press, 1998), pp. 6–11.

23. Sigmund Mowinckel, *The Psalms in Israel's Worship*, vol. 1 (Nashville, TN: Abingdon Press, 1962), pp. 86–192.

CHAPTER SEVEN

1. See Croner, *Stepping Stones to Further Jewish-Christian Relations*; Croner, *More Stepping Stones to Jewish-Christian Relations*; Eugene Fisher, ed., *Twenty Years of Jewish-Catholic Relations* (New York: Paulist Press, 1985).

2. Michael S. Kogan, "Jews and Christians: Taking the Next Step," *Journal of Ecumenical Studies*, no. 26 (Fall 1989): 703–13; Kogan, "Toward a Jewish Theology of Christianity," *Journal of Ecumenical Studies*, no. 32 (Winter 1995): 89–106, 152.

3. Buber, *Two Types of Faith*.

4. Rosenzweig, *Star of Redemption*.

5. Notably David Novak, *Jewish-Christian Dialogue: A Jewish Justification* (New York: Oxford University Press, 1989).

6. Reprinted with accompanying essays in Frymer-Kensky et al., eds., *Christianity in Jewish Terms* (Boulder, CO: Westview Press, 2000), pp. xvii–xx.

7. Ibid., p. xix (italics mine).

8. Ibid.

9. Ibid.

10. Ibid.

11. Reprinted with accompanying essays in Mary C. Boys, ed., *Seeing Judaism Anew: Christianity's Sacred Obligation* (New York: Rowan and Littlefield, 2005), pp. xiii–xix.

12. Ibid., pp. xiv–xvii.

13. Ibid., p. xiv.

14. Ibid., p. xvi.

15. Pope John Paul II, Seventh General Audience Talk, the Vatican, May 31, 1995.

16. John Hick, *A Christian Theology of Religions* (Louisville, KY: Westminster/ John Knox Press, 1995).

17. Paul F. Knitter, *One Earth, Many Religions: Multifaith Dialogue and Global Responsibility* (Maryknoll, NY: Orbis Books, 1996).

18. Sanhedrin 8b

19. Commission on the Philosophy of Conservative Judaism, "*Emet ve-Emunah*": *Statement of Principles of Conservative Judaism* (New York: Jewish Theological Seminary of America, 1988).

20. "Reflections," p. 2, citing addresses of John Paul II, first to the Jewish community in Mainz on November 17, 1980, and second to Jewish leaders in Miami on September 11, 1987.

21. Ibid.

22. Ibid., p. 3.

23. Ibid.

24. Ibid., p. 4.

25. Ibid.

26. Ibid., p. 5.

27. Ibid., citing an address by Cardinal Walter Kasper to the seventeenth meeting of the International Catholic-Jewish Liaison Committee, New York, May 1, 2001.

28. Ibid.

29. Phillip A. Cunningham, "A Response to Michael S. Kogan Concerning 'Reflections on Covenant and Mission,'" *Journal of Ecumenical Studies* 41, no. 2 (2004).

30. Avery Dulles, "Covenant and Mission," *America*, October 21, 2002, pp. 8–11.

31. Mary C. Boys, Phillip A. Cunningham, and John T. Pawlikowski, "Theology's 'Sacred Obligation': A Reply to Cardinal Avery Dulles on Evangelization," *America*, October 21, 2002, pp. 8–11.

32. Cardinal Joseph Ratzinger, *Many Religions, One Covenant: Israel, the Church, and the World* (San Francisco: Ignatius Press, 1999), p. 104.

33. "Reflections," p. 6.

CHAPTER EIGHT

1. Friedrich Schleiermacher, *On Religion: Speeches to Its Cultured Despisers*, trans and ed. Richard Crouter (Glasgow: Cambridge University Press, 1996), p. 48–49.

2. Søren Kierkegaard, *Concluding Unscientific Postscript*, in Bretall, *A Kierkegaard Anthology*, pp. 209–10.

3. Ibid., p. 253.

4. T. S. Eliot, "The Dry Salvages," in *T. S. Eliot: The Complete Poems and Plays*, p. 136.

5. Schleiermacher, *On Religion*, p. 22.

6. Kierkegaard, *Concluding Unscientific Postscript*, pp. 210–17.

7. Margaret Wise Brown, *The Little Island* (New York: Random House, 1946).

8. Immanuel Kant, *Critique of Pure Reason*, trans. Norman Kemp Smith (New York: St. Martin's Press, 1965), p. 131.

CHAPTER NINE

1. Michael S. Kogan, "Jesus the Jew: A Reappraisal," *Faith and Thought* 1, no. 1 (Spring 1983): 7–13.

2. *The Standard Prayer Book*, trans. Rabbi S. Singer (New York: Bloch, 1960), p. 232.

CHAPTER TEN

1. Talmud, Sanhedrin: 8b.

2. Kierkegaard, *Concluding Unscientific Postscript*, pp. 214–15.

3. T. S. Eliot, "Little Gidding," in *T. S. Eliot: The Complete Poems and Plays*, p. 145.

CHAPTER ELEVEN

1. John Hick, *A Christian Theology of Religions* (Louisville, KY: Westminster/John Knox Press, 1995).

2. Talmud: Berachot 31b.

3. Knitter, *One Earth, Many Religions*, p. 8.

4. Talmud: Sanhedrin 8b

5. Martin Buber, *Ten Rungs* (New York: Shocken Books, 1954), p. 106.

6. Midrash: Genesis Rabbah 38:13

7. T. S. Eliot, "Marina," in *T. S. Eliot: The Complete Poems and Plays*, p. 72.

8. David de Sola Poole, ed. and trans., *The Traditional Prayerbook* (New York: Behrman House, 1960), pp. 340–342.

Bibliography

Accattoli, Luigi. *When a Pope Asks Forgiveness: The Mea Culpa's of John Paul II.* Trans. Jordan Aumann, O.P. Boston: Pauline Books and Media, 1998.

Augus, Jacob B. *The Jewish Quest.* New York: KTAV, 1983.

Barth, Karl, *The Humanity of God.* Richmond, VA: John Knox Press, 1960.

Benamozegh, Elijah. *Israel and Humanity.* Trans. Maxwell Luria. New York: Paulist Press, 1995.

Boadt, Lawrence, C.S.P., Helga Croner, and Leon Klenicki, eds. *Biblical Studies: Meeting Ground of Jews and Christians.* New York: Paulist Press, 1980.

Borg, Marcus J. *Jesus in Contemporary Scholarship.* Valley Forge, PA: Trinity Press International, 1994.

Boyarin, Daniel. *A Radical Jew: Paul and the Politics of Identity.* Berkeley: University of California Press, 1994.

Boys, Mary C. *Seeing Judaism Anew: Christianity's Sacred Obligation.* New York: Rowman and Littlefield, 2005.

Bruteau, Beatrice, ed. *Jesus through Jewish Eyes: Rabbis and Scholars Engage an Ancient Brother in a New Conversation.* Maryknoll, NY: Orbis Books, 2001.

Buber, Martin. *Two Types of Faith.* Trans. Norman P. Goldhawk. New York: Harper Torchbooks, 1961.

Caroll, James. *Constantine's Sword—The Church and the Jews: A History.* New York: Houghton Mifflin, 2001.

Catechism of the Catholic Church. New York: Catholic Book Publishing, 1994.

Charlesworth, James H., ed. *The Messiah: Developments in Earliest Judaism and Christianity.* Minneapolis, MN: Fortress Press, 1992.

Cox, Harvey. *Common Prayers: Faith, Family, and a Christian's Journey through the Jewish Year*. Boston: Houghton Mifflin, 2001.

Croner, Helga, comp. *More Stepping Stones to Jewish-Christian Relations: An Unabridged Collection of Christian Documents, 1975–1983*. New York: Stimulus Books, 1985.

———, comp. *Stepping Stones to Further Jewish-Christian Relations: An Unabridged Collection of Christian Documents*. New York: Stimulus Books, 1977.

Croner, Helga, and Leon Klenicki, eds. *Issues in the Jewish-Christian Dialogue: Jewish Perspective on Covenant, Mission and Witness*. New York: Paulist Press, 1979.

Crossan, John Dominic. *The Historical Jesus: The Life of a Mediterranean Jewish Peasant*. San Francisco: Harper, 1991.

Cunningham, Philip A. *Proclaiming Shalom: Lectionary Introductions to Foster the Catholic and Jewish Relationship*. Collegeville, MN: Liturgical Press, 1995.

Davies, W. D. *Paul and Rabbinic Judaism*. New York: Harper and Row, 1948.

Duvernoy, Claude. *Controversy of Zion*. Green Forest, AR: New Leaf Press, 1987.

Eckhardt, A. Roy. *Christianity and the Children of Israel*. New York: King's Crown Press, 1948.

———. *Elder and Younger Brothers: The Encounter of Jews and Christians*. New York: Scribner's, 1967.

———. *Reclaiming the Jesus of History: Christology Today*. Minneapolis, MN: Fortress Press, 1992.

———. *Your People, My People: The Meeting of Jews and Christians*. New York: Quadrangle, 1974.

Evans, Craig A., and Donald A. Hagner, eds. *Anti-Semitism and Early Christianity: Issues of Polemic and Faith*. Minneapolis, MN: Fortress Press, 1993.

Fackenheim, Emil L. *God's Presence in History*. New York: Harper and Row, 1970.

Falk, Harvey. *Jesus the Pharisee: A New Look at the Jewishness of Jesus*. New York: Paulist Press, 1985.

Fiorenza, Francis Schussler, and John P. Galvin, eds. *Systematic Theology: Roman Catholic Perspectives*. Vol. 2. Minneapolis, MN: Fortress Press, 1991.

Fisher, Eugene J., ed. *Interwoven Destinies: Jews and Christians through the Ages*. New York: Paulist Press, 1993.

Flannery, Edward H. *The Anguish of the Jews: Twenty-three Centuries of Antisemitism*. New York: Paulist Press, 1985.

Flusser, David. *Judaism and the Origins of Christianity*. Jerusalem: Magnes Press, 1988.

———. *Jewish Sources in Early Christianity*. Trans. John Glucker. Tel Aviv: MOD Books, 1989.

Fredrickson, Paula. *From Jesus to Christ: The Origins of the New Testament Images of Jesus*. New Haven, CT: Yale University Press, 1988.

Gager, John G. *Reinventing Paul*. Oxford: Oxford University Press, 2000.

Goldberg, Michael. *Jews and Christians: Getting Our Stories Straight*. Valley Forge, PA: Trinity Press International, 1991.

Greenberg, Irving. *For the Sake of Heaven and Earth: The New Encounter between Judaism and Christianity*. Philadelphia: Jewish Publication Society, 2004.

Hagner, Donald A. *The Jewish Reclamation of Jesus*. Grand Rapids, MI: Zondervan, 1984.

Haight, Roger. *Jesus, Symbol of God*. Maryknoll, NY: Orbis Books, 1999.

Hargrove, Katherine T., ed. *Seeds of Reconciliation: Essays on Jewish-Christian Understanding*. N. Richland Hills, TX: Bibal Press, 1996.

Harrelson, Walter, and Randall M. Falk. *Jews and Christians: A Troubled Family*. Nashville, TN: Abingdon Press, 1990.

Herford, R. Travers. *Christianity in Talmud and Midrash*. New York: KTAV, 1903.

Heschel, Abraham J. *Between God and Man: An Interpretation of Judaism*. Ed. Fritz A. Rothschild. New York: Free Press, 1965.

Hick, John. *A Christian Theology of Religions*. Louisville, KY: Westminster/John Knox Press, 1993.

———. *Problems of Religious Pluralism*. London: Macmillan, 1985.

Hilton, Michael, with Gordian Marshall, O.P. *The Gospels and Rabbinic Judaism*. London: SCM Press, 1988.

Hirshman, Marc. *A Rivalry of Genius: Jewish and Christian Biblical Interpretation in Late Antiquity*. Trans. Batya Stein. Albany: State University of New York Press, 1996.

Isaac, Jules. *The Teaching of Contempt: Christian Roots of Anti-Semitism*. Trans. Helen Weaver. New York: Holt, Rinehart and Winston, 1964.

Jewish Theological Seminary of America, the Rabbinical Assembly, the United Synagogue of America. *Emet Ve-Emunah: Statement of Principles of Conservative Judaism*. New York: Jewish Theological Seminary of America, 1988.

Johnson, Luke Timothy. *The Real Jesus: The Misguided Quest for the Historical Jesus and the Truth of the Traditional Gospels*. San Francisco: Harper, 1997.

Kasimow, Harold, and Byron L. Sherwin. *No Religion Is an Island: Abraham Joshua Heschel and Interreligious Dialogue*. Maryknoll, NY: Orbis Books, 1991.

Katz, Jacob. *Exclusiveness and Tolerance: Jewish-Gentile Relations in Medieval and Modern Times*. New York: Schocken Books, 1962.

Klausner, Joseph. *Jesus of Nazareth: His Life, Times and Teaching*. Trans. Herbert Danby. New York: Bloch, 1989.

Klenicki, Leon, ed. *Toward a Theological Encounter: Jewish Understandings of Christianity*. New York: Paulist Press, 1991.

Knitter, Paul F. *One Earth, Many Religions: Multifaith Dialogue and Global Responsibility*. Maryknoll, NY: Orbis Books, 1996.

———, ed. *The Myth of Religious Superiority: Multifaith Explorations of Religious Pluralism*. Maryknoll, NY: Orbis Books, 2005.

Korn, Eugene B., and John T. Pawlikowski, O.S.M., eds. *Two Faiths, One Covenant? Jewish and Christian Identity in the Presence of the Other*. Lanham, MD: Rowman and Littlefield, 2005.

Levenson, Jon D. *The Death and Resurrection of the Beloved Son: The Transformation of Child Sacrifice in Judaism and Christianity*. New Haven, CT: Yale University Press, 1993.

Levine, Amy Jill. *The Misunderstood Jew: The Church and the Scandal of the Jewish Jesus*. San Francisco: Harper, 2006.

Lindbeck, George A. *The Nature of Doctrine.* Philadelphia: Westminster Press, 1984.
Martin, Vincent. *A House Divided: The Parting of the Ways between Synagogue and Church.* New York: Paulist Press, 1995.
Meier, John P. *A Marginal Jew: Rethinking the Historical Jesus.* Vol. 1. New York: Doubleday, 1991.
————. *A Marginal Jew.* Vol. 2, *Mentor, Message and Miracles.* New York: Doubleday, 1994.
Mendelssohn, Moses. *Jerusalem: Or on Religious Power and Judaism.* Trans. Allan Arkush. Lebanon, NH: University Press of New England, 1983.
Neusner, Jacob. *From Politics to Piety: The Emergence of Pharisaic Judaism.* New York: KTAV, 1979.
————. *The Incarnation of God: The Character of Divinity in Formative Judaism.* Philadelphia: Fortress Press, 1988.
————, ed. *Judaism and Christianity: The New Relationship.* New York: Garland, 1993.
————. *Judaism in the Beginning of Christianity.* Philadelphia: Fortress Press, 1984.
————. *Judaism in the Matrix of Christianity.* Philadelphia: Fortress Press, 1986.
————. *Messiah in Context: Israel's History and Destiny in Formative Judaism.* New York: University Press of America, 1988.
————. *Telling Tales: Making Sense of Christian and Judaic Nonsense.* Louisville, KY: Westminster/John Knox Press, 1993.
Neusner, Jacob, and Bruce Chilton, *Jewish-Christian Debates.* Minneapolis, MN: Fortress Press, 1998.
Neusner, Jacob, William S. Green, and Ernest Frerichs, eds. *Judaisms and Their Messiahs at the Turn of the Christian Era.* Cambridge: Cambridge University Press, 1987.
Oesterreicher, John M. *The New Encounter between Christians and Jews.* New York: Philosophical Library, 1986.
————. *The Unfinished Dialogue: Martin Buber and the Christian Way.* New York: Philosophical Library, 1986.
Patai, Raphael. *The Messiah Texts.* Detroit, MI: Wayne State University Press, 1979.
Pawlikowski, John T. *Jesus and the Theology of Israel.* Wilmington, DE: Michael Glazier Books, 1989).
————. *Sinai and Calvary: A Meeting of Two Peoples.* Beverly Hills: Benziger, 1976.
Pawlikowski, John T., and James A. Wilde. *When Catholics Speak about Jews.* Chicago: Liturgy Training Program, 1987.
Perelmuter, Hayim Goren. *Siblings: Rabbinic Judaism and Early Christianity at Their Beginnings.* New York: Paulist Press, 1989.
Ratzinger, Joseph Cardinal (Pope Benedict XVI). *Many Religions, One Covenant: Israel, the Church, and the World.* San Francisco: Ignatius Press, 1999.
Rosenberg, Stuart E. *The Christian Problem: A Jewish View.* New York: Hippocrene Books, 1986.
Rothschild, Fritz A., ed. *Jewish Perspectives on Christianity.* New York: Continuum, 1996.
Sacks, Jonathan. *The Dignity of Difference: How to Avoid the Clash of Civilizations.* London: Continuum, 2002.

Sanders, E. P. *Paul and Palestinian Judaism*. Minneapolis, MN: Fortress Press, 1977.

———. *Paul, the Law, and the Jewish People*. Minneapolis, MN: Fortress Press, 1985.

Sandmel, Samuel. *A Jewish Understanding of the New Testament*. Cincinnati, OH: Hebrew Union College Press, 1957.

Sandmel, David F., Rosann M. Catalano, and Leighton, Christopher M., eds. *Irreconcilable Differences? A Learning Resource for Jews and Christians*. Boulder, CO: Westview Press, 2001.

Setzer, Claudia. *Jewish Responses to Early Christian History and Polemics, 30–150 CE*. Minneapolis, MN: Fortress Press, 1994.

Shermis, Michael, and Arthur Zannoni, eds. *Introduction to Jewish-Christian Relations*. New York: Paulist Press, 1991.

Soulen, R. Kendall. *The God of Israel and Christian Theology*. Minneapolis, MN: Fortress Press, 1996.

Stendahl, Krister. *Paul among Jews and Gentiles*. Philadelphia, PA: Fortress Press, 1976.

Thoma, Clemens. *A Christian Theology of Judaism*. Trans. Helga Croner. New York: Paulist Press, 1980.

Vahanian, Gabriel. *Anonymous God*. Aurora, CO: Davies Group, 2001.

Van Buren, Paul M. *According to the Scriptures: The Origins of the Gospel and of the Church's Old Testament*. Grand Rapids, MI: Eerdmans, 1998.

———. *A Theology of the Jewish-Christian Reality*. Vol. 1, *Discerning the Way*. New York: University Press of America, 1987.

———. *A Theology of the Jewish-Christian Reality*. Vol. 2, *A Christian Theology of the People Israel*. San Francisco: Harper and Row, 1987.

———. *A Theology of the Jewish-Christian Reality*. Vol. 3, *Christ in Context*. San Francisco: Harper and Row, 1988.

White, Leland J. *Christ and the Christian Movement: Jesus in the New Testament, Creeds and Modern Theology*. New York: Alba House, 1985.

Williamson, Clark M. *A Guest in the House of Israel: Post-Holocaust Church Theology*. Louisville, KY: Westminster/John Knox Press, 1993.

Williamson, Clark M., and Ronald J. Allen. *Interpreting Difficult Texts: Anti-Judaism and Christian Preaching*. Philadelphia: Trinity Press, 1989.

Wilson, Marvin R. *Our Father Abraham: Jewish Roots of the Christian Faith*. Dayton, OH: Center for Judaic-Christian Studies, 1989.

Wilson, Stephen G. *Related Strangers: Jews and Christians, 70–170 C.E.* Minneapolis, MN: Fortress Press, 1995.

Witherington, Ben, III. *The Christology of Jesus*. Minneapolis, MN: Augsburg Fortress, 1990.

Wyschogrod, Michael. *The Body of Faith: Judaism as Corporeal Election*. Minneapolis, New York: Seabury Press, 1983.

Index

Aaron's line, 49–50, 62–63, 68,
      100, 115
"Abba," 164
Abednego, 28
Abel, 5, 16
Abelard, Peter, 23
Abihu, 115
Abraham, xii, 6–9, 16–18, 29,
      32–33, 167
   and adult education classes, 205
   and Christian reevaluation of
      Judaism, 122, 126, 134
   and Christian theologians
      Pawlikowski, John, 156, 158,
         160–61
      Williamson, Clark M., 108
   and core beliefs, 113, 115, 118
   and "Dabru Emet" (Speak the
      Truth), 169, 171
   and Jewish theologians
      Benamozegh, Elijah, 81, 84
      Buber, Martin, 91
      Greenberg, Irving, 147–50
      Mendelssohn, Moses, 80
      Rosenzweig, Franz, 89

   and Messiah question, 50
   and pluralism, 231, 241–42
   and "Theological Understanding"
      (1987), 218
   and truth claims, 185
Acts of the Apostles, 25–26, 46,
      83–84, 142
   and adult education classes, 201
   and Gamaliel, 78, 170, 173
   and pluralism, 245
Adam and Eve, 4–6, 11, 14–16,
      18, 22–23, 26, 76, 185,
      194–95, 203
"Adon Olam" (Jewish hymn), 4
adoption, 41, 219
adult education classes, 199–210
   church classes, 209–10
   doctors' class, 201–4
   objections from congregants,
      206–7
   synagogue classes, 199–201,
      204–6
adversus Judaeus tradition, 103–11.
      See also anti-Judaism
African American churches, 208–9

Ahaz, 41–42
ahistorical time, 88–89, 92, 94, 113
alcoholics, 20
Alexandria, 72
allegorical interpretation of Scripture,
    195
America (Catholic weekly), 181
Amos, Book of, 45–46
anachronism, 104
angels, 55–57
animals, cruelty to, 11, 82, 84, 233
anointing, 39–41, 49–50, 51, 58–59,
    62–63, 66, 100
"anonymous Christian" doctrine, 130
Anselm, Saint, 18, 22–23
anti-Christian polemic, 89
anti-incest command, 82
anti-Judaism, 72, 103
    and adult education classes, 205
    and Catholic Church, xi–xii, 103–4,
        121–24
    and Christian theologians
        Paul of Tarsus, 34, 105
        Pawlikowski, John, 156
        Williamson, Clark M., 103–11
    and Israeli-Palestinian dispute, 227–28
    and Jewish theologians
        Greenberg, Irving, 145–46
        Ha Me'iri, Menachem, 76–77
    and "A Sacred Obligation," 172–73
    and "Theological Understanding"
        (1987), 221–22
antinomianism, Christian, 206
antisemitism, xii. *See also* Holocaust
    and Christian reevaluation of Judaism
        Catholic Church, 124, 127
        Jewish response to, 140
        Protestant churches, 136
    and Greenberg, Irving, 146
    and Interfaith Thanksgiving services,
        208
    and Israeli-Palestinian dispute, 225
apocalypse, 60–63, 117

apocalyptic judge and redeemer, 25, 54,
    56–57
apocryphal Wisdom of Soloman, 59
apostasy, 113
Arab Christians, 217, 227–28
ark, 5, 17, 30
Assyrians, 85, 193
Ateek, Naim, 228
atheism, 151, 188, 194
atonement, 18, 116–17
Augustine, Saint, 16, 18–20, 22–23, 27, 71
Auschwitz, 101, 105, 144, 146, 227
Avodah Zarah (Idol Worship), 70
Azaz'el, 57

Babylonia, 44, 51, 73, 194
Babylonian Talmud, 64, 66
backsliding, 21, 27, 202
Baeck, Leo, 89
Balaam, 40
baptism, 19, 21, 26, 131, 141–42, 180,
    214, 219–20
"baptism of desire," 130
Bar Kochbar, 40
Barth, Karl, 108
"Basic Theological Issues of the
    Jewish-Christian Dialogue"
    (1979), 133–34
Beirut barracks bombing, 224
Belgian Protestant Council (1967), 138
Benamozegh, Elijah, 80–84
Benedict XVI, Pope, xii, 181
"Beth El," 9
Bethlehem, 46
Bishops' Committee for Ecumenical
    and Interreligious Affairs
    (Roman Catholic), 178
blasphemy, 11, 73, 232
*Body of Faith: Judaism as Corporeal
    Election, The* (Wyschogrod), 153
Book of Mormon, 186
Bossman, David, 156
boycott of Israeli products, 223–24, 229

Brantl, George, 185
Brennan, Frank H., Jr., 156
Buber, Martin, 90–95, 97–98, 112–13,
    147, 160–61, 168
Buddhism, 112
Bultmann, Rudolf, 95
burning bush, 91, 190
"burning fiery furnace," 28

Caesarea Philippi, 25, 37
Cain, 5–6, 16, 203
Caligula, 72
Calvin, John, xii, 23
Canaanite woman, 141
canon. *See* Hebrew Scriptures
catechesis, 128–29
Catholic Catechism, 22, 122, 135–36
Catholic Church, 22, 29
    and anti-Judaism, xi–xii, 103–4
    and Jewish theologians
        Buber, Martin, 94
        Greenberg, Irving, 147
        Heschel, Abraham Joshua, 97
        and Pawlikowski, John, 118, 152, 153,
            154–64
    and reevaluation of Judaism, 121–36,
        166, 213–14
        Catholic Catechism, 22, 122, 135–36
        local documents, 132–34
        Pope John Paul II, 128, 129–32
        in preaching and catechesis, 128–29,
            131–32
        Vatican II and *Nostra Aetate*, xi–xii,
            121–27, 131
    and "Reflections on Covenant and
        Mission," 178–82
    and "A Sacred Obligation," 172, 174–77
celibacy, 204
Center for Christian-Jewish Learning
    (Boston College), 172
Central Synagogue (New York), 208
ceremonial laws, 77, 79–80
Cesarea Philippi, 131

Chagall, Marc, 117
Chartres, 71
chosen people, xiii, 6–8, 10, 33, 41, 51,
    108, 139, 149, 176, 234–35
Christ. *See* Jesus
Christ Church Methodist (New York),
    208
Christian branch. *See* Jewish root and
    Christian branch
Christian Chamber of Commerce, 224
Christian cross imagery, 196
Christianity, xi–xiv, 11, 14–26, 32
    and guest sermons in churches,
        210–12
    Jewish theology of (*see* Jewish
        theologians of Christianity)
    and Messiah question, 38–39, 41
    reevaluation of Judaism, 121–42,
        166–67, 213–15
        Catholic Church, 121–36
        Jewish response to, 134, 138–42
        Protestant churches, 136–38
        "Reflections on Covenant and
            Mission," 178–82
        "A Sacred Obligation," 172–77
Christian messianism, 44, 46, 52–53,
    61, 63–68
"Christian Right" churches, 224–25, 227
Christian Scholars Group on
    Christian-Jewish Relations, 172
Christian theologians, 98–111. *See also*
    names of other Christian
    theologians
    Eckardt, A. Roy, 100–103, 143, 150,
        157–58
    Pawlikowski, John, 118, 152, 153,
        154–64
    van Buren, Paul, 99–100, 118, 150,
        157–58
    Williamson, Clark M., 103–11, 150,
        157–58, 172–73
Christian Zionists, 224
Christmas, 199–200, 210

christologies, 23, 24–26, 30–31
    and Jewish theologians
        Buber, Martin, 91
        Mendelssohn, Moses, 78
    and Messiah question, 37–38
    and Pawlikowski as Christian
        theologian, 152, 153, 157–60
Christomonism, xiii, 169
Chronicles I, Book of, 50
Church of the Rhineland, 138, 140
circumcision, 81, 84, 202
Claudius, 72
commandments, 10, 13–14, 29, 97, 99,
    151
communal experience, 28, 94–95, 105,
    139, 155, 157–58, 189, 204
Communion, 30
concretization, 102, 111, 153
Congregation for the Doctrine of the
    Faith (Vatican), xii
Congregation Shomrei Emunah, 199–200
Conservative Judaism, 178–79, 200–201
constellations of stars, 74–76
Consultation on the Church and the
    Jewish People (WCC 1977), 137
contempt for Judaism. See anti-Judaism
conversion of gentiles, xii, 83, 116, 131,
    150–52
conversion of Jews, 34
    and Christian reevaluation of Judaism
        Catholic Church, xii, 122, 125, 131–32,
            178, 181–82
        Jewish response to, 138–40
        Protestant churches, xii, 136–38,
            213–14
    and Christian theologians
        Pawlikowski, John, 156
        van Buren, Paul, 99
    and core beliefs, 114
    and Jewish theologians
        Greenberg, Irving, 144, 146
        Heschel, Abraham Joshua, 97
        Rosenzweig, Franz, 88, 90

    and "Reflections on Covenant and
        Mission," 178, 180–82
    and "A Sacred Obligation," 172, 176
    and "Theological Understanding"
        (1987), 219–21
conversion to Judaism, 10–11, 77, 116, 150
core beliefs, 111–18, 195
    of Christianity, 28, 114–18
Corinthians I, Book of, 19, 21, 25, 221, 245
Cornelius, conversion of, 46, 142
coronation anthem (Second Psalm), 25,
    39–41
correspondence theory of truth, 184,
    187, 191, 194
cosmopolitanism, 80
covenant, xiii, 5, 10, 14
    and Christian reevaluation of Judaism,
        166
        Catholic Church, 122, 125–32, 134, 213
        Jewish response to, 139–40, 215
        Protestant churches, 136–38
    and Christian theologians, 17, 19, 32–33
        Eckardt, A. Roy, 101
        Pawlikowski, John, 155, 158–59, 164
        van Buren, Paul, 99
        Williamson, Clark M., 108–10
    and core beliefs, 113, 115, 118
    and "Dabru Emet" (Speak the Truth),
        169, 171
    and Jewish theologians
        Benamozegh, Elijah, 82
        Buber, Martin, 91
        Greenberg, Irving, 144, 146–47,
            149–51, 153
        Heschel, Abraham Joshua, 98
        Rosenzweig, Franz, 90
    and Messiah question, 45, 50, 68
    opening of to include gentiles, 33–35,
        72, 75, 166–67
    and pluralism, 233, 239
    and "Reflections on Covenant and
        Mission," 178–82
    and "A Sacred Obligation," 172–74

and "Theological Understanding"
(1987), 218–21
creation, 4–6, 35–36, 76, 159, 185, 194
creation ex nihilo, 76
Cunningham, Phillip A., 180–81
Cyrus, king of Persia, 43–44, 51, 68

"Dabru Emet" (Speak the Truth), 168–71,
177, 179, 215–16
Daniel, Book of, 25, 28, 100, 117
and Messiah question
Messiahs who suffer and die, 59–60
Similitudes of Enoch, 56
"Son of Man" in the canon, 37,
53–54, 56, 149
David, King, 24–26, 37, 39–40, 46, 49.
See also David's line
David's line
and Messiah question, 68, 100, 149
Messiahs of the Qumran
community, 62–63
Messiahs who suffer and die, 62,
64, 66
priestly Messiah in the canon, 50
Psalms of Solomon, 57–58
royal Messiah in the canon, 39–48
Similitudes of Enoch, 56–57
Days of Awe, 206
Dead Sea community, 62
Dead Sea Scrolls, 100
Declaration on the Relationship of the
Church to Non-Christian
Religions. See Nostra Aetate
decoration of church and synagogue, 30
"de facto pluralism," 179–80
deicide, charges of, 71, 111, 121
demons, 25, 56, 148
Deutero-Isaiah. See also Isaiah, Book of
and Greenberg, Irving, 150
and Messiah question, 67
postcanonical Messianic
conceptions, 54
royal Messiah in the canon, 43

Similitudes of Enoch, 57
suffering servant in the canon, 51,
63, 65
Deuteronomy, Book of, 80, 108, 189,
202, 211. See also Deutero-Isaiah
"Dialogue: A Contemporary Alternative
to Proselytization" (Texas
Conference of Churches), 138
Diaspora, 83, 128
Dickinson, Emily, 20
dietary laws, 10, 79
Dignity of Difference, The (Sacks), 153–54
divestment of church funds, 223–24,
228–30
divine flame image, 88–89, 168, 196
divine-human encounter. See human
and divine
divorce, 221
"double covenant" theology, 158
"double-revelation" theory, 239
dragon of watery chaos, 194
dual messianic vision, 62–63, 66, 100
dual nature of Judaism, 82–83
Dulles, Avery, 181
dynamic conception of history, 72–73

Eagle Vision, 62
"ecclesiolatry," 242
Eckardt, A. Roy, 100–103, 143, 150, 157–58
Eckhart, Meister, 210
Eden story, 4–6, 15, 19, 24, 26, 31, 35, 160
Edom, 40
Egypt, 7, 10, 50–51
Ehrenberg, Rudolph, 87
election, 13, 27, 31
and Christian reevaluation of Judaism,
137
and core beliefs, 118
and Jewish theologians
Buber, Martin, 91, 93
Greenberg, Irving, 153
Mendelssohn, Moses, 80
and Messiah question, 55–57

election (*continued*)
 and pluralism, 234–35
 and "A Sacred Obligation," 176
 and Williamson, Clark M., 105, 108–10
Elijah, 65, 193
Eliot, T. S., 87, 187, 194, 210, 218
Emanu-El (God in our midst), 30
"Emet ve-Emunah" (Truth and Faith), 179
empathy, 50–51
emunah (Judaism's faith), 94
"end of days," 39. *See also* apocalypse
Enlightenment, 77, 79–80
Enoch, Book of, 25, 54–57, 100
"enthronement psalms," 163
Enumah Elish (Marduk), 194
Ephesians, Letter to, 209
Episcopal Church, 224
Esau, 9
eschatological speculation, 90, 118, 152, 162
 and Messiah question, 39–40, 48, 51,
  54, 60, 62–63, 67
eschaton, 157
Essenes, 171
Essex County (N.J.), 207
Etchegaray, Cardinal, of Marseilles, 133
"Eternal Birth, The" (sermon), 210
ethical and spiritual fruits, 36, 70, 133,
  166, 183–84
ethical law, 10, 13, 29
 and Golden Rule, 85–86
 and Jewish theologians
  Benamozegh, Elijah, 81–83
  Ha Me'iri, Menachem, 70, 73–74, 76
  Mendelssohn, Moses, 78–80
  Rosenzweig, Franz, 89
 and truth claims, 188
"ethnolatry," 7, 75–76, 242
etz hayim (tree of life), 35
Evangelical Lutheran Church, 224, 228
evolution, 194
exclusivism, xii–xiv, 33, 106–7, 144–45
 and Christian reevaluation of Judaism,
  128–29, 139, 214

and "Dabru Emet" (Speak the Truth),
  171
 and Interfaith Committee of Essex, 207
 and pluralism, 233, 237–38
 and "Reflections on Covenant and
  Mission," 181–82
 and "A Sacred Obligation," 173, 175
 and "Theological Understanding"
  (1987), 218
exilic period, 44–45
existential conception of religious
 truth, 188
Exodus, Book of, 4, 7, 10, 24, 29, 115, 160
 and Jewish theologians
  Benamozegh, Elijah, 82
  Buber, Martin, 91
  Mendelssohn, Moses, 79
 and Messiah question, 49–50, 64
 and pluralism, 235
 and truth claims, 190
Ezekiel, Book of, 45, 52–54
Ezra, Books of, 48, 60–62, 66, 68, 100,
  158, 193

facts, 114, 187, 191–94
"failed Messiah," 148–50, 152–53
Faith and Order Commission of the
 National Council of Churches, 172
"fall and redemption," 16–19, 22–23,
  26, 31–32, 90
Fatah, 228
Federici, Tommaso, 132–33
finite revelation of infinite reality, xiv,
  11–13, 15, 22, 79, 114, 164
 and guest sermons in churches,
  210, 212
 and pluralism, 237
 and truth claims, 183, 187–88, 190,
  195–96
First Assembly of the World Council of
 Churches (1948), 136–37
First Presbyterian Church (New York),
  175–76

Fleischner, Eva, 143, 207
flood, 5–6, 16–17, 73
Flusser, David, 158
France, 69, 161
fratricide, 16
free will, 4–5, 14–16, 19, 22, 31, 76, 78, 203
fundamentalists, religious, 72, 146, 174, 188, 193–94, 214, 224–25, 227

Gadarene demoniac, 141
Galatians, Book of, 16–19, 21, 29
    and adult education classes, 201
    and Christian reevaluation of Judaism, 138, 140–41
    and Jewish theologians
        Benamozegh, Elijah, 83
        Buber, Martin, 93
    and pluralism, 239
Gamaliel, Rabban, 78, 170, 173
gambling addicts, 20
Garden of Eden, 4–6, 15, 19, 24, 26, 31, 35, 160
General Conference of the United Methodist Church (1972), 138, 140
Genesis, Book of, 4–9, 26, 29, 31–32, 35–36, 73
    and adult education classes, 205
    and core beliefs, 115
    and Jewish theologians
        Benamozegh, Elijah, 81
        Rosenzweig, Franz, 89
    and Messiah question, 40, 50, 55
    and pluralism, 239
    and truth claims, 185, 188, 193–95
genocide, 137. *See also* Holocaust
gentiles, 13
    and adult education classes, 209
    and Christian reevaluation of Judaism
        Catholic Church, 123, 130–31, 135
        Jewish response to, 141–42
        Protestant churches, 137

and Christian theologians
    Eckardt, A. Roy, 101
    Pawlikowski, John, 155, 158–59
    Williamson, Clark M., 105, 108–10
and core beliefs, 113, 116, 118
and guest sermons in churches, 211
and Jewish theologians
    Benamozegh, Elijah, 81–84
    Buber, Martin, 92–93
    Greenberg, Irving, 144–45, 147, 149–53
    Ha Me'iri, Menachem, 69–73
    Heschel, Abraham Joshua, 95
    Mendelssohn, Moses, 77–79
    Rosenzweig, Franz, 88
and Messiah question, 68
    Davidic Messiah in Psalms of Solomon, 58
    royal Messiah in the canon, 43–44, 46
    Similitudes of Enoch, 56–57
    suffering servant in the canon, 52
and Noahide covenant, 73, 232–33
opening of covenant to include, 33–35, 72, 75
and post-Temple conditions, 166
and "Reflections on Covenant and Mission," 179, 181–82
and "A Sacred Obligation," 176
and "Theological Understanding" (1987), 219
Gethsemane, 49
Gibson, Mel, 226
Golden Rule, 85–86
Good Samaritan, parable of, 110
good works, 13, 16–17, 21, 28–29, 97, 109–11, 165, 202–4
goyim, 111, 181
"great commission," 131, 142, 181
Greeks, 12, 23, 26, 58, 95, 140, 194, 205
Greenberg, Irving, 143–54, 156, 161–62, 164

Guest in the House of Israel: Post-Holocaust Church Theology, A (Williamson), 103
Guidelines and Suggestions for Implementing the Conciliar Declaration *Nostra Aetate* (No. 4), January 1975, 124–27, 131–32

Habakkuk, Book of, 150
Hagar, 17
Haggadah, 7, 104
Haggai, Book of, 47, 49–50
Hai Gaon, 66
Haight, Roger, 31
halakha (Jewish legal system), 29, 69, 72
Halevi, Yehuda, 97, 113
Ham, 6
Hamas, 228
Ha Me'iri, Menachem, 69–77
Harnack, Adolf, 163–64
Hasmoneans, 57–58, 62
Hebrews, Letter to, 30, 50, 181
Hebrew Scriptures, xii, 14, 17, 26, 29–30. *See also names of Books of the Hebrew Scriptures*
  and adult education classes, 209
  and Christian reevaluation of Judaism, 126, 167
  and Christian theologians
    Pawlikowski, John, 159
    Williamson, Clark M., 109
  and core beliefs, 115–16
  and "Dabru Emet" (Speak the Truth), 169, 171
  and Jewish theologians
    Benamozegh, Elijah, 83
    Greenberg, Irving, 153
    Ha Me'iri, Menachem, 74
    Heschel, Abraham Joshua, 96
  and Messiah question, 39, 49, 57, 67
  and "A Sacred Obligation," 174–75
  and truth claims, 184, 186, 191
Heft, James L., 156

Heidegger, Martin, 189
Hellenized Hebrew Wisdom literature, 26, 58
Hellwig, Monica, 150
Herberg, Will, 101
Heschel, Abraham Joshua, 95–98, 112
Hezbollah, 224
Hezekiah, 42, 44, 46
Hick, John, 175–76, 233
"higher righteousness," 164
"Highwayman, The" (Noyes), 195
Hillel, xiv, 111
"History of the Jews from Mesopotamia to Montclair, The" (adult education class), 200
holiday foods, 74
Holocaust
  and Christian reevaluation of Judaism
    Catholic Church, 121–22, 124
    Protestant churches, 136–37
  and Christian theologians
    Eckardt, A. Roy, 101
    Pawlikowski, John, 156
    Williamson, Clark M., 103, 105–6
  and Greenberg, Irving, 144–46
  and Interfaith Committee of Essex, 207
  and Israeli-Palestinian dispute, 225–27
  and "Theological Understanding" (1987), 220, 222
Holy Spirit, 25–26, 58, 129–30
Holy Week, 103–4, 127, 177, 208
Hosea, Book of, 45–46, 80
human and divine, 159–61, 170, 176, 179, 189, 196, 210
human nature, 24, 26–27, 31, 77–78
"Hymn of Glory," 244–45

idolatry, xiv, 7, 11, 111
  and Jewish theologians
    Greenberg, Irving, 145–46, 151
    Ha Me'iri, Menachem, 69–70, 73, 75
    Maimonides, Moses, 70

and Noahide covenant, 73, 84, 232
and pluralism, 242
Immanuel (God in our midst), 41
incarnation, 23, 26, 30
and Christian reevaluation of Judaism, 132
and Christian theologians
Eckardt, A. Roy, 102
Pawlikowski, John, 159
and core beliefs, 114–15
and Jewish theologians
Buber, Martin, 91
Greenberg, Irving, 147, 153
and Messiah question, 41
inclusivism, 129–31, 135, 137, 141, 174–76, 180–81, 214, 219, 233
individual-in-community, 157–58
individualism, xiii, 12–13, 94–95, 97, 155, 167, 204
infinite reality. See finite revelation of infinite reality
"In Memoriam" (Tennyson), 243
Inquisition, 137
Institute of Jewish and Christian Studies (Baltimore, Md.), 168
Interfaith Committee of Essex, 207
Interfaith Thanksgiving services, 208–9
International Christian Embassy (Jerusalem), 224
interreligious marriage, 74
intertestamental period, 54, 56, 67, 117, 171
inward-looking Judaism, 88–89, 101, 103
Irenaeus, 23
Isaac, 8–9, 17, 29, 33, 50, 138, 158, 167, 185, 218
Isaac, Jules, 121
Isaiah, Book of, 29
and core beliefs, 116
and Jewish theologians
Greenberg, Irving, 150
Rosenzweig, Franz, 89

and Messiah question
priestly Messiah in the canon, 50
pseudepigrapha Messiahs, 57, 59
royal Messiah in the canon, 41–44, 46
suffering servant in the canon, 37, 51–53, 55, 60, 63, 65
and pluralism, 235
and truth claims, 194
Isaiah school, 25, 42, 44
Isaiah's servant songs, 51–52, 55, 57, 59, 63
Ishmael, 17, 138
Islam, 32, 69–70, 72–76, 83, 97, 231, 233, 237, 239
Islamist fanatics, 188
Israel, State of, 89, 102, 144–47, 151, 169, 172, 216–17, 223–30.
See also Zionism
Israeli checkpoints, 224
Israeli-Palestinian dispute and liberal Christians, 213–30
and Presbyterian National Assembly (2006), 228–30
and Presbyterian Resolution (2004), 223–28
and Presbyterian "Theological Understanding" (1987), 216–23
"I-Thou relationship," 161

Jacob, 9–10, 22, 33, 36, 40, 50, 115, 158, 160, 188–91, 193, 196, 218
James, Letter of, 28–29, 83–84
Jeremiah, 25, 44–45, 53, 63, 65, 80, 148, 173, 191
Jerusalem. See also Jerusalem Temple, destruction of
and Christian reevaluation of Judaism, 127
and Messiah question, 44, 46–48, 58, 62–63, 66
Jerusalem (Mendelssohn), 79
Jerusalem Temple, destruction of, 47, 60–61, 134, 144–45, 151, 165–66
Jesse, 45–46

Jesus, xiii, 13, 15–18, 20, 22, 24–34, 38.
    See also christologies
  and adult education classes, 200–202,
    204–5
  and Christian reevaluation of Judaism,
    214
    Catholic Church, 123–27, 129–32, 135
    Jewish response to, 138–42
    Protestant churches, 136–37
  and Christian theologians
    Eckardt, A. Roy, 101–2
    Pawlikowski, John, 154–56; 158–60,
      162–64
    van Buren, Paul, 99–100
    Williamson, Clark M., 105, 107,
      109–11
  and core beliefs, 112–18
  and "Dabru Emet" (Speak the Truth),
    169–70
  and Golden Rule, 86
  and guest sermons in churches, 211
  and Interfaith Committee of Essex, 207
  and Interfaith Thanksgiving services,
    208
  and Jewish reevaluation of Christianity,
    166
  and Jewish theologians
    Benamozegh, Elijah, 83–84
    Buber, Martin, 92–93, 168
    Greenberg, Irving, 144, 147–53
    Ha Me'iri, Menachem, 71
    Heschel, Abraham Joshua, 98
    Mendelssohn, Moses, 78–79
    Rosenzweig, Franz, 87
  and Messiah question, 67–68
    Messiahs of the Qumran
      community, 63
    Messiahs who suffer and die, 60–61,
      63–64
    priestly Messiah in the canon, 50
    royal Messiah in the canon, 37–38,
      40, 46, 49
    "Son of Man" in the canon, 37–38

  suffering and dying Messiahs in
    later Jewish texts, 63
  and opening of covenant to gentiles,
    33–34, 72, 75
  and pluralism, 233
  and "Reflections on Covenant and
    Mission," 180–82
  and "A Sacred Obligation," 172–75, 177
  and "Theological Understanding"
    (1987), 218–19, 221
  and truth claims, 185, 189
Jesus movement, 33, 78, 147, 156, 166.
    See also Jesus
"Jesus the Jew: A Reappraisal" (sermon),
    200
Jethro, 81
Jewish commentaries, 14, 116, 186
Jewish Messiah, 68, 99, 157
Jewish peoplehood, 75, 81
Jewish Reconstructionist Movement, 75
Jewish reevaluation of Christianity,
    166–71, 215–16
    "Dabru Emet" (Speak the Truth),
      168–71, 177, 179, 215–16
    "Reflections on Covenant and
      Mission," 178–82
    "Sacred Obligation: Rethinking
      Christian Faith in Relation to
      Judaism and the Jewish People,
      A" (Scholars Group), 216
Jewish root and Christian branch, xi,
    13–14, 35–36, 95, 99, 123, 134,
    149, 154, 164, 211
Jewish state of Israel. *See* Israel, State of
Jewish Theological Seminary, 98
Jewish theology of Christianity, 13,
    26–36, 69–84, 87–98.
    See also names of other Jewish
    theologians
  and Christian reevaluation of Judaism,
    134
  and Jewish theologians
    Benamozegh, Elijah, 80–84

Buber, Martin, 90–95, 97–98,
    112–13, 147, 160–61, 168
Greenberg, Irving, 143–54, 156,
    161–62, 164
Ha Me'iri, Menachem, 69–77
Heschel, Abraham Joshua, 95–98, 112
Mendelssohn, Moses, 74, 77–80
Rosenzweig, Franz, 87–90, 93–94,
    97–98, 101, 113, 126, 168, 181, 196
and pluralism, 231–46
"Jews and Christians: Taking the Next
    Step" (Kogan), 156
"Jews for Jesus," 220
Job, 81
Joel, Book of, 50
Johannine tradition, 23, 159
John, Gospel of, 18, 23, 26, 41, 87, 107, 159
    and Christian reevaluation of Judaism,
        127, 131
    and lectionaries, 104, 177, 221–22
    and "Theological Understanding"
        (1987), 221–22
    and truth claims, 194
John Paul II, Pope, 128, 129–32, 176–77,
    214
Johnson, Luke Timothy, 38
John the Baptist, 25, 142
John XXIII, Pope, xi
Jonah, Book of, 85, 158, 193
Joshua, 26, 50, 63, 158
Josiah, 158
Journal of Ecumenical Studies, 154, 156
Judah, royal tribe of, 40, 43–47
Judaism, xii–xiii, 4–14, 27–28. See also
    entries beginning with Jewish
"Judaism and Christianity: Covenants of
    Redemption" (Greenburg), 152–54
Judges, 26
judgment, 11–12
    and Christian theologians
        van Buren, Paul, 100
        Williamson, Clark M., 105
    and Messiah question, 55, 61–62, 67

Julius Caesar, 177
justice, 11, 14, 78
justification, 19–20, 27, 34

Kabbalistic texts, 80
kal goyim, 142, 181
kashrut, 74, 130
Kasper, Walter, 180–81
kerygma, Christian, 112, 115
kidnapping of Israeli soldiers, 224
Kierkegaard, Søren, 21, 80, 186–87, 191,
    195, 218
Kingdom of God, 11, 14, 68, 80, 97,
    162–64, 167–68, 177–78, 185, 189,
    205, 215
"Kingdom of God in Jewish Theology:
    Myth, History and Creation, The"
    (Kogan), 162
"Kingdom Present" (Kogan), 162
Kings I, Book of, 49
Kings II, Book of, 193
Knitter, Paul, 175–76, 237
kosher food, 74, 104, 204

Lamech, 5
Last Supper, 19, 22–23, 49
lectionaries, 103–5, 127, 177, 208, 221–22
legal system for non-Jews, 11, 26, 232–33.
    See also Noahide covenant
Lent, 127
Levine, Amy-Jill, 162
Leviticus, Book of, 28, 49, 73–74, 85–86,
    189, 211
Liaison Committee between the Roman
    Catholic Church and the
    International Jewish
    Committee for Interreligious
    Consultations (Venice 1977), 133
liberal Christians, xii, 22–23, 84, 97, 146,
    164, 175
    and Israeli-Palestinian dispute, 213–30
liberal Judaism, 12–13, 28, 146, 201
literalism, biblical, 193–95

Little Island, The, 191–93
liturgy, xi, 30, 47, 103–5, 125–27, 135,
    155, 159, 202, 208
lived experience, 20, 94, 105, 130, 176, 188
Logos. *See* Word of God
love relationship, 186–88
Luke, Gospel of, 22–23, 25–26, 86, 107,
    123, 162
    and Messiah question, 41, 60–61
Luther, Martin, xii, 23

Maccabees, Books of, 116–17
Magisterium, 181
Maimonides, Moses, 12, 70, 78, 81, 97,
    113, 126, 153
Malachi, Book of, 113
Manassah, 42
Marcionite heresy, 74, 95, 169
Marduk, 194
Mark, Gospel of, 22, 25–26, 33, 115, 131,
    152, 162, 211, 221
    and Messiah question, 37–38, 41, 49,
    59–61
martyrdom, 28, 148
Mary, 26, 79
Mass, 30, 104
Matthew, Gospel of, 15, 18, 22–25, 28,
    33, 93, 105, 115
    and Christian reevaluation of Judaism,
    131, 141–42, 181
    and Messiah question, 37–38, 41, 59–61
    and "Theological Understanding"
    (1987), 221
    and truth claims, 183
Melchizedek, 50, 81
Mendelssohn, Moses, 74, 77–80
Mennonite European Regional
    Conference (Netherlands 1977),
    138
menorah, 50
Meshach, 28
Messiah, 12, 14, 35, 37–68. *See also*
    messianic expectations

and postcanonical Messianic
    conceptions, 54–55
and priestly Messiah in the canon,
    49–50, 62–63
and pseudepigrapha Messiahs, 55–66
    Davidic Messiah in Psalms of
    Solomon, 57–58
    Messiahs of the Qumran
    community, 50, 54, 62–63
    Messiahs who suffer and die,
    59–66, 100
    Similitudes of Enoch, 55–57
and royal Messiah in the canon,
    39–49, 62–63, 166
and "Son of Man" in the canon, 25,
    53–54, 149
and suffering servant in the canon,
    37, 50–53, 57
messianic expectations, 54. *See also*
    Messiah
and adult education classes, 205
and Christian reevaluation of Judaism,
    214
    Catholic Church, 123, 125–27, 131,
    134–35
    Jewish response to, 138–39, 141
    Protestant churches, 136
and Christian theologians
    Pawlikowski, John, 157–59
    van Buren, Paul, 99–100
    Williamson, Clark M., 110–11
and "Dabru Emet" (Speak the Truth),
    169
and Jewish theologians
    Buber, Martin, 92
    Greenberg, Irving, 144, 148–50, 152
and post-Temple conditions, 166
and "Reflections on Covenant and
    Mission," 178
and "A Sacred Obligation," 177
and "Theological Understanding"
    (1987), 223
and truth claims, 185

metaphoric reading of sacred texts,
194–95
Metraton (angel), 64
Micah, Book of, 11, 46, 215, 232
Mid-Atlantic Academy of Religion, 213
Midrash, 241–42
Midrash Konen, 65
miracle births, 15, 29, 167, 185
miracles, 7, 25, 118, 184–85
mission, 10
  and Christian reevaluation of Judaism
    Catholic Church, 122–26, 128,
    133–34
    Protestant churches, 137–38
  and core beliefs, 116
  and Jewish theologians
    Greenberg, Irving, 147
    Rosenzweig, Franz, 89
  and Messiah question, 46
  and "Reflections on Covenant and
    Mission," 178–81
  and Williamson, Clark M., 106
"Mission and Witness of the Church,
  The" (Federici), 132–33
missionary activity, 106, 133, 137–39, 180,
  205, 214. *See also entries
  beginning with* conversion
"mission to the Jews," 97, 108, 114, 130,
  133, 237–38
mitzvot (commandments), 13–14, 29, 77,
  79–80
Moab, 40
Mojzes, Paul, 156
monotheism, 14, 79, 148, 155, 171
Montclair State University, 3, 109, 143,
  185, 199–200, 207–8
moral law, 5, 7–8, 10–11, 14, 16, 111
  and adult education classes, 204
  and Jewish theologians
    Buber, Martin, 92
    Ha Me'iri, Menachem, 70, 73–76
    Mendelssohn, Moses, 77
    Rosenzweig, Franz, 89

and "Reflections on Covenant and
  Mission," 178–79
and "A Sacred Obligation," 174
Mormons, 186
Mosaic covenant, 16–17, 19, 34, 81–84,
  179. *See also* covenant
Moses, xii, 7, 10, 13, 17, 50, 64, 80, 115,
  148, 150, 171, 184, 190, 218
Mowinckel, Sigmund, 163
multiculturalism, 146
Munich (film), 225
Muslims. *See* Islam
mystery, 95, 99, 125, 129–30, 139–40,
  219
mythic imagination, 39–40
  and Messiah question
    Messiahs who suffer and die, 59–61
    priestly Messiah in the canon, 50
    royal Messiah in the canon, 39–44
    Similitudes of Enoch, 56
    "Son of Man" in the canon, 54

Nadab, 115
Nathan, 39, 41
National Christian-Jewish Workshop
  (Pittsburgh), 102
National Council of Churches, 172
National Council of Synagogues
  (Conservative and Reform Jews),
  178–79
National Dialogue Newsletter, 156
nationalism, 94, 134, 146, 155, 227
natural-supernatural distinction, 184
nature, 184–85, 192
Nazarene movement, 67, 73, 100, 110,
  126, 148, 171, 173, 206, 237
Nazism, 169, 222
Nebuchadnezzar, king of Babylonia,
  28, 73
Nehemiah, Book of, 193
"new encounter," 144
"new Israel," 83, 92
"newness of life," 19–21, 27

New Testament, xii, 14–15, 17, 22, 24–26, 29
and adult education classes, 199–201, 205, 209
and Christian reevaluation of Judaism, 126, 131, 135, 167
and Christian theologians
Gamaliel, Rabban, 78
Pawlikowski, John, 159
Williamson, Clark M., 103, 107, 109
and core beliefs, 117
and Gamaliel, 78, 170, 173
and "Reflections on Covenant and Mission," 181
and "A Sacred Obligation," 173, 175, 177
and "Theological Understanding" (1987), 221
and truth claims, 184, 186
New Year service, 163
Niebuhr, Reinhold, 97
nihilism, 20–21, 96
Noah, 5–6, 11, 13, 16–17, 203. See also Noahide covenant
Noahide covenant, 11, 13–14, 73, 77–79, 81–84, 179, 215, 232–33, 238
"No Religion Is an Island" (Heschel), 95
Nostra Aetate, xi–xii, 121–27, 131
and Guidelines of 1975, 124–27
Notes on the Correct Way to Present the Jews and Judaism in Preaching and Catechesis in the Roman Catholic Church (June 1985), 128–29, 131–32
"Notzrim," 73
Noyes, Alfred, 195
Numbers, Book of, 40
and priestly Messiah in the canon, 49

objective uncertainty of faith, 114, 152, 187–88, 190–91, 195–97, 218
Office for the Conversion of Jews (Catholic Church), 176, 180
olam habah (world to come), 12, 19

Old Testament, 17, 83. See also Hebrew Scriptures
and adult education classes, 209
and Christian reevaluation of Judaism, 126, 135, 167
and "Dabru Emet" (Speak the Truth), 169
and Pawlikowski, John, 157
olive tree metaphor, 33, 35–36, 122–23
original sin, 14, 15–17, 22, 27, 31, 202–3, 219
Orthodox Judaism, 11, 28, 89, 143, 147, 153–54, 172
oxymoronic theology, 109

paganism, xiii, 7, 33
and Christian theologians
Pawlikowski, John, 155
Williamson, Clark M., 110
and Jewish theologians
Benamozegh, Elijah, 84
Ha Me'iri, Menachem, 69–72
Heschel, Abraham Joshua, 95
Maimonides, Moses, 70
Rosenzweig, Franz, 87–88
and post-Temple conditions, 166
Palestinian people, 216–17
parables, 105, 110
parallel redemptive purposes, 15, 29–30, 98, 167
Park Avenue Presbyterian Church (New York), 208
Parkes, James, 94
parochialism, 95
Parousia hope, 93, 99
particularism, 81–82, 106, 231–32
passion of Christ, 103, 110, 123–24, 152
Passion of the Christ, The (film), 226
Passover Seder, 103–4, 214
patriarchs, 7–9, 27, 40, 50, 113, 123, 131, 174–75
Paul of Tarsus, 15–25, 27–36, 245–46
and adult education classes, 201–4, 206

and Christian reevaluation of Judaism
  Catholic Church, 123, 131
  Jewish response to, 138–41
and Christian theologians
  Pawlikowski, John, 155, 159
  Williamson, Clark M., 105, 110
and core beliefs, 115, 117
and guest sermons in churches, 211
and Jewish theologians
  Baeck, Leo, 89
  Benamozegh, Elijah, 83
  Buber, Martin, 93
  Greenberg, Irving, 149–50
  Mendelssohn, Moses, 77, 80
and Messiah question, 68
and "Theological Understanding"
  (1987), 218–19, 221
Pawlikowski, John, 118, 152, 153, 154–64
Pelavin, Mark, 229
Penei-El ("face of God"), 188, 190–91
penitence, 17
Pentecost, 26
people Israel as collective individual, 15,
  29, 116, 167
and adult education classes, 204
and Jewish theologians
  Heschel, Abraham Joshua, 98
  Rosenzweig, Franz, 87–88
and Messiah question, 51–54
and truth claims, 189
persecution, xiv, 10
and adult education classes, 206–7
and Christian reevaluation of Judaism
  Catholic Church, 121
  Jewish response to, 138, 215
  Protestant churches, 136, 138
and Christian theologians
  Pawlikowski, John, 156
  Williamson, Clark M., 110
and core beliefs, 117
and Israeli-Palestinian dispute, 227
and Jewish theologians
  Greenberg, Irving, 144

Ha Me'iri, Menachem, 76
Mendelssohn, Moses, 78
and Messiah question, 60
and "Reflections on Covenant and
  Mission," 179
and "Theological Understanding"
  (1987), 220
Persian period, 47, 59
personification
  and Messiahs who suffer and die, 59
  Messiahs who suffer and die, 64
  and Similitudes of Enoch, 56
Pesiqta Rabbati, 65
Peter, 25, 37–38, 131, 142
Pharaoh, 7, 17, 64
Pharisees, 27, 54, 117, 126, 134–35, 157–60,
  162, 165, 170–71, 204, 206
Philippians, Epistle to, 24–25, 31
Philo of Alexandria, 29, 72, 195
philosemitism, 225
philosophy of religion, 176
Pilate, Pontius, 131
pistis (Christian faith), 94
Plato, 76, 194
pluralism, xii, xiv, 13, 35
and Christian reevaluation of
  Judaism, 214
  Catholic Church, 129, 131
  Jewish response to, 141, 215
and Christian theologians
  Pawlikowski, John, 161
  Williamson, Clark M., 107
and Interfaith Committee of Essex, 207
and Jewish theologians
  Greenberg, Irving, 146
  Mendelssohn, Moses, 78
and Jewish theology of Christianity,
  231–46
  affirmation of, 232–33, 238–39
  vs. exclusivism, 233, 237–38
  and revelation, 233–37
  and "Reflections on Covenant and
  Mission," 179–81

pluralism (continued)
and "A Sacred Obligation," 175–76
and "Theological Understanding"
(1987), 217–18
and truth claims, 183–84, 195
poetry, 194–95
pogroms, 72, 117
Pontifical Commission for the Religious
Relations with the Jews, 180
postbiblical texts, 63–66
postcanonical Messianic conceptions,
54–55
postexilic period, 44, 46–47, 50
postmodernism, 72
poverty, 204
praeparatio messianica, 97
preexistence, 25, 64
Presbyterian Church (U.S.A.), 216–30
National Assembly (2006), 228–30
Resolution (2004), 223–28
"Theological Understanding" (1987),
216–23
priestly Messiah in the canon, 49–50,
62–63
Promised Land, 153
prophets and prophecies, 13–14, 26
and Christian reevaluation of Judaism,
131
and core beliefs, 113
and Golden Rule, 85
and Jewish theologians
Buber, Martin, 91–92
Greenberg, Irving, 149–50
Heschel, Abraham Joshua, 95
and Messiah question
postcanonical Messianic
conceptions, 54
priestly Messiah in the canon, 49–50
royal Messiah in the canon, 39–49
Similitudes of Enoch, 55–57
"Son of Man" in the canon, 53–54
suffering servant in the canon, 51–53
and Pawlikowski, John, 157, 163

and "Theological Understanding"
(1987), 223
and truth claims, 186, 193
proselytizing, 90, 106, 108, 137–38, 213,
221. See also conversion of Jews
prostitutes, 21
Protestant churches, xii, 11
and Israeli-Palestinian dispute, 213–30
Presbyterian National Assembly
(2006), 228–30
Presbyterian Resolution (2004),
223–28
Presbyterian "Theological
Understanding" (1987), 216–23
and reevaluation of Judaism, 125,
136–38, 166, 213
and "Reflections on Covenant and
Mission," 182
and "A Sacred Obligation," 172,
174–75
Protestant Reformation, 22–23, 151
Psalms, Book of, 10, 18, 24–25, 81, 163,
182
and adult education classes, 203
and Messiah question, 25, 39–41, 50
and truth claims, 194
Psalms of Solomon, 57–58, 100
pseudepigrapha Messiahs, 55–66
and Davidic Messiah in Psalms of
Solomon, 57–58
and Messiahs of the Qumran
community, 50, 54, 62–63
and Messiahs who suffer and die,
59–66
and Similitudes of Enoch, 55–57
punishment
and Ha Me'iri, 76
and Maimonides, 78
and Mendelssohn, 77–78
and Messiah question, 51

Qumran community, 50, 54, 62–63, 68
Qur'an, 83, 186

rabbinic tradition, 11–15, 145, 149, 151, 157
  and adult education classes, 204
  and Christian reevaluation of Judaism,
    132, 134
  and "Dabru Emet" (Speak the Truth),
    168, 171
  and Messiah question, 67, 110, 126
  and post-Temple conditions, 165–66
  and "Reflections on Covenant and
    Mission," 179
  and "A Sacred Obligation," 173
Raheb, Mitri, 228
rainbow, 6
Rashi, 82
rationalism, 77–80, 82
Ratzinger, Joseph, xii, 181
Real Jesus, The (Johnson), 38
rebirth, 19, 27, 88–89, 202
recapitulation of history of Israel, 15,
    29–30, 167, 205
Reclaiming the Jesus of History
    (Eckardt), 101
redemption, 6, 8, 10, 15–16, 18, 25, 32,
    35–36
  and adult education classes, 205
  and Christian reevaluation of Judaism
    Catholic Church, 123, 126–28,
      130, 135
    Jewish response to, 139, 141
    Protestant churches, 137
  and Christian theologians
    Eckardt, A. Roy, 101, 103
    Pawlikowski, John, 155–56
    van Buren, Paul, 99–100
    Williamson, Clark M., 105–10
  and core beliefs, 113, 116–17
  and "Dabru Emet" (Speak the Truth),
    169
  and Jewish theologians
    Benamozegh, Elijah, 81
    Buber, Martin, 90–93
    Greenberg, Irving, 145, 148, 150,
      152–53

Ha Me'iri, Menachem, 70
Heschel, Abraham Joshua, 95–98
Rosenzweig, Franz, 87–88, 90
  and Messiah question, 67–68
  Messiahs who suffer and die, 59–63,
    65
  postcanonical Messianic
    conceptions, 54
  royal Messiah in the canon, 38
  Similitudes of Enoch, 57
  and opening covenant to gentiles, 72
  and parallel redemptive purposes, 15,
    29–30, 98, 167
  and "A Sacred Obligation," 174
  and "Theological Understanding"
    (1987), 218, 220
  and truth claims, 191
Red Sea, 184
"Reflections on Covenant and Mission,"
    178–82
Reformation, 22–23, 151
Reform Judaism, 89, 178–79
"Relationship of Judaism and Christianity:
    Toward a New Organic Model,
    The" (Greenburg), 145–52
religion and politics, 146–47, 225–27
religious bigotry, 180, 237
religious chauvinism, 134, 155
religious humanism, 85, 92–93, 193
religious liberty, 124–25
religious narratives, 184, 186, 191, 193–97
religious "other," 69, 74, 85–86, 106,
    111–18, 215
  and "Dabru Emet" (Speak the Truth), 170
  and Interfaith Committee of Essex, 207
  and Interfaith Thanksgiving services,
    208
  and truth claims, 191
renewal, 17, 95
repentance, 13, 17, 116, 173
resurrection, 15, 18–19, 24
  and Christian reevaluation of Judaism,
    142

resurrection (*continued*)
  and Christian theologians
    Eckardt, A. Roy, 101–2
    Pawlikowski, John, 157
    van Buren, Paul, 99
  and core beliefs, 114, 117–18
  and Greenberg, Irving, 144, 146–48
  and Messiah question, 40, 61, 66
  and "A Sacred Obligation," 175
revelation, 31, 35
  and Christian reevaluation of Judaism
    Catholic Church, 127, 131
    Jewish response to, 141, 215
    Protestant churches, 136
  and "Dabru Emet" (Speak the Truth),
    169–71
  and Eckardt, A. Roy, 101
  and Golden Rule, 86
  and Jewish theologians
    Benamozegh, Elijah, 82
    Buber, Martin, 91
    Greenberg, Irving, 144, 146, 153
    Ha Me'iri, Menachem, 70, 72, 75–76
    Mendelssohn, Moses, 77–79
    Rosenzweig, Franz, 88
  and pluralism, 233–37, 242–43
  and "A Sacred Obligation," 176–77
  and "Theological Understanding"
    (1987), 217
  and truth claims, 183, 186, 195
reverence for the earth, 11
reward, 13, 28, 76–78
righteousness, 11, 13, 17–19, 25, 27, 34,
    78, 83, 92
  and adult education classes, 201–5
  and Messiah question, 55–57, 59–60
  and "A Sacred Obligation," 173
ritual laws, 10, 13, 77, 79–80, 82–83,
    88–89, 204, 233
Roman Catholicism. *See* Catholic Church
Romans, ancient, 71–72, 100, 171, 173
  and Messiah question, 37, 58, 62,
    126

Romans, Epistle to, 16–20, 24, 27, 31,
    33–35, 93, 109
  and adult education classes, 203
  and Christian reevaluation of Judaism
    Catholic Church, 122–23, 131
    Jewish response to, 139–41
  and "Theological Understanding"
    (1987), 218
romanticism, 89
Rosenzweig, Franz, 87–90, 93–94,
    97–98, 101, 113, 126, 168, 181, 196
Rosh Hashanah, 163, 206
Rottenberg, Isaac, 156
royal Messiah in the canon, 39–49,
    57–58, 62–63, 166
Rudin, A. James, 156
Rue aux Juifs (Street of the Jews), 71
Ruth, Book of, 193

Sabbath observance, 10, 162, 204
  and adult education classes, 199–200
  and Christian reevaluation of Judaism,
    130
  and Jewish theologians
    Ha Me'iri, Menachem, 73–74
    Mendelssohn, Moses, 79
Sabeel Ecumenical Liberation Theological
    Center (Jerusalem), 228
Sacks, Jonathan, 153–54
sacramentalism, 29, 150–51
"Sacred Obligation: Rethinking Christian
    Faith in Relation to Judaism and
    the Jewish People, A" (Scholars
    Group), 172–77, 216
sacred texts. *See* religious narratives
sacrifice of Jesus, 17–20, 23, 34. *See also*
    atonement
  and Christian reevaluation of Judaism
    Catholic Church, 130, 135
    Jewish response to, 140
    Protestant churches, 140
  and core beliefs, 114, 116–17
sacrifices and priesthood, 49, 150–51

Sadducees, 54, 117, 165, 171, 204, 206
salvation
    and adult education classes, 201–2
    and Christian reevaluation of Judaism
        Catholic Church, 123, 125, 128–31, 133
        Jewish response to, 138–41
        Protestant churches, 136–37, 214
    and Christian theologians, xiii, 17–24,
        27–29
        Augustine, Saint, 71
        Pawlikowski, John, 157
        Williamson, Clark M., 105
    and core beliefs, 118
    and "Dabru Emet" (Speak the Truth),
        169
    and Jewish theologians, 11–12, 27–29
        Buber, Martin, 90, 92–93
        Greenberg, Irving, 144–45, 149–50,
            153
        Ha Me'iri, Menachem, 71
        Heschel, Abraham Joshua, 95, 97
        Maimonides, Moses, 78
        Mendelssohn, Moses, 78, 80
        Rosenzweig, Franz, 87–88, 93
    and Messiah question, 54, 68
    and "Reflections on Covenant and
        Mission," 180–81
    and "A Sacred Obligation," 173–75
    and "Theological Understanding"
        (1987), 219
    and truth claims, 189
same-sex unions, 221
Samuel I, Book of, 39, 49
Samuel II, Book of, 39–41, 49, 64
sanctification, 5, 11, 23, 28–29, 54
Sanhedrin, 135
Sarah, 7, 17, 29, 167, 185
Sartre, Jean-Paul, 20–21
Satan, 17, 26
Saul, 39, 49
Schindler's List (film), 226
Schleiermacher, Friedrich, 184, 191
Schoenveld, J. Coos, 150

Scholars Group, 172
"scriptolatry," 242
Sea of Reeds, 10
second coming of Jesus, 67, 141, 148–49,
    178
secularism, 145, 151
security fences, 223–24, 229–30
self-affirmation, xiv, 85–86, 102, 119
self-transcendence, xiv, 4, 7, 85–86, 119
    and Jewish theologians
        Ha Me'iri, Menachem, 75–76
        Heschel, Abraham Joshua, 95
    and pluralism, 239
    and "A Sacred Obligation," 176
    and truth claims, 183, 185, 188, 190,
        196
    and Williamson, Clark M., 107
separation of Church and State, 146–47,
    225–27
sexual morality, 5–6, 11, 21, 82,
    84, 233
Shabbat 156a, 74
Shadrach, 28
shepherd king, 45–46, 48–49, 59
Sherman, Franklin, 156
Shield of David, 196
Shinto history, 112
Shoah. See Holocaust
Similitudes, Book of, 55–57. See also
    Enoch, Book of
Sinai, Mount, 10, 33, 88, 115, 131, 158
"single-covenant" position, 158
Sisters of Scion, xii
skepticism, 141
social justice, 43–44, 86, 95, 105–6
Socrates, 194
Sodom, 7–8, 160
Solomon, King, 30, 41, 49, 57, 59–60
Solomon's Temple, 30
Song of Songs, 186
Son of God, 20, 23–25
    Israel as, 15, 24, 29, 64
    and Messiah question, 41, 59, 64

Son of Man and Messiah question,
    25, 37–38, 53–54, 56–57, 61, 149
soteriology, 11–12, 17–24, 27–29.
    See also salvation
Southern Baptist Convention, 140
Spielberg, Steven, 226
Spirit of God, 27
spirituality, 176, 188
spiritual narcissism, xiv, 105
star image (Numbers 24:17), 40–41
Star of Redemption, 88–89, 168, 196
Star of Redemption (Rosenzweig), 89
stars, 74–76
stereotypes, 108, 136, 144
strangers, 7, 10, 50–51, 96
St. Stephen's Episcopal Church
    (Charleston, S.C.), 209, 222
subjective certainty of faith, 114, 152,
    187–88, 191, 195–97, 218
suffering. *See* persecution
suffering servant in the canon, 37,
    50–53, 57, 116
suicide bombings, 224
supernaturalization, 54, 56, 132, 149,
    164, 184
supersessionism, 14, 101, 143–44, 165, 172–
    73, 181, 219
synagogues, 30, 130, 151, 157, 165
    and adult education classes, 199–201,
        206–7, 209
    and Interfaith Thanksgiving services,
        208–9
    and "Reflections on Covenant and
        Mission," 178–79
syncretism, 96, 155
Synod of Bishops on Reconciliation
    (Rome, October 1983), 133
Synod of the Protestant Church of the
    Rhineland, 138, 140
synoptic Gospels, 111, 131–32, 159, 201

table fellowship meals, 157
Talmud, 11, 14, 215

and Benamozegh, 80–81
and Ha Me'iri, 69–70, 72–74, 76
and Messiah question, 64, 66
Temple cult, 165–66, 173. *See also*
    Jerusalem Temple, destruction
    of
Tennyson, Alfred, Lord, 243
Texas Conference of Churches, 138, 140
textbooks of Catholic Church, xii
Text of the Seventh General Audience
    Talk of John Paul II, the Vatican
    (May 31, 1995), 129–32
Thanksgiving services, 208–9
theism, 73, 75, 78
"Theological Understanding of the
    Relationship between Christians
    and Jews, A" (1987), 216–23
Thomas, Gospel of, 185
tikkun olam (healing of a broken world), 14
Tillich, Paul, 97
Timaeus, The (Plato), 76, 194
time and space, 22, 87–88, 114, 162
tolerance, 69, 78–80, 97
Torah, 8, 12, 14–15, 17, 24, 27, 29–32, 34–35
    and adult education classes, 203, 209
    and Christian reevaluation of Judaism,
        139–42
    and Christian theologians
        Pawlikowski, John, 160, 163
        Williamson, Clark M., 111
    and core beliefs, 114–16
    and "Dabru Emet" (Speak the Truth),
        169
    and Jewish theologians
        Benamozegh, Elijah, 80–81
        Greenberg, Irving, 146, 149
        Ha Me'iri, Menachem, 74
        Heschel, Abraham Joshua, 97
        Maimonides, Moses, 70
        Mendelssohn, Moses, 79
        Rosenzweig, Franz, 87
    and Messiah question, 54, 65
    and pluralism, 234

and post-Temple conditions, 165
and "A Sacred Obligation," 173, 175
and "Theological Understanding"
(1987), 218
and truth claims, 194
Tosefta, 73, 215, 232–33
totality of the divine, 22, 78–79, 91, 105
"Toward Total Dialogue" (Kogan), 102,
156
trinitarian theory, 142, 217–18, 226
triumphalism, 87, 95–96, 99, 101, 145, 165
and adult education classes, 205
and Christian reevaluation of Judaism,
127, 133–34
truth claims, 170–71, 176, 183–97, 217–18
Two Types of Faith (Buber), 94
typology, 17
Tzur Yisrael, 9

Union for Reform Judaism, 229
Union Theological Seminary, 98
United Methodist Church, 138, 140
United Synagogue of Conservative
Judaism, 179
unity of God, 11, 13, 29, 82, 217–18
universalism, xii–xiii, 214–15, 231–32
and Christian theologians
Pawlikowski, John, 155–56, 158
Williamson, Clark M., 106
and "Dabru Emet" (Speak the Truth),
171
and Golden Rule, 86
and Jewish theologians
Benamozegh, Elijah, 80–82, 84
Greenberg, Irving, 144–45
Mendelssohn, Moses, 78
Rosenzweig, Franz, 89
and "A Sacred Obligation," 174–76
and truth claims, 193

Vahanian, Gabriel, 107
van Buren, Paul, 99–100, 118, 150,
157–58

Vatican Commission for the Catholic
Church's Religious Relations with
the Jews, 124, 128
Vatican II, xi, xiv, 36, 121–27, 143, 145,
156, 165–66
and Guidelines of 1975, 124–27
visions, 9–10, 22
and core beliefs, 117
and Messiah question, 39–50, 53–64

West Bank, 223, 228
White Crucifixion (painting by Chagall),
117
Wiesel, Elie, 109
Willebrands, Cardinal, 124
Williamson, Clark M., 103–11, 150,
157–58, 172–73
will of God, 12, 96, 98, 101, 139
wine, 74
wisdom, 32
and Messiah question, 55–59
and Williamson, Clark M., 111
Wisdom literature, 26, 58–60, 100
witnessing for Christ, xii, 89
and Christian reevaluation of Judaism
Catholic Church, 124–25, 137
Protestant churches, 137–38
witness people, 6–7, 10
and adult education classes, 205
and Christian reevaluation of Judaism,
127–29, 132–33, 135, 214–15
and Christian theologians
Augustine, Saint, 71
Pawlikowski, John, 155
Williamson, Clark M., 105–6
and Israeli-Palestinian dispute, 226
and Jewish reevaluation of Christianity,
168
and Jewish theologians
Greenberg, Irving, 144, 147
Ha Me'iri, Menachem, 71
Rosenzweig, Franz, 89
and pluralism, 234–35

witness people (*continued*)
  and "Theological Understanding"
    (1987), 220
women, 104, 204
Word of God, 23, 26, 30–31
  and Christian reevaluation of Judaism,
    132–33
  and Christian theologians
    Pawlikowski, John, 159
    Williamson, Clark M., 111
  and Messiah question, 41
  and "A Sacred Obligation," 175
Workshop on Jews and Christians, Central
    Committee of Roman Catholics
    in Germany (1979), 133–34
"works righteousness," 11, 109
World Council of Churches (WCC),
    136–38, 140, 224

wrestling match, 10, 22, 36, 115, 160,
    188–91, 196
Wyschogrod, Michael, 80, 153

Yisra-El (God-wrestler), 160, 189, 196
Yom Kippur, 17, 202, 206
Younan, Munib A., 228

Zadokite Document, 100
Zealots, 171
Zechariah, Book of, 47–50, 59, 61,
    62–63, 66
Zedekiah, 44
Zephaniah, Book of, 150
Zerubbabel, 47–50, 59, 63
Zionism, 102, 145–46, 185, 207,
    216, 226
Zohar, 65